PLOTS AND CHARACTERS
IN THE FICTION OF
JAMES FENIMORE COOPER

THE PLOTS AND CHARACTERS SERIES

Robert L. Gale
General Editor

PLOTS AND CHARACTERS
IN THE FICTION OF
JAMES FENIMORE COOPER

Warren S. Walker

Archon Books

Dawson

Archon Books, The Shoe String Press, Inc.
995 Sherman Avenue, Hamden, Connecticut 06514 USA

Wm Dawson & Sons Ltd, Cannon House
Folkestone, Kent, England

Library of Congress Cataloging in Publication Data

Walker, Warren S
    Plots and characters in the fiction of James Fenimore Cooper.

    (The Plots and characters series)
    Bibliography: p.
    1. Cooper, James Fenimore, 1789-1851—Plots.
2. Cooper, James Fenimore, 1789-1851—Characters. I. Title.
PS1441.W3   1978   813'.2   78-9469

30,280

Archon ISBN 0-208-01497-7
Dawson ISBN 0 7129 0763 7

Printed in the United States of America

CONTENTS

PREFACE

Partly because of the magnitude of Cooper's fictional canon—his thirty-two novels average more than 500 pages in length—few people besides specialists in early American literature have read all of his works. It is hoped that the present study will be of use both to those who have not yet read his fiction and to those who have read it but have forgotten its details. Plot summaries are provided for all of his novels as well as for four shorter pieces of fiction: "Imagination," "Heart," *Le Mouchoir . . .*, and "The Lake Gun."

Like Scott and other Romantic contemporaries, Cooper provided each of his stories with a whole gallery of characters, averaging more than forty per novel and eleven per piece of short fiction. Many of these characters have one or more aliases and/or nicknames and/or sobriquets. Some of his dramatis personae, especially his Indians, have names which appear both in their original form and also in translation into one or more other languages. Thus his 1,286 characters have a total of 1,536 names, all of which are listed in the last section of this volume. There each character is identified by the title or titles of the work or works in which he appears and then by the function he serves in that fiction. An abbreviated list of characters follows each plot summary; here appear only the real names of those characters who play active roles in that novel, not those who are present but only mentioned.

A word must be said about the texts on which this study is based. The Townsend edition (New York, 1859-1861) was used for the novels, and all page references are keyed to this widely distributed, uniform set of thirty-two volumes. "Imagination" and "Heart" appeared in 1823 in a small volume entitled *Tales for Fifteen* (New York, Wiley). Our text for this little-known work was James F. Beard's facsimile edition published by Scholars' Facsimiles and Reprints (Gainesville, 1959). *Autobiography of a Pocket Handkerchief* was first published in 1823 in *Graham's Magazine*. Later that year it appeared in book form retitled *Le Mouchoir; an Autobiographical Romance* (New York, Wilson Company). It was this first American edition of the book that was used as our text. "The Lake Gun" was written for a miscellany, *The Parthenon* (New York: George W. Wood, 1850). For this short piece our text was Robert E. Spiller's reprint published in New York by William Farquhar Payson in 1932.

CHRONOLOGY

1789   James Cooper, born on September 15 in Burlington, New Jersey, to William and Elizabeth (née Fenimore) Cooper.

1790   Moved with family to Cooperstown, New York, the village founded by and named for his father on Otsego Lake, the source of the Susquehanna River.

1801   Entered the preparatory school kept by Reverend Thomas Ellison, an Episcopal clergyman, at Albany, New York.

1803   Entered Yale College.

1805   Expelled from Yale after perpetrating several pranks.

1806   Sent to sea as a common sailor before the mast for a voyage to London and the Mediterranean on the merchant ship *Stirling*.

1808   Issued a midshipman's warrant in the United States Navy on January 1.

1809   Inherited $50,000 at the death of his father, who was fatally injured by an assassin while leaving a political meeting.

1810   Took furlough from Navy, to which he never returned for active duty.

1811   Married, on January 1, Susan DeLancey, daughter of wealthy landowners in Westchester County, New York.

1817   After six years of shuttling back and forth between Westchester and Otsego Counties, settled at Scarsdale and started construction of a home at Angevine Farm, on DeLancey lands.

1819   Became head of the entire Cooper clan after the death of the last of his five elder brothers; assumed full responsibility for Cooper estates then heavily in debt.

1820   Published his first book, *Precaution*, a society novel of the type then current in England; it was unsuccessful.

1821   Published *The Spy*, the first significant American novel and one highly praised by nearly all reviewers.

1822   Moved with his growing family to New York City.

1823   Published *The Pioneers*, the first of the Leather-Stocking Tales; his son Fenimore died; his household goods were seized by a sheriff at the behest of creditors but not sold.

1824   Published *The Pilot*, the first of his eleven tales of the sea.

1826   Continued the Leather-Stocking series with *The Last of the Mohicans*; added *Fenimore* to his name to keep alive his mother's family name; sailed for Europe after large testimonial dinner sponsored by The Bread and Cheese club of New York City and attended by a host of celebrities from the east coast.

1826-
1828   Lived at Paris, into whose society he was introduced by the Marquis de Lafayette and the Princess Galitzin; published *The Prairie* while there.

1828   Published, in London, *Notions of the Americans*, a book that offended both British and American critics; started, with his family, on a Grand Tour of the Continent that carried him through France, Switzerland, Italy, and Germany.

1830-
1833   Lived at Paris, where he became involved in French politics while assisting Lafayette; wrote *Letter to General Lafayette* for the Finance Controversy, a project which earned him unpopularity at home.

1833   Returned to America to find himself unwelcome in New York City; promptly left there to live again at Cooperstown.

1838   Presented the public with a defense of his Jeffersonian political and social philosophy in *The American Democrat* and two novels, *Homeward Bound* and *Home as Found*.

1839   Published his definitive *The History of the Navy of the United States of America* in two volumes.

1840   Published *The Pathfinder* in the Leather-Stocking series.

1841   Published *The Deerslayer*, the final volume in the Leather-Stocking series.

1842   Won judgments against both Thurlow Weed and Horace Greeley in two of the many libel suits he brought against newspapers during the last years of his life.

1843   Edited the autobiography of an old shipmate from the *Stirling*, Edward Myers, with whom he was reunited after more than thirty years: *Ned Myers, or a Life Before the Mast*.

1845-
1846   Published a fictional trilogy, *Satanstoe*, *The Chainbearer*, and *The Redskins*, in defense of the landlords' position in the Anti-Rent Wars in New York State.

1850   Published his last novel, *The Ways of the Hour*.

1851   Died on September 14, one day before his sixty-second birth-
        day, at Cooperstown.
1852   Memorial services held in February in New York City, presided
        over by Daniel Webster; letters read from Hawthorne,
        Melville, Emerson, Longfellow, and others; William Cullen
        Bryant read a memorable and perceptive tribute, "Discourse
        on the Life, Genius, and Writings of James Fenimore
        Cooper."

CHRONOLOGY OF COOPER'S FICTION

PLOTS

Afloat and Ashore: A Sea Tale, 1844.

The life story of Miles Wallingford, told in this novel and its continuation, *Miles Wallingford,* begins and ends at Clawbonny, the family estate in Ulster County, New York, on the west bank of the Hudson River some fifty miles above Newburgh. It is narrated in the first person by Miles when he is in his sixty-fifth year. After the death of their father (killed in a grist-mill accident) and their mother, Miles and his sister, Grace, become wards of the Rev. Mr. Hardinge, Anglican rector. In the Hardinge household are two children in the same age group, Rupert and Lucy. Miles is sixteen and Rupert seventeen when the two boys run away in September, 1797, and go to sea, taking with them the former's eighteen-year-old black slave, Neb (Nebuchadnezzar). Their respective families had expected Miles to attend Yale and become a lawyer, Rupert to assist and then succeed his father in the local church.

The boys sign aboard the *John,* an "Indiaman"—generic name for any freighter trading in the Orient; Neb goes aboard as a stowaway but is accepted as a green hand when Miles indicates that he will work without pay. Miles soon becomes a regular seaman while Rupert serves as Captain Robbins' secretary. After taking on a cargo of tea and silk at Canton, the *John* continues westward toward the Cape of Good Hope. Off Sumatra they are pursued by pirate proas and would have been boarded had not Neb swiftly cut the line of a grappling hook entangled in their rigging. As they continue westward, Captain Robbins' nautical incompetence becomes apparent. Indulging a pet theory about ocean currents, he wrecks the *John* on the rocky coast of Madagascar. The officers and most of the men survive in open boats and are taken aboard the *Tigris,* Captain Digges in command, a vessel bound for its home port of Philadelphia.

Off Guadeloupe the *Tigris* is pursued by a French privateer, *La Folie.* Being long-handed, with the addition of the *John's* crew to his own, Captain Digges engages *La Folie,* a heavily armed brig. A boarding attempt against the *Tigris* is repulsed in an unconventional manner as Neb trains boiling water on the Frenchmen with a hose attached to a pressure pump. The privateer now falls astern the *Tigris* and attempts to disable her by firing from close range at her rigging. Two guns quickly shifted to the stern of the *Tigris* turn the tables on the aggressor, and the combat is shortly ended. Since the engagement occurs in 1798, it is pictured as part of the quasi-war at sea between the United States and France during the last two years of the eighteenth century. [This phase of our naval history is underscored by having the *Tigris* hold a gam, off the coast of Virginia, with the *U.S.S. Ganges*, an Indiaman converted into one of the first regular warships of the new U.S. Navy.]

When a pilot boards the *Tigris* off Cape May, Captain Robbins, anxious to be the first to report to the owners the loss of the *John*, arranges to go ashore in the pilot's boat, taking with him Miles and Rupert. When they are within a league of shore, a gale, blowing from the northwest, drives the small boat to sea again despite the frantic rowing of the two Cape May men and the three from the *Tigris*. They are borne within one hundred feet of the *Tigris*, but the howling wind makes their shouts inaudible to those aboard the ship. Shortly afterwards they are run down in the dark by the *Martha Wallis*, a coastal schooner. Although all four of the seamen are saved, Captain Robbins disappears in the raging sea and is seen no more.

When the pilot discovers that his rowboat has not returned, it is assumed that all aboard it have been lost. In the meantime, most of the *John's* crew arrives at Philadelphia on the *Tigris* and proceeds to New York, where they report their disastrous voyage to the owners of the *John*. Someone—apparently the *John's* second mate, Mr. Kite—has had eulogistic obituaries for Miles and Rupert printed in a New York City newspaper, and Neb has taken passage on the *Wallingford* (the family sloop that shuttles back and forth between the city and Clawbonny) to apprise Grace, Lucy, and Mr. Hardinge of the tragedy. By boarding a faster boat, an Albany-bound packet, Miles and Rupert arrive home just as the girls are trying to extract the news from the frightened and speechless Neb. Great is the rejoicing at the safe return of the runaways.

After several days of happy reunion at Clawbonny, the group embarks on the *Wallingford* for New York City, where they enjoy a pleasant holiday. Rupert, having decided to make a career of law, is placed in the New York law office of a family friend. Miles, now eighteen and determined to return to the sea, signs aboard as third mate on the armed merchantman *Crisis*, outward bound on a voyage around the world. He accepts the post on condition that Neb be allowed to ship on the same vessel as a regular seaman. Knowing that Rupert's modest cash allowance from his father will never satisfy that youth's wants in New York City, Miles arranges with the owners of the *Crisis* that $20 of his

$30 monthly salary be paid to Rupert. Despite his generous gesture toward his friend, Miles is disappointed that Rupert does not have sufficient pride to decline the offer.

After a tearful farewell with his sister and Lucy (whom he now secretly looks upon as his beloved), Miles goes to sea on the *Crisis*. Although he is a young mate, issuing orders to seamen twice his age, Miles quickly adjusts to his new responsibilities and impresses all hands favorably with his cool manner and competent behavior. At mid-point in the North Atlantic, they engage a French-owned merchantman, *La Dame de Nantes*. She is a letter-of-marque vessel, like their own and capable of approximately the same fire power. After two and a half hours of steady artillery dueling, the two ships, both quite battered, drift apart as their crews set about repairing and replacing damaged spars and rigging. By the time the *Crisis* can resume its voyage, it has drifted much farther south, abreast now of the Bay of Biscay. Through a momentary opening in a heavy fog, the first mate, Mr. Marble, sees their French antagonist less than a mile away. Moving silently abreast of *La Dame de Nantes*, the Americans deliver a deadly broadside at close range, then board and capture the French merchantman. Below decks they discover several imprisoned members of the crew of the *Amanda*, an American vessel *La Dame de Nantes* had captured and sent on toward Nantes. These men, under the command of the *Crisis'* wounded second mate, are ordered to deliver the captured French vessel to New York, the value of the ship and its cargo to be "prize money" for the officers and crew of the victor.

Shortly after the *Crisis* sets sail once more for England, it overtakes a brig which refuses to show its colors. The ship proves to be the brig *Amanda*, which is now quickly captured by the *Crisis*. The brig is placed under the command of Miles, who is ordered to take it to London, hugging the British side of the English Channel to avoid French privateers. Within sight of the English coast the *Amanda* is overtaken by a French lugger. Unequipped to fight the privateer, Miles sails into a harbor where a larger ship lies anchored. The anchored vessel is not a man-of-war but the *Dorothea*, a West Indiaman. A much richer prize than the *Amanda*, the *Dorothea* is attacked and captured by the lugger. During the battle, the *Amanda* slips away and proceeds to London, where Miles delivers the vessel to the agent of the American consignee. He is promoted to the position of second mate on the *Crisis*.

While sight-seeing in London, Miles and Mr. Marble rescue one Major Merton, his wife, and their daughter, Emily, as the team pulling their coach becomes frightened and backs their vehicle into a canal. During the remainder of their layover in London, the two mates several times visit the upper-middleclass home of the Mertons and accompany this English family to the theatre and to other events novel to Miles.

The *Crisis* sails southward early in the year 1800, stopping at Madeira and Rio de Janeiro before attempting to beat around Cape Horn near the start of winter in those high southern latitudes. With only nine hours of sunlight each day and with heavy fog constantly before them, they pick their way among the islands of Tierra del Fuego and discover one morning that instead of doubling the Cape they have passed through the Straits of Magellan into the Pacific. For five months the *Crisis* moves slowly northward along the west coast of South America, smuggling merchandise of various kinds ashore and selling it. They have only minor skirmishes with the coast-guard vessels that often pursue them. The *Crisis* then sails north to the fifty-third parallel [now British Columbia north of Vancouver], where Captain Williams hopes to trade household wares and trinkets to Indians for sea-otter skins. A native "pilot," whom the seamen dub *Dipper,* comes aboard and guides the ship into a protected, almost circular bay of some three hundred yards in diameter. Soon after the anchor has been dropped, a canoe loaded with furs comes alongside, and its three savage occupants (given the names *Smudge, Tin-Pot,* and *Slit-Nose*) quickly trade their otter skins for blankets, beads, and frying pans. Through sign language the three primitive and seemingly degenerate Indians indicate that within two days more pelts will be available.

On a brief reconnaissance trip ashore Miles and Mr. Marble discover the remains of a burned ship and near it a slate on which is written the tragedy of the vessel and its crew. An American brig, *Sea Otter,* had been lured into the bay on June 9, 1797; two days later its crew had been overwhelmed by a greatly superior force of Indians. All officers and men had been killed, including, presumably, the writer of this last communication with the civilized world. Momentarily alarmed by this last entry in the *Sea Otter's* log, the captain exhorts his men to greater vigilance during their hours on watch. The following night, however, Miles is overpowered while on watch by Dipper and Smudge, two natives who had remained aboard seemingly with no other purpose than to enjoy the daily rations of pork and beef. After Miles has been tied up and gagged, more than a hundred Indians, responding to a signal from Dipper and Smudge, board the *Crisis,* kill Captain Williams, and trap the crew below decks. As the captors are working the ship toward shore and destruction by means of a line tied to a tree, the *Crisis* breaks loose and starts drifting seaward with the tide.

Totally unacquainted with the operations of a sailing ship, Smudge and his men depend upon Miles (whom they now free) to turn the ship around and bring it to shore. By means of sign language and figures drawn on the deck, Miles indicates the need of hoisting sails, a task for which the Indians provide the necessary manpower. Applying a lighted cigar to the primer of one of the loaded deck guns, Miles terrifies his captors with the resulting explosion. All but twenty-five jump overboard and swim toward land; those who remain aboard with Smudge, their chief, are all nonswimmers. As the *Crisis* moves farther from the land and as the anxiety of the Indians becomes intense, Smudge threatens to kill Miles unless he turns the ship shoreward. By this time there is little danger in doing just that, for they have by now progressed more than a league from the nearest land. Turning into the wind so aggravates the seasickness of the Indians that their alertness is greatly reduced. At an opportune moment Miles unlocks a forward hatch, and the crew, led by Marble (now *Captain* Marble), rushes out upon the surprised natives. Those not killed in the onslaught jump overboard to their deaths, Smudge alone being held captive. Over Miles's protest their chief is later hanged from a yardarm in full view of his people as a warning. Recovering its yawl and appropriating a cache of six hundred pelts, the Americans depart.

Following the ship's scheduled course, Captain Marble sails for the Sandwich Islands [now Hawaii] to pick up a cargo of sandalwood to be traded at Canton for tea. Miles is now Marble's first mate, and Roger Talcott has been promoted to third mate. Instead of sailing directly for China after leaving Honolulu, Captain Marble indulges one of his pet dreams for acquiring a quick fortune: a pearl-fishing expedition. Taking along with them four expert Hawaiian divers, the Americans sail south until they come upon an uncharted coral island and anchor for the night in the quiet waters of its lagoon. Exhausted from day-and-night exertions, everyone sleeps soundly, including (unfortunately) Harris, the man on watch. They awaken in the morning to find themselves captives of a shipwrecked crew of fifty Frenchmen who have come aboard in the dark and captured a rich prize. The tri-color already flies from the ship's gaff.

The Frenchmen were all from the *Pauline*, a privateer wrecked on the uncharted island. They had spent their time since this accident constructing a ninety-ton schooner from the timbers and decking of the grounded *Pauline*, planning to continue on their way to France in the smaller vessel. With chivalric sentiment Captain Le Compte declares that he will turn the schooner over to the Americans when he departs in the *Crisis*. One more surprise is in store for the American officers as they go ashore at Le Compte's invitation to breakfast with him in his tent. In an adjacent tent are housed their English acquaintances Major and Emily Merton. Having been assigned to a post in Bombay, the Major and his family had almost reached that distant city when the vessel on which they had sailed was taken by the *Pauline*. Mrs. Merton had died at Manila, but the Major and Emily are now being transported to Europe again. This reversal in directions does not occasion any personal discomfort for the Mertons aside from the annoyance of Le Compte's sallies of amorous gallantry toward Emily.

Captain Marble orders unremitting work to rig and outfit the newly launched brig, *Pretty Polly*, with a view toward using it to recapture the *Crisis*. Miles considers this hope little short of fantasy, remembering that the *Crisis* is well armed and that the *Pretty Polly* is equipped with only a chest of pistols and sabers salvaged from the ocean floor where the French had thrown surplus items from the *Crisis*. As the ship is being readied to sail, Miles, while swimming, discovers a bed of large pearl oysters and brings to the surface a basketful of these shellfish. When Marble learns of this, he sets his Hawaiian divers to work filling several bags and barrels with these marine creatures. Miles from his own catch extracts about two hundred pearls, some of considerable size, all of which he puts aside to be used as gifts rather than sold.

On the morning of the eleventh day of sailing toward the west coast of South America, they sight the *Crisis*. Near sunset the wind subsides so much that the schooner is sailing at a mere two knots. Taking the four Sandwich Islanders as oarsmen, Captain Marble proceeds in a whaleboat, at the rate of five knots, to approach the Indiaman and reconnoiter her movements under the cover of darkness. A sudden and severe thunderstorm arises, however, and the whaleboat is lost; search for it all of the following day is in vain. After another fifteen days of eastering, those aboard the *Pretty Polly* sight a peak of the Andes, and three days later they anchor in a roadstead on the coast of Ecuador. From Don Pedro, a smuggler with whom they had earlier done business, they learn that the *Crisis* lies only ten miles away in a protected cove. Using a local pilot, the Americans seek out and board the *Crisis* in the dark. So completely are the French surprised that the battle lasts for only three minutes before they ask for quarter. The Americans have nine slightly wounded (including Miles himself) and one dead; the French have sixteen killed (including Captain Le Compte) plus several wounded. Major Merton and Emily, who remained below decks during the brief action, are unharmed.

Leaving the coast as quickly as possible, lest they encounter Spanish coast-guard vessels, the *Crisis* and the *Pretty Polly* are by daybreak four leagues from land. The first ship they sight is a Spanish merchantman from whom they learn that the naval war between France and the United States has been terminated. Sailing shorthanded, the Spanish captain agrees to hire the French captives of the *Crisis* as crewmen on his own vessel—an arrangement agreeable to all hands. Soon thereafter a second ship appears on the horizon, an American whaler from which a boat is at once dispatched to the *Crisis*. As the boat approaches, everyone on the *Crisis* recognizes a figure in its bow as none other than Moses Marble! Although Miles tries in every way to return command of the *Crisis* to Marble, he fails. Marble insists that since the ship was in enemy hands for more than twenty-four hours, the man who led its recapture is legally its commander. On this point he remains resolute, but he does accept temporarily the captaincy of the smaller vessel, the *Pretty Polly*.

The two vessels return to the coral island, which they now call Marble Land, in order to salvage both the rich cargo and the valuable copper from the wrecked *Pauline*. While this freight is being loaded, primarily on the schooner, Miles, Marble, Major Merton, and Emily relax and enjoy the Edenic beauty of the island and its coral reefs. During one of their conversations Major Merton remarks whimsically that he would not mind spending the rest of his life in such an idyllic spot. What the Major says in jest Marble contemplates seriously. A foundling as an infant and a bachelor as an adult, Marble has no family ties; he has been ineffectual as a marine officer, an elderly man who had never risen to the rank of captain until the sudden death of Captain Williams; and then much to his professional mortification he had lost the *Crisis* shortly after taking command. All his misfortunes have frustrated and embittered Moses Marble to the point of withdrawal. He will become a hermit on his own island, Marble Land. All efforts to dissuade him from this course fail. Miles accordingly appoints another captain for the *Pretty Polly*, which sails for New York, and shortly afterward the *Crisis* departs for Canton. The remainder of the voyage is uneventful except for a brief running battle, on the way home, with twenty-eight pirate proas in Sunda Strait, where the *John* had earlier had a similar engagement. It is June of 1802 when the *Crisis* re-enters the harbor of New York.

With the *Pretty Polly* preceding the *Crisis* to New York by several months, news of the loss of the latter and its recapture by Miles had become a sensational news story. The valuable cargoes brought back in both vessels also add appreciably to Miles's reputation. His reception in New York, therefore, is enthusiastic. Mr. Hardinge, Grace, Rupert, and Lucy are in the city at the time of his arrival, making his return most gratifying.

His subsequent sojourn ashore, first in New York City and later at

Clawbonny, proves to be less satisfying. His family estate flourishes: Clawbonny's fields are productive, his grist mill earns substantial profits, and his investments (handled for him by Mr. Hardinge) pay good dividends. Assets so ample enable him to purchase a ship of his own, the *Dawn*, a year-old vessel of five hundred tons burden. His social relationships, however, grow complex and confusing. Miles always assumed that he would marry Lucy Hardinge and that his sister, Grace, would marry Rupert. The appearance of Emily Merton in New York and the information that she and her father had sailed with Miles for the past year—a fact to which he had made no reference whatever in his letters home—fill Lucy with doubts about Miles's intentions. The news that Lucy has rejected three suitors but is still seeing a fourth, one Andrew Drewett, gives Miles some pause. The Miles/Lucy association suffers primarily, though not entirely, from a failure of communication. Both Lucy and Rupert have recently been almost adopted by Mrs. Margaret Bradfort, the wealthy cousin of their father, and through this lady's influence they have been introduced into a higher social class in New York City. Rupert, who has been receiving two-thirds of Miles's sea pay, now finds it embarrassing to associate with a mere sea captain; although Lucy does not share this feeling, she has been moving in a social group closed to a person of Miles's education and occupation. Even the benevolent and kindhearted Mr. Hardinge acknowledges, when pressed for an honest answer, that there is some class distinction between the professional tradition of the Hardinges and the commercial tradition of the Wallingfords. It is with considerable frustration and some bitterness that Miles embarks on the *Dawn* for a short voyage to Bordeaux, France.

Reluctantly Miles agrees to carry three passengers, Wallace Mortimer Brigham, his wife, Sarah, and his sister-in-law, Jane Hitchcox. Inveterate gossips and name-droppers, these Salem Yankees bore Miles with inane chatter about acquaintances made in New York while they were awaiting passage to France. Among those mentioned in their frequently misinformed observations are Mrs. Bradfort and Rupert Hardinge. The only surprise produced during the crossing of the Atlantic is the reappearance of Moses Marble. Tired of his island hermitage, Marble had returned to civilization, and after several months he had worked his way toward home until now he is on the *Dundee*, a Scottish vessel bound for London. Captain Robert Ferguson agrees to his transfer to the *Dawn*, and there is a joyous reunion between Marble and his old shipmates, especially Miles and Talcott.

Instead of returning to New York directly from Bordeaux, Miles, awaiting a cargo destined for America, fills the time by carrying freight first to Cronstadt [then a Russian port on the Baltic] and later to various cities on the Mediterranean. While touring briefly in Italy, he again meets the Brighams, this time in Florence. They regale him with news and gossip brought to them by letters from home. Among the news is the information that Mrs. Bradfort has died and left her fortune to Rupert Hardinge, a fortune so substantial that its annual income is more than $6,000. Lucy, reportedly, has received nothing.

Hoping that he and Lucy will now be close enough in social status to permit a renewal of their mutual affection, Miles hastily contracts for a cargo and sails for New York. Soon after his arrival there he meets Rupert on the street and learns Mrs. Bradfort's estate had been left to Lucy and not to her brother (whose extravagance and irresponsibility with money had apparently alarmed their wealthy cousin). Later that evening Miles meets at the theatre the Hardinges, the Mertons, and Andrew Drewett and his mother. The following day he leaves for Clawbonny, distressed at the news that Grace is ill.

Miles finds his sister's condition more serious than he had supposed. Abandoned by Rupert in favor of Emily Merton, Grace, brokenhearted, has suffered a serious physical decline. Miles, shocked at her frailty, sends to New York City for a well-known physician. When the *Wallingford* returns with Dr. Post, it brings also Moses Marble and Lucy Hardinge, who has heard of Grace's illness. It is clear to Lucy at once how grave a sickness her childhood friend suffers, and she (as Grace had done earlier) exacts a promise from Miles not to take vengeance upon Rupert for his heartless behavior.

Among other remedies for Grace Dr. Post recommends a change of scene, and soon the whole party at Clawbonny—Miles, Grace, Lucy, Mr. Hardinge, Moses Marble, and Dr. Post—cruises up the Hudson toward Albany. One of the boats they come alongside en route is the *Orpheus*, a sloop which has among its passengers Andrew Drewett and his mother. Mrs. Drewett wishes to pass a small box to Lucy, and Andrew walks out on a boom to deliver the parcel to the *Wallingford*. He slips midway and falls into the river. Told that Drewett cannot swim, Miles dives into the water to rescue him but is himself pulled down and almost drowned. The powerful Neb, swimming beneath the two struggling bodies locked together, buoys them up long enough for Marble and several seamen to pull all three aboard a boat from the *Wallingford*. Although only half conscious, Miles will clearly survive, while Drewett's body appears to be lifeless.

Antoin [sic], Margaret Bradfort, Sarah Brigham, Wallace Mortimer Brigham, Chloe Clawbonny, Dido Clawbonny, Hiram Clawbonny,

Nebuchadnezzar Clawbonny, Pompey Clawbonny, Dale, Captain Digges, Dipper, Mrs. Drewett, Andrew Drewett, Robert Ferguson, Mrs. John Foote, Archibald Gracie, Greene, Rev. Mr. Hardinge, Lucy Hardinge, Rupert Hardinge, Harris, Jane Hitchcox, Dr. Hosack, Joe, Kite, Captain Le Compte, Mrs. John Little, Captain Moses Marble, Emily Merton, Major Merton, Mrs. Merton, Morgan, Don Pedro, Dr. Post, Captain Robbins, Slit-Nose, Smudge, Sweeney, Roger Talcott, Tin-Pot, Abraham Van Valtenberg, Mrs. Wallingford, Grace Wallingford, John Wallingford, Miles Wallingford, Miles Wallingford [the younger], Walton, Captain Williams.

[*Miles Wallingford*, published separately, is not so much the sequel that its subtitle declares as a continuation of *Afloat and Ashore*. It commences in the middle of this episode.]

The Bravo: A Tale, 1831.

Set in Venice in the early eighteenth century, the novel is a fictional treatment of the corrupting influences of power and wealth on all forms of government, even a republic. Exposition, ranging from the fading glory of the city's past to the gossip of the day, is provided in the conversation of two old friends, Gino Monaldi, a gondolier, and Stefano Milano, captain of *La Bella Sorrentina*, a felucca that has just docked. (Besides its commercial ventures, the vessel also carries out secret missions for the Venetian senate.) Almost all of the dramatis personae are introduced in this first chapter through the dialogue of these two men. Their discussion ends when Gino is called by his employer, Don Camillo Monforte, Duke of Sant' Agata.

Gino and his assistant gondolier, Giorgio, row Don Camillo to his palace. There the duke directs Gino to deliver a packet, just after sundown, to one Jacopo, giving Gino his own signet ring with which to identify himself to this person. The gondolier is reluctant to undertake this mission, saying that to be seen with Jacopo, the bravo, would ruin his reputation. Jacopo is known to be an underworld agent of the Venetian nobility in their machinations to circumvent the vaunted democratic processes of government in the island republic. En route to his meeting with the notorious bravo, Gino stops at the home of his sweetheart, Annina, daughter of a wine seller, in order to disguise himself in his carnival clothes and mask. When Annina, detecting his nervousness, insists on accompanying him, Gino pretends that his purpose is to visit Stefano Milano, whose ship, he tells the girl, contains rare wines which she may wish to buy for her father's shop.

Leaving Annina to bargain with Stefano, Gino slips away and approaches the Bridge of Sighs, where he hands the Duke's signet ring to someone he mistakes in the dark for Jacopo. It is the ne'er-do-well son of Senator Gradenigo, Giacomo, who flees with the ring. Subsequently Gino meets Jacopo himself and manages, even without the ring, to persuade Jacopo that he is a servant of the duke. Much to his chagrin, Gino discovers that Annina has returned from *La Bella Sorrentina* and witnessed his interview with the bravo.

While such a concern complicates the love plot of these menial characters, political forces threaten to affect an affair of the heart in which the orphaned heiress Violetta Tiepolo may become involved. Because of her wealth, with its economic implications for the state, Violetta is not at liberty to choose a mate. In behalf of security of the state, the government will determine whom she may and may not marry. A rigorously enforced law prohibits anyone of the patrician class from holding property or title outside Venice. Just as this law will control Violetta's future love life—she is presently an ingénue of sixteen—so it strongly influences the position of Don Camillo Monforte, a young Neapolitan duke, who has recently saved Violetta from drowning when her gondola was run down by a larger vessel. In ancient times his family had had a senate seat in Venice. When the family had inherited extensive estates in Calabria, a younger son (the ancestor of Don Camillo) was sent, with government approval, to possess and administer these properties. While the Calabrian branch of the family had thrived, the older branch had gone out of existence, and now Don Camillo, heir of both branches, seeks reinstatement of the Monforte senatorial rank. To achieve this end, however, the duke must, according to Venetian law, renounce claim to all his southern seigniories.

Accompanied by Donna Florinda, her governess and chaperon, Violetta calls upon her state-appointed guardian, Senator Alessandro Gradenigo. Besides paying her respects to her aged counselor, Violetta has come to request his influence in behalf of Don Camillo, to whom she feels indebted for having saved her life. Gracious and affable until he hears her request, the crafty old senator quickly changes roles to that of the suspicious and hedging politician. After warning her against involvement in such affairs of state, he promises her, falsely, to consider the matter. His duplicity becomes apparent almost immediately. After Violetta leaves, he warns his dissolute son, Giacomo, that he now has a rival for the hand of Violetta in the person of Don Camillo. Giacomo replies that he has effectively eliminated this rival by filing an anonymous accusation against the stranger, an accusation to which the court will give credence because it was accompanied by Don Camillo's own signet ring. The senator's uneasiness at hearing this is caused not by the falseness and injustice of the charge but by the possibility that Giacomo's treachery may somehow be exposed. Soon after his son departs, the senator is visited by his foster brother, Antonio Vecchio, a poor, ragged, but proud old fisherman. Refusing the money offered to him, Antonio requests a favor of the senator: his help in securing the release of the fisherman's fourteen-year-old grandson from his servitude as a galley slave in a Venetian warship. Antonio has lost all five of his sons, the father of this boy having been killed in the continuing wars with the Turks. Although Antonio makes his request with dignity, his problem is obviously deserving of sympathy. Gradenigo's lack of compassion and his refusal of assistance are measures of the man's moral values.

Yet further dimensions of the senator's character are revealed in his continuing interviews of the evening, the next with a disguised figure who, unmasked, is recognized as Jacopo. The bravo, an undercover agent for the government, warns Gradenigo that Giacomo is borrowing money at high interest rates from Jewish brokers. Declaring that he will attend to this problem himself, the senator orders Jacopo to warn Antonio against making remarks critical of the state; Jacopo is also to promote among the common people discussion of the state's recent demonstration of justice in awarding reparations to a Genoese wronged by a Venetian. The bravo departs, and Don Camillo enters the senator's chamber. Having contacts in the Vatican and in other states, the duke is used by the Venetian nobility to further their interests abroad. Gradenigo advises him that securing for the republic better relations with Spain will be Don Camillo's best means of influencing the senate to restore the Monforte position in Venice. Some time later comes the last visitor of the night, Hosea, a Jewish jeweler and financier. Gradenigo advises Hosea to warn the Jewish moneylenders against charging unreasonably high interest rates to young patricians lest the senate take action against such usury. The senator then rewards Hosea with a hundred sequins for identifying the purchaser of an amatory signet, the information being useful in some way in the intrigues of state.

Although the senator now retires, his agent Jacopo works on into the night. Finding Antonio near the doge's palace, he cautions the old man against his outspoken criticism of the state. Unmoved by this warning, the fisherman declares that he will sleep there on the pavement in order to intercept the doge early on the morrow and plead his case against the state before its highest official. Antonio also appeals to Jacopo, the son of an old comrade in arms, to renounce his role as informer and assassin for the senate. Remaining masked and using the alias *Roderigo,* Jacopo next

confers with Stefano Milano about some secret work which the Calabrian captain is to carry out for the senate.

All of Venice turns out on the following day to watch the festivities of
the annual regatta. As the doge leaves his palace for the colorful event, he
listens to Antonio's petition and seems sympathetic until he understands
the exact nature of the old man's case; at that point his compassion fades
and he dismisses the fisherman peremptorily. After the traditional
marriage of Venice to the Adriatic—the doge casts a precious ring into
the sea and pronounces the nuptial service—the gondola races along the
Grand Canal begin. In the most important event, one open to all
contenders, Venetian and foreign, Jacopo places second, deliberately
allowing Antonio to come in first; Gino finishes third. The three winners
are brought before the doge, who rides in a splendid galley, surrounded
by Venetian officials and the diplomatic corps, to receive their awards.
Although Gino accepts the third prize, a miniature boat, Antonio refuses
to take the first prize, a golden oar, and Jacopo declines the silver oar
which is the second prize. Both request that their reward be the liberation of Antonio's grandson from galley duty.

The assembled aristocrats reject this request as a mark of disloyalty to
the state. They are even more alarmed, though they carefully conceal
their feelings from public view, when a large body of fishermen rallies
around the ragged old Antonio and calls for the restoration of his
grandson. Although the fishermen are afterwards permitted to return to
their homes in the Lagunes, at the conclusion of the regatta, their ranks
are infiltrated by gondolas of the secret police, among whom is Annina.

That night Jacopo meets Antonio by appointment, disguises him
appropriately, and conducts him to the presence of the secret, dreaded,
and most powerful executive arm of the government, the Council of
Three, of which Senator Gradenigo is a member. (Minor responsibilities
are delegated by the senate to its council of three hundred; heavier
responsibilities fall upon its Council of Ten; the most crucial matters are
decided upon by the Council of Three, whose power and authority
exceed those of the doge himself.) Both the Council members and their
subordinates are masked. After Antonio is questioned about his supposedly disrespectful efforts that day to have his grandson released, he
makes his final bid to please the tribunal: he presents them with the
valuable ring with which the doge had wedded the city to the Adriatic.
Marking with a small buoy the spot in the bay where the ceremony had
been conducted, he had returned and recovered the jeweled ring. Finding
the Council unmoved either by the Vecchio family sacrifices for the state
or by his own well-earned claims to special consideration, Antonio at last

speaks bluntly of the injustice he suffers. Bound to secrecy about his appearance before the Council, the old man is dismissed to await their verdict. In their subsequent deliberation a decision is made on Antonio's case, but the reader, like the Venetian public, is not to be informed about it until later. Among the other actions of the Council are the removal of Violetta Tiepolo's guardianship from Senator Gradenigo and a decision to place Violetta herself in a convent for better security. (These decisions had been made before Gradenigo had joined his colleagues.) Both actions may have been prompted by the anonymous accusation made against Don Camillo warning that the Neapolitan duke intended to abduct the heiress.

This same evening Don Camillo serenades Violetta beneath her balcony, later enters her palace, and proposes to her in the presence of Florinda and Father Anselmo, the Carmelite monk who is the girl's spiritual adviser. Violetta pledges that if she is not permitted to marry the duke, she will spend the rest of her life in a convent. This scene is interrupted by a state messenger who announces to Violetta that she has been removed from the supervision of Senator Gradenigo, and that her new guardian will soon be determined. Don Camillo is hidden in a chapel of the palace by Father Anselmo during this intrusion of the senate's agent. As he leaves the Tiepolo palace, the messenger requires the monk to accompany him.

The Carmelite is taken in a state gondola to the gondola of Antonio, who is fishing by moonlight for a meal to appease his hunger, where he is told to shrive the old man. Although alone now, the old man had been visited by Jacopo, who had offered him fine food; the fisherman had refused it because it had, he said, been bought with blood. After hearing Antonio's confession and blessing him, Father Anselmo declares to the state agent that an error was made, that the criminal they sought must have escaped. As the large boat moves away, however, one of its crew ties to it the little gondola of Antonio. The sudden and unexpected movement tumbles the old man into the bay, where he drowns before the returning Jacopo can rescue him.

So shocked is Father Anselmo by the assassination of Antonio that he agrees to flee, if that is possible, with Don Camillo, Violetta, and Florinda to the duke's Calabrian castle. Another official courier arrives at the Tiepolo palace to inform Violetta that she is to be removed from her family home temporarily—no mention of a convent is made—and that her only servant henceforth will be Annina, whom he has brought to begin her duties. After Annina and the courier leave the room, the four refugees hastily prepare to depart. What Don Camillo mistakes for the boat he ordered is a state-owned duplicate of the vessel. After his group is aboard the large gondola, Don Camillo is seized and thrown ashore by two gondoliers. Violetta, Florinda, Father Anselmo, and Annina (who jumps aboard) are whisked away before Don Camillo can take action. His own large gondola, commanded by Gino, pulls up to the palace water gate seconds too late. Unable to discover the whereabouts of Violetta, Don Camillo, in deep melancholy, walks among the tombs in the Jewish cemetery where he comes upon the equally melancholy Jacopo. The now proscribed bravo and the duke, formerly hostile toward each other, exchange accounts of their grievances against the corrupt state of Venice and become friends.

On the following day Jacopo, disguised, calls at the infamous dungeon opposite the doge's palace. There he is admitted by his sweetheart, Gelsomina, who, though the jailer's daughter, is a simple and innocent girl. She has no knowledge of Jacopo's occupation, and she knows him only as Carlo. She is Jacopo's means of visiting his father, Ricardo Frontoni, long a political prisoner there. It is obvious to Jacopo during this visit that his father is near death, close to the liberation which the senate cannot prevent.

Leaving the prison at dusk, Jacopo meets Don Camillo briefly and then proceeds to *La Bella Sorrentina*, where he learns from Stefano that the ship is that night to transfer from Venice a lady of high estate. Back on land again, he encounters Hosea, who, mistaking him for Giacomo Gradenigo, also informs him of the senate's plan to move Violetta that night to some destination in Dalmatia. After Jacopo leaves, Giacomo himself approaches Hosea in haste to borrow a thousand sequins. His urgent need for money is soon explained: he has his own plan to abduct Violetta that night.

Gino calls upon Annina and tells her of a nearby gondola laden with rare wine smuggled into Venice from Calabria. Although she is in great haste, and although she declares that her friendship with Gino is at an end, Annina cannot resist the opportunity to buy duty-free wine for her father's shop. When she steps into the canopied gondola, however, Annina finds herself the prisoner of Don Camillo, who demands that she disclose the present whereabouts of Violetta. Their conversation is interrupted by a mob of fishermen come to protest the murder of Antonio. Sweeping past Don Camillo's gondola on their way to the doge's palace, they intercept and capture a state boat. Aboard are no officials against whom they can take vengeance but only Violetta, Florinda, and Father Anselmo, none of whom they know. Taking the boat in tow and having the Carmelite chant prayers over the corpse, they proceed on their way. Following the instructions of the Council of Three, the doge listens to the fishermen's complaints and their demand for justice. He denies the state's responsibility for Antonio's death. Senator Soranzo, a young patrician in the official party, suggests that Jacopo, whom Antonio surpassed in the regatta, may have killed the old man for revenge. Erroneous and ironic as this suggestion is, it strikes the fishermen as plausible, and a roar goes up for the death of the bravo. The frightened patricians can now afford to be generous, and continuous prayers throughout the night are ordered for Antonio as he lies in honor in the Cathedral of St. Mark.

During the riot the state gondola, still bearing Violetta and Florinda, is neglected, and the two women make their escape. Gelsomina, seeing their distress, gives them temporary sanctuary in the prison. The jailer's daughter then agrees to bear a message to Don Camillo, but she is intercepted at the duke's palace by Annina, who persuades her simple cousin that Don Camillo is a rake and Violetta a strumpet. The gullible and confused girl does not, therefore, give the message to the duke when he appears and asks her mission. When Jacopo, posing as a gondolier, rows Gelsomina and Annina from the duke's palace, he learns from his sweetheart, sotto voce, that Violetta and Florinda are at her quarters.

Jacopo rows first to *La Bella Sorrentina*. Having served as the senate's contact man (using the name Roderigo) with her captain, Stefano Milano, Jacopo finds it easy to give orders that Annina be held aboard as part of the ship's secret cargo for the night. He then rows Gelsomina to the prison from which he takes Violetta and Florinda, whom he also delivers to the felucca. En route to pick up Don Camillo, he is stopped by Giacomo and Hosea, who hire him to assassinate the duke. Inasmuch as he is proscribed now, Jacopo agrees to undertake this bloody job lest he be exposed by Giacomo. Once free of his would-be employers, Jacopo locates Don Camillo and rushes him to *La Bella Sorrentina*, now ready to sail. The ship has already been cleared by the police for departure (supposedly to carry Violetta to a Dalmatian convent), and thus its leaving is unhampered. Jacopo accompanies the ship until it reaches the open waters of the Adriatic and then, over their strong protests, bids his friends farewell and rows his gondola back to Venice.

On the following day Jacopo visits his father, whose condition is deteriorating rapidly. In attempting to leave the prison he is trapped on the Bridge of Sighs and taken into custody. It is then that Gelsomina learns that her beloved Carlo is the feared and detested bravo, Jacopo Frontoni. His case is brought before the Council of Three and before a larger, more representative group of senators. Although penalties are given to Giacomo Gradenigo and Hosea for their attempt to have Don Camillo assassinated, no formal decision is reached concerning the bravo. The two older members of the Council of Three, however, distrusting the judgment of Paolo Soranzo, the humane and still idealistic patrician who replaced Alessandro Gradenigo on that tribunal, secretly order the execution of Jacopo the following morning. During a recess in the hearings, Jacopo has been permitted to visit his father during the old man's dying moments.

To Jacopo's own cell is now sent Father Anselmo to hear his last confession. Both the Carmelite and Gelsomina are surprised to learn that Jacopo has never committed any of the murders attributed to his hand. Using threats to torture his imprisoned father, the senate had forced him to accept the blame for all the murders committed by the secret police; even the privilege of visiting his parent has been made conditional upon his assuming the reputation of an assassin. His greatest sin has been his serving as messenger for the state in its nefarious activities.

Father Anselmo and Gelsomina go directly to the doge's palace and insist on an audience with the prince, but before he listens to their plea, the aged figurehead of power invites a nearby member of the Council of Three to audit the interview. The monk and Jacopo's betrothed explain so persuasively the injustices suffered by the Frontoni family that the doge, moved to tears, promises a further hearing on the matter. Gelsomina and Father Anselmo leave with confidence that there will be a stay of execution. Even as Jacopo is led to the block the next morning, they expect a last-minute reprieve to be signaled by the doge, but at the prescribed moment the axe glitters in the air and the head of Jacopo rolls on the pavement. Gelsomina loses her mind at the horrible spectacle, and the Carmelite is stunned into immobility. He is led by a friend to the outskirts of Venice and started on a journey to the Papal State. He eventually becomes a member of the household of Don Camillo, Duke of Sant' Agata.

Father Ferdinand Anselmo, Bartolomeo, Father Battista, Enrico, Senator Enrico, Florinda, Jacopo Frontoni, Ricardo Frontoni, Gelsomina, Giorgio, Giulio, Senator Alessandro Gradenigo, Giacomo Gradenigo, Hosea, Olivia Mentoni, Captain Stefano Milano, Gino Monaldi, Duke Don Camillo Monforte, Pietro, Giulietta Soranzo, Senator Paolo Soranzo, Violetta Tiepolo, Annina Torti, Giuseppe Torti, Tommaso Torti, Antonio Vecchio.

The Chainbearer; or, The Littlepage Manuscripts, 1845.
[This is the second volume in a trilogy, preceded by *Satanstoe* and followed by *The Redskins*.]

Mordaunt, or Mordy, Littlepage, the narrator, the only surviving son of Cornelius and Anneke Mordaunt Littlepage [central characters in *Satanstoe*], participates—as do his father and paternal grandfather—in various battles culminating in Independence. Mordy's maternal grandfather, a Tory, dies during a visit to England; his paternal grandfather, General Evans Littlepage, dies of smallpox at the end of the Revolutionary War, and the General's friend Brom Follock (Abraham Van Valkenburgh) is killed and scalped by Indians while returning to quarters after a week-long drunken carouse. The surviving members of the family are at last reinstated at Lilacsbush, one of the family's estates along the Hudson River, following the war.

After his graduation from Nassau College [later Princeton], Mordy is assigned the responsibility of subdividing the two extensive family patents northeast of Albany, Mooseridge and Ravensnest; the subdivision is to be effected by his selling parcels of Mooseridge and leasing parcels of Ravensnest to land-hungry Yankees. Mordy's older sister, Anneke, is happily married to Mr. Kettletas; Mordy's spirited younger sister, Kate, has been courted and won by Tom Bayard. Mordy, uncomfortable under the family pressure—especially from his grandmother—urging him to marry Priscilla Bayard, Tom's sister, whose manner seems to Mordy both insincere and dominating, is determined not to be rushed. Pris Bayard's fulsome praises of Dus (Ursula) Malbone, the niece of Andries Coejemans (Chainbearer), and Pris's knowledgeability of the land-settlement situation in upstate New York arouse Mordy's curiosity and prompt Mordy's grandmother to express doubt that a young girl reared by a chainbearer under such circumstances could in any respect be ladylike. Motivated both by duty and by interest, Mordy takes Jaap Satanstoe, his personal slave, with him and sets out for his work on the land patents. On the sloop Mordy takes to Albany are a number of landseekers, readily identifiable by their axes and their packs of settlers' effects: these men soon learn through Jaap the errand on which Mordy is engaged, and within the week the sloop requires to reach Albany, all the would-be settlers have determined to lease land at Ravensnest, reserving their small cash holdings for purchase of various farmstead necessities.

Mordy leaves Albany for the patents immediately upon his arrival there, stopping at the log tavern near Ravensnest. Apprised of his identity, Mrs. Tinkum, garrulous squatter landlady of the tavern, expresses to Mordy her disappointment that the Littlepages did not side with the British and thus lose their patents following the colonists' victory. By her comments about Chainbearer, Mordy discerns that the unschooled but diligent surveyor—Mordy's superior officer during the

recent war—is one of the few truly high-principled men in the area, and
he voices this view to Mrs. Tinkum, prompting a derisive remark about
the unwarranted pride of Chainbearer's niece. Mordy, disgusted by the
landlady's vulgarity, leaves the tavern and strikes out for Ravensnest, to
be followed by Jaap when the latter has finished eating. En route, Mordy
hears a girl's beautiful singing in Onondago; subsequently he sees an
Indian emerging from the wooded area of the singing, but he is unable to
see the singer herself. The Indian proves to be Susquesus, a longtime
friend of the Littlepage family [the details of the friendship are furnished
in *Satanstoe*], and the two walk together to Ravensnest, talking of both
past and present land-settlement problems. Susquesus owns no property
and envisions being reduced to broom-making for a living; Mordy
resolves that Susquesus and Chainbearer (a friend of both Mordy and
Susquesus) will each have enough land for self-support.

An overview of Ravensnest shows Mordy the small hamlet, 'Nest
Village, with its mill seats and scattered, well-cultivated farmsteads,
surrounded by virgin hardwood forest. When Mordy and Susquesus
arrive in the village, Jason Newcome, Yankee owner of the mill seats as
well as local agent for the Littlepages, is conducting an election to
determine the denomination of the church to be established in the
village; the building itself is already under construction. Mordy, unidentified, observes Newcome's tactics with keen interest: Newcome clearly
supports majority rule and maneuvers adroitly to achieve the appearance
of majority rule. By degrees eliminating those eligible to vote against his
own preference in the matter, Newcome manages to muster sufficient
support for the Congregational denomination. Newcome, made suddenly aware—by Jaap's arrival—of Mordy's identity, is decidedly embarrassed but is reassured that Mordy had just arrived. Mordy determines to
keep a watchful eye on his opportunistic agent and to replace him as soon
as possible.

The denomination of the church being decided, the settlers complete
the church building, with both Chainbearer and Mordy aiding in the
difficult and dangerous business of putting the roof into position. At the
moment when it appears that the roof must collapse upon the builders, a
young woman sees the danger and supports a prop herself, averting the
falling of the roofbeam. Mordy and Chainbearer walk to the fort at Nest-
house, where Mordy hears the same girl singing and learns she is not an
Indian, as he had supposed from the language, but Dus Malbone, of
whose gentle breeding and intellect he has heard from her former
schoolmate Priscilla Bayard; the orphaned Dus is the daughter of Chainbearer's half-sister, and is totally dependent upon her half-uncle for her

support. Distressed to learn that Dus herself has performed the arduous labor of carrying chain for Chainbearer (who cannot afford to hire such help), and observing that the girl has indeed excellent breeding as well as a tender interest in her half-brother Frank Malbone's opportunity for advancement, Mordy transfers the position of agent at Ravensnest from Jason Newcome to Frank Malbone, placing the latter in sufficiently sound circumstances to court the girl he has long loved, Priscilla Bayard.

Jason Newcome, acceding graciously enough to his replacement by Malbone, engages in a long and wordy wrangle with Mordy as to the former's right to *own* the mill seats he has developed, succeeding at last in his real objective: a renewal of the lease for three lives at a very low rent. The rest of the tenants at Ravensnest opt also to renew their leases rather than to purchase land at Mooseridge, a decision perplexing to Mordy.

A visit by Chainbearer, Dus, Susquesus, and Mordy to a pigeon roost on Mooseridge patent occupied by millions of birds affords the author an opportunity to express his distrust of rule by the majority, a lengthy diatribe frequently broken by comments on the marvel of the birds. Shortly after the pigeon hunt, Jaap, Susquesus, and Chainbearer go to find and mark the graves of the surveying party murdered and scalped during the original surveying of the patent [the grisly murders are recounted in *Satanstoe*], Mr. Traverse, Pete, and the others. While they are gone, Mordy seeks out Dus and declares his love for her, a love she says she cannot accept because she is pledged to another whose identity she does not reveal (the pledge is later revealed as that of her loyalty to Chainbearer). Distraught by Dus's rejection of his suit, Mordy plunges into the forest, wanders until exhausted, and then sleeps; he wakes to find that Susquesus has covered him with a blanket. At Susquesus's report that he heard a sawmill, the two go to locate it. Since none of Mooseridge has been sold, the mill is an illegal operation and must be investigated.

The lumber thief proves to be an old Vermont squatter named Aaron Timberman, commonly called Thousandacres, one to reckon with. After some amiable conversation, during which Mordy identifies himself only as Mordaunt, the squatters become suspicious and confine both Susquesus and Mordy in the impregnable storehouse, to protect the lumber the squatter and his family have labored to mill. Susquesus escapes but is presumably recaptured. Meanwhile, Jason Newcome, the purchaser of the lumber, comes secretly, and he and Thousandacres bargain (within Mordy's hearing) over the price to be paid by Newcome. Common terms are not reached, and Newcome leaves hastily as three of Thousandacres' sons appear in the clearing with the recaptured Susquesus. Susquesus, placed in the storehouse with Mordy, tells Mordy he has reported the capture to Jaap and then allowed himself to be recaptured, to allay Thousandacres' suspicions. After a bitter struggle, Chainbearer, suddenly appearing on the scene, is throttled by Thousandacres but throws him, and then is imprisoned in the storehouse by Thousandacres' boys. Dus, Mordy is told, has accompanied her uncle and is standing guard with Jaap in the woods while Frank and the rest go to secure arrest warrants from Jason Newcome.

Dus has sent a note to Zephaniah Thousandacres by Chainbearer, a note he passes out to the young man through a chink in the log wall. Zephaniah, unable to read Dus's elegant handwriting, asks Mordy to read it to him; in it, Dus urges Zephaniah to keep the peace between Chainbearer and old Thousandacres and to ensure the protection of Major Littlepage. Zephaniah refuses, on Mordy's petition, to allow the prisoners to escape, despite an offer of fifty acres of land of his own. When Zephaniah is called away for a family conference, Lowiny (Lavinia) Thousandacres, one of Aaron's daughters, comes near the storehouse and at Mordy's request carries a note to Dus urging her to return to safety. Lowiny is gone for more than an hour, on the pretext of berry-picking. In the meantime, Zephaniah releases Susquesus to roam in the clearing, under restrictions the Indian promises to observe. Neither Chainbearer nor Mordy is to be released, a circumstance prompting sharp words from Chainbearer.

At last the two prisoners are led to Thousandacres' hut. The argument that ensues between Thousandacres and Chainbearer is heated and acrimonious, and results in Chainbearer's being reconfined in the storehouse. Under cover of the bustle, Lowiny assists Mordy into the cellar, searched thoroughly by the Thousandacre boys without Mordy's being detected thanks to his own assiduous assistance in the search under cover of the shadow deliberately cast by Lowiny into the cellar area. As they go outside to look for Mordy, Lowiny advises him to run and hide in the mill, which he does. Thousandacres and his sons meet in the mill to discuss the feasibility of various plans for disposing of their troublesome prisoners and of safeguarding their lumber, but they do not detect Mordy in the loft. After they leave, Lowiny urges Mordy to flee to Dus and safety. Mordy finds Jaap and then Dus, and Mordy and Dus confess their love for one another. While they are still talking, they are surprised by Tobit, Zephaniah, and Lowiny Thousandacres. Mordy and Dus are captured; Dus is put into the custody of Tobit's wife, and Mordy is returned to the storehouse. There Mordy and Chainbearer discuss

Mordy's suit for Dus's hand, and Chainbearer declares she is too far
beneath him for a suitable marriage. While they are still discussing this
point, Thousandacres' sons come to fetch the two for another council in
Thousandacres' hut; Susquesus is left behind.

The council begins amicably enough, and Dus is brought to join the
group. After a long preamble, Thousandacres proposes to bring peace
between his family and Chainbearer by marrying Dus to Zephaniah, a
proposal Chainbearer greets with scorn and indignation. He starts to
lead Dus out of the house; a rifle cracks, and Chainbearer falls. Dus
moves immediately to his side, and Thousandacres and his wife Prudence
are the only ones who remain in the room with the grieving girl and her
uncle. Suddenly, more shots are heard; a posse led by an under-sheriff
and including Frank Malbone has come to rescue Mordy Littlepage. In
the excitement, old Thousandacres is shot—by Susquesus, Mordy suspects—and Prudence hastens to him. The rest of the Thousandacres
family escape under cover of darkness except for Lowiny, who remains to
comfort Dus and caution Mordy against exposing himself to Tobit. In a
conversation between Jason Newcome and Mordy, Newcome realizes
that Mordy may have overheard from the storehouse the conversation
the old squatter had had with Newcome concerning the purchase of the
lumber, a matter of embarrassment to the erstwhile agent but one on
which his curiosity and anxiety are never satisfied. Frank Malbone, on
learning of Mordy's capture, had posted a letter to Mordy's parents, a
circumstance that will require earlier disclosure of Mordy's plan to marry
Dus than he intended, but Mordy is determined to declare the facts, as he
tells Dus in a brief conversation. She then goes inside the hut to offer last
prayers for old Thousandacres; Frank and Mordy kneel during the
prayer, but Prudence Thousandacres and her daughter Lowiny remain
upright, disdaining formalistic prayer. Not long afterwards, Chainbearer
extracts a promise from Dus that she will not marry Mordy Littlepage
against his family's wishes; Mordy will not make that pledge. Meanwhile,
Thousandacres dies, still sullen and fierce in his resentment, and un-
shriven. The following morning, Chainbearer dies peacefully.
Thousandacres is interred on his squatter property; Chainbearer is taken
to Ravensnest for burial. As Mordy has promised Prudence Thousandacres, all the family members' personal property is packed into a boat that
is set adrift downriver from the mill, and she is gracious enough to
acknowledge its receipt. Neither the members of the Thousandacres
family nor Jason Newcome is prosecuted for losses incurred through the
squatters' lumbering.

Mordy's family proves warm and responsive to Dus as Mordy's prospective bride, and they are soon married. Subsequently, Pris Bayard marries Frank Malbone, the culmination of a courtship of several years' standing but awaiting Frank's improved financial circumstances, the consequence of a substantial inheritance from a Malbone relative; Kate Littlepage marries Tom Bayard. All three marriages are happy and fruitful ones, attended by bequests on one side and another that remove all cause of financial worry. Lowiny, after several years as Dus's household servant, is suitably married to a respectable Ravensnest tenant. The death of Chainbearer is not forgotten, but he is felt to be safe with the Lord.

Ravensnest becomes the site for Mordy and Dus's new home, as Mordy's parents have urged. Not far from that home live Susquesus and Jaap, comrades in their later years.

Priscilla Bayard, Thomas Bayard, Captain Bogert, Captain Andries Coejemans, Major Hosmer, Anneke Littlepage Kettletas, Mrs. Light, Anna Cornelia Mordaunt Littlepage, General Evans Littlepage, Mrs. Evans Littlepage, Katrinke Littlepage, Major Mordaunt Littlepage, Francis Malbone, Ursula Malbone, Jason Newcome, Mrs. Jason Newcome, Jacob Satanstoe, Mrs. Jacob Satanstoe, Susquesus, Aaron Timberman, Daniel Timberman, Lavinia Timberman, Moses Timberman, Nathaniel Timberman, Prudence Timberman, Tobit Timberman, Mrs. Tobit Timberman, Zephaniah Timberman, Tim Trimmer, Major Dirck Van Valkenburgh, Mary Wallace, Willis.

The Crater; or, Vulcan's Peak : A Tale of the Pacific, 1847.

Born in Bristol, Bucks County, Pennsylvania, Mark Woolston, protagonist of the novel, is the oldest child of one of the village's two physicians. After attending Princeton for three years, Mark hears the call of the sea and, in 1793, ships aboard the *Rancocus* (Captain Crutchely, Master), a vessel in the China trade. Adapting quickly to nautical life, Mark advances in station so rapidly that he returns, still not quite nineteen, as second mate with the promise of being first mate on the next voyage.

Back in Bristol, Mark now seriously courts Bridget Yardley, only child of Dr. Yardley, aggressive and somewhat paranoid medical competitor of Dr. Woolston. When Dr. Yardley learns of this relationship, he orders Mark out of his home, more for economic reasons than for any personal dislike of the youth. The doctor cannot bear the thought that his professional rival might benefit from the considerable wealth left to Bridget by her mother, who had died while Mark was at sea. Although

Yardley suspects Mark of courting Bridget for her money rather than for herself, the young suitor is not even aware, at this point, of the girl's inheritance. The prospect of lengthy separation during Mark's next voyage encourages the couple to marry; but because of parental disapproval, the wedding is a secret one held aboard the *Rancocus* and conducted by a young minister who had been a college friend of the groom. When they break the news to their families, they experience the displeasure of both Dr. Woolston and Dr. Yardley. A compromise is reached, however, when these two professional rivals confer on the matter. In view of the tender age of the bride—she is sixteen—it is agreed that the marriage will not be consummated until Mark returns from his imminent voyage to the Orient. Dr. Yardley secretly hopes that he will not return.

Rounding Cape Horn and sailing north past Valparaiso, the *Rancocus* approaches uncharted reefs in the Pacific. Refusing to believe either the lookout's or Mark's warning of white water ahead, Captain Crutchely, drinking with the second mate, Hillson, runs the ship aground. When Crutchely is swept overboard from the canting vessel, Mark launches a jolly boat in an attempt to rescue him; but neither the captain nor the six-man boat crew is seen again. While Mark is preparing to drop anchor, Hillson gathers all but one of the remaining ten crew members and departs in the launch of the *Rancocus,* leaving Mark and the "old salt" Bob Betts the sole occupants of the vessel. When morning comes, the two leave the ship in a dinghy to explore what appears to be an island some two leagues away. Upon arriving there, they discover it to be an almost barren reef at the center of which is the cone of an extinct volcano. The crater within the cone covers about a hundred acres.

With no hope of maneuvering the *Rancocus* against the wind to extricate her from the maze of shoals and reefs, and with no illusions about sailing the crewless vessel to civilization even if they could free her, Mark and Bob decide to bring the ship in as close as possible to the crater islet and then ferry ashore in the dinghy its usable stores. They are obliged, as Betts says, to "Robinson Crusoe it a while" (p. 61). A small collection of livestock—pigs, a goat, chickens, and ducks—are taken ashore to fend for themselves as much as possible. All kinds of seeds are found in the ship's supplies (intended as items to be traded with the Fijis for sandalwood), but the reef is void of soil in which to plant them. They laboriously begin amassing a substitute for ordinary soil, a mixture of seaweed, volcanic ash, guano, and humus, a pocket of which Bob finds in the large cavity of a nearby reef. They plant as many seeds as their supply of soil substitute will accommodate, and within a few days they are gratified to see their first crop sprouting. While it grows, Bob catches great quantities of fish with which they feed both themselves and their livestock. Boatloads of seaweed are also brought ashore as fodder for their animals and fowls. As more humus is hauled to the crater and its salt content leached out by gentle rains, Mark gradually sows the slopes with grass seed.

After three months, with food for the future now assured, the two men search the hold of the *Rancocus* for parts of a prefabricated pinnace, about which Bob had heard the owner, Abraham White, speak while the ship was being loaded. Supposedly, the boat was to be assembled for use while the officers traded with the natives of the Fiji Islands. Mark doubts the existence of such a vessel, but among the lumber in the hold, they do indeed find the carefully cut and marked pieces of a pinnace. This thirty-foot boat—small enough to thread the shoals but large enough to be fairly seaworthy—they now begin to assemble on shore, close to the water's edge to permit easy launching. When the construction is completed, the *Neshamony* (as they name the pinnace) is outfitted and provisioned from the ship's stores. A tropical storm now begins and threatens to inundate much of the lower levels of the reef. While Mark carries tools and other valuables up to the crater, Bob goes to secure the new boat. Before Mark can return to aid the old seaman, a large wave lifts the *Neshamony* from her ways and launches her prematurely. The gale drives the boat to sea with Bob Betts aboard.

Soon after the hurricane subsides, Mark becomes seriously ill with a tropical fever. Sick aboard the *Rancocus* for several weeks, he requires more than two months to recover fully. During that time, he reflects upon his solitary condition and the minimal chance of his ever being rescued. His survival is no longer in question, however, for he finds his garden lush with melons and many kinds of vegetables.

Using lumber and some ready-cut parts found in the hold of the *Rancocus,* Mark puts together another boat, an eighteen-foot craft which he christens *Bridget Yardley.* Sailing her among the reefs and shoals on a trial cruise, Mark hastens home at sunset after observing a strangely ominous sky. In the middle of the night an earthquake rocks the area, and a volcano erupts, casting a lurid glow and emitting noxious fumes. When dawn arrives, Mark discovers that the quake has thrown upward some ten or fifteen feet a nearby reef. Later he finds that his own reef, crater and all, has risen the same amount without any discernible damage to its surface. Climbing to its summit, Mark is able to see numerous new islands around him, most of them shoals or reefs that have been thrust upward by the convulsion of the earth. Some of these now connect with his own reef, thus adding extensively to his domain; from one of these newly risen areas bubbles a freshwater spring which soon forms a small lake. In the distance, near the volcano erupting in the sea, towers a mountain to the height of a thousand feet or more. When he sails the sixty miles to this mountain, which he names Vulcan's Peak, Mark realizes that its upper section must have been above the surface of the sea for many years, for it is heavily wooded with trees of many kinds, including coconut palm, fig, and breadfruit. For ten days Mark explores the region in the *Bridget Yardley*, naming all its topographical features.

One day while he is on Vulcan's Peak, Mark is amazed to see, at no great distance, the *Neshamony* manned by Bob Betts and a companion. It had been fourteen months since Bob and the pinnace had vanished in the hurricane, and Mark had had little hope of ever seeing him again. Firing his musket, Mark attracts the attention of his old friend, and the two are soon reunited. So great are the surprise and shock to Mark that Bob relates his story slowly lest it overcome the distraught young man.

Carried away from the crater reef by high winds, Bob had sailed the *Neshamony* to an island populated by friendly natives. Ooroony, leader of these people, had transported Bob to a distant island where a Spanish pearl-fishing ship lay at anchor. Joining this ship's company, Bob had sailed with them to the Isthmus of Panama and had, in several stages of travel, made his way to Bristol, where he had given accounts of the fate of the *Neshamony* and the plight of Mark Woolston. Bridget, whose father had taken unsuccessful legal action to force a divorce on her, at once organized and funded an expedition to rescue Mark. Besides Bob Betts and his newly wed wife, Martha, the party of twelve included Mark's sister, Anne, her husband, Dr. John Heaton, and a shipwright named Bigelow. Bob guided the group, retracing his course, step by step, until he reached Ooroony's island and repossessed the *Neshamony* (which during his absence had been isolated and protected as a taboo object by the tribesmen). The pearl fishermen who had brought them to this island had also transported for them horses, cattle, and ample equipment for farming. From there, Bob had carried the passengers in the *Neshamony* to an island not far from Vulcan's Peak while native catamarans transferred the freight.

After a joyful and emotional reunion of Mark and Bridget and the introduction of Mark to his new brother-in-law, Dr. Heaton, the entire group rests for a week. Then begins the final stage of their trip, the ferrying of people, animals, and equipment to the Edenic loveliness of the lower slopes of Vulcan's Peak. The *Neshamony* shuttles back and forth for several days until the move is completed.

It soon becomes evident that this pristine site may not be entirely safe as a dwelling place. While Mark is at the crater reef, a large flotilla of war

canoes and catamarans is sighted offshore. Studying the boats with field
glasses, Bob sees in the lead boat one Waally, a fierce and treacherous
native chief hostile to Ooroony. Bob thinks he can also distinguish
among the occupants of that canoe two white men. To reconnoiter their
movements and equipment, Bob circles them, at a distance, in the
Neshamony, and later that night he has the temerity to land on their home
island to gather additional information. To his great surprise, he is met
near the shore by two former whalers, Peters and Jones; both had been
guests and then captives of the islanders. Peters had married a native girl,
Petrina, but now both he and Jones are ready to leave and join the new
colony. It is the intention of Waally, they claim, to massacre the white
settlers and plunder their equipment and supplies. Back at Vulcan's Peak,
Mark, Bob, and their friends decide to mount strategically (so that they
will command the landing places) two of the eight carronades stored in
the *Rancocus*. These are brought and readied for service in any crisis that
may develop.

The settlers now begin to build houses with lumber hewn from trees
on the Peak, and Bigelow begins the construction of an eighty-ton
schooner, which will provide both a means of traveling anywhere in the
Pacific and greater protection against any attack made by the Kannakas.
For months, however, nothing menaces the tranquillity of the new Eden.
Children are born to Anne and John Heaton, to Bridget and Mark
Woolston, and to Martha and Bob Betts. Jones marries Martha's sister,
Joan, and Peters pleads for a boat with which to visit Waally's island and
carry off his lost Petrina. Mark so pities Peters (remembering his long
separation from Bridget) that he agrees to take him back in the *Neshamony*.
En route, they swing wide from their course in order to examine the
volcano still erupting from the sea. After landing on the outer, cool edge
of the cone, Mark and Bob hear a shout from Peters aboard the pinnace,
and at the next moment they see the seaman rush ashore and embrace his
Petrina. When Waally had assembled a hundred canoes and a thousand
warriors to attack the settlement on Vulcan's Peak, Petrina and her
brother Unus had departed, under the cover of darkness, paddling in the
direction of the smoking volcano, knowing that the mountain isle Waally
was to attack must be nearby. Petrina felt certain that this was the place
where her husband had taken refuge. With the news of imminent
invasion, Mark and his companions immediately return to defend Vulcan's Peak. Even with the addition of Unus, the settlement's fighting
force now numbers only eight men.

When Waally's armada comes close to shore, a cannon is fired into the
air. Although some of the natives have heard artillery fire before, none

has experienced the phenomenon of echo, and the reverberations rolling several seconds along the shores and among the heights frighten them. Fearing that the local gods are angry, they paddle away in terror; but no one doubts that sooner or later they will return. Completion of the schooner now becomes crucial, for it will provide a vehicle of pursuit. Leaving men to handle the carronades at Vulcan's Peak, Mark sails with four men to the crater reef to push forward the work on the new vessel. As they approach the reef, near sunset, however, they are shocked to find that it too has been discovered by Waally's men, many of whom are camped on an adjacent island. The governor, as Mark is now called, calms the momentary panic of his handful of men with his quiet and confident preparations for defense. Earlier, Mark had learned from Jones of seven additional white sailors held by Waally, captives Jones had never seen but whose descriptions, as he had them from others, fitted those members of the *Rancocus'* crew lost three years ago. Now as they await Waally's attack, Mark and his men are pleasantly surprised to be hailed in English from the darkened waterfront. There they find Jim Wattles, crewman, and Bill Brown, ship carpenter, of the *Rancocus,* who had made their escape from Waally's warriors. They describe in detail their protracted stay with the savages and their method of escape during the present expedition; they also corroborate Jones's report that there are five additional members of their crew still in captivity.

At dawn, work is resumed to launch *Friend Abraham White,* the new schooner named after the Quaker owner of the *Rancocus.* Before it is quite in the water, a force of 1,200 to 1,500 Kannakas attack from the next island. They are raked with grapeshot from carronades, and then when the schooner goes down the ways, pursued into the open sea by the new ship. In the course of this chase, the settlers run down a canoe and capture its crew, among whom is a favorite son of Waally. After extended dickering, Waally agrees to exchange his five white prisoners for his son's release. Accompanying the canoe fleet to its island base, Mark recovers his long-lost shipmates; and while there, he also strengthens the hand of Ooroony, Waally's rival, by providing the friendly chief with supplies of various kinds. This, Mark feels, will reduce the likelihood of future attacks on Vulcan's Peak and the crater reef.

Back at his colony, Mark begins to be bothered by a matter of conscience. With his greatly improved circumstances, does he not owe some return to the owners of the *Rancocus?* Abraham White, its original owner, had collected insurance for it after the *Rancocus* had been unheard from for a year; but there is still a moral obligation to the underwriters. Mark now has fourteen men under his command and could hire additional help from among Ooroony's people. The ship, though still locked among the reefs, might now, with the manpower and skill available, be somehow hauled into clear water. Mark has been using the ship's supplies for three years, but the *Rancocus* itself is still intact. It is decided, therefore, to complete, however belatedly, the original sailing plan: picking up sandalwood among the islands, selling it at Canton—the Chinese cherish it for making idols and other religious objects—and returning to Philadelphia with a valuable cargo of tea. This plan Mark proceeds to put into effect.

While at Canton, Mark purchases the *Mermaid,* an old ship of two hundred tons burden, and sends it to the crater reef, piloted by Bigelow and loaded with Americans who, for a variety of reasons, have been stranded in China and are now quite willing to join the Woolston colony. Back in Philadelphia, Mark reports to the insurance company which has legal rights to the *Rancocus.* After recovering their losses, with interest, the underwriters give the vessel to Mark plus $11,000, the value of the tea that exceeds their own claims. While back in Bristol, Mark is received by Dr. Yardley, who has recanted sufficiently to make available to his son-in-law extensive funds from Bridget's estate.

Mark is now able to return to his islands with a ship loaded with settlers, additional livestock, and supplies of all kinds. Enlisting first an old friend, John Pennock, he delegates to him authority to select willing settlers of good moral record and a wide variety of skills. Exactly 207, plus more than fifty children, embark on the *Rancocus* for a new life in the Pacific. As they appproach the volcanic isles of Mark's domain, they are met by the *Mermaid,* manned not by settlers but by Kannakas. Capturing the ship and driving off the natives, Mark finds imprisoned in the hold Saunders, Bigelow, and a steward; from these men he learns certain news: Ooroony had died, and his son had been quickly deposed by Waally, who immediately began to organize forces to move against Vulcan's Peak. Capturing the *Mermaid* was but a minor part of the intended invasion. Betts, commanding a launch, is sent with a force of twenty-five well-armed men to reinforce the defenders of the crater reef, who are attacked the following morning. Retreating upward into the mouth of the crater, the settlers hold an impregnable position. The siege is soon lifted as the *Rancocus* and the *Mermaid,* approaching from two different directions, come into view.

With the military crisis at an end, the process of settling all of the colonists (soon to number more than five hundred) begins. Governor Woolston declares that the land belongs to the state, not to him and Bob Betts. Besides his garden in the crater, Mark accepts a thousand acres on

Vulcan's Peak and an unsettled island of the same size. Betts refuses to take more than a hundred acres on the crater reef. Each other man of twenty-one or more years receives a grant of fifty acres on Vulcan's Peak and a hundred acres on an unsettled island. Farming soon flourishes throughout the group of islands, especially on Vulcan's Peak, and there is never any doubt that the colony can be self-sustaining. There is some concern, for a while, about a source of cash income for the colony now that the sandalwood forests have been largely depleted. At the suggestion of a Nantucket whaler, Walker, a couple of whaling ships are fitted out, and within six months valuable cargoes of whale oil are being shipped to Hamburg.

As the colony grows and develops, Mark can no longer govern it without help. Accordingly, a council of nine members is appointed to advise the governor. Mark's brother Charles becomes the colony's first Attorney General; his brother Abraham becomes its first Secretary; and an independently wealthy settler named Warrington becomes its first judge. To accommodate such governmental functions Mark personally finances the building of a large public structure named Colony House. One of the tokens most indicative of the tiny nation's coming of age is the establishment of a postal system serviced by a packet boat that calls regularly at all populated islands.

Such positive processes of society are suddenly threatened by a negative force from the outside world: piracy. A frigate-rigged ship tended by two armed brigs sails directly for Vulcan's Peak guided in its course by Waally and several of his subordinate chiefs. When their demand for great quantities of meat and other supplies is rejected, hostilities commence. Although the firepower of the three vessels exceeds that of the colonists, the pirates have the disadvantage of operating in strange and treacherous waters. Waally can lead them to Vulcan's Peak but is ignorant of the natural labyrinth of reefs, shoals, and blind passages throughout the group of islands that constitute the colony. Using his several small vessels strategically, always just beyond the range of buccaneer guns, he finally leads the frigate into a cul-de-sac where it runs aground while tacking to escape. A single shore battery now pounds the vessel steadily until two hot shots [cannon balls heated red-hot in a forge] set it afire. As the flames spread, the ship is abandoned by all those able to flee; shortly afterwards its magazine explodes, completely demolishing the vessel. Among the wounded left aboard was Waally, whose body is found, missing an arm, as the brigs escape to the open sea and disappear.

A more serious threat to the colony comes from within. A few months after the conclusion of the "Pirate War," a group of fifty new immigrants arrives. These are not applicants screened by either the governor or his council, according to the requirements for citizenship, but the relatives and friends of older settlers. Among them are a printer, a lawyer, and clergymen from four denominations (Baptist, Methodist, Presbyterian, Quaker) to compete for souls with the Episcopalian Mr. Hornblower. All six of these newcomers create discord and wrangling among the settlers. There begins a great clamor for "rights" of all kinds, many of them running counter to the constitution and the laws of the little nation. The newspaper founded quickly by the printer constantly agitates the citizens, often with false or irresponsible editorials. Mark is ousted from the governor's office and replaced by John Pennock, the first settler he had recruited for the colony. Claims are made against Mark's property by newly arrived immigrants totally unaware that Mark and Betts had converted much of the land from barren waste to its present state of productivity. (Extensive authorial intrusions draw obvious parallels between the abuses of democracy here and in the United States of the 1840s.)

Partly from disgust at these developments and partly because they wish to see their homeland again, the Woolstons, the Heatons, and the Bettses decide to visit the United States. This they do, arriving home in Pennsylvania after a long absence. Before the whole party is ready to return to the Pacific isles, Mark decides to take a shipload of supplies to his colony; Bob Betts accompanies him, this time as a passenger. When they reach the destined latitude and longitude, however, they cannot find the colony. Finally they identify just the tip of Vulcan's Peak and the upper rim of the crater above the water level, the whole area having sunk into the sea to the depth of a hundred fathoms in some places. Discussing the catastrophe with young Ooroony, whom they visit on the way home, Mark and Bob learn of a recent devastating earthquake, apparently part of the titanic shift in the earth's crust that had submerged their paradise in the Pacific Ocean. Although the disaster seemingly was caused by a freak of nature, there is a suggestion of divine retribution against a people gone astray, political and social behavior throughout the novel having been viewed in terms of their religious implications.

Robert Betts, Bigelow, Teresa Bigelow, Bright, Mary Bromley, Bill Brown, Charlton, Captain Crutchely, Dickinson, Dido, Dighton, Dunks, Edwards, Harris, Dr. John Heaton, Hillson, Rev. Mr. Hornblower, Johnson, Jones, Juno, Ooroony, Ooroony [the son], John Pennock, Peters, Petrina, Phoebe, Saunders, Socrates, Thomas, Unus, Waally, Walker, Warner, Warrington, Joan Waters, Martha Waters, James Wattles, Abraham White, Wilmot, Dr. Woolston, Abraham Woolston, Anne Woolston, Charles Woolston, Mark Woolston, Dr. Yardley, Bridget Yardley.

The Deerslayer; or, The First Warpath, 1841.

[This is the first of the five Leather-Stocking Tales in relation to plot, the last in order of composition.]

In the year 1740 two woodsmen are traveling together in central New York near Lake Otsego, then often called Glimmerglass. Henry March, nicknamed Hurry Harry, is a large, powerful, and handsome young man of twenty-eight. Nathaniel (Natty) Bumppo, whose Indian sobriquet at this point is Deerslayer, is several years younger and of slighter build, though no less able than his companion. From the beginning, their moral views are revealed to be quite different. March acknowledges no law beyond his own strength and will; Deerslayer has respect both for Indian justice as he has learned it among the Delawares and for Christian values as he has learned them among the Moravian missionaries to these Indians.

The conversation of the travelers introduces us to three other central characters: Thomas Hutter and his two daughters, Judith and Esther (Hetty). The father is rumored to be a former pirate now eluding the law by living on the frontier. Harry confesses that he has unsuccessfully courted Judith, strikingly beautiful but flirtatious and fickle. She has been too familiar with officers at British garrisons to escape gossip. The younger sister, Hetty, is feebleminded but virtuous to the point of piety.

On the shore of Glimmerglass, Harry removes from a hollow linden log a birchbark canoe which the two men launch and paddle toward a strange structure a quarter of a mile offshore. It is "Muskrat Castle," one of Tom Hutter's two abodes. Having been burned out three times on shore and having there lost his only son in a conflict with Indians, Hutter has grown wary of the land. Muskrat Castle is a log fortress built on piles driven into a shoal; his alternate home is mobile, an ungainly but practical houseboat known as "The Ark." When the two woodsmen reach the castle, they find no one there.

Searching for the ark, they locate it just beyond the outlet of the lake on the headwaters of the Susquehanna River, where Tom Hutter is tending his muskrat and beaver traps. When the old man learns that the French-allied Canadian Indians are preparing to go on the warpath, he realizes the vulnerability of the present position of the ark. With the aid of Harry and Natty, he hastily pulls the vessel upstream by means of a rope attached to an anchor in the lake. As they pass the last clump of trees at the outlet of Glimmerglass, six of a large force of Indians spring from the overhanging branches toward the ark. Only the first manages to land on the scow, and this invader is pushed overboard by Judith, who rushes from the safety of the cabin to perform this act of bravery. The Indians are Hurons, of Iroquois stock and language but living farther north than the Six Nations of the Iroquois Confederacy. [Throughout the novel they are referred to as Hurons, Iroquois, and Mingoes, the last being a pejorative name.]

Once away from the treacherous shore and out of danger, Tom Hutter switches from defensive to offensive strategy. Knowing that the colony is paying a bounty for enemy Indian scalps, just as the French are buying British scalps, he suggests that they locate the Huron camp and scalp its women and children before the warriors return. March agrees at once to participate in this raid, but Deerslayer opposes it as being unchristian. In rebuttal March repeats the two premises of his frontier ethic: first, that the Indians are only animals, not human beings; and, second, that you should "do as you're done by" (p. 91). Tom accepts Natty's decision not to engage in the scalping foray, and is grateful for his willingness to guard the ark and the girls during his own absence. Overhearing this discussion, Judith and Hetty are morally in sympathy with Natty's position. As Tom and Harry conspire together from their rowing position near the bow, Judith moves to the stern, where Natty now serves as helmsman. Her interest in Natty is evident both in her warm response to his honest simplicity and in her effort to gainsay any malicious reference Harry March may have made about her past.

Arriving at the castle about an hour before sunset, Hutter suggests that they make that fortress more secure by removing from the shore the two additional canoes he has hidden there. They go ashore in a canoe, retrieve from hollow logs Hutter's two additional canoes, and set them adrift to float away in the gentle offshore breeze. Paddling around a point, the three men now locate the Indian camp when they see the dying embers of a fire glowing in the dark. Harry and Tom now pursue their plan to collect scalps, leaving Deerslayer in the canoe to pick them up later at a given signal. Both the invaders are captured, however, and they warn Natty away, Tom again admonishing him to guard the castle and the girls.

Wishing to pick up the two drifting canoes at daybreak, before they fall into Huron hands, Natty paddles his own canoe into deep water and permits it to drift while he sleeps. At dawn he recovers one canoe quite quickly and then proceeds cautiously to the beach where the other boat has drifted. As he reaches it, he is fired upon by an Indian. Aware of the easy target he offers while afloat so close to shore, Natty lands the canoes and slips into the protective brush. Catching off guard his assailant reloading his rifle, Natty could easily have shot the man, but his sense of chivalry forbids his taking this kind of advantage of his enemy. Waiting until the Indian starts toward the shore, Natty steps into the path and confronts him in a friendly manner. In seemingly amiable fashion, the two haggle over the ownership of the canoes until Natty shows the brave that these light craft have been constructed not as Indians but as white men build such vessels. With a quick thrust of his foot Natty sends one of the canoes skimming many yards away from shore. The Indian, whose name is *Le Loup Cervier* (Lynx), pretends that he is convinced by Deer-slayer's argument, turns his back, and walks away into a thicket. As the woodsman is about to step into his canoe, however, his peripheral vision detects that the Indian is again taking aim at him from behind a bush. Only the face and the rifle of Lynx are visible. With the quick reflexes of a successful hunter, Deerslayer wheels about and fires at the spot in the brush where the man's body should be. Their two rifles discharge simultaneously. Natty's side is grazed, but his opponent is mortally wounded. With what remains of his ebbing strength, Lynx rushes at Deerslayer, hurls his tomahawk at close range, and then collapses. The tomahawk has little force behind it, and Natty catches it by the handle as it sails past. Carrying the Indian to the water's edge so that he can drink, Natty assures him of his forgiveness and promises not to scalp him— scalping being a proper practice for Indians but not for Christians. [Here, as elsewhere in the Leather-Stocking Tales, Natty refers to the values and conditioned traits of ethnic groups as "gifts."] The expiring Indian gives Deerslayer a new and more appropriate name, Hawkeye. Musing about having killed his first human being, Natty paddles toward the drifting canoe. Discovering that it contains an unarmed Indian who, while lying in the bottom, is quietly urging the boat toward the shore, Hawkeye refrains from shooting the man and is satisfied to allow him to swim ashore with impunity.

Returning to the castle with the canoes, Natty informs the Hutter girls of the captivity of their father and Harry March. It is hoped that at the appropriate time it will be possible to ransom them with furs or other valuable goods. Judith's admiration of Natty now becomes more appar-ent as she talks with him long and earnestly. Late in the afternoon Natty and the two girls leave the castle and proceed in the ark—they travel in zigzag fashion hoping to confuse the Hurons—towards the large flat rock near the outlet of the lake where, by prearrangement, Natty is to meet the Delaware chief Chingachgook, his adopted brother, at exactly sunset. The purpose of their mission in this area is the liberation of Wah-ta-Wah (English: Hist-oh-Hist), the betrothed of Chingachgook (English: Great Serpent) from Huron captivity.

When the scow edges up to the designated place of rendezvous,

Chingachgook leaps aboard pursued by twenty Hurons. Pulling hard on the grapnel line, Deerslayer and the Delaware quickly move the ark into deeper water beyond the reach of their enemies. As darkness settles around the vessel, the two men and Judith are discussing their next strategy when they are startled by the sound of a canoe paddle in the water. Fearing that the barely visible canoe contains Huron warriors, Natty, ready to fire upon it, calls out a challenge. The response is made in a woman's voice. To their surprise, the sole occupant of the canoe is Hetty Hutter, setting out to rescue her father and "Hurry Harry" March, the man for whom the feebleminded girl has an unspoken and hopeless infatuation. They try to catch Hetty and halt her mad endeavor, both for her own safety and to prevent her from unwittingly supplying the Hurons with the only equipment they need to attack the castle: a canoe. While cruising along the shore searching for her, they find her canoe (deliberately set adrift) and even talk with her briefly. Telling those on the ark that with her Bible she is going to teach the Hurons Christian forgiveness, Hetty plunges into the darkened forest and is heard no more. Natty and Judith take some comfort from the knowledge that Indians hold in religious awe the mad and feebleminded.

When she is brought before the Huron chief, Hetty reads to him from the Bible and pleads for his forgiveness of her father and Harry March. Failing in this effort, she is successful in serving as a messenger between the captive Hist-oh-Hist and Chingachgook. She apprises Hist of Chingachgook's presence in the area; later, after she has been brought back to the castle on an Indian raft, she informs the chief of the time and place on shore where he can find his beloved that night in order to rescue her.

As soon as Judith, Deerslayer, and Chingachgook return to the castle, after Hetty has gone ashore, they start searching for objects which might be used to ransom Hutter and March. Finding little that would tempt Indian cupidity, they finally decide to look in Tom Hutter's old sea chest, the contents of which Judith has never seen. There, beneath a layer of expensive clothes, they discover a pair of silver-mounted pistols and an ivory chess set. Deerslayer feels certain that the Hurons will be fascinated by the ivory elephants on which the castle-shaped rooks are mounted. The young Indian boy delivering Hetty to her home is allowed to examine at length one of these chess pieces. Soon afterwards, Rivenoak and a lesser chief raft out to the castle to bargain with Deerslayer for the release of their two prisoners. The ransom finally decided upon is four of the elephant-borne rooks. Just before sunset, Rivenoak returns with his captives, and the exchange is completed.

Natty, with his chivalric sense of honor, prevents the liberated men from shooting the Indians who delivered them to the castle.

An Indian boy later places on the porch of the castle a bundle of blood-covered sticks, a Huron declaration of war. Again Deerslayer thwarts Hurry Harry's attempt to kill an enemy emissary. Despite their narrow escape from death, Hutter and March again undertake a scalping foray—this time joined by Chingachgook—but find the old Indian camp deserted. As Deerslayer and the Hutter girls stand offshore in the ark, Judith makes a strong appeal for the affections of the white hunter.

While the exhausted Hutter and March sleep aboard the ark, Deerslayer and Chingachgook go ashore in a canoe to meet Hist-oh-Hist. When the girl does not appear at the appointed time and place, the two friends find her, guarded closely by an aged squaw, at a new campsite. While throttling the squaw, Natty relaxes his stranglehold often enough to permit her to breathe; during one of these respites, the woman manages to shriek an alarm. Racing to the canoe, Natty shoves it from the shore with such great force that it is out of sight in the dusk before his many pursuers arrive at the beach and fall upon him.

Although he fully expects to be tortured, perhaps killed, unless he can escape or be rescued, Deerslayer refuses to buy his freedom by returning to the ark and betraying its occupants. As he and Rivenoak, the foremost Huron chief, spar verbally, they are both amazed to discover Hetty Hutter standing beside them. She has been brought in a canoe by Judith so that she can ask Deerslayer what, if anything, can be done to save him. After assuring Hetty that he will in no way betray the white group, he instructs her to warn those on the ark to remain vigilant and to keep the vessel in motion to avoid attack. Judith later picks up Hetty and paddles toward the position of the ark. As she does so, a shot from across the water (fired by Harry March) kills a Huron girl. Discovering that the scow has disappeared, Judith and Hetty move to the lake for protection and spend the night there in the canoe.

As the ark approaches the castle the next morning, Chingachgook suspects that the building has been occupied by Hurons during their absence. He and Hist refuse to leave the ark. With his usual braggadocio, Harry March scoffs at them as he and Hutter proceed to embark. Once inside the castle, they find it filled with warriors who, after a furious hand-to-hand struggle, subdue both of them. As the Delaware couple cast off, Hist urges Harry to roll from the dock, where he lies pinioned, into the scow. This he attempts to do but, missing the boat, falls into the water bound hand and foot. Grasping with his teeth and then one hand the coil of rope which Hist throws to him, Harry is towed to safety and hauled aboard the ark.

Judith and Hetty approach the castle while the struggle is still in progress. Suspecting that both castle and scow are in enemy hands, they cautiously keep their distance. Three Hurons soon emerge from the castle and pursue the girls in one of Hutter's canoes. Although competent canoers, Judith and Hetty are being gained upon when the Indians break a paddle and quit the chase. They return to the castle where all of the Hurons now enter canoes and go ashore. When, soon afterwards, the girls arrive at their home, they find there their father scalped and fatally stabbed but alive. Before dying he tells Judith that the woman they had buried in the lake had indeed been the girls' mother but that he was not their real father. After Chingachgook, Harry, and Hist arrive with the ark, the group weights Hutter's body and buries it in the lake beside the girls' mother.

Again Harry March proposes to Judith, and again Judith tells him that she cannot accept him as her husband. She asks him to travel to the nearest garrison on the Mohawk River, report their desperate situation, and request military aid. She also requests that the relief force be led by anyone but one Captain Thomas Warley—another indication that gossip about her past may not be entirely baseless. Ready to leave the area anyway after his rebuff from Judith, Harry prepares to start northward for the Mohawk.

In a canoe above the watery grave of their mother and Thomas Hutter, Judith tries to explain to Hetty why it is no longer possible for them to remain in the wilderness. The younger sister, who has lived all her life here and has associated the beauty and bounty of Nature with the Divine Being, is deeply disturbed by the news. Much like Deerslayer, she can see only wickedness in the settlements. As they are returning to the ark, they are astonished to see Deerslayer paddling toward them. They are even more astonished to learn that he intends to honor the terms of the "furlough" given him by the Hurons and to return willingly to their savage hands at noon of the following day. His torture has been delayed to permit him to serve as messenger for proposals which the Hurons wish to make to the remaining occupants of the castle and ark. To Chingachgook they offer the opportunity to return unmolested to his tribe if he will leave Hist-oh-Hist with them. To Judith and Hetty they offer a home if they will consent to become the wives of a Huron widower. To Harry March the Hurons (thinking that his narrow escape has probably intimidated him) offer an open road to escape. The Delawares and the Hutter girls indignantly decline the proposals made to them; Harry had already decided to decamp, and Natty paddles him ashore for that purpose. Before they part, Natty urges the reckless giant to guide a force from a British fort to rescue the Hutter sisters. It was Harry's scalp hunting with Hutter, Natty observes pointedly, that had led to the present orphaned status of the girls.

When he returns to the castle, Deerslayer assists Judith in examining the contents of Hutter's trunk. The girl's primary concern is to discover evidence that will reveal her and Hetty's real identity. Who are they? Letters and other papers in the chest indicate clearly that the name Thomas Hutter was an alias for Thomas Hovey, a proscribed pirate, but the exact relationship between this man and the girls' mother is not wholly revealed. Although most personal and place names, along with dates, have been erased or excised, Judith is able to piece together a partial account of her origins. Her mother, of an educated, affluent family, had been deserted by the father of her two children, a European military officer who had never married her. Motivated by resentment, she had married the coarse and semiliterate Thomas Hovey partly to disgrace herself further and thereby heap coals of fire on the head of the man who had wronged her. Disappointed at being unable to ascertain more than this vague familial background, Judith is doomed to additional frustration as she tries to suggest to Natty that they be married. So sincere is his humility that he cannot believe that Judith is really serious in saying that she could accept as husband an illiterate man of lowly status.

In the early dawn of the following day Chingachgook and Hist pledge themselves to do everything possible to rescue Deerslayer from the Hurons, despite the hunter's remonstrance that such an effort by only two people would be sheer madness. Testing Killdeer, the fine Hutter rifle Judith had given him, Deerslayer brings down an eagle from a great height only to be embarrassed then by his wanton slaying of the bird. As noon and the end of his "furlough" approach, Natty bids a solemn farewell to his friends; then Hetty paddles him to the shore, where he willingly returns to Indian captivity. He has honorably kept the terms of his agreement.

Although some of the Huron chiefs are surprised at Natty's voluntary surrender of himself, Rivenoak had expected this unusual paleface to honor his "furlough." After some debate among themselves, the chiefs offer Natty an alternative to torture and death: adoption by the Hurons and marriage to Sumach, the widow of Lynx. Natty's refusal of this proposal so angers the chief Panther, brother of Sumach, that he hurls his tomahawk at the prisoner's head. Dextrously catching the weapon by its handle, Natty returns it with such force and accuracy that it brains its owner before he can raise a hand in defense. As the astonished Indians rush to aid the fallen chief, Deerslayer bolts from their camp and escapes into the forest. Soon pursued by the whole band of warriors, Natty doubles back to the lake, jumps into a canoe, and pushes it vigorously from the shore. Without a paddle, he relies on the wind to carry him away from the land as he lies in the bottom of the canoe in order to expose the smallest possible target for rifle fire. The fickle wind shifts, however, and carries him to another point of land, where he is once again captured.

After Rivenoak and Sumach again urge him to accept Huron adoption, and after he for a second time rejects this offer, Natty's ordeal begins. At first it is a form of mental torture as the Hurons tie him to a tree and demonstrate how close they can come to hitting him with thrown tomahawks and rifle bullets. Hetty now appears and berates the Indians for their cruelty. When the physical torture is about to begin, the Hurons are interrupted by a stunningly beautiful woman, dressed in exquisite clothes and bearing herself with the demeanor of a princess, who demands the release of Deerslayer. The ruse fails, however, when the innocent Hetty identifies the newcomer as only her sister. The torture is next delayed by the unexpected arrival and attempted intervention of Hist. The small, sharp knife which she secretly passes to Judith is relayed to Hetty, but the younger girl's attempts to cut Deerslayer's withes fail. Hist then stalls for time by pouring invective upon Briarthorn, the renegade Delaware who had abducted her and joined the Hurons. After Rivenoak silences the loud bickering between Hist and Briarthorn, the attention of the Hurons is yet once more diverted by the appearance of Chingachgook, who bounds into the ring of startled warriors, cuts Deerslayer's bonds, and hands him Killdeer. Briarthorn identifies Chingachgook as the Hurons' mortal enemy and throws a knife at the naked chest of the chief, but Hist spoils his aim by grabbing his arm. Chingachgook retaliates, burying his weapon in the heart of the former Delaware. Their amazement now broken, the Hurons move to surround their two armed and dangerous foes when the rapid tread of marching feet is heard, and sixty British redcoats enter the camp at double time.

Although Deerslayer, Chingachgook and Harry March use their rifles, the British regulars, having trapped the Hurons on a point projecting into the lake, advance in a deadly bayonet charge. The result is a massacre from which few escape. It is discovered that during the battle Hetty was mortally wounded by a stray bullet. She dies the next day after a protracted and pathetic death scene at the Hutter castle and is buried in the lake beside her mother.

Also at the castle, now the temporary headquarters of the British troops, are Captain Thomas Warley and several of his officers. It becomes evident that Judith's earlier relationship with this officer was more than an innocent flirtation. A confirmed roué bachelor, Warley, struck anew by Judith's beauty, talks lightly with a fellow officer of his intention of renewing an affair with the girl now that there are no longer parents to interpose.

As the troops prepare to leave the following morning, Judith and Deerslayer paddle to the watery graves of the Hutters, and there Judith proposes that the two be married at once and take up permanent residence at the castle. Natty refuses her offer, at first protesting that it would be taking unfair advantage of her to consider such an offer while she is so bereaved. Upon further urging, Natty says that he cannot feel sufficient love for any woman to marry. Later, as they are bidding each other farewell on shore, Judith presses Natty with her final question: had the rumors of her moral misconduct, passed along by Harry March, influenced his feelings toward her? Although he utters no word, the answer is unmistakably revealed in Natty's honest face. Certain now that her past has doomed her hope of real love, Judith turns and follows the soldiers marching toward their garrison on the Mohawk. Tempted to follow and console her, Natty finally moves in the opposite direction to join Chingachgook and Hist-oh-Hist.

Although the three are warmly welcomed in the Delaware village, it requires months of activity to lighten the deep sorrow of Natty, now known among the Indians by his recently earned name, Hawkeye. During the French and Indian War, which soon erupts in full fury, both he and Chingachgook earn military distinction. It is fifteen years before the two friends revisit Lake Glimmerglass. With them is a son borne by Hist not long before her death, a boy named Uncas and destined to be the last of the Mohican Delawares with that family name. Hawkeye finds the castle and the ark in ruins, both shoal and shore having reverted to nature. All traces of the Hutters have disappeared, and at the garrison Natty can gather no reliable information about Judith, but instead only vague and contradictory rumors about her life with ranking British officers.

Bounding Boy, Briarthorn, Nathaniel Bumppo (Deerslayer), Catamount, Chingachgook, Lieutenant Craig, Dr. Graham, Thomas Hovey (Hutter), Hetty Hutter, Judith Hutter, Lynx, Henry March, Moose, Panther, Raven, Rivenoak, Shebear, Sumach, Ensign Arthur Thornton, Wah-ta-Wah, Captain Thomas Warley, Sergeant Wright.

The Headsman; or, The Abbaye des Vignerons, 1833.
On the quay in Geneva, impatient to set sail for Vévey before the fickle

winds on Lake Leman lose their force, Baptiste, the greedy owner of the new but overloaded *Winkelried*, is thrice delayed. Mob action of the passengers, led by a leather-lunged Neapolitan street juggler, opposes the rumored embarkation of the abhorred Balthazar, holder of the hereditary post of headsman, or official executioner, of the canton of Berne. During this protest, a furious battle also occurs between two passengers' dogs—Uberto, a St. Bernard accompanying a cheerful Augustine monk, and Nettuno, a Newfoundland dog attached to a hardy Italian erstwhile seaman courageous enough to halt the fight.

The passengers' anxiety concerning their safe passage is relieved by Baptiste's agreeing to submit all passengers to the scrutiny both of the Genevese port official and of a panel selected from among the passengers. The panel members selected have their own credentials cleared: Pippo, the Neapolitan rabble-rouser; an unnamed Westphalian student on literary pilgrimage to Rome; and the pompous, prosperous Bernese burgher Nicklaus Wagner, owner of much of the cargo aboard the *Winkelried*.

Conrad, an openly hypocritical "pilgrim" en route to Rome, is passed and, unasked, assumes a fourth screening post. Maso, owner of the Newfoundland dog, claims his papers are already aboard ship and by sheer effrontery passes both the official and the panel; he and the faithful Nettuno board the vessel.

One after another, various unnamed passengers are cleared by the port official, cross-examined by the deputation, and allowed to board, with the cunning Baptiste so maneuvering matters that none will be rejected. Then the venerable Melchior, Baron de Willading, his lovely but ailing daughter Adelheid, and their liveried servants are respectfully greeted and passed, as is Monsieur Sigismund, a Swiss soldier normally in foreign service but presently accompanying the de Willadings and attentive to Adelheid. Next comes a meek, unassuming man whose papers gain him a hasty clearance from the Genevese official. Pippo, eager to provoke a little fun, questions whether this one must not be the bloody Balthazar, a charge so patently ridiculous that it prompts laughter and further mockery from Pippo. With no untoward reaction, the victim of these sallies duly embarks, followed shortly by the last prospective passenger, the respected Augustine monk and his dog Uberto.

With none identified as the detested Balthazar, Baptiste hastens to weigh anchor. But, noting two prosperous-looking travelers hurrying to the quay, the greedy owner delays the sailing further until these two Genoese gentlemen have been painstakingly identified (as a last resort, by a document whose contents are not revealed but are clearly awesome to the port official) and safely put aboard.

While the *Winkelried* gets under way, Adelheid learns that one of the
Genoese, Signor Grimaldi, is her father's dearest youth-time friend, and
she listens as the two reminisce and fill in the details of the thirty years
since they last met. The Baron's concern about the health of this sole
survivor among his nine children is matched by Signor Grimaldi's grief
that his only son is, though not dead, irretrievably lost to him. During
this and succeeding conversations, the two men's camaraderie, their
strong Christian faith—though one is a Calvinist and the other a
Catholic—their respect for tradition and for family position, and their
shared philosophic bent become apparent; too, Adelheid is revealed as a
sincere, sensitive, appreciative, well-educated, thoughtful, and strong-
willed young woman.

As the *Winkelried* continues her journey, Baptiste becomes increasingly
aware that his failure to depart—as promised—from Geneva at dawn
bodes ill for the safety of the voyage; the fickle winds and the peculiar
situation of Lake Leman make it subject to strong and sudden gales
perilous to an overloaded ship. Toward sunset, despite the crew's earnest
maneuvers, the *Winkelried* is becalmed, and the exhausted crewmen and
Baptiste go to sleep, to await the northern breeze normally following
sunset by two hours.

Maso, or "Il Maledetto" ["the accursed"], is of all passengers the only
commoner not cowed by the ill-tempered Baptiste; with Baptiste asleep,
the lesser passengers bestir themselves and respond heartily to the antics
of Pippo, quick to sense a ready audience. Maso gives but slight attention
to the show, maintaining rather a serious watch on the sky and the lake,
and the more aristocratic passengers soon tire of the Neapolitan's
buffoonery, so Pippo and the coarser passengers continue their merri-
ment at the opposite end of the ship. (Pippo's comments at Conrad's
expense allow a castigation of various practices of the Catholic Church
during the period in question, the early eighteenth century.)

Soon the genteel passengers in the stern invite the meek, mild-
mannered stranger, the butt of Pippo's mocking accusation that he is the
dreaded Balthazar, to join them. When Herr Müller (as Baptiste has
earlier termed him) hesitates, Sigismund offers his arm in assistance, and
Herr Müller quietly joins the group. On questioning, he admits to being
from Berne; but soon he diverts questions from himself to the Augustine
monk, whose calling to succor those lost in the Great St. Bernard portion
of the Alps is valued by all. Even Maso interjects a comment on the
monks' hospitality, and Signor Grimaldi, detecting in the watchful young
man "better stuff" than his outward appearance suggests, includes him
briefly in the conversation; the exchange develops such biting implica-

tions that Maso himself changes the subject to that of the peculiar calm on Lake Leman. The scene, ever changing and awesomely beautiful, temporarily erases all other concerns.

But Herr Müller's remarks prompt further questioning and lead to his comment that one living under the displeasure of his fellows comes at last to a chastening of his spirit. Sigismund, normally devoted to Adelheid, appears drawn to Herr Müller and his remarks, and Adelheid is puzzled by his single-minded concern with the stranger. At last, in response to Baron de Willading's query "I fear thou hast taken life?" Herr Müller cautiously reveals that he is Balthazar, and prays the Baron's aid if the truth should be discovered by those aboard who have already shown deep-seated superstition. After initial surprise mixed with aversion, the Baron agrees to afford this unjustly tormented man protection if it should be needed.

After a brief conversation with the pensive Westphalian student, Maso descends to the stern, where he tells Signor Grimaldi in Italian the hazards posed by the unnatural calm of the sea and the unnatural light in the sky, signs which have also been troubling Father Xavier, the monk. Signor Grimaldi privately conveys this bad news to the Baron, who—despite the encouraging glow of the beacon from his friend Roger de Blonay's castle above Vévey—now fears the worst.

Maso rudely awakens Baptiste and finds him immobilized by fear. Saying he has one in the ship whom he would save even at some peril to his own life, Maso takes command of the ship and, to make it more secure during the coming storm, orders the jettisoning of the cargo. All set to work—except the infuriated Baptiste and Nicklaus—to heave overboard cargo that had taken an entire day at Geneva to load. Maso, once this labor is initiated, takes further steps to safeguard the ship and its occupants, putting out the anchors, rolling up the canvas, and tying the women securely to the main masts. Seeing the Westphalian student attempting to roll a bale into the sea, he lends a hand, only to glimpse the student helplessly cast into the water with the bale by the sudden lurching of the ship; entangled in the bundle, the student cannot be rescued, a misfortune only Maso views.

Fear grips the passengers, who only twenty minutes earlier roared with laughter at Pippo's antics. They cry for religious symbols, for a light for the Virgin's picture—then someone mentions the curse that might lie on the *Winkelried* because of Baptiste's intention to transport Balthazar. Concerned for his own safety, Baptiste exposes the headsman and then retreats. The frenzied passengers, led by Conrad and Pippo, grasp Balthazar to throw him overboard; meanwhile, Baptiste and Nicklaus grapple in vicious combat. The Baron and Signor Grimaldi, attempting to break up the latter fight, are close at hand when Balthazar, caught by Sigismund in midair and swung back to the deck, collides full force with Baptiste and Nicklaus, and sweeps not only the two contenders but also the Baron and Signor Grimaldi into the lake. At that moment, a tempest of hurricane force strikes Lake Leman.

By the dull unnatural light overhead, all aboard witness the horrifying event and sense the hopelessness of the victims' situation. When Adelheid desperately calls out his name, Sigismund plunges into the raging lake to save the Baron, father of his beloved Adelheid. Meanwhile, Maso, having provided supporting ropes for all passengers, lashes the tiller down; finding that the anchors are indeed holding the ship head to wind, he calls Nettuno, who immediately leaps into the water to rescue the imperiled men. Maso repeatedly casts a loop of rope into the waves and hauls it back on the chance that it will afford support to one of those struggling to reach the ship. Sigismund, despite his skill and determination, cannot manage to reach the Baron; fortunately, Nettuno approaches Sigismund, and the young soldier, grasping the dog's tail and swimming vigorously alongside him, is guided to the Baron and Signor Grimaldi. The Genoese is rescued by Nettuno, and Sigismund, with the timely aid of Maso's rope, saves the Baron; all three men are pulled aboard alive. Maso persists in casting and pulling back the life-saving rope, calling continuously to Nettuno. Finally, during a brief lull in the storm, he hears the barking and then the ominous growling of the dog; Baptiste and Nicklaus, threatening and cursing one another, still locked in furious combat, refuse to loose their hold even to save their own lives, and drown. The tempest returns with renewed force; in the ensuing lull, Maso raises no response from Nettuno, though he calls ceaselessly. Bereft of his sole companion, the mariner weeps uncontrollably, beyond comfort even by Father Xavier.

A steady north wind succeeding the spent hurricane draws Maso from his grieving to the business of pulling up anchors, setting the sails, and steering for the harbor of La Tour de Peil, near Vévey. Within an hour, the *Winkelried* is safely docked, to be greeted both by those human friends who have anxiously watched its perils and by Maso's faithful Nettuno, the latter still carrying in his teeth a lock of hair from one of the quarrelsome pair washed ashore following the storm, still locked in vengeful embrace.

After a brief reception by self-important Peter Hofmeister, hereditary bailiff of Vévey, and by the Baron's longtime friend Roger de Blonay, de Willading's party, now by invitation including Maso, ascends to de

Blonay's castle, escorted by the bailiff. That official's deferential treatment of Signor Grimaldi mystifies the Baron but amuses Gaetano.

Following a pleasant meal, de Blonay and his guests view the peaceful lake, and, recalling Maso's agency in their safe arrival, the Baron and Signor Grimaldi and de Blonay all offer the mariner large sums of money for his services. Refusing all such offers, Maso asks only the blessing of Signor Grimaldi, which the noble gravely gives, wishing his own lawless son might be the recipient of the benediction. Kissing Signor Grimaldi's hand, Maso abruptly leaves, obviously moved by the scene.

The following morning, Adelheid and the Baron discuss the possibility of her marrying Sigismund, who had declared his love but acknowledges the formidable barrier presented by their vastly different social stations. Both Adelheid and her father recognize the seriousness of the barrier and seek to remove it. Adelheid has confessed that her ill health is caused by despair concerning the unlikelihood of their marriage; she loves Sigismund, but will not marry him without her father's consent. The Baron discusses the marriage with Signor Grimaldi, who shows concern at such an unequal yoking: his own life has been thus blighted, he reveals, baring the story of his unhappy marriage to Angiolina, wed against her will to the wealthy Gaetano. The discovery that Adelheid loves Sigismund persuades Signor Grimaldi that Sigismund's service in saving both Adelheid's life (in an unrecounted accident) and the Baron's should outweigh the disadvantage of his lower social station. Further discussion of the matter with de Blonay strengthens the Baron's support for the marriage.

With the Baron's assurance of his approval, Adelheid summons Sigismund and declares her love for him. To her distress, he is disturbed by her avowal, protests that their marriage is unthinkable, and at last reveals that he is the son of Balthazar. On her insistence, he tells her all the facts: his father has inherited the post of headsman and his mother is herself the daughter of the headsman of Neufchâtel; to protect Sigismund from the odious office, they have had him reared from infancy apart from his family and have concealed his existence from all except his only living sibling, his sister Christine, to be married at Vévey to one who insists on the secrecy of her parentage as part of the price of marrying her; if Christine's secret is uncovered—perhaps by the cousin forced otherwise to inherit the post—Sigismund will be honor-bound to acknowledge his identity and to succeed his father in office.

Adelheid, assuring Sigismund she loves him nonetheless, promises to discuss this discovery with her father, supporting Sigismund's cause but abiding by her father's decision. The Baron and Signor Grimaldi, pre-

sented with the horrifying information, doubt the wisdom of the marriage, though they discuss it long and earnestly, and will continue to
consider it together.

Meanwhile, preparations have been made for the colorful Abbaye des
Vignerons held every six years at Vévey, attracting thousands of visitors
from all parts of Europe. Central to the neo-Bacchanalian festival is a
lengthy procession representing all of Switzerland's agricultural activities, especially those associated with the production of wine. Erected
in the city square is a platform reserved for honored guests, including the
worthy bailiff, de Willading and his party, and Roger de Blonay.

Just before the guests enter, Father Xavier appears to greet the throng,
which welcomes him and his dog Uberto, throwing the latter bits of food.
Nettuno, now a close companion of Uberto, incenses the crowd by eating
some of Uberto's scraps; and Maso's dog is roundly abused and at last
injured by a sizable rock thrown from the crowd by Conrad. Maso
immediately throttles Conrad, the halberdiers intercede, three witnesses
(including Pippo) offer contradictory evidence in the matter, and—to
keep the peace—Maso, Conrad, and the three witnesses are hustled off
to jail.

As soon as the bailiff and his guests are seated, the procession begins,
with actual shepherds, gardeners, mowers, reapers, and vine-dressers
demonstrating their various jobs, each group with its own songs and
dances, and each honoring a pagan god or goddess or demigod—Ceres,
Flora, Pales, Bacchus, Silenus, Hymen—with special attention reserved
for Bacchus and for the group accompanying Hymen. Response from the
multinational audience is enthusiastic, especially for the realistic performance of the part of the satyr Silenus, played by Antoine Giraud, well
supplied already with the wine he is commending. Great interest is
shown in the identity of the young couple actually to be wed at the
conclusion of the performance; the bride-to-be is Sigismund's sister,
Christine, whose worth, despite her beauty and demeanor, is questioned
because of the bridegroom's paltry gift, a single gold chain, in contrast to
the huge dowry she brings him. As the procession circles the city, it
passes the jail where Maso, Conrad, and the three witnesses are confined; Maso has enticed his fellow prisoners into heavy intoxication, and
the moment the bridal group has passed, he escapes, followed by those
others not too drunk to run. An outcry reaches the bailiff, and at his
order they are apprehended. The prisoners are brought to the square just
in time for the celebration of the nuptials; their sentencing is deferred, at
Signor Grimaldi's suggestion, until after the wedding ceremony. A
genuine notary officiates; the bridegroom, Jacques Colis, signs the

papers in the presence of several of his friends as witnesses. When the bride is to sign and no witnesses appear, Balthazar and his wife Marguerite come forward. Christine is about to sign when Pippo, still under guard, identifies the girl as a headsman's daughter. Immediately, Jacques Colis tears up his signed statement, refusing to wed Christine. Shocked silence is succeeded by public approbation of Jacques's action; despite Balthazar's and Marguerite's protests, the marriage is canceled. Signor Grimaldi's informing the bailiff of Maso's significant service during the voyage causes that official to release all five of the prisoners, after which the bailiff and his male guests hasten to the fine feast awaiting them.

Adelheid, after winning Marguerite's confidence, goes secretly to their housing in Vévey to comfort the stricken Christine. After a long conversation, during which she discovers Sigismund has informed his family on every point of their relationship except her declaration of love for him, Adelheid invites the abused girl to accompany the de Willading party to Italy, an offer gratefully accepted.

Early the following morning, de Willading's party, including Christine, leaves for the late-season passage through the Alps, riding sure-footed mules along the trail, and accompanied as far as Villeneuve by Roger de Blonay. Through scenes of mixed beauty and barrenness they travel until nightfall, staying overnight, as planned, at Martigny. There de Willading hires Pierre Dumont, the most reliable mountain guide, to lead them to Aoste, Italy. Dumont reports that a few have gone ahead of them: Pippo, Conrad, Maso, and Jacques Colis, whose behavior at Vévey has become known already throughout the pass.

The party's leisurely pace is gradually quickened by the guide as he detects the threat of worsening weather, a concern communicated only to Signor Grimaldi. Following a rest stop at Liddes, they hurry even faster, increasingly feeling the chill in the shaded glens and finally becoming so cold that they are in danger of freezing to death. Snow begins to fall, making walking even more difficult; desertion of the party by a hired muleteer causes the unmounted mules to wander, and in going to recover the mules, the party loses the path. Sigismund and Pierre, seeking the trail, encounter Maso and Nettuno, also lost; the last two join the de Willading party. Just as hope has been abandoned, Uberto locates the party and leads them to the wayside Refuge provided by the Bernardine monks, a shelter which saves their lives. All the members of the party and their animals sleep that night within the Refuge. Uberto, once the party is safely housed, goes to the convent to summon help; Father Xavier and several convent servants meet them at the Refuge the next morning to guide them to the convent.

Adelheid and Christine's inquiring about four travelers "sleeping" in the smaller hut near the Refuge—a discovery made during their early-morning walk just after Maso's departure with Nettuno—prompts Pierre's examination of the "bone-house" sheltering unclaimed corpses and the revelation that the fourth body is that of the murdered Jacques Colis. Since the matter requires immediate legal attention, Sigismund is sent ahead to the convent with the female members of the party while the rest remain to investigate the murder.

Sigismund, after seeing the women to the convent, observes three men and a dog leaving the convent. Suspecting Maso's involvement in the murder, he accosts the three, and with the aid of a young monk and the convent dogs has Maso, Conrad, and Pippo placed in confinement for questioning. Soon afterwards, while visiting the convent chapel, Sigismund receives a note that Balthazar has been found hiding in the bone-house and is therefore, suspected of the crime, being brought in chains to the convent. Greatly agitated, Sigismund tells Adelheid and Adelheid tells Christine the distressing news; all express confidence in Balthazar's innocence, but all three are uneasy about the outcome of the formal trial, for which the châtelain of Sion, in Upper Valais (the official in whose area the murder has occurred), and Peter Hofmeister, bailiff of Vévey (concerned with the welfare of the accused, an official in his canton), have been called.

On his arrival three days later, the bailiff frankly confesses to Sigismund that only Signor Grimaldi's distinguished presence has persuaded him to make the hazardous journey through the pass, a statement the Vévey official repeats to Father Michael, Prior of the convent, when he is greeted by the latter. After a hearty meal, all the dignitaries go directly to the chapel, where the trial is to be held; the châtelain is to serve as judge and inquisitor. The corpse of Jacques Colis is present but concealed. Also attending are the bailiff, all members of the Bernardine brotherhood currently at the convent, and all members of the de Willading party; among the women at one side is Marguerite, come to support her husband at his trial.

Balthazar's answers to the judge's questions are given openly and honestly, and the headsman's statements are supported by Signor Grimaldi and Marguerite. When the judge requires Balthazar and Marguerite and then Christine to view the corpse, their responses are free from evidence of guilt or rancor. Christine's concluding testimony convinces the judge of Balthazar's innocence.

Pippo and Conrad, summoned next, produce testimony sufficient to acquit them of the charge; the two would have been released entirely except for Signor Grimaldi's recommendation that all remain until the proceedings are completed. They therefore agree to detention until the following morning.

Maso, the last to be interrogated, gives ready, open answers to the questions asked; and testimony in his behalf is volunteered by Melchior, Father Xavier, Signor Grimaldi, and Sigismund. Since his apparent poverty does not accord with his well-known traffic in contraband and since Jacques Colis is known to have been carrying jewels not found on his corpse, Maso is questioned on this point. After the chapel has been cleared of all not directly concerned, Maso removes from Nettuno's body a belt containing a valuable necklace, to be sold to a Milanese noble. The judge, detecting a second packet in Nettuno's fur, orders its removal—a packet obviously surprising also to Maso—and in it are found most of Colis's missing valuables. Despite Maso's claims that the second packet is not his and that he is innocent of the murder, both the judge and the bailiff agree that he is to be held responsible for the crime. Knowing the seriousness of the case, Maso reveals that Signor Grimaldi is the powerful Doge of Genoa; identifies himself as the Doge's son, Bartolomeo; proves his statement by presenting a signet ring given him by the Doge; recounts the Doge's unhappy marriage, the untimely death of his young wife, and the abduction of his only child by the wife's vengeful lover; restates his own innocence of the murder; and proclaims that the only son of the Doge of Genoa "has little to fear from the headsman's blow!" (p. 458).

At this point, Balthazar interjects some information: the Doge's real son may instead be Sigismund, adopted (without Marguerite's knowledge) by the headsman when their own son Sigismund died in infancy; the child, surrendered to Balthazar when Signore Pantaleone (abductor of an unnamed Italian noble's son) was to be executed by the headsman for murder, was left with a substantial sum in gold and with various personal items sufficient to identify him; the child's given name was Gaetano; for the child's mother the abductor had deep love but for the child's father equally deep hatred; Sigismund himself has not been told of his adoption and assumes he is in truth the headsman's son.

Earnest searching for physical resemblances poses more problems than it solves, and the Doge's hopes are further dashed by Maso's reminder of certain papers proving his paternity and of a similar declaration from the lips of a dying priest. Balthazar, urged to produce evidence, brings the clothing and trinkets left with the abducted child, among which Gaetano finds an heirloom he himself had hung around the infant's neck. On this discovery, Adelheid appeals to Maso to reveal the truth she feels certain he is still concealing, and at length Maso agrees to exchange this further information for his release.

During the three days spent awaiting the bailiff's arrival, Adelheid has won her father's consent to her marriage with Sigismund if Balthazar's innocence of the murder can be proved (the alternative she offers is her unmarried state until death, an option unacceptable to the Baron). Therefore, the morning following the trial, Adelheid and Sigismund are married in the convent chapel by Father Xavier, with Sigismund's paternity still in doubt but clearly not through Balthazar's line of descent.

After the wedding, Pippo and Conrad are encouraged to leave for Italy; they are not to be parties to Maso's last revelations or to his release from bondage for the murder. As the de Willading party, having left the convent, stand on the Italian border, Maso reveals that he is indeed the son of the Doge, but born out of wedlock to a poor but beautiful young woman, now dead, named Annunziata Altieri. The papers furnished to Maso by a confederate of the abductor rightly belong to Sigismund, born Gaetano to the unhappy Angiolina.

Before the Doge is able to make atonement to Maso for the wrong done his mother, Maso leaves via a rocky shortcut, determined to outdistance Conrad and Pippo. Papers later secretly delivered to the Doge allow Sigismund's recognition as the Doge's son and heir; despite earnest efforts, no one ever hears of Il Maledetto again. The charge of murder is subsequently removed from Maso by Pippo's confession, before his own execution for another murder, that he and Conrad had killed Jacques Colis and had hidden his valuables on Nettuno's body for undetected transport into Italy.

> Balthazar, Baptiste, Herr Bourrit, Christine, Jacques Colis, Conrad, Bartolomeo Contini [Maso], Roger de Blonay, Adelheid de Willading, Melchior de Willading, Pierre Dumont, Benoit Emery, Etienne, Antoine Giraud, Signor Gaetano Grimaldi, Gaetano Grimaldi [Sigismund Steinbach], Henri, Peter Hofmeister, Enrico Marcelli, Marguerite, Mariette Marron, Father Michael, Pippo, Nicklaus Wagner, Father Xavier.

"Heart," 1823.

"Heart" is the second of two stories in *Tales for Fifteen*, a slight volume of fiction written by Cooper under the pseudonym Jane Morgan. The story opens with a street scene in New York City. As Maria Osgood, twenty, and her friend and distant relative Charlotte Henley, seventeen, are walking along a busy street on a wintry day, they observe a crowd gathered around a man writhing on the sidewalk. Maria declares him a drunkard and urges that they pass on without delay. Charlotte thinks the man ill rather than drunk and she is distressed that none of the onlookers makes any move to assist the afflicted stranger. Seymour Delafield, a wealthy young bachelor in the crowd, observes both Charlotte's beauty and her sympathy for the sufferer, and admires her greatly for both these qualities. When George Morton appears on the scene, Charlotte is confident that this young man, who is all heart, will aid the stricken stranger. Her good opinion of him is justified as George places the man, who has suffered a fit, in a hired hack and takes him to an almshouse where he can be given medical attention. As the carriage drives away, Charlotte expresses her concern that George, in frail health, is not wearing any overcoat. Maria then introduces Charlotte to Delafield, who walks the girls home, engaging them en route in witty conversation.

At the dinner table that evening Maria tells Mr. and Mrs. Henley that their daughter has made a great conquest in winning the admiration of the city's most prominent and most eligible young bachelor, Seymour Delafield. Like many another young lady, Maria herself was interested in Delafield, but in vain, she admits. The elder Henleys, concerned that Charlotte, the only survivor of their six children, be happily married, take note of a possible relationship between their daughter and young Delafield. George Morton, finding his family gone out, comes to the Henley home for supper. He is obviously chilled from his exposure to the weather but he insists that he is quite well.

On the following evening the Osgoods have a music party to which they invite many fashionable guests. Mr. and Mrs. Osgood hope that such social occasions will further the matrimonial interests of their thirteen children, most of whom are daughters. Among those who play solos is Seymour Delafield, who attends the party primarily because he knows that Charlotte will be present. He plays the flute superbly but soon realizes that his performance moves Charlotte far less than the mediocre flute playing of George Morton that follows. George is really too ill now to perform at all, but he feels an obligation to carry out a commitment to contribute to the entertainment. Charlotte persuades George, after his performance, to return home for proper medical treatment and rest.

Shortly after Maria arrives at the Henley home next morning, both George and Seymour pay social calls. George quickly excuses himself, declaring that he is not in fit condition to be good company. A few minutes later, Maria, aware of Delafield's growing infatuation with Charlotte, finds an excuse to leave the room. Alone now with Charlotte, Delafield declares his love for her and makes a proposal of marriage.

Greatly surprised at such a definite avowal of affection from a man she has known for only three days, Charlotte politely but firmly declines his offer.

Having been pursued by many young women (and their parents) for his wealth and personal attractiveness, Seymour Delafield is stunned that his first marriage proposal is rejected. He continues for a short time to call at the Henley home, but piqued at last by Charlotte's aloofness, he declares the girl heartless. As the winter progresses, his attention is shifted to Maria, who becomes first his confidante and then his fiancée.

In the meantime George Morton's cold worsens, and an inflammation of the lungs develops. By early spring the doctor pronounces his case incurable. As warm weather returns, however, the Mortons and the Henleys move to their adjacent country houses, both families filled with renewed hope for George's recovery. Such hope is short-lived. The medical prognosis is borne out, and George dies on a balmy day in June. In a deathbed scene, George and Charlotte declare their love for each other, a love which they understand to be eternal.

Maria and Seymour are soon married, but Charlotte remains single, " . . . showing how much Imagination is inferior to Heart" (p. 223). George died for "heart," his fatal illness having commenced during his rescue of the stricken stranger from the cold street, and now Charlotte remains faithful to him as a matter of "heart."

> Seymour Delafield, Henley, Mrs. Henley, Charlotte Henley, George Morton, Maria Osgood.

The Heidenmauer; or, The Benedictines—A Story of the Rhine, 1832.

Set in the Kingdom of Bavaria during the early sixteenth century, this sociopolitical novel pictures a power struggle among three forces: the church, the aristocracy, and the rising commercial class. The principal exponents of these forces are, respectively, Father Bonifacius, Abbot of Limburg; Emich Leininger, Count of Hartenburg; and Heinrich Frey, Burgomaster of the town of Deurckheim. It is a bitter struggle which often reveals the worst sides of the adversaries, and none of the three principals emerges as a really attractive character. Beyond the passing performance of these individuals lies the more protracted drama of the Reformation.

The opening scene introduces two menials in the employ of Count Emich: Gottlob Frinck, cowherd, and his friend Berchthold Hintermayer, forester and huntsman. Old companions, they meet as Berchthold is bringing home to the castle some hunting dogs he was exercising and as Gottlob is rounding up cattle which he was illegally grazing in the pasturelands of the Abbey of Limburg. They discuss guardedly the growing conflict between the count and the abbot. After they kennel and stable their animals, the two meet again and walk toward the mountain hermitage of the Anchorite of the Cedars, a holy man who is new in the area. This religious recluse has made his abode among the Roman ruins at Pagan Camp near a large circular wall known as the Heidenmauer or Pagan's Wall. The place has an additional overtone of paganism because it was reputedly the site of the winter quarters of Attila the Hun during the fifth century. Contributing further to the spookiness of the ruins is the Devil's Stone, an outcropping of rock about which a legend, rich with supernatural lore, has survived for several centuries. Just before Gottlob and Berchthold reach the hermit's hut, they are overtaken by Father Siegfried, a Benedictine from the nearby Abbey of Limburg, who is bound to the same destination.

As the three enter the dimly lighted hut, they find the anchorite giving advice to a young lady. At a signal from Berchthold, Gottlob involves Father Siegfried in a discussion of a controversial nature in order to allow the huntsman and Meta Frey, daughter of the burgomaster, to slip away. Whatever business it is that Father Siegfried has at the hermitage we are not told; but as he walks away with Gottlob, the monk promises gold to the cowherd if he will ascertain the size of the armed force which Count Emich is accumulating at Hartenburg Castle. Siegfried's interest in such information reflects the insecurity felt by the Benedictines at this time.

Berchthold and Meta converse in whispers as the latter's aged nurse, Ilse, naps after her long climb to the Heidenmauer. From their gossip the reader infers some of the tension that exists between the castle and the town of Deurckheim. More explicit in their conversation is the fact that the strange new hermit has chosen these young people as his special students, each having already visited him several times in this out-of-the-way place.

At the castle, Gisela, daughter of the warden, Karl Friedrich, talks with Count Leininger about the rough and uncouth character of the soldiers being assembled in that stronghold. She also reminds the count several times that it was in his military service that her father had lost a leg. The count chafes at her saucy manner but gives her only a light reprimand, realizing that his wife, Ermengarde (absent from the castle at this time), has spoiled the girl. He is preoccupied with matters of more moment as he prepares to entertain Wilhelm of Venloo, known as Father Bonifacius since he became Abbot of Limburg. At the banquet the count is flanked by two aides: his cousin, Albrecht of Viederbach, a Knight of St. John, also called a Knight of Rhodes, one who was present at the fall of Rhodes to the Ottoman Turks in 1523; and Abbé Latouche, a Parisian cleric who is a politician in church circles rather than a devoutly religious person. Emich has invited these two worldly churchmen to his castle to provide it with a facade of sanctity at a time when he plans to destroy the Abbey of Limburg. During his visit to the castle the abbot is supported by two of his fellow Benedictines, Father Siegfried and Father Cuno. As the meal progresses, the count and the abbot discuss a vineyard to which they both lay claim. They decide to settle the ownership not by resorting to arms but by means of a drinking bout. Each signs a quitclaim on the disputed property, and the man who can walk away from the winefest will take both documents with him. As the carouse continues, the six men grow more garrulous and quarrelsome. One by one the four subordinates are overcome by alcohol, and either collapse in their chairs or fall beneath the table. Of the two principals, Bonifacius seems to be enduring the trial more comfortably than Emich, for the count has all but lost command of his power of speech. The abbot has requested that the count's huntsman come to the hall so that he can congratulate the man for the choice game he had provided for their feast. When Berchthold appears, the young man recognizes at once the precarious condition of his master and, to the count's great relief, carries the burden of conversation with the guest. Berchthold's outspoken support for the doctrines of Martin Luther, by now the most controversial churchman in Germany, infuriates the abbot, who, losing his self-possession, swallows several goblets of wine and lapses into unconsciousness. The count, still unable to speak, picks up the quitclaims and, supported by Berchthold, staggers from the banquet hall, the victor.

The following day is the Sabbath, and high mass is performed at the abbey, attended by the Burgomaster of Deurckheim and by Count Emich and numerous followers. Although Brothers Bonifacius, Siegfried, and Cuno manage to attend the service, they do not participate actively. The sermon is preached by Father Arnolph, Prior and spiritual leader of the Benedictines cloistered in the abbey. Both in his sermon and afterwards in his conversation with the count, Father Arnolph proves to be at once a reasonable and a benevolent man. He acknowledges the shortcomings of churchmen as human beings, not trying to defend the behavior the night before of the abbot and his drinking cronies. He reminds the count that his noble ancestors had helped found the abbey and that succeeding generations of Leiningers had contributed to the maintenance and defense of the establishment. So assuaged are the count's feelings of hostility toward the convent that he experiences some serious misgivings about his designs upon abbey lands. At that crucial moment, the vindictive Father Johan interrupts with a threat of damnation against the count, thus shattering the last chance of rapprochement between church and state in the district.

After the conclusion of the service, Gottlob, the count's cowherd, is detained for questioning by the abbot. How many armed men are now garrisoned in Hartenburg Castle? This was the information Father Siegfried had enlisted Gottlob to secure, but now the cowherd is unwilling to commit himself on this matter. Instead, he gives evasive answers to all of the abbot's queries. Thinking at first to extract the desired information by means of torture, the abbot decides against this course and, instead, orders Gottlob confined in the convent for a period of penance.

As the count leaves the abbey, he invites to dinner at the castle Heinrich Frey, his family, and his attendants. Flattering the Burgomaster of Deurckheim in every possible way, Emich solicits his support in a move against the Benedictines. At one point during the social hour preceding the meal, Frey's wife, Ulrike, talks privately with the count about a domestic dilemma she faces. Her daughter, Meta, and Berchthold Hintermayer are in love; but their betrothal is blocked by the burgomaster, who refuses to allow his daughter to marry into a family of ruined fortune. The count, who once admired this woman for her beauty and now respects her for her ability, makes a proposal to Ulrike: if she will persuade her husband to support his campaign against the Benedictines, Emich will elevate Berchthold to a more responsible position, thus making him a more worthy suitor for the hand of Meta. Too devout to abet any conspiracy against the church, Ulrike refuses the offer. Later she visits the nearby Hintermayer cottage where she relates to her old friend Lottchen, Berchthold's mother, the discussion she has had with the count. Both women are shocked at the suggestion of physical hostility against the Abbey of Limburg, and their conversation turns to a notorious instance of such hostility twenty years earlier. Baron Odo von Rittenstein, then betrothed to Ulrike, had let his zealous interest in church reform carry him into violence. Under the influence of alcohol, he and a group of his followers had invaded the Abbey of Limburg and committed various sacrileges culminated by Odo's trampling on the divine host.

Suspecting that the Anchorite of the Cedars, about whom she has heard so much from Meta and the others, may be Odo von Rittenstein, Ulrike, accompanied by Ilse, goes at ten o'clock that evening to the Heidenmauer to call upon the hermit. She is not mistaken. The penitent who prays in the ruins is indeed Baron Odo, though greatly changed from the youth whom Ulrike had known years earlier. He had become an outcast and wandered for years, seeking various forms of expiation for his sins. He has returned and by means of gold has made his peace with the monks who this night will offer a special mass for his absolution; his peace with God is something not yet achieved. As the two old friends talk, the chapel bells ring announcing the midnight mass for the benefit of the anchorite. Ulricke and Ilse follow Odo to the abbey and, after his intercession with the sentinel, are admitted to the chapel. Part way through the mass a trumpet is heard at the gates, and a large body of armed men bursts into the abbey grounds, one hundred of them citizens of Deurckheim led by their burgomaster, and thrice that number soldiers from the castle commanded by Berchthold Hintermayer.

The attacking forces meet no real resistance, for the troops of Duke Friedrich, Elector of Saxony, which usually guard the abbey, had been recalled, earlier in the day, to defend their own hard-pressed lord. Moving to the chapel, the invaders confront the assembled monks; and the Burgomaster of Deurckheim voices the community complaints against the Benedictines: their heavy assessment against the economy of the area, their encroachment on the lands of others, their arrogance of behavior. Abbot Bonifacius begins to enunciate a malediction against the intruders when Ulricke interposes—much to the surprise of her husband, who had supposed her safely out of the way at the Heidenmauer. Pleading first with Bonifacius not to excommunicate the mad offenders, she then turns her competent rhetoric against her husband and Berchthold, urging them to desist from their present folly. As she jousts verbally with these men, Ulricke effects a virtual stalemate until the belated arrival of Count Emich. At that point her challenge to the invaders collapses, and she is led away to safety.

Pillage of the abbey progresses as the peasant followers of Count Emich and the citizen soldiery of Deurckheim set fire to one after another of the buildings. They overturn altars within the church; Dietrich, the blacksmith who serves as Frey's lieutenant, smashes tombstones and marble images with rapid blows of his hammer. Twice the plunderers falter in their destructive work, once when Bonifacius utters a malediction and again when Father Johan displays the convent's collection of religious relics. The spell is broken each time by a raucous blast from the cow horn of Gottlob. Following his second blare, the troops put their torches to the chapel itself, and all retreat from the spreading flames except the prostrate Odo and the fanatic Father Johan, who remains in prayer before the chest of relics. Albrecht, the Knight of Rhodes, and Berchthold rush into the fiery building and try to carry the mad monk to safety. When he escapes their grasp and returns to the altar, Albrecht abandons the effort to rescue him. Berchthold, seemingly transfixed by the wild scene, remains and, along with Johan and Odo, disappears in the conflagration when the roof collapses.

On the following day the town council of Deurckheim meets to consider the demands for reparations made by the Benedictines, most of whom are housed in the abbey of an adjoining district. There is a mixed air of defiance and remorse among the burghers and artisans assembled. The demands of Bonifacius for gold and penance are heavy, and Heinrich Frey remonstrates with the mild-mannered Father Arnolph, the abbots' representative. Upon the arrival of Count Emich, however, the decision is made to satisfy the Benedictines' requirements in most respects, though there is a consensus that the Abbey of Limburg must never be rebuilt. Having achieved his political end and established his authority, the count is ready now to salve his conscience with whatever obeisances may be required. A large sum of gold—much of it plundered from the abbey itself—is paid, and all of the leading persons of the castle and town undertake a long and arduous pilgrimage to the Benedictine convent and Our Lady of the Hermits shrine at Einsiedlen, Switzerland. Among the penitents who make this Alpine pilgrimage are Lottchen and Meta, both in mourning for the death of Berchthold. Upon their arrival at Our Lady of the Hermits, a shrine famous for miracles and redolent of saints' legends, each pilgrim passes before Father Rudiger, the local abbot, and Father Bonifacius, who stand by the sacristy, and deposits one or more gifts for the convent.

Later that evening the reality of the Reformation is more clearly rendered than on any occasion previously. Ulricke, Meta, and Lottchen are brought before the two abbots by Father Arnolph to plead for a mass on behalf of the soul of Berchthold. The petition is refused because of the forester's known Lutheran sympathies. In private the two abbots discuss, quite objectively, the activity of Martin Luther and the growing strength of the schism. At midnight Father Rudiger, mindful of the Benedictine tradition of hospitality, hosts a dinner for his most prominent guests (Bonifacius, Emich, Albrecht, Latouche, Frey, and Dietrich) at which the current rebellion within the church becomes the subject of heated controversy. The count himself now requests a special mass for Berchthold but is refused after Bonifacius, remembering the forester's words at the drinking bout, declares him a heretic. Only the timely chimes announcing a special pre-matin service prevent the issue from erupting into renewed hostilities.

When the pilgrims return home, traveling down the Rhine by boat, they find the citizens of Deurckheim filled with superstitious dread.

Berchthold's hounds have been heard baying on the trail of game.
Reports have been made by some who claimed that they actually saw the
dogs, and a few have even gone so far as to insist that they saw the form
of Berchthold flying along behind the pack. On the following morning
the newly returned pilgrims lead the people of Deurkheim to the ruins of
the Abbey of Limburg where they find only the bones of Father Johan.
All in the assembled multitude are startled to hear the hounds of
Berchthold baying from the direction of the Heidenmauer, and to this
eerie place they all now hesitantly proceed. After a careful buildup of
suspense by the narrator, Berchthold himself bursts from the woods
alive and well to tell his story. After the collapse of the chapel roof,
Berchthold had grabbed the prostrate Odo and dragged him to the crypt
below. There the two men had been found the following morning by
monks returning to their demolished abbey. The Benedictines had
nursed the injured men but had exacted from them a vow of silence until
the pilgrims had returned from Switzerland. (Unfortunately Fathers
Cuno and Siegfried had failed to keep their part of the bargain, which was
to inform Lottchen, Ulricke, and Meta of Berchthold's safety.) Now there
is great rejoicing for the restoration of one mourned as lost.

Despite his pleasure at discovering the physical well-being of young
Hintermayer, Heinrich Frey still cannot bring himself to accept a mere
forester as a son-in-law. Ulricke now turns to her last hope for help in
this domestic crisis. She proceeds to the hut of Odo von Rittenstein and
appeals to the noble hermit to aid the impoverished Berchthold. To her
surprise and joy she discovers that Odo has anticipated her request, for
he hands her documents in which he has willed to his rescuer and former
pupil both his castle and his lands. Still moved by barely repressed love
for Ulricke, Odo himself departs, declaring that he cannot remain near
the woman who has meant so much to him and also continue the
religious penitence to which he is committed. Ulricke's unrestrained
sobbing at his departure reveals that the youthful passion has not passed
entirely from her heart either.

Berchthold's new wealth makes him at last acceptable to the materialistic burgomaster, and his marriage to Meta occurs on the following
day. The ceremony and its consequent celebration are quickly passed
over in two brief sentences as the author hastens to reaffirm the
sociopolitical thesis of the book: " . . . the reluctant manner in which the
mind of man abandons old, to receive new, impressions" (p. 464).

Albrecht of Viederbach, Father Arnolph, Father Cuno, Dietrich,
Heinrich Frey, Meta Frey, Ulricke Hailzinger Frey, Karl Friedrich,
Gottlob Frinck, Gisela, Berchthold Hintermayer, Lottchen Hinter-

mayer, Hugo, Ilse, Father Johan, Abbé Latouche, Emich Leininger, Ludwig, Odo von Rittenstein, Rudiger, Father Siegfried, Father Ulrich, Wilhelm of Venloo, Wolfgang.

Home as Found, 1838.

[This is the second of the two Effingham novels.]

The cousins Edward and John Effingham and the former's daughter, Eve, return from a lengthy stay abroad to their town residence in New York City. There Eve is welcomed home by her cousin and former schoolmate, Grace Van Cortlandt, the orphaned daughter of a prominent family who becomes a ward of Edward Effingham. Delighted to see each other again after several years, both girls are aware, nevertheless, of certain differences now in their attitudes and manners. As they are talking, they are surprised by a caller, one Aristabulus Bragg, a Yankee lawyer moved to New York, who is now the agent and attorney for the Effinghams' upcountry estate at Templeton. It soon becomes apparent from Bragg's comments on contemporary American life that he is an extreme egalitarian, feeling that even one's personal life should be governed by what the majority of people approve. This becomes apparent in his mild censure of the Gothic features in the architecture of the Wigwam, the Effingham mansion at Templeton; a majority of Americans, he advises Eve, now favor the style of the Greek Revival.

At dinner that evening the Effinghams entertain Captain John Truck, master of the packet *Montauk* on which they had returned (quite circuitously) from Europe, Sir George Templemore, British baronet who was a fellow passenger, Grace Van Cortlandt, and Aristabulus Bragg. During the repast Bragg demonstrates in their crudest forms some of the vulgarities to which Americans of the time are prone. He is presumptuous and coarse in his manner, arrogant in his provincialism, utterly scornful of tradition, and consistently materialistic in his "go-ahead-ism." The other two male guests often serve as foils to this pronounced American type. Sir George is urbane, deferential, and humanistic in his outlook. Captain Truck, though a man of action and a hearty "old salt," is modest, courteous, and warmhearted. The old seaman is surprised and moved almost to tears by the gifts presented to him by the Effinghams as mementos and tokens of appreciation for his courageous behavior during their recent voyage together: a silver punch bowl from Eve, a silver watch from her father, and a pair of silver tongs from cousin John. Bragg rudely hefts each of these gifts and announces his estimates of their respective market values.

To Sir George Templemore's question as to whether the upper class in America, like its counterpart in England, breaks down into social cliques and coteries, Grace and Eve respond affirmatively; and to prove their point, they invite the baronet to join them in visiting those socialites keeping open house that evening: Mrs. Jarvis, Mrs. Hawker, and Mrs. Houston. They are also accompanied on their calls by John Effingham and the reluctant Captain Truck, who feels out of his element among the social elite. The brash Aristabulus Bragg they leave behind temporarily with Edward Effingham to discuss business matters relating to the Templeton estate. The party stops first at the Jarvis home, where they are met by the steady, practical master of the house and his wife, Jane, who is a showy, aggressive social climber. To the great amusement of the Effingham group, they find being lionized there as a renowned traveler Steadfast Dodge, the narrow-minded, provincial newspaper editor who has become an authority on all Europe in six months. A fellow voyager of theirs on the *Montauk*, he is well known to them as a pretentious fraud. At their next stop their hostess is the widowed Mrs. Hawker, a gracious and dignified lady in her seventies, a descendant of one of the oldest families in the state. They are all fascinated at the Hawker home by the witty intellectual conversation of one Mrs. Bloomfield. They proceed next to the most fashionable home in New York, that of Mrs. Houston, where a ball is in progress. The banality of the occasion is relieved by the absurd behavior of Miss Ring, supposedly a typical belle of the time. After carrying on an exaggerated and demonstrative flirtation simultaneously with five men she has cornered, she mistakes Bragg for the visiting Englishman of rank said to be among the Effingham guests; even more ridiculous, she concludes that Truck must be an Anglican clergyman traveling with the distinguished visitor. If either of the gentlemen concerned is aware of her errors in identity, he mercifully forbears exposing them.

Mistaken identity becomes highly farcical at the next soiree attended by the central characters. The satire this time is directed not at the pretension and snobbery of a shallow, upperclass society but at the jejune nature of the city's literati. After being mistaken for an English clergyman, Captain Truck is thought now, quite unbeknownst to him, to be a prominent English writer. Accordingly, a reception is arranged for him at the home of Mrs. Legend, a patroness of letters, who invites the leading authors to meet this literary star from abroad. A score of writers fawn before Truck and ply him with questions about literature old and new. Quite ignorant of the poets and novelists to whom they refer, Truck makes evasive and noncommittal answers, all of which are interpreted as being shrewd witticisms and subtly ambiguous critical thrusts. Besides the Effingham group, only four young wags are aware that poor Truck is a simple seaman beyond his depth in conversation. When Steadfast Dodge arrives, however, he moves about the gathering and whispers the truth about Truck's occupation, whereupon most the the guests make a hasty and embarrassed exit. Quite oblivious to the whole contretemps, Truck thanks his mortified hostess for a pleasant evening and invites her to come to the dock to inspect his packet ship.

American materialism, especially the mania for money, is the next object of Cooper's satire. Under the guidance of John Effingham, Sir George visits the New York Stock Market and Wall Street, where he is introduced to the rage for speculation which animates American finance. In a symbolic gesture of wish fulfillment, Cooper has that section of the city destroyed that night by a fire that runs out of control for many hours.

On May 31 the Effingham group, including Grace and Sir George, leaves New York City bound for Templeton. They travel up the picturesque Hudson by steamboat, at what they consider breakneck speed, to Albany and thence westward through the Mohawk Valley on a canal boat. The last stage of the journey is made by carriages. All along the way to Templeton they see in the architecture ample evidence of the popularity of Greek Revival, structures for even the most mundane purposes bearing a resemblance to classical temples. On the outskirts of Templeton they are met by Paul Powis (alias Paul Blunt), a traveling companion who [in *Homeward Bound*] had suddenly left the *Montauk*, as it had come within American waters, and had boarded a British cruiser; although an American newspaper report had labeled him a deserter from the English navy, the report was baseless, for he was an American citizen. Powis is a great favorite with all of the Effinghams for having been of great service to them in Europe and en route to the United States, and there are frequent clues to the romantic interest that has developed between him and Eve. The arriving travelers are, in a sense, greeted by the dead as well as by the living, for there are still echoes at Templeton of the Leather-Stocking, Natty Bumppo, and other early settlers in the area.

The Wigwam, Edward Effingham's mansion, to which they all now retire, is an architectural monstrosity. Constructed originally [in *The Pioneers*] by two amateur Yankee builders, it was said, euphemistically, to be of the "composite order." Almost fifty years later John Effingham has restyled the building, removing some of its ugliest features but giving it a flat roof which will not withstand the winter weather of such a high northern latitude. Everyone has his say about the architecture, including the townspeople, who are offended that it does not conform to the popular Palladian principles.

Most of these citizens are strangers to the Effinghams, the westward flow of migration having filled, emptied, and filled the town again several times during the twelve years that Eve and her father were abroad. These birds of passage have little respect for property and still less for the privacy of the individual. A group of apprentice boys, shouting and swearing, gather to play ball on the front lawn of the Wigwam until they are urged to move elsewhere. The local barber requests permission to take down the fence around the front yard in order to haul manure across it for his potato patch. The fact that Bragg, manager of the Effingham property, sees nothing unusual in the request is an indication of the temper of the times.

On the third day after their arrival at Templeton, the Effinghams hold open house for their friends and neighbors. Among those who call are Tom Howel and Mr. Wenham, both American types during the second quarter of the nineteenth century. Howel is a hopeless Anglophile, so affected by the "colonial complex" that he values only English opinion on any subject, regardless of opposing evidence. Thus he is certain that Emperor Nicholas of Russia is a monster because the czar was so described in an English journal. The fact that his old friends the Effinghams have met Nicholas and attest to his humanity does not sway Howel a jot from his opinion. Wenham, who mistakenly supposes America completely liberated from the influence of European culture, maintains a rigidly nationalistic point of view on every issue. In this attitude he is frequently supported by Dodge. The extreme and simplistic views of Howel and Wenham often provide comic preludes to more serious consideration of national characteristics.

Next to be treated satirically is a popular religious trend of the day. A group of mechanics calls upon Edward Effingham to solicit his support in changing the interior of the church to which they all belong. They wish to make the arrangements within the church structure more democratic, they say, by lowering the pulpit and the altar while raising the congregation in banked seats like those in a theatre. It is not proper, they feel, to have the parson placed so far above the heads of his parishioners. Bragg agrees with the mechanics on this matter. He goes even further in his ideas about church reform, contending that all kneeling should be eliminated. It is un-American, he says, for God never intended Americans to kneel.

On a fair day the Effinghams and their guests take a boat ride on Otsego Lake [the real lake on which Cooperstown, New York, is located], enjoying all of its scenic splendor. Appreciation of its present beauty is increased by an awareness of the antiquity of the scene. Historical references go farther back in time than the period of Natty Bumppo and the pioneer settlers. A magnificent tree known as the "Silent Pine"—misnamed, really, for it has an eloquence of its own—surely stood on this spot, Eve observes, when William the Conqueror invaded England; perhaps even earlier, another suggests, when Columbus first ventured westward into unknown seas. Balancing the solemnity of such thoughts is the comic tone of their encounter with a droll fellow known only as Commodore. Still agile in his seventies, this local character spends all of his time fishing; he now regales the party with both factual data about the lake and some of its folklore, among the latter a tall tale about a "sogdollager," a great fish that cannot be caught. At the group's last stop, near the "Fishing Point," a favorite picnicking place, Eve learns from John Effingham the disturbing news that this part of the family estate is now being claimed as public property.

During the Effinghams' absence a rumor had circulated that the Fishing Point had been given to the citizens of Templeton by Edward Effingham's father. By the time that the present owner returned, this unfounded rumor had become accepted as fact, and there is deep public resentment that John Effingham has planned to hold a private entertainment on the property. Learning from Bragg of the citizens' determination to claim the Point as their own, Edward Effingham posts a notice that the public should not trespass on that part of the lake front. This triggers a mass meeting at which resolutions are passed reiterating the claim that the Point had been willed to the public and censuring Edward Effingham for his alleged usurpation of public property. After Edward shows Bragg both his title deed and a copy of his father's will, both of which provide clear proof of his ownership, the attorney doubts that such information will satisfy public feeling about the matter. Presented as typical of that public is Mrs. Widow-Bewitched Abbott, gossip, rumor-monger, and busybody. When she declares that the Fishing Point has been public land for as long as she can remember, we are told that she has lived in the county all of fifteen months. Despite the clamor of such people as Mrs. Abbott and the threats of less vocal residents of Templeton, Edward Effingham retains all rights to the disputed territory. [The conflict over the Fishing Point is a lightly veiled fictional treatment of the "Three-Mile-Point Controversy" in which Cooper became embroiled in 1837, the year before *Home as Found* was published; it was a dispute settled more quickly than the tangled mass of slander suits which grew out of it, litigation which the novelist pressed resolutely for many years.]

To leaven the society found at Templeton, the Effinghams entertain guests from the outside world: Mrs. Hawker, their gracious New York City hostess; Mrs. Bloomfield, the brilliant conversationalist, and the nonentity who is her husband; Captain Truck of the *Montauk;* and Captain Charles Ducie of His Majesty's cruiser *Foam.* These newcomers are soon busy observing the life-style and social dynamics of a small rural community as they attend a picnic, a Fourth of July oration, and an evening of fireworks. They also inject a cosmopolitan air into the lively discourse at the Wigwam on the mores and manners of contemporary Americans.

By this time, two courtships among the central characters have progressed to formal engagements. Grace Van Cortlandt accepts the marriage proposal of Sir George Templemore; and Eve, after rejecting the presumptuous offer of Aristabulus Bragg, accepts that of Paul Powis. Edward Effingham confers his blessings upon the betrothals of both his daughter and his niece. In the final stage of the courtship between Paul and Eve much of the mystery about the former—his birth, family, background, and nationality—is clarified. [It was this mystery that had provided a cliff-hanger ending to *Homeward Bound.*]

Seemingly orphaned in his infancy, Paul Assheton was cared for at first by hirelings and then by a kindly disposed guardian, Francis Powis, whose name he later adopted. Paul's deceased mother and Charles Ducie's mother, both Americans originally, were sisters upon whom had devolved jointly a British peerage. Wishing to secure this rank for herself but even more for her son, Mrs. Ducie, now married to an Englishman and living in England, had refused to acknowledge Paul as her sister's legitimate child. While in the United States navy, Paul had fought a duel with his British cousin, Charles, because of a reflection the latter had cast upon the virtue of Paul's mother. (This confrontation ended only in flesh wounds.) Ducie, having discovered thereafter his error about the circumstances of Paul's birth, intended to find him and make proper amends. By then, however, Paul had left the navy, after Francis Powis had died and left him a competency, and thus he was not easily located. Ducie discovered him by pure coincidence on the *Montauk,* the vessel from which he was recovering an embezzler for trial in England. After a hasty private conference with Ducie, Powis (much to the mystification of the Effinghams and his other fellow voyagers) transferred from the *Montauk* to the British cruiser *Foam* to sail back over the very ocean which he had just crossed. His object in doing this was of great importance to both Ducie and himself. He was willing to sign papers renouncing all claim to the peerage—as an American citizen he could hardly expect to acquire it anyway—for the truth from Mrs. Ducie about his birth and parentage. His aunt, who had been present both at the wedding of his parents and at his own subsequent birth, finally helped him to achieve a partial sense of his own identity. His mother had died at the time of his birth, but about his father and what had become of him he still knew nothing. Soon after this, Mrs. Ducie acquired the suspended peerage and became Lady Dunluce. The reader must piece together the story from the two accounts Paul gives of himself, the first to John Effingham (who had, in an unofficial way, virtually adopted Paul and secretly made him heir to half of his estate) and the second (a more emotional recital) to Eve. Only to Eve does Paul remember to mention that his original surname was Assheton. Shortly afterwards, when John Effingham is apprised of this surname, a further and even more startling identification is made. Paul is revealed to be the son of the supposed bachelor John Effingham.

John and Edward Effingham had loved the same girl. When Edward had married her, John had left home in blind despair and had hastily married the orphaned Mildred Warrender, the sister of the woman who would later become the mother of Charles Ducie. Quite beside himself, John had taken his mother's family name, Assheton, and it was by this name only that he was known to the wife from whom he soon parted to travel in the West. Not really in love with the woman he had married on the rebound, he did not know that her death during his absence had resulted from childbirth or that a son had survived. This failure in communication is now explained. Mildred's brother had taken a strong dislike to John when he confused him with another John Assheton, a ne'er-do-well and bigamist; supposing that his sister had unknowingly wedded a bigamist, Mr. Warrender had doubts about Paul's legitimacy, doubts which were reflected in some of the letters that Paul later came to possess. It was remarks he found in these letters which had caused Paul to wonder about his mother's moral position and about his own legal status. Eventually the Warrenders realized their error in thinking Paul's father a bigamous John Assheton. As if probability had not already been pushed to the utmost limits of credulity, there is one further coincidence which sheds light on some of the otherwise obscure aspects in the identity of Paul Blunt-Powis-Assheton-Effingham. The papers of the deceased Mr. Monday [killed by Arabs in *Homeward Bound*] describe an orphaned infant cared for by Monday's mother in return for an annuity provided by Mrs. Ducie, Paul's aunt. The infant was Paul, and the Monday letters provide still further evidence attesting to the virtue of Paul's mother.

There follows soon a double wedding at New St. Paul's Church, Sir

George and Grace being married at the same ceremony that unites Paul and Eve. Secure in their domestic happiness, the central characters indicate their reservations about "home as found" as they plan to visit Europe again the following year, sailing from New York in Captain Truck's *Montauk*.

Bianca-Alzuma-Ann Abbott, Orlando Furioso Abbott, Rinaldo-Rinaldini-Timothy Abbott, Roger-Demetrius-Benjamin Abbott, Widow-Bewitched Abbott, Annette, Mrs. Annual, Bale, Bloomfield, Mrs. Bloomfield, Miss Brackett, Aristabulus Bragg, Brutus, Julius Brutus, Lucius Brutus, Ordeal Bumgrum, Commodore, D. O. V. E., Dickey, Steadfast Dodge, Captain Charles Ducie, Edson, Edward Effingham, Eve Effingham, John Effingham, Paul Effingham, Florio, Fun, Gray, Abijah Gross, Hammer, Mrs. Hawker, Mrs. Houston, Thomas Howel, Jarvis, Jane Jarvis, Jenny, Julietta, Captain Kant, Mrs. Legend, Longinus, Monday, Miss Monthly, Moreland, Moseley, Peter, Pierre, Pindar, Pith, Miss Ring, S. R. P., Ann Sidley, Summerfield, Sir George Templemore, Tom, Captain John Truck, Grace Van Cortlandt, Mlle. Viefville, Walworth, Joe Wart, Wenham, Writ.

Homeward Bound; or, The Chase, 1838.

[This is the first of the two Effingham novels.]

Passengers board the American packet *Montauk,* first at London and then at Portsmouth, as she is being prepared for a scheduled October 1 sailing to New York. Introduced first are three of the best educated and most affluent passengers: John Effingham, a bachelor of fifty; his cousin, Edward Effingham, the same age to the very day; and the latter's daughter, Eve. Now twenty, Eve is returning home to America after a twelve-year residence in Europe, where she had taken her education. The Effinghams are accompanied by Eve's nurse, Ann (Nanny) Sidley, and by her French governess, Mademoiselle Viefville. As the other passengers arrive, the Effingham party amuses itself by guessing their occupations and backgrounds. This is all done in good nature except for the harsh and ungenerous comments of John Effingham, who is often cynical about his contemporaries.

As the *Montauk* is embarking from Portsmouth, Mr. Grab, a British bailiff, and Mr. Seal, a British attorney, come aboard with a warrant for the arrest of one Robert Davis. Davis and his wife, steerage passengers, have been married against the wish of her guardian uncle, who has filed suit against Davis to recover debts allegedly incurred by Mrs. Davis during her childhood. Captain Truck, master of the *Montauk,* does not try to prevent the agents of British law from searching the vessel but refuses to delay the departure of the ship for their convenience. Although Truck and several of the passengers know the identity of Davis, all refuse to betray him. Grab and Seal are still aboard as the ship moves out of the harbor into the English Channel, and their position is soon reinforced by the appearance of a British cutter whose crew prepares to board the packet. As the cutter is overtaking the *Montauk*, Captain Truck dismisses his harbor pilot, unfurls more sail, and determines to take the vessel to sea himself rather than submit to force.

Although Truck cites articles of international maritime law for his decision, his action is questioned by a passenger named Steadfast Dodge, a Yankee newspaper editor and ultra-democrat. Dodge has polled all of the passengers and demands that a committee be appointed to decide whether or not to surrender to the cutter. Truck humors Dodge and passengers of his persuasion by appointing a committee, knowing well that it will be ineffectual. As her sails fill, the *Montauk* leaves the cutter far behind; and Grab and Seal, realizing that they will soon be taken to sea, depart hastily in their small boat.

While congratulating themselves on having escaped the clutches of English law, the crew sights a more formidable pursuer, a cruiser named *Foam*. The cruiser's mission is a mystery to the people aboard the packet, for it seems most unlikely that a man-of-war would be dispatched to apprehend a debtor like Davis. Again opinion aboard the *Montauk* is divided about the proper action to be taken: flight or surrender. There is never any doubt in the mind of the only real authority aboard, Captain Truck, who adds more sail, hoping to elude the *Foam* during the night as they pass out of the Channel and into the Atlantic Ocean. He underestimates his adversaries, however, for the dawn shows them still dogging his wake. The cruiser, a sharper-hulled vessel than the *Montauk*, has the advantage while sailing against the wind; conversely, the kettle-bottomed packet can outdistance the *Foam* when scudding before the wind, and this is the tactic that Truck immediately employs. Unfortunately, the wind remains, day after day, in the northwest, driving the *Montauk* off course, down the coast of France, past the Bay of Biscay, Lisbon, the Azores, and the Canary Islands.

The unusual southerly course and the pursuit by a foreign naval vessel draw the cabin passengers of the *Montauk* more closely together than they might otherwise be. Of the three Effinghams, Eve (not surprisingly) is the most sought after socially. When the occasion permits, she is engaged in conversation by Mr. Sharp, an Englishman, and his cabin partner, the supposedly American Paul Blunt. The latter seems to be

preferred by Eve, partly because he had rescued both her and her father
from a boating accident on the Continent; it is clear that Eve knows but
discreetly protects the real identity of the man who goes by the name
Paul Blunt. Sharing another cabin are the newspaper editor Steadfast
Dodge, whose name suggests his equivocal character, and, quite his
opposite, the bluff British baronet, Sir George Templemore, traveling to
America to hunt bison on the Great Plains. Pictured in even sharper
contrast with Dodge, however, is Captain Truck, though both men are
Connecticut Yankees. Dodge constantly moves about the ship sampling
passenger opinion, canvasses support for his every move, and insists on
the infallibility of a majority. Truck seldom counsels with others during a
crisis, always acts with courageous independence, and cares little for his
public image. Despite certain grotesque features—his mania for introducing both strangers and acquaintances, his incessant quoting of Emer-
ich de Vattel (an authority on international law), his excessive fondness
for cigars—Truck is clearly a sympathetic character, while Dodge is made
despicable at almost every turn. (The author's antipathy toward excessive leveling tendencies of Jacksonian Democracy is voiced in this second
novel he published after his own fall from popular favor in the early
1830s.)

A gale that arises off the coast of Africa proves to be a mixed blessing: it
separates the *Foam* from its quarry, but it also carries away the *Montauk's*
masts and leaves it a crippled hulk. When the storm abates somewhat,
two jury masts are rigged, making the ship maneuverable if not seaworthy. A sail is now sighted, and the vessel which approaches the packet
proves to be a supply ship for the American naval squadron stationed in
the Mediterranean. Returning empty to New York, she had met the gale
off Madeira and had also been borne southward by its force. Unlike the
Montauk, however, she has sustained no damage, and her captain readily
takes aboard as many of the packet passengers as wish to sail home in his
ship. On the following morning all the steerage passengers and most of
the cabin-class passengers are transferred to the freighter, which sails
westward on the now tranquil sea and soon drops below the horizon.

When the *Montauk* approaches the shore of Africa, where Truck
halfheartedly hopes to find timber for new masts, a grounded Danish
vessel is discovered without a soul aboard but with ample evidence of
having been plundered recently. On the beach they find the body of a
Dane dead no more than a day, killed by natives who, apparently, have led
off the rest of the ship's complement to captivity. Truck decides at once to
equip the damaged *Montauk* with the masts and spars of the abandoned
wreck; for this purpose he takes ashore thirty men, along with tools and

all available arms, leaving the women on the packet guarded by the two Effingham men, Paul Blunt, and Sharp.

During the night, Captain Truck and his first mate, Mr. Leach, detect two Arabs scouting the beach. One they catch, but the other escapes on a camel; since this second man will spread the alarm among his people, they release his companion too. Next day, as the workmen are removing the last poles from the wreck, a band of more than two hundred armed Arabs appears mounted on horses and camels. Stalling for time, Truck sends to them a dubious delegation composed of the alcoholic Monday, who takes along a case of liquor for bargaining purposes, and Dodge, persistent advocate of citizens' committees. Predictably, Monday becomes tipsy and the cowardly Dodge runs back to the wreck in fear. By this time, the salvaged masts are lashed together to form a rude raft, and the men, in their own small boats and the Dane's launch, begin towing it to sea. Much to the surprise of Captain Truck, the Arabs have not lifted a hand or fired a shot to prevent their departure. The seamen work against a stiff onshore breeze as they move their cumbersome load seaward, and they can progress only by means of warping: anchoring a boat firmly and then hauling the raft abreast of it while another boat is anchored farther out to repeat the process. Working thus slowly and laboriously, hampered too by a rising sea, they anchor at nightfall only a league from shore.

Aboard the *Montauk*, in the meantime, all remains tranquil throughout the day, and the ship rides easily in a cove protected by reefs. During the night, however, an attempt is made by a small group of Arabs to enter the packet by crawling up the anchor chain. Blunt frustrates their efforts by releasing more chain, thus submerging its whole length. The situation of those aboard the ship is now recognized to be most perilous, for at low tide one of the reefs forms a virtual land bridge to shore. The anchorage is more vulnerable than Captain Truck had realized. The Arabs, given to plundering helpless ships borne ashore by tropical storms, have been watching and waiting for the most opportune time to capture the *Montauk* and its valuable cargo of supplies and personnel. This explains the question that had puzzled Truck: why they had not bothered to attack the crew salvaging masts from the Dane. Possessed of a pair of field glasses (booty from some earlier shipwreck), the tribesmen are aware that the packet is shorthanded, having aboard but five men including the steward and the two elder Effinghams. What they do not know is that the ship is without rifles or even pistols, all available small arms, powder, and shot having been taken by the salvage crew, who had expected hostilities ashore. The light cannon mounted on the forecastle deck is charged with powder but not shotted, since it was intended as a signal gun. Blunt and Sharp fire the blank charge hoping that its report will reach the ears of Captain Truck and alert him to the fact that they are endangered. As they discover later, the noise did not carry far enough to serve their purpose.

Under the pressure of imminent danger, the identities of Paul Blunt and Sharp are revealed. Stunned by the news that they are beset by semicivilized Arabs, Eve calls both men by their real names. Paul Blunt is actually Paul Powis, and Sharp is Sir George Templemore, who has, for the voyage, permitted a stranger to usurp his name in what the baronet supposes is a mere caprice.

Wishing to take the ship before low tide (or before Truck and his men might return), the Arabs build a large pontoon to serve as a floating bridge over those parts of the reef still inundated. It seems certain to those aboard that it will be but a short time before the Arabs reach the *Montauk* by means of this device. Paul Blunt [Powis], who turns out to be an experienced seaman, takes command now and directs a last-minute effort to swing the heavy launch over the side of the *Montauk* and into the sea. This they finally manage to do; and when food, water, sails, and the swivel are placed aboard the launch, the group sails away in a hairbreadth escape. After supper on a small islet, where Saunders, the steward, manages to build a fire and prepare tea, the refugees try to find the passage through the reefs that leads to the open sea. Fearing that Truck and all his men have been killed or captured, they hope to leave the area and reach the Cape Verde Islands. Throughout the night they are hampered by Arabs, shifting winds, and hidden shoals until, near morning, they come upon Truck and the crew of the *Montauk* in their small boats.

After hasty explanations on both sides, the entire company of the *Montauk* moves back toward their ship. Leaving Mr. Effingham and the women in a boat out of sight from the Arabs' positions, the remainder of the party attack their foes, first those on the reef and then those aboard the now grounded packet. The single small cannon taken from the *Montauk* provides the balance of firepower; after a bloody struggle, a truce is declared, and the Arabs withdraw, taking with them their dead and wounded. They have suffered heavy losses, mainly from the grapeshot of the swivel fired with deadly accuracy by Paul Blunt [Powis]. Only two of the boarding party become casualties, a young seaman, Brooks, killed instantly by a rifle ball, and Monday, shot through the shoulder and then fatally wounded in the chest by an Arab spear.

Knowing that the Arabs will return, probably in even greater numbers, the crew works feverishly to replace the *Montauk's* masts with those from the Danish ship. Then as the tide rises, they man the capstan to warp the packet off the sand bar where it is lodged. By the time she is freed, the shore and reef are covered with Arabs who scream, gesticulate wildly, and maintain a steady rain of musket fire at the vessel. One seaman is killed while carrying rigging to the top of a mast, and the helmsman dies clinging to the wheel after being struck in the back by an Arab rifle ball. At long last, however, the *Montauk* is once more at sea bound west for New York.

Monday lingers for another day before he dies, attended during his last hours by John Effingham. Both the kind acts and the religious counsel of the latter mitigate for the reader the impression this man often gives of aloofness and insensitivity to the sufferings of others. Monday leaves in his care a parcel of papers to be probated when the packet arrives in New York.

Now out of danger, Dodge reverts to his old activist and self-promotional tactics. Though he had hidden in fear during the battle, he now tries to persuade the stewards it was he who had mounted the cannon and driven off the Arabs. He now solicits support for his contention that it was the passengers who repossessed the *Montauk* and that they therefore have a just claim for compensation from the ship's owners. During the toasting and conviviality enjoyed on Saturday night—it was a common custom on sailing vessels—Dodge is invited to divert the company by reading from the journal he has kept of his European travels, a journal to be published in the pages of his *Active Inquirer*. He accedes to this request with great alacrity, though the audience response that is forthcoming has a motivation quite different from what Dodge supposes. Most of the passengers are amused at the confident ignorance and provincialism of this Yankee editor, but Dodge is quite oblivious to the thrust of their ironic comments.

As the *Montauk* comes within American waters, it meets the cruiser *Foam* bound for London. Captain Charles Ducie's request for a meeting with Captain Truck is granted, and the British commander comes aboard the *Montauk*. He has two petitions, one stated at once to Captain Truck, and the other reserved for someone else. His first is for permission to remove from the *Montauk* the embezzler Henry Sandon, who has been masquerading under the title and name of Sir George Templemore. Sandon has absconded with £40,000 of government funds. Although Truck orders from his vessel the bad-mannered Green, the civilian agent accompanying Captain Ducie, he surrenders the culprit to the British authorities. He makes the point, however, that he is responding to a request and not acquiescing to a demand. The desperate young Sandon attempts unsuccessfully to commit suicide; a second attempt, made a month later while he is in an English prison, succeeds.

The real Sir George Templemore, who has been traveling under the name Sharp, is an old friend of Ducie, and the two are glad to see each other again. Ducie is far less pleased to see Paul Blunt [Powis], to whom his second request is apparently addressed. After Ducie and Paul talk apart, quietly but with animation, the latter has his luggage transferred to the *Foam's* boat and bids farewell to everyone on the *Montauk*. Remembering his gallant action against the Arabs, all are sorry and puzzled at his unexplained departure—not least Eve Effingham. On the day after the *Montauk* docks in New York, the mysterious behavior of Powis is partially clarified. A newpaper article reporting the arrival of the packet notes the removal of two passengers shortly before the ship had landed, one an embezzler and the other "a deserter from the king's service, though a scion of a noble family" (p. 531). An account of how Eve Effingham felt and acted when she received this information is promised in the story's sequel [*Home as Found*].

Paul Blunt [Powis], Brooks, Mrs. Davis, Robert Davis, Steadfast Dodge, Captain Charles Ducie, Edward Effingham, Eve Effingham, John Effingham, Grab, Green, Handlead, Leach, Monday, Henry Sandon, Saunders, Seal, Sharp [Templemore], Ann Sidley, Tom Smith, Sir George Templemore [Sandon], Toast, Captain John Truck, Mlle. Viefville.

"Imagination," 1823.

The first of two tales for adolescent girls written by Cooper under the pseudonym Jane Morgan, "Imagination" is a piece of light fiction 124 pages in length. It begins along the Hudson River on the outskirts of New York City at the summer home of Miss Margaret Emmerson, where that lady's niece and ward, Julia Warren, sixteen, is bidding farewell to her closest friend, Anna Miller. The Millers, a large family, are, for economic reasons, moving from New York City to the banks of the Genesee in the western part of the state. The two boarding-school companions are distressed at the necessity of parting, and Anna is further disturbed about leaving the metropolis to live in a frontier village. They promise to write to each other frequently. As the Miller carriage disappears from view, Julia rushes to her room to give vent to her feelings.

An hour later Julia, composed again, descends to the parlor to join her aunt and Charles Weston, a distant relative of Miss Emmerson and a frequent visitor in her household. Charles, not yet twenty-one, is enamored of Julia, but the girl shows no interest in him at all. In the conversation that ensues, Miss Emmerson indicates her wish that Julia would renew her friendship with her other niece, Katherine, daughter of Miss Emmerson's brother, an affluent attorney in whose office Charles is studying law. With an excellent education and a position among the city's social elite, Katherine would, Aunt Margaret thinks to herself, have a better influence on Julia than does Anna Miller. A conversation develops concerning affection for others. Julia takes the position that her affection for her cousin Katherine is that natural love due between relatives but that her affection for Anna Miller is of a superior kind, a love born of mutual sympathy, a kind of "innate evidence" (p. 18).

Julia waits for some time for her first letter from Anna, and at last it arrives, delivered on horseback from the local post office by Charles Weston. Taking this missive to the summerhouse in the garden, Julia locks herself inside to read and reread Anna's message several times. Besides requesting an invitation to winter with Julia and her aunt in the latter's Park Place residence, Anna writes at length about Edward Stanley, a young man she has recently met. Of special interest to Julia is the comment that Edward has expressed admiration of her after hearing Anna describe her former schoolmate. So absorbed has Julia become in Anna's letter that she has not noticed the gathering thunderstorm outside. When she emerges from the garden, she is whisked into the home of her aunt by Charles lest she be drenched by the downpour then commencing. During a series of thunderclaps that follow, Charles candidly acknowledges that each loud peal frightens him momentarily. Outwardly, Julia mocks Charles for his unheroic timidity; inwardly, she compares him unfavorably with Edward Stanley, who is, according to Anna, very brave.

In the exchange of letters that follows, the girls use the code name Antonio for Edward Stanley. Anna is soon able to report to her friend that Antonio has declared his love for Julia. Anna also reveals that she too has a beau, a resident of New York City to whom she gives the code name Regulus. This is also exciting news to Julia, and she begins to scrutinize surreptitiously every young man she sees in an effort to determine if he might perhaps be Regulus. Anna wants especially to winter with Julia and her aunt, she says, in order to be near her paramour, and in every letter she presses Julia to secure for her an invitation from Miss Emmerson to be their houseguest. But, as Aunt Margaret tells Julia, there is only one spare room in the Park Place house, and she would like to offer it to her other niece, Katherine, who will be alone when her parents spend the winter months in Carolina. They agree not to invite either potential guest until September.

Late in the summer Miss Emmerson announces her intention to take Julia and Charles to see Niagara Falls, stopping for a night en route at the Miller home. Julia receives this news with delight, for the stop along the Genesee will enable her both to visit with Anna and to meet Antonio. In a subsequent letter Anna informs her that Antonio, upon learning of the projected trip to the Falls, has rushed to New York to accompany and protect the party of travelers. He will, of course, be in deep disguise to protect the secrecy of their love, and Julia will probably have great difficulty in recognizing him.

The first leg of the journey, from New York City to Albany, is made by steamboat. Along the way they pass a sloop carrying, among other freight, the horses and carriage hired to take them westward across the state from the capital. When Julia learns that the coachman is named Anthony Sandford, she is certain that he is her heroic Antonio assuming a menial role in order to be close to her. She resents the fact that Charles calls the driver Tony and treats him like a servant. The man attending the horses on the sloop is tall, stout, and swarthy; he appears to be middle-aged, and he wears a large green patch over one eye. All of these features Julia attributes to appearance only, a clever disguise.

Throughout the overland leg of their trip Julia indulges in a love fantasy, giving every word and act of the coachman a romantic interpretation. The farce is able to be sustained at length because it exists entirely in the imagination of Julia.

When the traveling party reach the Miller home, they are welcomed by the whole family, and it is some time before Anna and Julia have privacy in which to exchange girlhood confidences. When at last they are alone, Anna's main concern is to learn if and when she will receive an invitation to spend the winter in New York City with her old schoolmate. Julia is more interested in talking of their secret lovers, Antonio and Regulus. This wish-fulfillment fantasy is shattered when Anna reveals that Antonio and Regulus are straw men she had created to add excitement to her letters. The coachman is but a coachman, says Anna, " . . . and an ugly wretch he is" (p. 122). Sobbing for an hour in the arms of her aunt (who never learns the cause of all this grief), Julia pulls herself together sufficiently to take leave of their hosts with composure and respect. Reality is reinforced when Julia mounts the step of the coach and sees a brown liquid stain her new shoes and stockings—tobacco juice drooled by the driver and carried back by a gust of wind. The same gust blows aside Anthony's patch to expose a face deformed by disease and lacking one eye.

The author spares the reader the details of the remainder of the trip, telling him only that the group returns by boat, down Lake Ontario and the St. Lawrence to Montreal, then southward over Lake Champlain and Lake George to the headwaters of the Hudson. It is not until Julia has been married to Charles Weston for more than a year that she can admit, even to herself, that " . . . she had once been in love, like thousands of her sex, 'with a man of straw'" (p. 124).

Katherine Emmerson, Margaret Emmerson, Miller, Anna Miller, Henry Frederick St. Albans [Regulus], Anthony Sandford, Edward Stanley [Antonio], Julia Warren, Charles Weston.

Jack Tier; or, The Florida Reef, 1848.

Set during the time of the Mexican War, *Jack Tier* is a much more realistic sea story than the nautical romances Cooper wrote in the 1820s and 1830s. It begins in New York City where the *Molly Swash,* tied up at an unattractive wharf near beer halls and an almshouse, is in the process of departure for Key West. Although a sleek, clipper-built brig, the *Molly Swash,* like her captain, Stephen Spike (now fifty-six), shows signs of age. Most of the crewmen too are beyond the prime of life, and the Negro steward and cabin "boy," Josh, is sixty. The only young man among the ship's company is Henry (Harry) Mulford, the first (and only) mate. Three passengers are aboard the brig: Rose Budd, an intelligent and beautiful girl not yet nineteen; Mrs. Budd, her aunt, in late middle age but already failing mentally; and the latter's Irish maidservant, Bridget (Biddy) Noon. It is Mrs. Budd's opinion that Rose has incipient tuberculosis and that a sea voyage will cure her malady. She does not tell this to her niece, however, but pretends that she herself has pulmonary problems that a cruise may relieve. Mulford is certain that neither woman has any lung disease. He soon does discover, though, that the widow has a less serious failing, a confirmed case of nautical malapropism. Her late husband, a sea captain, had, with a perverted sense of humor, carefully mistaught her shipboard terms and seaman's lingo in order to amuse himself and his cronies at her expense.

As they cast off, Captain Spike exhibits a degree of anxiety that suggests he has something to hide. He is disturbed by the appearance nearby of a customs vessel. When the brig is only a few feet from the dock, he is hailed by a tall man who wants the job of harbor pilot to carry the brig through Hell-Gate, a narrow channel in the East River. He is also hailed by a short, fat, waddling little figure with a cracked, dwarflike voice, a seaman who, claiming to be a shipmate of twenty years earlier, asks Spike for a berth aboard his ship. Spike rejects both bids for employment and directs the *Molly Swash* toward Hell-Gate, which he intends to navigate with his own skill. When the would-be employees follow, however, in a smaller but faster boat, Spike grows so upset that he permits his vessel to graze a dangerous rock in the passage.

The glancing blow sustained by the *Molly Swash* does not damage her hull. After having the pumps sounded to verify the ship's tightness, Captain Spike sets sail once again. In the meantime, a skiff comes abeam bearing the stubby seaman who had called from the dock. Eager for a place among the brig's crew, the man identifies himself as Jack Tier, one of the *Molly Swash's* original hands who, having been accidentally left on an island twenty years ago, had shipped on numerous other vessels since. Spike cannot clearly recall the man, but his story is confirmed by Josh, who remembers Tier as a handy steward's assistant. Although not very presentable or overly clean, Jack Tier is hired as a cabin steward for the ladies' quarters.

It now becomes apparent that the *Molly Swash* is being pursued by a large armed steamship in the customs service. Spike tells his mate that since he owes no revenue of any kind, he is determined to avoid the delay that a boarding and search would entail. Mulford takes the captain at his word and diligently supports his efforts to elude the steamer. At dusk they rearrange the sails to convert the brig into what will pass, from a distance at night, as a schooner. When a shot is fired over the *Molly Swash*, Spike hoists all sails to get a head start before the revenue ship can get up a head of steam. As the government ship begins to gain speed, the brig darts into an anchorage known to Spike and Mulford, a roadstead backed by high, dark bluffs against which the tall masts of the *Molly Swash* will be all but invisible. The customs vessel, its course revealed by the glow from its stack, sails past the roadstead and temporarily disappears. The following evening the brig escapes both the steamer and a schooner which have laid a trap for her off Block Island.

During all of this maneuvering, Rose Budd begins to have misgivings about the nature of the vessel on which she and her aunt have taken passage. Rose is not deceived by Spike's explanations for his unusual movements, explanations which are patent falsehoods. She is not alone in her second thoughts about the *Molly Swash*. Mulford had doubts about Spike's character even before the voyage started—he had been first mate for a year by then—but having no tangible evidence of misconduct, he had allowed his penury, his interest in Rose, and his attachment to the ship itself to persuade him to sign on for another voyage. Like Rose, he is mystified by Spike's antipathy to all contact with government ships; for, as he tells her, the *Molly Swash* has in her hold nothing but flour, hardly a cargo to cause anyone concern.

Several days later the *Molly Swash* is overtaken by the U.S. cruiser *Poughkeepsie*, commanded by Captain Adam Mull, who sends aboard an officer, Lieutenant Wallace, to inspect the freight. Blockading the Mexican coast, the navy is examining all vessels that might bear contraband destined for enemy use. Lieutenant Wallace finds nothing in the hold but what Captain Spike's papers list: eight hundred barrels of flour. There remains a nagging doubt in the mind of Captain Mull, however, when his junior officer reports his findings. Flour for Florida and Gulf ports normally comes, more directly, down the Mississippi River, not down the Atlantic coast from New York. The *Poughkeepsie's* commander determines to make a closer scrutiny of Spike's flour in a day or two, but once the *Molly Swash* is out of sight, he does not see it again for some time. Mulford's suspicions about the business motives of Spike now deepen as the captain first orders the mate to surrender all his navigational instruments and then sets about disguising the brig by repainting her and altering dramatically the configuration of her sails. About Spike's personal motives for taking aboard his passengers, Mulford now has no doubts at all, for he has overheard the captain's declaration to Mrs. Budd that he wishes to marry Rose.

The *Molly Swash* now approaches a cluster of islets among the Dry Tortugas, off the Florida Reef, and anchors near a fully equipped lighthouse that seems to have been very recently deserted. At dusk, Spike enters the lighthouse, trims the lanterns, and lets them burn throughout the night. Harry and Rose discover that this is a signal to a Mexican schooner waiting in the distance for the arrival of the brig. (The lighthouse keeper and his assistant are held imprisoned on the schooner.) A Mexican agent, the gentlemanly Don Juan Montefalderon y Castro, comes aboard the *Molly Swash* and closes a deal, initiated in New York, for the brig's cargo. Both crews work diligently to transfer the flour to the schooner as quickly as possible. In their haste, they drop a barrel from the gangplank to the deck of the schooner, where it bursts and reveals amidst the flour a keg of gunpowder. The nature of Stephen Spike's mission is now disclosed: he is traitorously selling munitions to the Mexican government with which his own country is at war. He is also interested in selling the brig itself and settling in Mexico, he tells Don Juan, with his new bride-to-be, Rose Budd. The Mexican is shocked at the depth of Spike's depravity and responds evasively to his request for assistance in entering Mexico. Much of this discussion, overheard by Rose, is repeated to Mulford, and the young people now begin to watch for an opportunity to escape from the evil power of Spike.

A tornado strikes the anchorage and sinks the schooner with all hands on board. Spike offers to salvage the Mexican ship for half of the gold it contains, and Montefalderon readily accepts the proposal. By the end of a day the American crew has moved the schooner into an upright position on the sandy bottom and begins to raise her with a number of block-and-tackle purchases swung from the masts of the brig. Pumping starts, and many barrels of flour are moved from the hold of the vessel to its deck.

Before the work can be resumed the following morning, Lieutenant Wallace of the *Poughkeepsie* comes alongside in a gig and boards the *Molly Swash*. He is undeceived by Spike's claim that Don Juan, to whom he is introduced, is a Cuban, but he gives no indication of his disbelief. After an outwardly cordial exchange between Spike and Wallace, the latter departs after promising to send forty or fifty men, if needed, to assist in the salvage operation. Upon his return to the *Poughkeepsie*, however, he sends not men but heavy shells toward the two ships at the anchorage. When the cruiser's guns begin firing, Spike and his boatswain, Ben Clench, are neck-deep in water in the cabin of the schooner trying to locate Don Juan's doubloons. They find one of two bags of gold there and then abandon their efforts as the *Poughkeepsie's* guns begin to get the range of their target. As the *Molly Swash* prepares to sail, Spike, accompanied by Jack Tier, rushes to an islet to recover the passengers who have been tenting there comfortably during the salvage work. When Mrs. Budd and Biddy, reduced to hysterics by the shelling, refuse to budge, Spike begins to carry away Rose until he is struck on the head and then held at pistol point by Jack Tier. A shell falls among a hundred barrels of flour drying on the islet, detonating the kegs of gunpowder they contain. Recognizing the danger to his ship posed by the barrels of flour that cover her deck, Spike, forgetting about the women and Jack Tier, rushes back to the brig and directs the work of casting overboard the now-lethal cargo. As the last of these are being dumped into the sea, a heavy shell passes between the masts of the *Molly Swash* and then explodes. No damage to the ship is discernible; but apparently Mulford, who had been standing near one of the masts, has been swept away in the vortex of the passing missile. Such is not actually the case; for Harry, determined not to desert Rose under any circumstances, has jumped aboard the small boat Spike vacated and, unobserved, has left the ship during the consternation caused by the near miss of the cruiser's heaviest gun.

Without searching for his first mate or concerning himself further about the fate of Jack Tier and the women, Spike takes the *Molly Swash* through an opening in the reef and out of the range of the *Poughkeepsie's* guns. As the two vessels disappear over the horizon a distance of twenty-five miles is between them. The five people left behind (Mulford, Tier, and the three women) finish bailing out the Mexican schooner and restoring it to its former condition. It is Mulford's intention to sail the schooner to Key West, only sixty miles away, staying within the Florida Reef lest, shorthanded, they should be carried away by heavy weather in the open sea. With only two or three sails in use, and those at the lowest functional levels of the masts, the mate thinks that they can handle the craft safely. All goes well until Mrs. Budd takes her watch during the night. With officious ineptitude she tries to retie the ship's dinghy and in the process loses it. Then, failing to waken Harry at the time he had specified, she is responsible for the capsizing of the schooner in a squall.

For two days the five refugees live on the upturned hull of the schooner, which is kept afloat by the air trapped in the hold. They have only a handful of food among them and no water. When their thirst grows almost intolerable, they are given some relief by a brief shower. Once a sail is sighted, and the ship approaches close enough so that they can recognize it as the *Poughkeepsie*. Despite their frantic signals, however, they are too low in the water to be seen by the lookouts on the warship. Toward the end of the second day, Harry, watching the steady stream of bubbles rising along the waterline, realizes that air has been escaping continuously from the hold. The ship has actually sunk several inches lower in the water, a fact which he keeps to himself. The lost dinghy, shifted back and forth (as they themselves are) by the movement of the tides, had floated by earlier in the day, but sharks had prevented them from pursuing it. Now, as it grows dark, the boat is sighted again; after the others have retired for the night, Harry decides that it must be recovered at any hazard. After much arduous swimming, during which he is several times menaced by sharks, the mate reaches the boat and rows back to pick up his companions just as the schooner is submerging. The group stops momentarily to scoop rainwater from cavities in an exposed reef. As they are about to depart, they are sighted by a lookout on the *Molly Swash*, which, having barely outrun the cruiser, has returned to the area. After being chased for some time by a boat with Spike at the helm, they are finally captured. Spike leaves Mulford stranded on a bare rock and returns hastily to the brig, which is once again within range of the *Poughkeepsie's* guns. Knowing these treacherous waters far better than those aboard the cruiser can possibly know them, Spike soon eludes his persistent enemy.

Back aboard the *Molly Swash*, Jack Tier tries unsuccessfully to persuade Josh and Simon, the Negro cook, to accompany him that night in the ship's boat to rescue Mulford, the handsome mate. They would return to the brig themselves and then let Harry escape in the boat. Although the two blacks like the mate and are sympathetic to Jack's effort in his behalf, they are too intimidated by Spike to become active accomplices. They do arrange to have the boat in readiness, though, and they stand Jack's watch while he, Rose, and Biddy sail back to the rock and rescue Harry.

Under the cover of darkness Biddy is taken back to the *Molly Swash* to attend to the needs of Mrs. Budd; then Harry, Rose and Jack proceed to the abandoned lighthouse. Still unaware that Rose and Jack Tier are missing from his ship, Spike later that night awakens and, taking Don Juan Montefalderon with him, goes ashore himself and lights the lanterns in the lighthouse tower. He does this in order to give the impression of normality to any ship that might be in the area. The refugees hide in the keeper's living quarters; but Harry, recognizing in Don Juan a gentleman who would not ordinarily associate with a degenerate like Spike, speaks to the Mexican as he goes to visit the graves of his drowned countrymen. Harry secures from Don Juan a pledge of whatever assistance he can possibly render. True to his word, Don Juan returns the following night to ferry Jack Tier back to the *Molly Swash*. (There is a striking ambivalence throughout the novel in Jack Tier's attitude toward his captain. Although he mutters repeatedly, "Spike is a willian" [p. 343], he refuses to leave the villain.) As the brig is about to leave the isle and its lighthouse, the crew spots Mulford, who has carelessly exposed himself by walking into the moonlight. They think it is the ghost of the first mate left on the barren rock. Spike fires two musket shots, neither of which affects the figure on the shore. Even more ominous, his second shot seems to echo twice and its charge seems to return, singing above the heads of the crew and striking the open water beyond the ship. The shot whose whine they hear is actually return fire from the islet, where boats from the cruiser have just arrived. The *Poughkeepsie* itself is too far away to see the *Molly Swash*, much less bring its guns to bear upon her, and again Spike escapes. During the time that elapses before the arrival of the warship, Harry and Rose are united in marriage by the Rev. Mr. Hollis, a naval chaplain who has accompanied Lieutenant Wallace and the sailors in the small boats.

When the cruiser arrives, Lieutenant Wallace reports to Captain Mull on everything that has occurred at the lighthouse, as well as on Mulford's separation from the *Molly Swash*. At first dubious about Harry's integrity, Mull is soon won over by the mate's frankness and directness. The young man agrees to guide the cruiser to the site of the sunken schooner, to which Spike has gone to recover the lost bag of Mexican gold.

During this time, the *Molly Swash* has sailed directly to the wreck, and Spike commences at once to raise the vessel just far enough to make accessible the cabin containing the doubloons. There is no intention this time of trying to salvage the schooner itself. A ship carpenter who cuts a hole in the deck above the cabin is ordered to enter the opening and bring out the money. One of the poles propped under the schooner breaks, and the vessel sinks back to the bottom. No effort is made to rescue the trapped carpenter, who, Spike knows, cannot swim. Such cruel disregard for human life shocks Don Juan, but Spike yawns at his remonstrance and observes that carpenters are expendable. The captain's only concern is the gold still in the schooner.

The *Poughkeepsie* arrives with the dawn, and the quest for gold is abandoned. Spike pilots his ship among the rocks of the reef as shells from the cruiser begin to destroy its rigging. Without masts and spars from which to swing tackle, it is impossible to get the ship's launch over the side. Instead, the yawl is lowered, and into this much smaller craft everyone rushes when the *Molly Swash* founders on a bank of projecting coral. Greatly overloaded with its eighteen passengers, the yawl cannot possibly escape the four cutters from the man-of-war. Three of these cutters return to the *Poughkeepsie* when the *Molly Swash* breaks apart on the rocks; but the fourth, commanded by Lieutenant Wallace, who is accompanied by Mulford, continues the pursuit. As the distance lessens between the cutter and the yawl, a brutal drama of self-preservation begins on the latter. To lighten the load of his boat, Spike forces overboard, one at a time, its defenseless occupants, first Josh, Simon, and Don Juan, then five of the crewmen who attempt to save the Mexican, next Mrs. Budd (whose wrist is slashed to release her grip on the boatswain's hand) and Biddy Noon, and finally Jack Tier. Of these helpless victims only Jack is saved as he swims stoutly into the path of the oncoming cutter. As the pursuers continue to gain on the pursued, a desperate struggle begins among the six remaining seamen, each trying to keep his place in the yawl while forcing others overboard. When the frantic fight has ended only Clench, the boatswain, remains in the boat with Spike. A volley of musket fire from the cutter kills Clench and fatally wounds Spike.

Spike is taken to a small naval hospital at Key West where he is attended by Jack Tier and Rose Budd. While Rose is out of the sickroom, Jack Tier, now wearing woman's clothing, reveals to the dying captain that she is Mary Swash, the wife he had left on an island twenty years earlier when he had become interested in another woman. She nursed a seaman dying of yellow fever who had accidentally been left behind on the same island, a short stubby man name Jack Tier. Pretending to be Jack Tier herself, she while still in her late twenties had assumed the mien and role of a man and had sailed on ship after ship, knowing eventually she would find Spike again. This had taken her twenty years, during which time she had aged markedly and had grown coarse in her features. Only Rose Budd and her aunt had, until now, known her real identity.

The dying man is forgiven by his long-suffering wife before he expires, but his final moments are horrible as he mingles cursing and shouts of fear, sullen defiance and cries for mercy. After Spike's death and burial, Harry and Rose return to New York City, where they make Jack Tier—she still goes by that name—part of their household, more a companion than a servant. Although Spike's illegally gained gold is confiscated, his honest earnings go to his wife and heir, Mary (nicknamed Molly), and these are invested for her in a way to make her fairly independent. As she recovers from her years of hardship, she becomes more feminine, even to the point of forsaking chewing tobacco for snuff!

With funds from Rose's fortune, increased now by the inheritance of her late aunt's estate, a ship is purchased for Harry to command. A son born to the couple provides the final tie of affection to hold Jack Tier to the Mulford home and a settled life ashore.

Midshipman Archer, Barlow, Bill, Mrs. Budd, Rose Budd, Ben Clench, Rev. Mr. Hollis, Josh, Don Juan Montefalderon y Castro, Henry Mulford, Captain Adam Mull, Bridget Noon, Sam, Simon, Captain Stephen Spike, Strand, Jack Tier [Mary Swash Spike], Tom, Lieutenant Wallace.

"The Lake Gun," 1850.

The central story in this brief political allegory is presented twice, first in expository form by a narrator, then in more dramatic form by a cast of three characters. Set on Seneca Lake in Central New York, it is based partly on a real Indian legend and partly on a fictitious tale which Cooper endowed with some of the qualities of legend. For centuries Seneca Lake has periodically emitted loud explosive sounds, detonations from what the white settlers call "The Lake Gun." This documented phenomenon has never been scientifically explained, but the Indians consider it the voice of the Manitou, their god. Equally mysterious is the author's invention called the "Wandering Jew," a tree trunk that is said to have floated for ages on the lake, moved back and forth by winds and currents.

Early in the nineteenth century one Fuller, a traveler in the Finger Lakes region, hears accounts of the "gun" and the "Jew," and sets out to investigate these two wonders of nature. For this purpose he engages a small sailboat owned and operated by an aged mariner, Peter, who is well acquainted with both of these phenomena. Together the two men cruise along the shore of Seneca Lake looking for the "Wandering Jew," which

Peter has not seen for the past three years, and listening to tales about the area told by local residents.

One morning as Fuller is returning to the boat, having lodged the previous night at a farmhouse, he sees a motionless human figure, statuesque in appearance, gazing steadily out over the lake. Approaching this individual, he discovers him to be a young Iroquois of the Seneca tribe. The unidentified Seneca, a college graduate, speaks fluent English, but in most other respects he has reverted to the ways of his people. Clad in buckskin leggings and draped in a light, summer-weight blanket, he has returned to visit the land of his ancestors. He has been gazing at the Swimming Seneca, which the palefaces call the "Wandering Jew"; and he points out this strange being, a mere spot in the distance. As the two men strain their eyes to see this object, they hear a deep booming noise, the angry voice of the Manitou, the palefaces' "Lake Gun." Thereupon, the young Seneca recounts the Indian explanation of these two phenomena.

Long ago there arose among his people a dangerous demagogue, a young chief named See-wise. He broke many of the traditions that had been given to the Senecas by the Great Spirit. He declared that fishing could be carried on at any time of the year and need not be restricted to a prescribed season. Flattering the masses and appealing to their vanity, he told them what they wanted to hear: that they were as wise as the Manitou and did not have to obey his laws. By such demagoguery See-wise gained the support of half the young braves, a matter of grave concern to the older chiefs. Then suddenly See-wise disappeared, never again to be seen in human form. Shortly afterwards, however, the trunk of a tree was observed floating in the lake, and this, proclaimed a wise old chief, was See-wise metamorphosed for his wickedness. A cursed creature, he would float for a thousand years, a wanderer on the waters of Seneca Lake. Whenever he dives deeper in the water to catch fish out of season, the Manitou warns him in a voice of thunder to desist.

Fuller now proposes that they board the sailboat and approach the wanderer to get a better look at him. His companion agrees at once; for as an enlightened man, he seeks the truth, he says. But when pressed to state whether or not he believes the legend, the young Seneca gives a carefully qualified answer. "I cannot say. The things learned in childhood remain the longest on the memory. They make the deepest marks. I have seen the evil that a demagogue can do among the pale-faces; why should I not believe the same among my own people?" (p. 48).

When Peter sails close to the large trunk, he points out to his two passengers the curious configuration of one end of the log, a shape that resembles a human face. Its features include a retreating forehead and a

hatchet-shaped face. [As Robert E. Spiller has pointed out in his Introduction, these were facial characteristics of William Seward, the demagogue whom Cooper had many specific reasons to dislike, though
contemporary readers failed to penetrate the allegory sufficiently to
recognize this butt of his satire.] The tale ends in a discussion of the
dangers of demagoguery, especially as it misleads man from divine truth.
Such false prophets will be punished: "The man or the people that trust in
God will find a lake for every See-wise" (p. 54).

Fuller, Peter, [Seneca Indian].

The Last of the Mohicans: A Narrative of 1757, 1826.

[This is the second of the five Leather-Stocking Tales in relation to
plot, and the second in order of composition.]

As the French and Indian forces under Montcalm press southward
from Canada into the English colony of New York in 1757, General Webb
dispatches 1,500 British reinforcements from Fort Edward, near Glens
Falls, to nearby Fort William Henry, at the southern tip of Lake George.
Traveling with the troop movement and personally escorted by Major
Duncan Heyward go Cora and Alice, daughters of Lieutenant Colonel
Munro, commander of Fort William Henry. They are joined by David
Gamut, a comic, hapless Yankee teacher of sacred music, especially psalm
singing. Their Indian guide is Magua, a Huron exiled among the
Mohawks, allies of the British, but recently reinstated as a chief of the
Hurons, who support the French cause. He promises to take Heyward,
Gamut, and the Munro girls to Fort William Henry by a route shorter
than that to be used by the heavily encumbered contingent of troops, but
his real intention is to lead them into an Indian ambush. In the late
afternoon they encounter along the trail Natty Bumppo and his two
Mohican Indian friends, Chingachgook and the latter's son, Uncas, who
apprise Heyward of Magua's deception. When they try to capture
Magua, the Huron escapes; Natty Bumppo is certain that he will soon
return with hostile Indian forces.

Natty agrees to guide the four travelers to safety in the morning; at
night no one could safely pass through the forest filled with predatory
Indians. Heyward's and Natty's groups move, via canoe, to an island in
the turbulent waters at the foot of Glens Falls, a position more easily
defended than a camp in the woods. Before they retire for the night,
David Gamut leads them in singing a psalm of thanksgiving. They
repulse the first Indian attack, led by Magua, but are then rendered
helpless by the theft of the canoe in which all their ammunition is stored.
Hiding Heyward, the now wounded Gamut, and the Munro girls in a

cave, Natty, Chingachgook, and Uncas escape (by swimming down the river) to bring help.

After searching the cave in vain for some time, the Indians locate and capture their prey. As the Hurons lead their captives away, the women on horseback, the two men on foot, Heyward pretends that he has always trusted Magua as their protector and promises a substantial reward for the safe delivery of the party to Fort William Henry. As they travel, the resourceful Cora takes every opportunity to break small branches along the way to leave a more visible trail.

Magua offers his captives the choice between death for all and freedom for Heyward, Alice, and David Gamut if Cora will consent to become his wife. His interest in the girl is not sensual but vengeful. Once a scout for Colonel Munro, Magua had broken a military regulation by going to his commander's tent intoxicated. Flogged for this offense in the presence of the garrison, Magua had suffered irreparable injury to his pride. Now Magua envisions continuous vengeance against Munro by enslaving and abusing his daughter, knowing too that he could, at any time he might wish, kill her. Cora rejects this offer, and the captives are prepared for death. In a supreme effort to protect the women, Heyward bursts his bonds but is immediately overpowered. As a Huron raises his arm to stab Heyward, he is felled by a rifle ball before he can deliver the blow. The shot has come from *La Longue Carabine*, an epithet applied both to Natty Bumppo and to his rifle, otherwise called "Killdeer."

Natty and his two Indian companions, having replenished their supply of powder and shot, have returned to rescue the white prisoners. After a brief battle, they defeat the four remaining Hurons, but Magua again escapes. Recapturing their horses, the party proceeds again toward Fort William Henry. Unaware that Montcalm's lines have already outflanked the British fortifications, they are almost intercepted, just before dawn, by French pickets; but when Heyward and Cora answer the guards' challenges in fluent French, they are allowed to pass. Later they are pursued, in heavy fog, to the very gates of the fort before their safety is assured.

How long anyone will be safe within the fort, however, grows increasingly doubtful. The earthen walls have been severely damaged by French field artillery; many of the fort's antiquated and poorly maintained cannon have become unusable; and the defenders are now greatly outnumbered by the attacking French and Indian forces. On the fifth day of siege Natty is delivered to the fort by a French officer. He had been sent by Colonel Munro to Fort Edward to request additional reinforcements from General Webb. Bearing Webb's letter, Natty, to his great mortification, had been intercepted by a French sentinel. Montcalm, with the benefit of information Munro lacks, requests a parley with the British commander. Munro sends Heyward as his representative with orders to determine, if possible, the import of Webb's letter; but in the guarded military repartee that ensues, Heyward learns none of the specifics of Webb's intercepted message.

Returning to his commander's quarters, the major finds Munro talking affectionately with his daughters. After the girls' departure, Munro insists upon discussing personal rather than professional matters. He grants Heyward's earlier request to be allowed to court his daughter, supposing that it is Cora in whom he is interested. Learning that it is Alice's hand that Heyward seeks, Munro again consents but only after an intense emotional struggle with himself that reflects some anguish. He tells Heyward that as a young officer in Scotland he had won the heart but not the hand of Alice Graham, for her parents had disapproved of their marriage. Later serving in the West Indies, he had married a girl of mixed British and Caribbean ancestry, from which union had come the dark-eyed beauty, Cora. After an absence of twenty years, Munro, by then a widower, had returned to Scotland; there Alice Graham, still single, had waited for him. They had married immediately, and a year later a daughter, Alice, had been born to them at the cost of the mother's life.

After this domestic interlude, the two officers return to a consideration of the military crisis at hand. Heyward informs Munro that it is he, the commander of Fort William Henry, with whom General Montcalm wishes to confer. Attended by Heyward as interpreter, Munro meets Montcalm halfway between the fortress and the French front lines. To his bitter chagrin, Munro reads, in the intercepted letter which Montcalm now hands him, that Webb has refused to send additional reinforcements to Fort William Henry. Montcalm now makes a generous military proposal. If the British will surrender the fort, they will be guaranteed an unmolested retreat, departing in freedom, bearing their arms, and flying their national colors. It is a chivalric gesture that will permit the British to abandon the doomed fort with honor, and Munro gratefully but reluctantly signs a treaty which includes these concessions. Control of the fort is to change hands the next day.

On the fateful morning that follows, the British, numbering nearly three thousand (including women and children), begin their withdrawal, taking their many wounded troops with them. They are suddenly fallen upon by two thousand French-allied Indians whom Montcalm tries to dissuade from their bloody purpose but does not forcibly restrain—if, indeed, such restraint lies within his power. Dissatisfied with Montcalm's generous surrender terms, the savages, led by Magua, had waited in the forest to wreak their fury upon the enemy and plunder their provisions. [The massacre is more historical than fictional.] In the midst of the slaughter, Magua finds Cora and Alice and again abducts them, followed, at a distance, by David Gamut, the girls' ineffectual "protector."

On the third day after the massacre, five men move in pursuit of Magua, his Huron band, and his captives: Heyward, Munro, Chingachgook, Uncas, and Natty Bumppo (Hawkeye, as his Indian friends call him, and *La Longue Carabine* to his Indian foes). They, in turn, are pursued by other Hurons and by Oneidas, whose tribe is a member of the powerful Iroquois Confederacy. [Behind much of the action here lies the confusion of Indian alignments during the French and Indian War. The French are supported by Hurons, the British by most of the Six Nations of Iroquois, though Hurons and Iroquois derived from the same stock. The numerous and widely distributed Delawares or Lenni-Lenape also fight on both sides—the Mohicans and other Southern Delawares (Delawares of the Hills) aiding the British and the Northern Delawares (Delawares of the Lakes) supporting the French—partly because of their hatred of the Iroquois. The Northern Delawares refuse, however, to participate in the battle for Fort William Henry, in which they would have to fight other Delawares; they inform Montcalm that they need more time to sharpen their tomahawks—an obvious subterfuge. (Cooper here distorts history somewhat for his own fictional purposes.)]

After tracking Magua and his group for some time, the five pursuers approach the Huron village. As they view the Indian settlement, they are alarmed by the sudden splashing of numerous bodies in a nearby stream. Cautiously investigating the source of the noise, they discover that it is being made by beavers diving furiously to escape the instructions in psalm-singing offered by David Gamut. David is dejected by their negative response to his efforts. From the psalmodist they learn that Magua has gone moose hunting, that he has left Cora as his prisoner at a camp of Northern Delawares, and that he has kept Alice in captivity at his own Huron village. David himself has enjoyed immunity from harm, Natty conjectures, not because of his musical ability but because of Indian awe of and reverence for insanity. Taking his cue from this bit of Indian lore, Heyward has himself made up as a madman in order to gain safe entry into the Huron village with David, and then to try to rescue Alice. Chingachgook remains with Colonel Munro, whose age and recent losses have deranged him perceptibly; the two hide in an unoccupied beaver house. Natty and Uncas go to the camp of the Northern Delawares to negotiate for the release of Cora.

Entering the Huron village with David, Heyward is readily accepted in the role he now chooses to play, that of a French medicine man. His discussion with the elders of the tribe is interrupted by the arrival of warriors bearing a pole covered with scalps and leading two captives: Uncas and Reed-That-Bends, a craven Huron who had fled from Uncas. Uncas successfully runs a gauntlet to the sanctuary of a sacred post before the council lodge; there he awaits the final judgment of the council. Reed-That-Bends, resigned to his fate, uncovers his breast to receive the knife of his chief.

Magua, back from the hunt, enters the council of chiefs to smoke a pipe with them. Discovering that the Delaware captured during his absence is Uncas, Magua delivers a powerful oration demanding the death of the prisoner. He then leaves the council lodge without recognizing Heyward in his antic attire.

A chief requests Heyward to cure an ailing Huron woman whom their own medicine man has been unable to aid. As they proceed to the cave where the patient is kept, Heyward is astonished to find them being followed by a growling, fierce-looking bear. The Indians, recognizing the bearskin worn by their conjurer, know that the bear is not real. What they do not know is that inside the skin is Natty Bumppo, who has bound and gagged the conjurer and left him in another part of the cave. Left alone with the sick woman, who is in a coma, Natty reveals his identity to Heyward and leads him to that section of the cave where Alice is imprisoned. When Magua surprises them, he is overpowered and, like the conjurer, tied up and left in the cave. Wrapping Alice in blankets, Heyward and Natty (still playing the bear) smuggle her from the cave by pretending that she is the sick woman being moved beyond the reach of the evil spirits which have possessed her. Once they have safely cleared the Huron settlement, Natty directs Heyward and Alice to the nearby Delaware camp where they will find asylum from the Hurons who will surely pursue them. Natty himself returns to try to rescue Uncas.

Along with David Gamut, Natty visits Uncas in the tent in which he is imprisoned and cuts the young man's bonds. Uncas then dons the bearskin and Natty the clothes of David in order to effect their escape. Wearing the scanty garb of Uncas, David is tied up in his place to deceive the guards temporarily. When, shortly afterwards, Magua is released and David's identity is detected, two hundred Hurons set out on the trail of the woodsman and the young Mohican. The fugitives reach the safety of the Delaware camp, however, before they can be overtaken.

Magua soon visits the Delaware camp to claim as his prisoners Cora, Alice, Heyward, Uncas, and *La Longue Carabine*. With well-placed gifts and carefully calculated rhetoric, Magua influences the council of chiefs in his favor. The issue has too many implications, however, to be decided by the council. It must be aired before the Delaware nation presided over by the venerable sage Tamenund (Tammany). When Tamenund asks the prisoners which of them is *La Longue Carabine*, Heyward claims the title in an effort to protect Natty. Natty resents this and insists that the title is his. In a shooting match arranged to establish the identity of the famous marksman, Natty easily outdoes the major's best shots. Listening to Magua's claims for the return of his prisoners, Tamenund rules initially in his favor. Cora's plea before the sage for compassion fails, but she does succeed in drawing to the attention of the aged leader the Delaware among the prisoners, Uncas.

The proud young Mohican's censurious comments so anger the mass of Delawares that they demand permission to torture him. As they rush upon Uncas, they are suddenly frozen in superstitious awe, staring, with mingled fear and reverence, at the totemic turtle tattooed in bright blue on his chest. Uncas is not slow to remind them of the Indian creation myth that the earth was formed by the Manitou upon the back of a great sea turtle and that his lineage symbolically supports the world. It is then revealed that Uncas is the last of the most noble line of chiefs among the Mohican tribe of the Delawares. Tamenund, more than one hundred years old, gives thanks to Manitou for being able to see again before his death a direct descendant of the first great and, by now, legendary Uncas.

The youthful Uncas demands the release of the prisoners of Magua. All are freed except Cora, who was personally delivered into the custody of the Delawares by Magua. Tamenund rules that Magua's claim on Cora must be honored if Indian justice is to prevail. To the grief of all observers, both red and white, Cora is led away the captive of Magua, who says that she will henceforth live in his wigwam.

Uncas leads a ritualistic war dance as the Delawares await the three hours' truce before they can justly pursue Magua. Preparation for war apparently is not one-sided, for several Huron snipers hiding in the adjacent woods have already found their range. David Gamut enters the Delaware camp to confirm the fact that Hurons have gone on the warpath and that Cora has been confined to the cave in which Alice was imprisoned earlier. Knowing well the cave and its various entrances, Natty Bumppo, accompanied by twenty braves, is to attempt the rescue of Cora while the rest of the Delawares engage the Huron forces and keep them occupied.

Before this rescue operation can be carried out, however, a full-scale battle develops. Three units of Delawares and whites now attack the Hurons. One is led by Natty and Heyward, one by Uncas, and one by Chingachgook and Munro, who have now emerged from their hideout among the beavers. The Hurons are soon routed, and the action shifts to the pursuit of four fugitives: Magua, Cora, and the two Hurons who drag the girl along their escape route.

When the four reach a rocky ledge above a steep precipice, Cora declares that she will go no farther, regardless of the penalty. Bidding her choose between flight and death, Magua twice raises his hand to stab her and twice hesitates to strike. Just at that moment, Uncas, leading the pursuit, rashly jumps from above to the ledge, where his prostrate body is fallen upon and stabbed in the back by Magua. In the meantime, one of Cora's Huron attendants takes this opportunity to bury his knife in her bosom. With his remaining strength Uncas arises and kills Cora's murderer, and then, powerless, is himself slashed in the breast three times by Magua. Thus ends the life of the last of the ruling family of the Mohicans' turtle clan. Magua, attempting to escape by jumping across a narrow ravine to the opposite cliff, is struck by a shot from Killdeer, and his body hurtles downward to destruction.

Funeral ceremonies are held for Uncas and Cora by the Delawares and the handful of whites present. In the elegies that are recited over the dead, the suggestion is made that an affinity between the two will unite them in the next world. Natty alone demurs at this notion, though he unhesitatingly renews his pledge of undying friendship with the bereaved Chingachgook. The venerable Tamenund closes the story with a broader elegy, one that goes beyond the fate of individuals to that of the race: "Go, children of the Lenape, the anger of the Manitou is not done. . . . The pale-faces are masters of the earth, and the time of the red-men has not yet come again. . . ." (p. 443)

> Nathaniel Bumppo, Chingachgook, David Gamut, Major Duncan Heyward, Magua, Marquis of Montcalm, Lieutenant Colonel Munro, Alice Munro, Cora Munro, Reed-That-Bends, Tamenund, Uncas, Uttawa, General Webb.

Lionel Lincoln; or, The Leaguer of Boston, 1825.

Set in Boston in 1775, the action of this novel is played out on the first stage of the American Revolution. Young Lionel Lincoln, a major in the British army, arrives from England for duty in the city of his birth and infancy. He lands with one of his shipboard acquaintances, a strange and moody old man toward whom he unaccountably feels some vague tie of affection. On the waterfront Lionel rescues a simpleminded boy, Job Pray, from the abusive treatment of carousing soldiers, and then employs the unfortunate child to guide him to the Tremont Street home of Mrs. Priscilla Lechmere, the young officer's great-aunt, who awaits his arrival. The major's aged fellow passenger soon falls in with them as they walk along. Taking a circuitous route to Tremont Street, Job stops first at his own squalid quarters in an empty warehouse where his mother, Abigail Pray, is introduced. Mrs. Pray, a friend of Priscilla Lechmere, gazes at Lionel Lincoln and tells him that he has the smile of his mother and the terrible eyes of his father. She goes on to tell the surprised young man she had not only known his parents but also had attended his own birth. When Lionel's aged traveling companion makes his presence known, it is Abigail's turn to be surprised. She is so startled, in fact, that she collapses in a chair and for several minutes is unable to speak. From such circumstantial evidence and from innuendoes made by the old man, it can be inferred that there is some relationship among these four characters not yet clear either to the young man or to the reader. As Job prepares to take Lionel to his destination, the oldster declares that he will make his lodging right where he is, in the impoverished home of the Prays.

At the residence of his great-aunt Lionel meets that lady's granddaughter, Cecil Dynevor, his own cousin twice removed, and Agnes Danforth, Mrs. Lechmere's great-niece. Agnes is an ardent and outspoken patriot who refuses tea in a gesture of defiance to British authority. The manner in which Cecil and her grandmother savor their bohea suggests their loyalistic inclination. Twice during his conversation with his American relatives Major Lincoln offers seemingly commonplace observations which upset Mrs. Lechmere to the point of fainting. One is a remark about the condition of his father, long confined in an English mental institution, and the other is his report that he has already encountered and talked with Abigail Pray and her retarded son. Lionel's casual comments about Abigail Pray so unnerve his seventy-year-old great-aunt that she has to be helped from the room. What sensitive matter has he touched upon unwittingly?

Just before sunrise the following morning Major Lincoln climbs Beacon Hill to view his native city. There he meets Job Pray and then his elderly shipboard acquaintance, who is now called Ralph. Job and Ralph will henceforth often be seen together, partly because they now live under the same roof, partly because they share a zeal for liberty and a love of country above king. Each takes every opportunity to point out the oppression and abuse under which the colonists live. When Lionel is hailed by Captain Peter Polwarth, a friend from his own regiment, Ralph and Job disappear. The two officers (schoolboy companions who had attended the same college at Oxford) talk briefly about the gathering storm of rebellion and then turn to happier and lighter subjects, personal and social.

That evening after Lionel has excused himself from Mrs. Lechmere's parlor to finish writing an important letter, he discovers Ralph in his bedroom reading this uncompleted epistle. Lionel is indignant at this impertinence until he sees that the startled old man is weeping profusely over what he is reading. Again Ralph intimates that there is some undefined affinity between them. Ralph then conducts the major, whose raincoat and cape conceal his uniform, to a patriot meeting from which the younger man returns more fully aware of the calm, intelligent kind of commitment that characterizes much of the revolutionary movement.

A few days later Lionel Lincoln entertains two of his best friends, Captains Polwarth and M'Fuse, at dinner in the quarters he rents from one Seth Sage. (Although the major sleeps at the home of his doting aunt, he takes his meals and carries on his social commitments at this boarding-house.) His guests are character types, M'Fuse being a professional soldier whose only interest is warfare, Polwarth being the good-natured, Falstaffian gourmet of the group. Their feasting and fellowship are suddenly interrupted by orders from the British headquarters for a night march into the New England countryside by two thousand troops, among them the companies commanded by Polwarth and M'Fuse. Lionel secures permission to accompany the expedition as a volunteer, his real purpose being to observe for himself the temper of the time and the mood of the local citizenry. The objective of the large-scale troop movement, he discovers, is the capture of stores of arms and munitions being collected at Lexington and Concord by the minutemen of Massachusetts. What begins as a routine action by confident British forces turns into disaster for them as they are routed by angry farmers gathering along their twenty-mile retreat route to Boston. This is the historical Battle of Lexington.

In this episode, as in most others in the novel, Ralph and Job play active but mysterious roles. Before leaving Boston, Lionel calls upon Ralph and finds the old man abed, seemingly too ill to stir. Job he observes entering a small boat at the waterfront in order, he says, to catch fish for his mother. Lionel is therefore astonished when he encounters both of these individuals momentarily in the thick of the battle at Lexington. Although he is annoyed by their duplicity, his resentment is overcome by gratitude when the two save his life during the very height of the conflict. The oldster and the simpleton are not his only Boston acquaintances who manage to participate in the engagements at Concord and Lexington, Lionel discovers when he returns to his quarters, for there he finds Seth Sage under arrest for treason. The landlord makes no attempt to deny his involvement. Lionel arrives at the boardinghouse just before Job appears with the message that Ralph wishes to speak to the major.

When the young man enters the warehouse where Ralph and the Prays live, he overhears a strange conversation between Abigail Pray and (to his great surprise) Priscilla Lechmere. He observes his aunt give Abigail a handful of silver to relieve her poverty, apparently not the first such dole. From their remarks he infers that both women are guilt ridden for their involvement in some crime. Ralph appears and accuses Mrs. Lechmere of somehow causing the insanity of Sir Lionel Lincoln, the hero's father. Later, when Lionel visits Ralph in his quarters in a loft of the warehouse, he asks the old man for some explanation of the conversation he has just heard. Ralph refuses to satisfy his curiosity, saying that the time is not appropriate for such a revelation.

Back at the officers' quarters, Lionel finds Seth Sage at liberty again but being forced by M'Fuse and Polwarth to sign an elaborate contract to supply victuals for their table. As Seth leaves the building, Lionel steps into the street to speak to him, but the landlord has moved away too swiftly. Vainly pursuing Seth, the major encounters in the dark the unidentified man he had heard speak at the patriot rally. Near Copp's Hill Cemetery he meets Job Pray. As he and Job talk, Lionel hears muffled noises which the wise fool claims are the sounds of the dead moving about, as is their wont, at night. What he actually hears is the movement of patriot militiamen fortifying nearby Breed's Hill, known in history as Bunker Hill.

On the following day, Lionel, in the company of General Burgoyne and General Clinton, watches the first charge of British troops up the slopes of Bunker Hill thrown back with heavy losses. Although his company is involved in the attack, Major Lincoln has not been included in it, the high command wishing to use him instead in the more delicate work of liaison with the enemy. When the British are repulsed a second time, however, the major cannot refrain, regardless of orders to the contrary, from rushing into the fray. In the third and successful onslaught Lionel is so seriously wounded that it is seven months before his life is out of danger.

When, at last, he becomes fully conscious, he finds himself at the home of his great-aunt, where he is attended by Cecil Dynevor. He had sent Cecil a love letter, when the Battle of Bunker Hill seemed imminent; now, thankful that he has survived, the young lady avows the reciprocal love she feels for him. A few minutes later his friend Polwarth comes to cheer the patient, and, typical of the gourmet, he has brought a choice steak to hasten his convalescence. Polwarth himself had lost a leg in the battle, and their mutual friend Dennis M'Fuse had been killed.

During his recovery, Lionel discovers, the British position in Boston has grown increasingly precarious as thousands of colonial troops, regulars and guerrillas, surround the beleaguered city. Governor Gage has been replaced as commander-in-chief by General Howe, and the latter is contemplating the evacuation of all British forces from the city. Lionel, anxious about the safety of Cecil in such an unpredictable situation, urges her to marry him as soon as possible. When the two consult Mrs. Lechmere about the propriety of such a move, they are surprised at her insistence that the marriage take place that very day. Cecil's only condition is that the ceremony be performed at a church rather than at home. Accordingly, Lionel hastens to the home of the Rev. Dr. Liturgy, Anglican rector of King's Chapel, and arranges for the wedding that evening. Because the sexton has contracted smallpox and is unable to carry out his janitorial duties, it is necessary for Lionel to find someone else to light the furnace and warm the church on this cold, snowy day. He commissions Job Pray to perform this task, giving him money with which to buy candles and kindling. Unfortunately, the family from whom Job purchases these supplies is also afflicted with smallpox, and Lionel fears that this may have exposed the simpleton to the dread disease.

The wedding itself is marked with awesome Gothic qualities. It takes place on a snowy, blustery night in an almost vacant church, the only witnesses being Captain Polwarth, Agnes Danforth, and Job Pray. When Dr. Liturgy requests a response from anyone who knows any reason why this man and woman should not be united, the huge shadow of a human being with outstretched arms moves across the ceiling; the silent shadow appears each of the three times that this request is made. Agnes and Polwarth are so shaken by this eerie experience that they neglect to congratulate the bride and bridegroom at the conclusion of the service. Even the rector is aghast and departs as quickly as he can do so without being rude. Polwarth drives Agnes and the newlyweds to the Lechmere residence but remains only long enough to mumble the appropriate good wishes.

Lionel and Cecil go to Mrs. Lechmere's sickroom and receive that lady's congratulations. Cecil leaves the room after a few minutes so that her grandmother may speak in confidence with Lionel. As she begins to discuss the Lincoln family history, Mrs. Lechmere is interrupted by a sepulchral voice, and Ralph appears, seemingly from nowhere, with a note from her physician, who has been called away on another case. The missive contains bad news. Mrs. Lechmere's illness has advanced more than the doctor had at first thought, and it is likely that she will die during the night. Shocked by this announcement of her impending death, Priscilla Lechmere vacillates between confessing her sins, preparatory for entering the next world, and maintaining her hold on her position in this world. As she intimates her involvement in some scandal within the Lincoln family, Ralph demands repeatedly and loudly that she reveal the whole truth about the matter, and Lionel, who has lived under a shadow all his life, pleads for more information on the subject. The woman dies, however, without making any helpful revelation.

When Cecil returns to her grandmother's room, she finds there only the ghastly corpse. Still troubled by the ominous shadows that had cast gloom over her wedding, the frightened girl rushes to the bridegroom's room and finds it empty. The embers still burn in his fireplace, but Lionel Lincoln has vanished. Cecil screams and faints. Her cry is heard by Agnes, who comes to her assistance and then, baffled herself by what has happened, sends a servant to bring her suitor, Peter Polwarth.

Hearing the accounts given by Cecil and Agnes, Captain Polwarth determines to find his old friend. He is given by Agnes an ornamental metal collar she had found on the grate of Lionel's fireplace after he had disappeared. This gorget, which Polwarth at once identifies as that of the dead M'Fuse, has a bullet hole through it. Remembering now Job's remark about having shot the Irish grenadier officer—a remark he had not taken too seriously before—and remembering Job's attachment to Lionel Lincoln, Polwarth goes to the simpleton's rude quarters hoping that there he may learn something of the major's whereabouts. At the warehouse he comes upon a wild and gruesome scene. A crowd of irate Irish grenadiers are about to lynch the helpless Job, already critically ill with smallpox. Beaten and bleeding, he lies on a pallet at the mercy of his tormentors. Polwarth forestalls the violence temporarily by conducting a simple trial of the accused killer of Captain M'Fuse. Job does confess that he was the patriot at Bunker Hill who had shot M'Fuse, and the enraged soldiers again clamor for his life. This time they are prevented from taking their vengeance by the appearance of Cecil, who, as the lady of an officer, threatens them with punishment for their cruel and criminal behavior. Grumbling, the soldiers reluctantly depart. Cecil is accompanied by Lionel's valet, Meriton, and a stocky, muscular stranger. After Cecil calms the fears of Job and his mother, the stocky stranger proceeds to question the stricken boy in a kind and quiet manner. He elicits from Job the information that Lionel Lincoln had left the city and gone into patriot territory with Ralph. Armed with this information, Cecil and her two male companions leave.

Polwarth, who remains with the Prays, now learns that Job has been employed by Seth Sage to go into the country and buy food for Major Lincoln's table. To his horror, he discovers that Job and Abigail have not eaten for many hours even though they are protecting in the warehouse a large supply of Major Lincoln's provisions. Moved to tears by this pitiable situation, Polwarth cooks mother and son a hearty meal with some of these provisions, breaking up his own wooden leg to provide the necessary fuel. Food is this gourmet's cure for all ills, but in fact he may be hastening the death of Job by feeding him thus while he runs a high fever.

Cecil, Meriton, and the stranger take a boat, manned by British sailors, and land across the bay near a road leading to Cambridge, where they hope to gain news of Lionel. Cecil ingenuously imagines that she may locate her lost husband by appealing for help from the American commander-in-chief. Because the siege of Boston is growing more intense, security measures are too severe to permit free movement of unidentified persons, and Cecil is arrested almost as soon as she arrives in patriot territory. She and her companions are nevertheless transported by coach toward Washington's headquarters. En route, however, they are intercepted by the seemingly ubiquitous Ralph, who takes Cecil to the jail cell on the Harvard campus where Lionel is being held. The old man is training troops for the patriot cause, and he moves freely about the American installations. He secures the release of Meriton; then, disguising Lionel in the overcoat and large hat of the stocky stranger, he conducts Meriton, Lincoln, and Cecil to freedom. Ralph guides the trio to the grave of Lionel's mother, and there he reveals part of the Lincoln family tragedy. When they return to Boston proper, the four go to the warehouse, where Job is dying and where the distraught Abigail discloses the remainder of the calamity that befell the Lincolns.

Sir Lionel Lincoln, father of the titular hero, had wed a beautiful girl named Priscilla who was a ward of his aunt, Priscilla Lechmere. This greatly displeased Mrs. Lechmere, who, wishing to keep the title and wealth in the family, had hoped he would marry her own daughter, Cecil Dynevor's mother; Mrs. Lechmere was equally displeased with her daughter for having wed Colonel Dynevor. Called to England on urgent business connected with his estate, Sir Lionel did not return to Boston for two years, during which time his wife had borne him a son, Lionel, and had shortly died. Mrs. Lechmere again hoped, perversely, to interest Sir Lionel, her nephew, in her daughter or even in herself as a mate; but he rejected such proposals. To take her vengeance against him, Mrs.

Lechmere had then told Sir Lionel that the wife for whom he grieved had been unfaithful to him, that she had during his absence borne an illegitimate son as well as young Lionel. This he had not believed until Abigail Pray, his former mistress, swore under oath that Mrs. Lechmere's account was true. They showed him the demented infant Job and told him that this was the bastard child of his dead wife. Job, however, older than Lionel, was the natural son of Abigail, a poor girl, and Sir Lionel, who had left his mistress when he had wed and knew nothing of her having a child by him. The shock sustained by the baronet upon being persuaded of his wife's infidelity and dishonor had driven him temporarily insane. The vengeful aunt then took this occasion to have him committed to an English madhouse where he had been held for more than twenty years.

At the conclusion of Abigail's story, Ralph seizes the woman to force her to swear upon a Bible to the accuracy of the account she has just given. When Lionel moves to quell Ralph, Cecil warns him against striking his own father. Major Lincoln is so stunned by this revelation that he stands speechless and dazed, unable to move. At this moment the door of the warehouse bursts open and the stocky stranger reappears, released from the patriot jail after he had shown his credentials as the keeper of the mad Sir Lionel, whom he has been pursuing since his escape from a lunatic asylum. Sir Lionel grapples with his keeper (whom he had deliberately left in jail at Harvard) and with maniacal strength throws the stranger and starts to strangle him; the baronet is not the aged person he had seemed but a man in his early fifties. When none of the petrified observers moves to aid the keeper, he pulls from his pocket a knife, stabs Sir Lionel in the breast three times, and flees. The dying baronet extends his arms in silent benediction over the benumbed major and his wife, and in this gesture they recognize the shape of the shadow they had seen on the ceiling of King's Chapel during their wedding.

In a double funeral ceremony Sir Lionel and his natural son, Job (Major Lincoln's half brother), are buried in the family vault in King's Chapel. Abigail Pray remains after the service, and is consoled by Major Lincoln and Captain Polwarth. The former leaves with the disconsolate mother a large purse of gold; but it is of no use to her, for, unbeknownst to the two men, she dies in the deserted chapel. Her body is not discovered for several days, for the entire area is in great turmoil as the British evacuate Boston and the American forces move into the city.

As Major Lincoln, Cecil, and Captain Polwarth are about to sail for England, they are bidden farewell by the vivacious Agnes Danforth. For the fiftieth time, Polwarth proposes to her, and for the fiftieth time she refuses his offer. She marries an American officer the following week.

Although they were both born in America, the new Sir Lionel and his wife remain in England and settle down on the Lincoln estate. In time the baronet becomes a peer and ultimately an earl. The leaguer (siege) of Boston and its dramatis personae have by then passed into history.

Allen, General [John] Burgoyne, Cato, Agnes Danforth, Sergeant Doyle, Cecil Dynevor, Admiral Graves, Hopper, Priscilla Lechmere, Lionel Lincoln, Sir Lionel Lincoln, Rev. Dr. Liturgy, Captain Dennis M'Fuse, Meriton, Major Pitcairn, Captain Peter Polwarth, Abigail Pray, Job Pray, [William] Prescott, Seth Sage, Shearflint, Terence, Tom.

Mercedes of Castile; or, The Voyage to Cathay, 1840.

The air of mystery with which this sea adventure of late fifteenth-century Spain begins is soon dispelled: the fortunes of two of the four leading kingdoms within Spain—Aragon, ruled by John II, and Castile, ruled by Henry IV—are to be united in 1469 by the marriage of cousins six months secretly engaged, brave young Ferdinand, heir to Aragon's throne, and beautiful and reverent Isabella, heir to the more powerful throne of Castile. The prospective bridegroom, disguised as a servant in what appears to be a merchant caravan including his merry friend Don Andres de Cabrera, arrives safely at Valladolid, where Isabella has taken refuge during this period of severe political unrest. Accompanying Isabella in her elegant quarters is her childhood friend, Beatriz de Bobadilla, lovely, loyal, and more lighthearted than her mistress. Beatriz, too, is to be wed, to Don Andres de Cabrera; so both await the arrival of the young men with anxiety and eagerness. To pass the time, they discuss both current conditions in the two kingdoms and nineteen-year-old Isabella's previous suitors, chosen by her half brother Henry IV and roundly rejected by the queen-to-be.

The political expediency of Ferdinand and Isabella's marriage is fortunately accompanied by strong affection between the two heirs, evidenced in their first actual meeting, and the serious matters of property and of protection of the individual rights of the two kingdoms are thus amicably settled prior to the marriage. A papal bull sanctioning the consanguineous union is secured by the Archbishop of Toledo, and the two are wed. During the first twenty years after this strategic alliance, Ferdinand and Isabella both deal successfully with various civil disruptions, and Ferdinand makes good progress toward fulfilling a significant clause in their marriage contract: that he assume leadership in expelling the Moors from Spain. The conquest of Granada marks the achievement of that important purpose, a welcome conclusion to a campaign that had drained the treasuries of Aragon and Castile. On January 2, 1492, Christian symbols replace the Moslem ones in that sumptuous capital, and the royal couple await possession of the city formerly belonging to the last Moorish king, Boabdil.

Among the throng of spectators at the formal occupation of Granada are two men whose subsequent actions provide the heart of the novel: Christoval Colon [Christopher Columbus], a middle-aged, devout Christian, and twenty-year-old Don Luis de Bobadilla, Beatriz de Bobadilla's handsome and adventurous nephew, reputed a scapegrace and a rover. Young Luis's attention is drawn to Columbus by the venerable Father Pedro de Carrascal, deeply committed—as is Queen Isabella's companion Beatriz de Bobadilla—to Columbus's bold proposal of sailing west across the unexplored Atlantic to reach the Orient. Further details about the grave, dedicated mariner prompt Luis to secure through Fray Pedro an introduction to the upright Genoese dreamer-scholar-mapmaker himself. This first encounter wins Luis to Columbus the man; a subsequent interview with his beloved Mercedes de Valverde, orphaned niece and ward of Beatriz de Bobadilla, wins Luis to Columbus's cause. To prove his worthiness as the suitor for Mercedes's hand, Luis will accompany the intrepid Columbus on his proposed voyage of discovery, a journey that Columbus, Beatriz, Mercedes, and Queen Isabella view as a means of carrying the Christian faith to the heathen. Mercedes, who has promised Queen Isabella that she will not marry without the sovereign's consent and presence, reveals to Luis both this vow and her own wholehearted love for the impetuous young cavalier, who has countless times professed his devotion to the deeply religious, beautiful, and wealthy Mercedes. Beatriz herself, determined that Luis must demonstrate stability and dedication as well as daring, is satisfied that Luis's service in Columbus's holy cause will win the queen's approval of Luis as Mercedes's husband.

Isabella, learning that Luis proposes to accompany Columbus, asks her wary, mercenary consort, Ferdinand, to investigate the feasibility of supporting Columbus's venture through the combined houses of Aragon and Castile; a royal commission is felt necessary for this significant undertaking. Ferdinand, not at all inclined to favor Columbus's project, immediately summons Fernando de Talavera, the new Archbishop of Granada, and commissions him and selected nobles to investigate Columbus's proposals and report to him. The Archbishop, detecting Ferdinand's coldness toward the proposal, receives Columbus at a hearing attended by the chosen noblemen; after questioning the mariner closely and then reading his written demands for his own rewards for this arduous and dangerous venture, he ridicules Columbus's lofty conditions. Assured that Columbus will not reduce his demands—to be named Admiral as well as Viceroy over all lands discovered, to receive one-tenth of all proceeds, and to make his title and fees hereditary—the Archbishop promises to report to the king and queen, and Columbus is dismissed. Queen Isabella's recommendation, conveyed through the Archbishop, that Columbus temper his demands is rejected by the Genoese navigator, and Columbus is therefore refused the support he seeks.

Having failed to win aid in Spain, Columbus determines to appeal to the ruler of France. Those who strongly support Columbus's cause— among them, Alonzo de Quintanilla, Luis de St. Angel, and Luis de Bobadilla—thus meet with Columbus in February, 1492, to express their regret for the shortsightedness of the Spanish monarchs in rejecting his proposal and to bid him farewell. Young Luis accompanies the dejected navigator as long as he is permitted to do so, vowing that he will be among Columbus's crew when the daring Genoese has secured the support he seeks, no matter what country may choose to send him west to the Orient. While Columbus journeys toward France to seek support from Louis XII, Luis returns to the Spanish court to discover that Quintanilla and St. Angel have succeeded by their bold speaking in assuring both Ferdinand and Isabella of the folly of allowing France or any other nation to gain the undoubted benefits of Columbus's voyage; appeals made to Ferdinand's political jealousy and to Isabella's piety effect the object Columbus had sought in vain. Though Ferdinand refuses to provide sums from Aragon, Isabella pledges the full support of the Castilian kingdom, so the loyal Luis de Bobadilla is dispatched to bring Columbus back to the Castilian court. By the time Luis and Columbus appear before Isabella, Ferdinand has given his consent to Isabella's supporting the bold venture.

By special concession, Luis is permitted to speak alone with Mercedes, a conference monitored only by Mercedes's duenna, Pepita, who graciously allows the door to be closed between her and the enamored pair. The two talk eagerly of their love and of the projected voyage; the hour's conversation closes with Mercedes's presenting Luis with a jeweled crucifix to wear, and with Luis's giving Mercedes a brilliant necklace, once the property of a queen, as a pledge of his love. After an affectionate farewell, Luis leaves, assuming at his aunt's request a common citizen's name, Pedro de Muños, or Pero [Pedro] Gutierrez.

The ships, or caravels, needed for the voyage are promptly commandeered by royal order from the small harbor town of Palos de Moguer, a short distance from the convent of La Rabida, long hospitable to Columbus and his sons, Diego and Fernando. Luis, en route secretly to Palos to join Columbus, travels thence with Martin Alonzo Pinzon, his former shipmate and admirer; and Luis wins the support of Pinzon for Columbus's cause. Strong reluctance on the part of Palos residents to commit either property or their lives to this mad venture has delayed preparations until July, despite sharp royal reprimands; but the decision of the highly respected Palos resident Pinzon to furnish a third caravel himself and to assume personal command of a vessel heartens prospective crew members, and work on preparation and staffing of the three caravels is undertaken with much greater speed and enthusiasm than before. By August 2, the full complement—officers and crew—make their final confessions, celebrate Holy Mass, and embark at Palos for the transfer to a more suitable sailing point off Huelvas, with Columbus confident that God has appointed him to this mission. The following day, a Friday, the *Pinta*, the *Niña*, and the flagship *Santa Maria* set off for the Canary Islands, from which they will sail due west for Japan and fabled Cathay.

Even before the *Santa Maria*—the slowest of the three—goes a full day's journey, Columbus is assured of the sturdy support of two Palos mariners: Pepe, a young married seaman, and Sancho Mundo, a mercenary bachelor sea-dog nearing fifty. The latter, an expert and widely traveled mariner, proves useful to Columbus even during the passage to the Canaries; among other services, he confirms Columbus's statement that the sight of Teneriffe spouting fire is not a sign of God's disapproval of the voyage but merely a volcano, thus allaying the fears of the crew. The *Pinta's* rudder comes loose twice during the run to the Canaries, and its repairs and slowed pace greatly increase the time required to reach the last known land on the Atlantic en route to Cathay. The vessels wait for the *Pinta* to be thoroughly repaired at Grand Canary, and all vessels take on additional supplies at Gomera. At the latter stop, Columbus and his highest-ranking officers, including Luis, are entertained by the mother of the Count of Gomera, Doña Inez Peraza, from whom Luis learns that gossips have reported his absence on another roving adventure, no one knows whither, but surely one that displeases the queen. No one penetrates Luis's disguise, but he is resolved to earn a respite from such scurrilous talk by his heroism on the voyage to the Orient. Before Columbus boards the *Santa Maria* for departure, Sancho Mundo's old Portuguese friend José Gordo reports, for a suitable tip, that three armed Portuguese caravels have been sent to intercept Columbus's fleet.

Columbus, determined not to be undone by the Portuguese, directs his fleet out of the Canaries unseen by the Portuguese warships, despite an inauspicious calm that hampers the Spaniards' efforts. As Ferro, the last of the Canaries, disappears from sight on September 9, the sailors show deep fear of the uncharted voyage ahead of them. At Sancho Mundo's request, Columbus identifies Cathay as their destination, their probable westward sailing time as thirty days, and their rewards—both material and spiritual—as ample for the risk undertaken. After conferring with the other two commanders (Martin Alonzo Pinzon, of the *Pinta,* and Vincente Yañez Pinzon, of the *Niña*) on the need for the fleet to remain together during the voyage, Columbus dismisses them to their ships and reveals privately to Luis that he plans to understate to the men each day the distance the ships have traveled, to reduce their occasion for fear as much as possible. The efforts of the helmsman to turn toward Spain are readily detected and corrected by Columbus, as are other attempts to jeopardize the success of the voyage. Even the unsettling discovery that the compasses deviate from true north as indicated by the position of the North Star, the dramatic passage and sinking of a meteor, and the appearance of birds normally found near land are explained to his men by Columbus in such a way that their concern is substantially reduced. The hope of land nearby, aroused by floating weeds and the presence of tuna fish, is dispelled by Columbus, who is prepared for these peculiar manifestations by his reading of Aristotle. Columbus's serene confidence in the midst of whatever unusual signs alarm the men, coupled with Sancho Mundo's firm backing (gained by occasional gold coins) of Columbus's interpreting these signs as evidences of the support of a divine Providence, carries the men of all three crews through the uncertainties of many days at sea. Martin Alonzo Pinzon's cry of "Land!—Land! Señor!" on September 25 arouses all hands to thankfulness and songs of praise to God, songs in which Columbus joins though he is far from confident that the mass seen is land; the next day, the "land" proves to have been a cloud bank, a matter of grave disappointment met by Columbus with the explanation that such optical illusions are not uncommon at sea. For several days afterwards, the sight of pelicans and more weeds and the softening of the air tantalize the crews, but land still is not seen. The variations in the compass are still apparent, but Columbus's explanation that the North Star itself moves is cited by the seamen as a counter to their anxiety on this score.

On October 5, despite favorable winds and good progress, Martin Alonzo Pinzon comes aboard the *Santa Maria* to urge a change in course to the south, since most of the recent discoveries have been made in the southern latitudes. Columbus rejects this plea, and orders a continued westward course; but from this point on he detects increasing signs of disaffection in this influential commander.

Since an annuity of ten thousand *maravedis* [a *maravedi* was equivalent to one-thirtieth of a silver *real* at that time] will be paid by Ferdinand and Isabella to the man who first discerns land, all are alert to signs suggesting the nearness of land; another signal of land sighted proves to mark only another optical illusion. Columbus, noting large flocks of birds flying southward, orders a change of direction for the three vessels to a west-south-west course. As the fleet follows this changed course, more encouraging signs of land are detected; Columbus, distressed by the frequent mistaken cries of "Land!" declares that any man who calls it carelessly will be ineligible for the reward.

On October 10, distraught that land has still not been reached, more than twenty men aboard the *Santa Maria*, with Juan Martin as spokesman, threaten mutiny, demanding that Columbus return with his ships at once to Spain. Sancho Mundo, Pepe, and Luis range themselves on the side of the Admiral, who—not one whit swayed by the crew's mutinous words and looks—warns them that food and water aboard will not suffice now for a return to Spain and that the fleet must complete the task set by the sovereigns: to sail west to Cathay. His calm manner spreads to the would-be mutineers, and they desist. Fortunately, the next day brings renewed signs of nearness to land—green rushes, a floating roseberry bush, a piece of cane-plant, a large tree trunk, a walking-stick fashioned by the hand of man. Columbus, certain that the soundest course lies due west, orders the fleet on October 11 to head westward, and the ships move with a favorable wind at the satisfying speed of nine miles an hour. That night Columbus sees a light and calls Luis to confirm his sighting; Luis sees it also, and the Admiral quietly asserts that the light marks land. Few are inclined to be certain of the fact, though all are hopeful. That night at midnight, Martin Alonzo Pinzon fires a gun from the *Pinta* as a signal that land is sighted, and soon all men can see the unmistakable outline of land on the horizon—an island, Columbus says, but the Indies, nonetheless.

The following morning—October 12—confirms the midnight conclusion, and the commanders of the three ships, with Columbus leading, carry ashore the flags bearing crosses and the initials of the king and queen, an act observed by hundreds of awed, naked red-skinned men certain that the strangers have come from Heaven. Columbus takes possession of the land, gives thanks to God, and then prepares to examine the island he names San Salvador. The crew members offer both congratulations and apologies as they crowd around Columbus, as calm in the face of adulation as he had been in the face of near-mutiny.

After well over a month of exploring and claiming various islands, including Cuba, for the sovereigns, and of observing that everywhere the natives are living in the simplest of conditions, a number of the men tire of sight-seeing and determine to search for the reputed riches of the Indies. On November 21—the same day on which Sancho Mundo is introduced by the natives to the smoking of tobacco—Columbus discovers that Martin Alonzo Pinzon, the *Pinta,* and that caravel's crew have defected to seek gold by themselves, a defection that has been brewing for some time because of friction between Columbus and Pinzon.

About two weeks after the *Pinta's* departure, Columbus and his remaining men leave Cuba for Haiti (Española, or Little Spain), where they find the inhabitants even more docile and more hospitable than those in the earlier islands. Gold appears to be abundant; and the island houses Guacanagari, the Great Cacique, or king of kings, of a number of tributary peoples. When an ambassador is sent by Guacanagari to Columbus, Luis and Sancho Mundo with Columbus's permission accompany Mattinao, the ambassador's attendant, by canoe to his own area of the island, where he himself proves to be a tributary cacique. While Sancho Mundo is entertained by the intrigued village Indians, Luis is led to meet Ozema, Mattinao's beautiful eighteen-year-old sister, a virgin so like Mercedes that Luis's first exclamation is "Mercedes!" Sheltered and thus fairer than her compatriots, Ozema is destined to mother the next cacique, and Mattinao and Ozema envision a match between Ozema and Luis. Luis remains faithful to Mercedes but is charmed by the lovely girl, who obviously adores him. During the several days spent with the cacique and his family, Luis endeavors to win the girl and her relatives to Christianity. Sancho, meanwhile, is inquiring about the source of the gold he daily acquires in trade for hawks' bells brought as items for gift or barter, as well as thoroughly enjoying himself. An attack by the dreaded cannibalistic Carib cacique Caonabo, intent on capturing the beautiful Ozema as one of his wives, leads Luis to defend the girl—who at one point interposes herself between Luis and enemy arrows—and Sancho Mundo appears with his arquebuse to complete the rout of the invaders. At her urging, Luis takes Ozema with him and Sancho Mundo in a hasty retreat by canoe to a landing near the *Santa Maria,* which Luis finds shipwrecked and being converted into a fort to house the bulk of Columbus's men as colonists while he and the rest return to Spain with the good news of the mission's accomplishment. Ozema, determined never to become the wife of Caonabo, agrees—with Mattinao's consent—to accompany Columbus to Spain (with several other high-born natives) as examples of the inhabitants of the Indies. Having ensured fortification of the stranded *Santa Maria,* Columbus and his party board the *Niña* on January 4, 1493, for the voyage back to Spain.

On January 6, the *Pinta* reappears, and the two commanders are prudently reconciled, to travel in company across the broad Atlantic. Pinzon has secured many gold objects but has not succeeded in locating the mines. Taking on supplies for both ships, the two crews set sail for home, leaving Haiti on January 16. The *Niña* proves a fine ship, less sluggish than the *Pinta*, the latter having a sprung after-mast that cannot carry full sail. The voyage, begun with favorable winds, offers little difficulty until February 12, when the weather becomes increasingly stormy. The *Pinta's* commander, unable to find his own way home, stays close to the *Niña;* none but Columbus knows the true location of the vessels, and Columbus intends not to share his information with Pinzon, whom he suspects of intending to claim discovery of the Indies himself. The storm worsens to such a degree that Columbus and Luis prepare two identical copies of the record of the discovery, wrap each record in waxed cloth, and secure each packet in a separate barrel. Columbus's barrel is solemnly cast into the hissing ocean; Luis's barrel is placed on the poop of the *Niña*, to survive the ship if it should sink. None but Columbus and Luis know the contents of either barrel; all the others assume that a religious vow is being kept. Even in this tempest, the *Pinta* travels in company with the *Niña*, but neither ship can bear canvas before the screaming wind. The danger to all aboard is so great that divine assistance is sought by the drawing of a single cross-marked pea from a capful of peas; the man who draws the marked pea is to make a given holy pilgrimage. Columbus draws the pea. A second drawing, prompted by the increased severity of the storm, falls on Pedro de Villa, of whose piety none feels confident. A third drawing falls again on Columbus. Since the storm still does not abate, Columbus directs all water casks to be filled with seawater, to add ballast; the ship becomes more stable following the completion of this undertaking, and sail is added. During the tempest, the *Pinta* disappears, and most believe she has been lost.

The following day, February 15, land is sighted, precisely where Columbus had anticipated it. Conjectures concerning its identity vary, but Columbus's declaration that it is an island of the Azores proves accurate. Unfavorable winds prevent a landing, however, and the *Niña* makes its way the following day to a Portuguese-owned port on another island. Attempts by the Portuguese to seize the *Niña* fail, and she proceeds toward Spain. Ill winds and an evil storm—the worst yet encountered—drive the ship instead toward Portugal.

In the midst of the terror, Ozema appears at the door of the women's cabin and appeals to Luis to protect her. Tenderly holding her, he kisses the cross which Mercedes had given him and which he has worn close to his heart ever since. Saying that the cross will protect her, he places the chain around her neck, saying, "That cross is a sign of undying love" (p. 433). His intention is to reassure her religious faith; unfortunately, she misinterprets his feeling for that of love for her. (Luis's reassurance of Ozema is quietly observed by Columbus.) Murmuring "Mercedes"—the word she understands as meaning all that is good and beautiful because Luis shows such emotion when he says it—she goes inside the cabin again. Despite the fierceness of the storm, skillful work at the helm by Sancho Mundo and Vincente Yañez Pinzon under Columbus's direction enables them to enter the safety of the Tagus River, in Portugal. The ship anchors on March 4, and leaves the harbor for Spain on March 14, following a gala reception by the generous but envious Portuguese.

The scene shifts now to the sovereigns' court in Barcelona. After an authorial summary of events that have meanwhile occurred in Spain— chiefly, expulsion of the Jews and an assassination attempt on Ferdinand—attention turns to the expedition led by Columbus, and the queen learns Columbus has been reported back following the most boisterous marine winter that any can recall. At that moment, Sancho Mundo awaits, with a letter he has carried overland from the harbor in Portugal to be certain it would not fall into the wrong hands. The letter, read first by Isabella and then by Ferdinand, astounds and delights them. Columbus has indeed returned from the Indies! The wary king retires with the queen, Luis de St. Angel, Alonzo de Quintanilla, and the Archbishop of Granada to his own cabinet for a conference, leaving Sancho Mundo, the Marchioness of Moya (Beatriz de Bobadilla) and Mercedes alone. Sancho Mundo's comments about the beauty of Ozema and of Luis's defense of her against Caonabo lead both Beatriz and Mercedes to conclude that Luis has transferred his affections to the Indian maiden. In a private conversation with Sancho afterwards, Mercedes is distressed to learn that Luis has not mentioned anyone but the sovereigns and his aunt to be greeted on his arrival with the letter.

The news of the successful voyage brings Columbus much honor, and on his arrival at court a month later he is graciously received by the king and queen. Luis's arrival at Barcelona is overshadowed by the preparations being made for the reception of Columbus, though some observers comment that the marchioness seems strongly displeased with her nephew; none know that he has accompanied Columbus on the famous voyage to the Indies except Isabella, the marchioness, and Mercedes. Sancho relishes his own popularity, and is regaling Peter Martyr and a number of young nobles with an account of the voyage when Luis enters. Sancho and Luis are introduced to one another by Peter Martyr, and each shows pleasure at the introduction. Luis, still concealing his part in the voyage, listens as Sancho tells a lively tale of the wonders seen. Then Luis, saying Columbus himself has given him full details of the journey, talks for over an hour, detailing the voyage as if he has actually heard the story from the admiral rather than experienced it himself; Sancho Mundo solemnly confirms Count Llera's narrative. In fact, Luis's remarkable ability in recounting the narrative and Columbus's obvious respect for him improve the young courtier's public image decidedly.

The scene changes to Isabella's quarters, where, after prayer, she is joined by Ferdinand; the two discuss the awesome change in their fortunes as a result of Columbus's successful venture. Following this lengthy conversation, the queen visits her daughters and then the Marchioness of Moya. Not sensing the coldness of Beatriz on the matter, Isabella declares that Luis has exonerated himself in the westward voyage and will now be allowed to marry Mercedes. At Isabella's request, Beatriz leads the queen to Mercedes's quarters, where Isabella tells the startled and distraught girl that she is now to marry Luis. Mercedes, tearfully refusing such a marriage, leaves Beatriz to explain that Luis has lost his heart to a beautiful Indian princess. Not having seen a beautiful maiden among the Indians displayed, Isabella is perplexed until Mercedes, after preparing Ozema to receive the queen, leads Isabella to Ozema's quarters. The queen, astounded by Ozema's beauty and by her aristocratic bearing, suspects that Mercedes is mistaken about Luis's infidelity; she questions Ozema alone for over an hour. Ozema confesses not only to her love for Luis but to their actually being wed, information that Isabella immediately shares with Beatriz.

The scene changes again to reveal the banquet given by Cardinal Mendoza for Columbus. Following Columbus's recounting of his voyage to the respectful listeners, as well as a toast to him by Luis de St. Angel, a jealous noble, Juan de Orbitello, questions whether Columbus is the only man who could have performed such a feat. In answer, Columbus, after others fail, causes an egg to stand on end, a demonstration effectively silencing the envious courtier.

Both Columbus and Luis are suddenly summoned from the banquet by the queen; as Luis hopes, the summons concerns his marriage to Mercedes. But that matter is far from secure, for Luis finds the queen and the marchioness both convinced of his marriage to Ozema. Ozema herself reveals the cause of error when she describes Luis's presentation of the cross, an incident witnessed by Columbus and declared by him a pious act rather than a marriage. Further testimony from Luis confirms that he has never envisioned any spouse but Mercedes. Satisfied on this score,

Beatriz rejoices at her nephew's innocence. Isabella remains to talk alone with Ozema. In her earnest conversation with the Indian princess, the queen explains the error into which Ozema has fallen by her misinterpretation of Luis's concern and protection, his use of the name "Mercedes," and his presentation of the crucifix. Ozema is entirely unstrung by the discovery that Luis has not in fact wed her but has long been pledged to Mercedes. Immediately, Ozema falls into deep illness and is felt to be close to death.

Luis, summoned to an interview with Mercedes, learns that Mercedes will relinquish Luis to marry Ozema and will herself become a nun, a suggestion that stuns the young count. By degrees, he restores Mercedes's confidence in his love for her alone. Fearful that Luis will feel differently when she sees the dying Ozema, she leads him to the Indian princess's apartment, where Columbus, Isabella, and Beatriz await his arrival. He is shocked at the maiden's evident decline but reports that others of the Indians from Haiti, at Seville and at Palos, are also sick unto death; all except Ozema are by now, however, baptized. Ozema agrees to accept baptism on the condition that Luis and Mercedes first be married in her presence. Although the suggestion of an immediate marriage seems highly inappropriate, all present feel that Ozema's soul must be secured to the Lord through the rite of baptism. After an hour of prayer and preparation, Mercedes, adorned in a white veil, is brought to be married to Luis, whose love she now knows she fully possesses. Ferdinand drapes Luis with the collar of one of his own orders, and then the ceremony is held, with Columbus giving away the bride.

Ozema, requesting and receiving the crucifix hanging at Luis's breast, holds it and submits to baptism by the archbishop. Then, assured she is a Christian, she asks the archbishop to wed her to Luis as his second wife! The archbishop's sharp reprimand is interrupted by the marchioness, who observes that Ozema, aware from the archbishop's words that she can never marry Luis, has died, a somber beginning for Isabella's pious mission of taking the Cross to the Indies.

Seagoing suddenly becomes not only proper but socially mandatory for young gentlemen following Columbus's successful first voyage to the Orient. Columbus' second westward voyage, shortly undertaken, includes seventeen vessels with crews drawn from among the finest families in Spain; many young nobles twit Luis for his lack of courage in not being one of the company. Luis and Mercedes, in the little felucca they have named *Ozema,* sail out to bid the Admiral bon voyage; Columbus takes this occasion to urge Luis to guard Columbus's interests against the jealous and malicious intents of Fonseca, of one of the house of Bobadilla, and even of Ferdinand himself. After Columbus's fleet has left Cadiz, Luis and Mercedes sail to Palos, where they learn from Pepe's wife, Monica, that Martin Alonzo Pinzon has died of grief at Columbus' having arrived before him to report success in the Indies. After visiting the church to pray for the success of Columbus's second voyage, the bride and groom return to the *Ozema* and thence home to Valverde, where they live happily, secure in their love for one another. [Presumably, among their children is one named Ozema, who dies young.]

Diego de Ballesteros, Boabdil, Doña Beatriz de Bobadilla, Don Luis de Bobadilla [Luis], Don Andres de Cabrera, Caonabo, Father Pedro de Carrascal, Admiral Christoval Colon [Christopher Columbus], Father Alonso de Coca, Dama, Diego, King Ferdinand, Fonseca, José Gordo, Guacanagari, Queen Isabella, King John II, Father Juan Perez de Marchena, Juan Martin, Martin Martinez, Duke of Medina Celi, Cardinal Mendoza, Monica, Sancho Mundo, Pedro Alonzo Niño, Alonzo de Ojeda, Ozema, Juan de Orbitello, Pepe, Pepita, Doña Inez Peraza, Pero, Francisco Martin Pinzon, Martin Alonzo Pinzon, Vincente Yañez Pinzon, Alonzo de Quintanilla, Christoval Quintero, Gomez Rascon, Roderique, Bartolomeo Roldan, Sancho Ruiz, Luis de St. Angel, Rodrigo Sanchez of Segovia, Sancho, Archbishop Fernando de Talavera, Doña Maria de las Mercedes de Valverde [Mercedes], Pedro de Villa, John de Vivero.

Miles Wallingford: Sequel to Afloat and Ashore, 1844.

[Although published separately and described as a sequel to *Afloat and Ashore, Miles Wallingford* is in fact a continuation of that novel, and hence no exposition is provided. It begins in the middle of an episode suspended at the end of *Afloat and Ashore.*]

Through the efforts of Dr. Post, Andrew Drewett is revived and put to bed to recover aboard the *Wallingford.* His mother and his two sisters, Helen and Caroline, come aboard the same vessel, and all four members of the Drewett family are carried to Albany. There they encounter yet another sloop containing friends and acquaintances: Major and Emily Merton and Rupert Hardinge. Asking about the welfare of several on the *Wallingford,* Rupert makes no inquiry whatever about Grace, an unkind cut or oversight which worsens markedly the invalid's condition. When Lucy signals Miles to avoid further contact with Rupert and his party, Miles starts the return voyage down the river. He learns subsequently from Lucy that though the betrothal of Grace and Rupert had not been formalized, the young couple had considered themselves engaged for four years before Rupert's fickle fancy had settled upon Emily Merton.

Miles and Marble go ashore near Coeymans at the point where they anchor at the end of the first day. Near the river they admire an old stone house—the year 1698 is visible on one of its iron braces—and its surrounding garden. There they fall into a conversation with its seventy-year-old owner, a widow named Katharine Wetmore. When the old lady tells them her life story, it becomes quite apparent that she is the mother of Moses Marble! Secretly marrying, against her parents' wishes, a Yankee schoolteacher, George Wetmore, she had had their child put out to nursing care. The heartless nurse had received her fee and then abandoned the infant boy on a slab of marble in a stonecutter's yard. Acknowledging their marriage and the loss of their child, the Wetmores had spent thirty years and all their means seeking their lost son, even mortgaging their home for funds necessary to carry on their search in England, where a false clue had led them. But now, after many difficult years, Providence has brought her son to her very door. Moses is ecstatic at identifying one of his parents after a lonely, homeless life, though he is somewhat disconcerted by his true name: Oloff Van Duzer Wetmore. He enjoys a second surprise when he discovers that he also has a niece, Kitty Huguenin, who lives with his mother.

Before his death George Wetmore had paid off the mortgage to a greedy usurer named Van Tassel. The payment receipt has been lost or misplaced and Van Tassel, claiming that the note has never been redeemed, is proceeding to foreclose on Mrs. Wetmore. Miles and Moses determine to take whatever steps are necessary to settle the mortgage issue, even if that means attending the mortgage sale and themselves buying Willow Cove, as the Wetmore estate is called. With this possibility in mind, Moses again joins the company on the *Wallingford* to sail down the river to New York and there pick up the necessary money. En route they realize that the ship moves too slowly for Marble's purpose, that he must take a coach to the city and back if he is to arrive at Coeymans in time for the mortgage sale. He lands at the town of Hudson and continues his journey by land.

Though Miles had intended to sail slowly down the river to New York City, he is persuaded now by Grace to do otherwise. He is shocked to see how much his sister has failed, and he acquiesces quickly to her plea to be taken back to Clawbonny at once. There her condition grows steadily worse, despite advice from another medical specialist, Dr. Wurtz, and despite Lucy Hardinge's tender day-and-night care. Grace calls her brother to her side several times for long and intimate discussions. Since she is not yet of legal age to come into her inheritance, she cannot have a will executed, but Miles assures her that he will dispose of her property as she directs. He is stunned to discover that after leaving modest gifts to Lucy, to the family slaves, and to charity, Grace wishes to have the bulk of her estate, some $20,000, bestowed upon Rupert. She has written a long and forgiving letter to accompany this bequest which will make Rupert independent of Lucy's wealth. The inheritance for Rupert is to be arranged by Miles in such a way that neither Lucy nor Mr. Hardinge will be apprised of it.

There is a protracted death scene as Grace grows weaker, lapses tranquilly into unconsciousness, and a few minutes later passes quietly away. Because Miles has fixed in his mind the angelic features of his beautiful sister during her last hour, he refuses to look upon the corpse she has left behind. A large funeral is held, attended by the numerous Clawbonny blacks and by a group of mourners most of whom are identified only as relatives. One relative who is identified is Miles's cousin, John Wallingford, who just happened to be in the area and, hearing of Grace's death, appeared at the last rites. (A land speculator in Western New York, Cousin Jack is a bachelor of fifty whose primary interest in life seems to be money.) Mr. Hardinge, himself innocent and saintly, had sent for Rupert as Grace had begun to sink, not realizing that the girl was dying of a broken heart caused by his son's desertion. Fortunately, Rupert does not arrive until the day of the funeral, after which he coolly accepts Miles's note on a New York City bank for $20,000 and departs hastily.

That night Miles walks alone in the moonlight to Grace's grave, and there he finds another mourner, Lucy Hardinge. Although Miles still loves Lucy, he has, according to Mr. Hardinge, waited too long to declare his affection—the implication being that she is now committed to Andrew Drewett. Although there is evidence to make the reader suspect that this is not the case, Miles resigns himself to bachelorhood. He tells Lucy that he will never marry, that he will go to sea again until he has recovered from the loss of his beloved sister.

In New York, Miles again meets his cousin, John Wallingford, whom he admires for his directness and for his apparent interest in the Wallingford family and name. So thoroughly is Miles persuaded on the latter point that he rewrites his will to make Jack his sole heir. Now that Grace is dead and Lucy lost to him, he neither has nor will have, he assumes, any other heirs. The two relatives, who had not seen each other for years until Grace's death, now discuss Miles's forthcoming voyage. With no cargo available for him at the moment, Miles contemplates the advisability of purchasing a cargo himself, perhaps a shipload of sugar and coffee to be sold in northern Germany, where these commodities are selling at high prices. After paying off his $20,000 to Rupert, however, Miles has but $10,000 in ready cash plus some $20,000 worth of stocks and securities from Grace's share of the estate. Cousin Jack offers Miles a $40,000 mortgage on Clawbonny and his securities, a note payable in six months. Saying that he will now make Miles *his* heir, Jack indicates that he will not file the mortgage claim but simply keep it with his personal papers. Miles subsequently has some second thoughts about this whole arrangement but hopes for the best.

As Miles's ship, the *Dawn,* is being loaded, Moses Marble arrives to serve as first mate on the ship. He had repurchased Willow Cove at the mortgage sale, and later, after Mrs. Wetmore had found the receipt for the original mortgage settlement, had recovered his money from Van Tassel. While Moses takes his mother and niece for some last-minute sight-seeing in the city, Miles lunches at a popular restaurant in the business district. In a compartment next to his—the stalls are separated by only a thin partition—are Rupert Hardinge, Andrew Drewett, and a mutual friend named Norton. When the conversation among these three turns to the news of Grace's death, Rupert is quite diffident; he acknowledges once knowing her but dismisses her as a rural girl of only modest charm. Drewett, on the other hand, praises her great beauty and describes Clawbonny as a most respectable estate. Less gratifying to Miles's ears is Andrew Drewett's observation that although he once considered Grace's brother a rival for the hand of Lucy Hardinge, he no longer has any fears on that score. Upon hearing this, Miles leaves the restaurant at once and orders the immediate sailing of the *Dawn.*

Now, in 1803, a renewal of hostilities has begun between France and Great Britain, and the sea phase of this conflict requires a substantial increase in manpower for the British navy. This, in turn, leads to another period of impressment of seamen from the vessels of neutral countries, especially the United States. Miles becomes aware of the seriousness of this situation while just barely clear of the New York harbor as the departing pilot points out to him the distant sail of the *Leander,* a British man-of-war that has been prowling the area for weeks. The *Dawn* manages to outrun the *Leander* only to fall captive to the *Speedy,* a British frigate, which promptly impresses or imprisons all but four of the Americans and confiscates the ship's cargo, sending the vessel toward Plymouth, England, manned by a "prize crew." Lord Harry Dermond, Captain of the *Speedy,* justifies this illegal seizure of a neutral ship by two very specious claims: 1) that its destination, Hamburg, now lies within the sphere of enemy influence, and 2) that the sugar aboard came from Santo Domingo, a French colony. It does Miles no good to protest that he

had bought the sugar in New York or that when it had been produced in
the West Indies, England and France were not at war. An ill-mannered
supernumerary lieutenant named Sennit is placed in command of the
"prize" with a crew of ten British sailors. Once the *Speedy* is out of sight,
the four Americans aboard (Miles, Moses, Neb, and Diogenes, the black
cook) recapture the vessel, by means of a carefully planned ruse, and set
the "prize crew" adrift in a well-provisioned yawl. Before they lose sight
of the yawl, they see that it will make contact with an English West
Indiaman bound for some Caribbean port.

With almost superhuman exertion, the four Americans manage to
operate the ship, but they are soon overtaken by the French lugger
Pollison, a privateer. Expecting help from the *Pollison*, since they had been
abused by the enemy of France, Miles is unpleasantly surprised by their
being made French captives and by the strategy Captain Gallios adopts to
rationalize his own cupidity. He claims that the *Dawn* is still legally a
British prize and that it is his duty to capture it as enemy property. By
means of another ruse, Miles and his three men recapture their ship for
the second time. Off the coast of France they are pursued by a French-
built British frigate named *Fortunée*. This would-be captor they elude by
flying a tricolor and sailing within the range of powerful French shore
batteries where the *Fortunée* dares not follow.

As they near the English Channel on the following day, they sight no
fewer than six sails. One is that of the *Pollison*, which is about to retake the
Dawn when it is beset by a British sloop-of-war and flees southward. The
remaining sails belong to two British frigates (the *Speedy* and the *Black
Prince*) and two French frigates (the *Cerf* and the *Désirée*) which now
engage in a five-hour battle finally won by the British. While the crew of
the *Speedy* is occupied in this conflict, several of her American captives
from the *Dawn* make their escape in an open boat, but they are soon
chased by a well-manned cutter. Desperately in need of more hands and
anxious to aid his former crewmen, Miles sails within range of the *Speedy's*
guns in order to throw a line to his men. Immediately tacking, Miles is
beginning to pull his captured crewmen out of the clutches of the cutter
when the towline detaches and the escapees are recaptured.

Realizing the virtual impossibility of carrying the shorthanded *Dawn*
through the heavy ship traffic of the English Channel, Miles and Moses
now decide to bypass Great Britain on the west instead, by way of the
Irish Channel. After outdistancing a brig that gives chase off Wales, they
are forced to seek a safe anchorage along the Irish coast in order to ride
out a rising gale blowing from the northeast. The tempest increases so
much that their anchor cables part, and the *Dawn* is driven back down the

Irish Channel and into the Atlantic again. Still rising, the fury of the storm finally carries away most of the ship's rigging and spars. While they are trying to clear the wreckage, huge seas crash upon the deck of the *Dawn,* sweeping overboard Neb in the ship's launch, Diogenes in the caboose [galley], and Moses Marble in a great tangle of spars and sails, and leaving Miles the sole member of the ship's company. With six feet of water in the hold of the wreck, Miles, abandoning all hope of saving either the *Dawn* or himself, lapses into a stupor in which he sees alternately the faces of Lucy and of his three lost shipmates. As the *Dawn* settles deeper and deeper in the water, Miles finally rouses himself and constructs a raft of spars decked with a hatch cover. He abandons the ship just a few hours before it sinks. After drifting for some time and wondering just how long the raft will hold together in the still rough seas, Miles is picked up by Moses and Neb in the ship's launch.

All three men are moved to tears by their almost miraculous survival and their unlikely reunion on the open sea. Although their physical safety is assured when they are picked up by a passing ship, their prospects are still not very cheering. As they are taken aboard the British frigate *Briton,* they are immediately declared prisoners by Captain Rowley for having stolen a British "prize ship" (their own vessel, the *Dawn!*) and for having caused the deaths of the "prize crew" by setting them adrift in a small boat. No credence is given to Miles's statement that he saw the prize crew picked up by a West Indiaman. For three months they are well-treated captives aboard the *Briton,* and during that time they witness a sea battle in which the *Briton* vanquishes a French frigate. When the *Briton* meets the *Speedy,* however, and the prisoners are transferred to the latter vessel, the situation of the Americans worsens. Miles is placed in loose-fitting irons, and Moses and Neb, set to work as regular seamen, are put under steady pressure to join the British service. Another five months elapse before the *Speedy* completes her patrolling assignment and returns to Plymouth, where the three Americans are to be tried by an Admiralty court. In the excitement of docking a French captive of the *Speedy,* Miles and his companions escape and proceed up the English Channel in a launch. Being passed unobserved by an English vessel, they are picked up by an American tobacco ship and carried to Hamburg, their original destination, where Miles expects to find letters from home and papers which will establish his credit in Germany. His expectations are not realized; no communication of any kind awaits him at Hamburg. Penniless now in a foreign land, the three sign aboard the *Schuylkill* of Philadelphia in order to earn their passage back to America. This they do, after a lateral voyage to Spain, arriving in their own country on September 7, 1804; pooling their pay, they find that their total combined assets are one hundred and thirty-two dollars.

Proceeding to New York City, they take quarters at a low-cost rooming house for seamen. Long thought dead, the men create a small stir by their return, though their homecoming this time is not as happy as those from earlier voyages had been. During their absence John Wallingford had died, apparently intestate, and the administration of his estate had passed into the hands of a distant relative, one Thomas Daggett. Most of Cousin Jack's papers and securities have not been acquired by Daggett, but he had come into possession of the mortgage note on Clawbonny. When this note had been long overdue, Daggett had placed Clawbonny, worth $35,000, on mortgage sale and (through an agent) had purchased the estate for a mere $5,250—the only bid. Miles is financially ruined. Besides having lost his ship, its cargo, and his ancestral home, Miles is now indebted for the remaining $35,000 of the loan from his cousin.

Miles and Marble meet Rupert outside the mansion where he and his wife, Emily, now live. Supported by an allowance from Lucy and the $20,000 bequest from Grace, Rupert condescends to speak briefly with his former friend and benefactor and to explain why he cannot entertain such members of the lower class as seamen. As they continue their walk Miles and Moses are interviewed by two newspaper editors, one blindly pro-British (who attributes all of Miles's suffering at sea to the French) and the other blindly pro-French (who blames the British for Miles's losses). Back at the rooming house they are accosted by Mr. Meekly, Thomas Daggett's attorney, and a sheriff's deputy who, armed with a court order, arrest Miles and take him to a debtors' prison where he is to remain until he can pay his debts or have someone post a bond for $60,000. He has little hope of such help from anyone. He quickly rejects the patronizing gesture of Rupert, who sends him in his great distress a $20 bill; it is returned via the same messenger who bore it to the jail.

When Lucy and Mr. Hardinge learn of Miles's predicament, they rush to his side with strong but mixed emotions. Grateful and delighted that Miles has returned alive, they are shocked at his sudden fall from fortune. When her father leaves to seek the assistance of the family lawyer, Mr. Harrison, Lucy exacts a promise from Miles that he will accept bail bond from whatever person she sends to his cell for that purpose. Soon after Lucy's departure, Andrew Drewett appears, and the jailer receives an order to release Miles. Andrew thanks Miles again for saving his life on the Hudson near Albany but informs Miles that his present posting of bail bond was done at the request of Lucy Hardinge. Even more important pieces of news that Andrew divulges are the facts that he is not (as Miles was led to believe) engaged to Lucy and that Lucy does not love him. Andrew and Lucy are simply good friends. Elated but dazed, Miles rushes to Lucy's house, declares his love, and proposes to her. Having awaited this offer for several years, she accepts without hesitation. The young lovers are for some time lost to the world in tearful reconciliation. When he returns to a sense of reality, Miles feels presumptuous in asking Lucy to marry the beggar that he now is.

At dinner time Mr. Hardinge returns with Mr. Harrison, and an even more striking reversal of fortune is revealed. Harrison, also John Wallingford's attorney, had not heard of his client's death in the "Genesee Country" of Western New York until apprised of this just now by Mr. Hardinge. He informs Miles that Cousin Jack had indeed left a will and furthermore that Miles is Jack's sole heir. Clawbonny, then, had not legally been disposed of and will be repossessed by Miles. Miles will, moreover, inherit the remainder of his cousin's estate in properties and securities valued at more than $200,000. This day of incredible reversals is rounded off by Miles's returning to the rooming house to spend the night with his two most faithful retainers, Moses and Neb. These two simple-hearted (though at times grotesque) friends had spent the afternoon assembling rope ladders and other equipment with which to spring Miles from the debtors' prison.

While Miles remains in the city to attend to business and legal matters with the aid of Mr. Harrison, Lucy and Mr. Hardinge proceed at once to Clawbonny to restore that estate to its former activity and to make preparations for the wedding. An invitation is sent to Rupert, but he declines with the excuse that both Emily and her father are in too poor health to make the trip up the river. The nuptials, which take place in St. Michael's Episcopal Church, are presided over by Mr. Hardinge. Moses, in appropriate attire, serves as an attendant and is quite convinced that he has been the bridesmaid. During the several days of celebration following the marriage of Miles and Lucy, a second wedding occurs, that of Neb and Chloe.

After Moses Marble's mother dies and after his niece, Kitty, marries Horace Bright, a neighbor's son, Moses grows restless and again hears the call of the sea. Miles purchases a ship, which he names the *Smudge,* and appoints Marble to serve as its first captain. The old salt makes many profitable voyages on the *Smudge* and dies aboard her during a return passage from Europe. Miles, Lucy, their three children, and Neb, all passengers on that voyage, are with Moses during his last moments. At his request, he is given a sea burial.

The life story of Miles in the two novels ends where it had begun, at

Clawbonny. By the time Miles pens his memoirs, he and Lucy have four grown children and several grandchildren. In their old age they enjoy all those comforts of home, family, and affluence associated with the life of the landed gentry.

Diogenes Billings, Chloe Clawbonny, Cupid Clawbonny, Hector Clawbonny, Nebuchadnezzar (Neb) Clawbonny, Romeo Clawbonny, Venus Clawbonny, Vulcan Clawbonny, Lieutenant Clements, Thomas Daggett, Lord Harry Dermond, Diggins, Andrew Drewett, Caroline Drewett, Helen Drewett, Mrs. Drewett, Captain Gallios, Rev. Mr. Hardinge, Lucy Hardinge, Rupert Hardinge, Richard Harrison, Nathan Hitchcock, Kitty Huguenin, Jared Jones, Le Gros, Terence McSwale, Meekly, Captain Menneval, Emily Merton, Major Merton, Signora Montiera, Norton, Colonel Positive, Dr. Post, Lieutenant Powlett, Captain Rowley, Lieutenant Sennit, Michael Sweeny, Van Tassel, Abraham Van Vechten, Voorhees, Grace Wallingford [sister of protagonist], Grace Wallingford [daughter of protagonist], John Wallingford, Lucy Wallingford, Miles Wallingford [protagonist], Miles Wallingford [son of protagonist], Colonel Warbler, Sir Hotham Ward, Katharine Wetmore, Oloff Van Duzer Wetmore, Dr. Wurtz.

The Monikins, 1835.

Described in the introduction as a manuscript sent to the author in Geneva, Switzerland, by a Viscount Householder in gratitude for the author's having saved the Viscount's beautiful wife from accidental death, this novel uses the framework of a south-polar voyage to two unknown countries, Leaphigh [markedly similar in its institutions to England] and Leaplow [singularly like the United States in its principles and practices], to satirize the social, political, and judicial systems of the two Western countries. The "voyage" appears to have been imaginary, the product of the manuscript writer's delirium during an illness in Paris, but the points made are indelible ones. The first-person narrative device [in the voice of John Goldencalf, Viscount of Householder] adds verisimilitude to the account.

The narrator initially traces his ancestry, one known generation on his father's side and two known generations on his mother's side. His father, a foundling discovered in the late eighteenth century by a London orange seller and named Thomas Goldencalf after a sign outside a nearby butcher shop, was very early apprenticed to the bachelor owner of a prosperous variety shop. Proving an apt learner, Thomas won his master's favor, assumed and magnified his master's mercenary tactics, and on his master's death was made executor of the merchant's substantial estate and guardian of his adopted infant foundling daughter, Betsey, sole heiress of the estate and thirty years Thomas's junior. Ostensibly to protect his ward from unscrupulous suitors, Thomas married Betsey himself when she had reached eighteen years of age and had inherited £400,000. This union, of fourteen years' duration, produced five children, among whom only the fifth—John Goldencalf, the narrator—survived infancy. His mother, dying shortly after John's birth, exacted from Thomas Goldencalf the promise that he would entrust the rector, Dr. Etherington, with the care and upbringing of their child and that he would provide for the education of two poor but worthy scholars—at a total cost of £10,000—a promise reluctantly given and even more reluctantly kept by the mercenary Thomas Goldencalf. (By dint of clever management, Thomas almost doubled the amount of Betsey's inheritance by the time of her death.)

At the age of twenty, John Goldencalf has completed his schooling at Eton and at Oxford, with his vacations spent happily at the rectory with Etherington and his lovely daughter, Anna. Stung by his exclusion from a birthday party attended by Anna and given by the son of the baronet Sir Harry Griffin—on the grounds that John is the son of an untitled stockbroker rather than a member of the landed gentry—John comes to recognize the advantage of social rank, a distinction scorned by his father but respected by the rector. On Thomas Goldencalf's death, at the age of seventy-five, John inherits all his father's property and is made sole executor of the will, to the disappointment and despair of a score of his father's false friends. Shortly after the prompt settlement of his father's estate, John leaves London for the countryside to ponder his proper conduct, well aware of his late father's monetary wealth but spiritual poverty (his final cry on his deathbed was "gold—gold!") and consequently unpromising eternal prospects. Halting overnight at an inn in the borough of Householder, John hears an impassioned election-campaign speech by Sir Pledge and, moved by the stake-in-society principle expressed in that newly appointed government minister's address, he purchases the independent borough of Householder and promises its support for the reelection of Sir Pledge. In an ensuing conversation with the grateful candidate, John mentions his regret at his own lack of social rank; Sir Pledge, true to his promise to attend to the matter, arranges John's elevation to the rank of baronet. John's return to the rectory provides an opportunity for his declaration of love for Anna, a suit his beautiful lifelong comrade alternately encourages and discourages. John, unaware of the depth of Anna's real affection for him but deeply aware of what he considers his obligations to mankind, determines to travel for a year or two, and takes affectionate farewell of the rector and Anna. His sole aim, he explains to the reader, is "a life of useful and active benevolence, a deathbed of hope and joy, and an eternity of fruition" (p. 81).

To effect the end of establishing stakes in society everywhere and thus enlarging his compassion for mankind, John invests vast sums from his fortune in real estate in all parts of Great Britain and in many portions of its far-flung Empire; he hires agents to manage a wide range of business enterprises around the world, convinced that he who has social stakes will be better able to administer wisely the interests of his fellow citizens. Thus allying his own interests with those of others, he sets out to examine personally his many enterprises, and returns with firm confidence in the stake-in-society principle but painfully aware of weaknesses lurking in it if it is misapplied. Arriving in Paris in 1819, he encounters a neighbor of the Etheringtons who informs him Anna has just refused the hand of a highly eligible young peer. John, with his hopes for Anna's love renewed, writes her an amorous letter indicating that his travel is merely strengthening his susceptibility to her charms. Her eagerly anticipated response, a cryptic note, dashes his hopes and arouses his jealousy: she proposes to expand her own affections and thus prepare herself to be a more worthy wife for a man whose affections embrace the whole world!

Endeavoring to regain his composure, John walks hither and yon for many hours, not even pausing to eat. The following morning, still distraught, he breakfasts at a street café, where he encounters a Connecticut seaman, Captain Noah Poke, whose open manner and common-sense comments arouse his interest. Poke, early orphaned, and sent to sea at the age of four, has traveled widely, but—having lost his vessel, the *Debby and Dolly of Stunin'ton* [Stonington], by shipwreck on the coast of Russia—is now penniless and seeking means for a new venture. After a thorough canvass of one another's backgrounds and experiences, Gold-encalf and Poke agree to undertake an expedition together, outfitted by Sir John and captained by Poke, to test in new territories the merits of the baronet's stake-in-society principle. En route to John's quarters, the men see two ragged, gypsylike Savoyards and their four costumed monkeys. Sensing an audience, the Savoyards put the monkeys through their tricks, a performance that serves to align John's sympathies with the abused animals, of which one appears to be considerably more sensible than its tattered masters. Aware that he has not yet invested in quad-rupeds and therefore does not share their concerns, John buys the monkeys from their exhibitors; he and Captain Poke take the compliant primates to John's hotel.

Once there, John gives the hotel personnel directions for the proper care both of Poke and of the monkeys, and then settles down to read his mail. Each letter, from one quarter of the globe or another, represents one of Goldencalf's "stakes in society" and prompts a cogent letter to the appropriate British minister or business representative or member of Parliament, letters intended to effect correction of the situations of which John's agents have sent reports. [His own financial involvement in the various enterprises causes John to bend truth and principle to suit each situation in turn, a basic defect in his stake-in-society proposition of which he is ingenuously unaware.] His correspondence finally completed to his satisfaction, John looks in on the four monkeys—well fed and sound asleep in the anteroom—and then goes to his own bed, where a confusion of images causes great difficulty in his settling into sleep.

The following morning, John awakens in a state of reverie. Overhearing a quiet but earnest conversation in the anteroom in a language that he is unable to identify, he enters the anteroom and addresses the only occupants, the monkeys, in French; the apparent leader of the four monkeys responds in flawless French. In answer to Sir John's self-introduction, the speaker introduces the younger male as Lord Chatterino, the younger female as Lady Chatterissa, her duenna as Mistress Vigilance Lynx, and himself as Dr. Reasono, philosopher, the traveling tutor of Lord Chatterino; the young lord is heir of one of the most ancient and illustrious families of the kingdom of Leaphigh, in the monkey (monikin) territory. Intrigued by the grave monikin philosopher, John questions him about Leaphigh and discovers the cause of the ladies' embarrassment in his presence: monikins prefer the unclothed state. To make his visitors more comfortable, John returns to his room and removes all but his slippers and nightcap! The more John learns about Leaphigh, the more eager he becomes to have his new comrade, Captain Poke, hear about the interesting features of monikin culture. With the monikin philosopher's permission, John dresses himself sufficiently to order breakfast for his guests and to fetch Poke to attend Dr. Reasono's promised lecture. Poke's resistance to discarding his clothes just to hear a lecture by a monkey is discreetly overcome by their allowing him to wear a bison-skin, a natural garment in John's possession; John himself, subject to colds, avails himself of a similar garment. After a guarded but heated argument between the monikins and the humans on certain matters of protocol governing the lecture, Dr. Reasono begins his learned comments on the philosophical, scientific, political, social, and historical aspects of monikin civilization [a lecture that continues throughout two chapters of the novel].

Interrupted occasionally, as agreed beforehand, by questions or demurrals from John and from Poke, the grave philosopher outlines the monikin classifications of elements, vegetation, and animals (listing humans above sponges but below monikins), explains the monikins' stress on the tail as the seat of reason, accounts for the revolution of the earth and the development of the salubrious steam-heated environment of monikin territory at the south pole (an environment once threatened by ill-advised capping of the steam vent but restored by an eruption that carried away the perpetrators of the mischief and forty thousand square miles of monikin territory), expounds the monikin theory of the evolution of species, and hints at other subjects too vast to be explored by other than an actual visit to monikin territory. Then, well aware of John's eagerness to learn further details of monikin philosophy, Dr. Reasono proposes that Sir John, being wealthy, provide a suitable ship, navigated by Captain Poke—half of whose life has been spent sailing in the south-polar regions in quest of seals—to carry the monikins home and there to see for himself the blessings of a superior society, one in which he might well be happy to have a stake. At length, John persuades Poke to undertake such a voyage; and the two men and the monikins forthwith journey to England and arrange for a suitable vessel, the *Walrus*, for the polar expedition, on which they subsequently set sail.

Captain Poke proves an excellent mariner, and the crew members amiably accept as clothing the animal skins which John provides for them in view of the monikins' aversion to human dress. As the *Walrus* approaches the south-polar area, Poke constructs a globe of a peeled pumpkin, outlines the principal land masses, and has Dr. Reasono locate the island of Leaphigh, as well as Captivity Island—the island on which he and the other three were captured by sealers, and subsequently sold first to an Indiaman and then to the Savoyards at a handsome profit. With this guide as a chart, Poke continues sailing confidently southward. As the *Walrus* arrives among mountainous icebergs, he navigates so expertly that—despite Dr. Reasono's error in the location of Captivity Island—the ship slips through one channel after another, with the ice closing in immediately behind the vessel. When field ice is encountered, Poke orders the ship hove to, and the entire crew works to attach to the *Walrus* an outer skeleton of beams prefabricated precisely to protect the ship from the crush of the ice. Shielded thus, the ship works its way to the clear waters marking the edge of the monikins' domain, comfortably steam heated; the humans shed their animal skins for cooler dress fashioned to resemble the discarded pelts. In due course, the *Walrus* arrives in the harbor of the city of Aggregation.

The port officers, intent on placing the monikins' customary brand—personal identifying color and number—on the seats of the human visitors, are persuaded by John's discreet bribe to allow the numbers to be painted instead of burned. Safely home again, Lord Chatterino, Lady Chatterissa, and Mistress Vigilance Lynx are utterly scornful of their human benefactors; members of the nobility in Leaphigh, they and their friends mock the humans and the cultures from which they come. Even Dr. Reasono, although he appears friendly, shows a lofty disregard for the truth regarding the circumstances of the four monikins' safe return to their homeland, turning every development in the whole affair to the advantage of the monikins. He reports to the learned academy that while he and Mistress Vigilance Lynx were guiding Lord Chatterino and Lady Chatterissa on the Journey of Trial required before their marriage, he encountered a party of sealers and, desirous of exposing his young charges to human society and of bringing back to the academy information of immense scientific and philosophical value, he engaged the sealing vessel to transport the monikin party northward. Finding that vessel's accommodations inadequate, he transferred the party to a better ship, which landed at the island of St. Helena, an island Dr. Reasono is convinced had been formed by portions of the land carried away by the south-polar eruption; to prove this point, the speaker presents several rocks obtained there—clearly of the same mineralogical content as that of a mountain near Aggregation. He also describes the monkeys with whom he talked on St. Helena, obviously of monikin origin but with intellects sadly blunted by their ancestors' fearsome concussion during the eruption and by the viscissitudes of climate; these monkeys, he suggests, would undoubtedly prove of economic importance if imported in large quantities into Leaphigh as domestic servants. Arriving shortly thereafter in Portugal, he engaged two Savoyards as guides for their party for a tour he proposed of Europe; a full report of the momentous discoveries made during that tour is promised by Dr. Reasono for delivery at a later date. Feeling the obligation of returning to Leaphigh with Lord Chatterino and Lady Chatterissa, he reluctantly terminated their travel in Great Britain, where he engaged a vessel to transport the party to monikin territory. At the request of the king of England, he included the Prince Royal, and at the urging of the British Lord High Admiral, that dignitary was allowed to take command of the expedition.

Finishing his formal address, Dr. Reasono presents Bob Smut, the *Walrus's* cabin boy, as Prince Royal, Poke as Lord High Admiral, and

Goldencalf as traveling tutor and personal attendant of the Prince Royal! For his singular services, Dr. Reasono is awarded the titles of F.U.D.G.E. and H.O.A.X. John finds no support among his own men, all elated with their elevation in rank and importance; even Poke, though sympathetic, has little time to waste on the Prince Royal's attendant. Stung by this reversal in fortunes, John is greeted as Sir John Goldencalf by Judas People's Friend, envoy-extraordinary and minister-plenipotentiary of the republic of Leaplow to the kingdom of Leaphigh. People's Friend appears to know all about Sir John and his discomfiture, and invites him to sup with him and his attendant, Brigadier Aaron Downright. During the meal at the inn, paid for by promises—the currency of Leaphigh— John and his new friends discuss the salient features of Leaplow, an offshoot of Leaphigh that was established on purely republican princi- ples. In a lengthy chapter, People's Friend bares many interesting facts about Leaplow: The docked tails of the Leaplowers indicate the republic's disdain for an aristocracy based on intellect. Their conducting of elec- tions by pure chance and their limiting of offices to a year's duration avoid the danger of corruption. Proper deference to public opinion is expected, though in Leaplow there are two separate and equally accepted public opinions. The newspapers are supplied with the intelligence extracted from all the cropped tail portions in order to represent the average sense of the citizens. [In the details given of Leaphigh and of Leaplow throughout the novel, the author allegorically satirizes the characteristics of Great Britain and of the United States respectively, much in the manner of Swift's Lilliputian portion of *Gulliver's Travels*. For example, in Leaplow one demonstrates patriotism and political astute- ness by the finesse with which one executes fixed gymnastic feats (including complete reversals of position) while still managing to "toe the line."]

John, eagerly pursuing the features of Leaplow's political philosophy, is summoned—with People's Friend and Downright—to witness the wedding of Lord Chatterino and Lady Chatterissa. Attired in "formal dress"—i.e., wearing an oxtail borrowed for him by Dr. Reasono from the cabinet of natural history—John goes with Poke, similarly decked, to an elaborate reception at which Bob, now Prince Royal, affronts John by naming Jack Coppers, Negro cook aboard the *Walrus*, as the member of the human party most useful in getting the *Walrus* to Leaphigh, where- upon Jack is duly knighted. Before and after the wedding, John is provided both by Downright and by the distinguished Archbishop of Leaphigh with extensive information about religious patterns and prac- tices among the monikins; Downright continues the account during a private supper following the wedding, appending to each description of a patently absurd detail [reflecting a recognizably human foible, also] the comment "[N]o doubt, men manage better" (p. 294).

Captain Poke having committed during the wedding reception two serious crimes—one by stating that the king of Leaphigh has a memory and the other by stating that the queen of Leaphigh lacks a memory—is placed on trial before the High Criminal Court of Leaphigh. Defended by John Goldencalf and Brigadier Downright as next of kin (the former hastily adopted as mother and the latter as father to meet the legal requirements), Poke is immediately at the mercy of a court that violates every accepted principle of justice, including a highly prejudicial charge to the jury by the chief justice on each of the two counts. Instantly found guilty on both counts and condemned to amputation of his tail and to beheading for the respective crimes, Poke is counseled by Downright (actually an attorney in Leaplow) to submit to decaudalization while Downright manages to extricate him from punishment by beheading. Promptly upon the report of Poke's decaudalization, Downright declares his client, now non compos mentis [by virtue of the reason's having resided in the tail], entitled to release from punishment for the second charge, and the attorney's claim is honored. Poke, thus spared execution, hastens to the *Walrus*. John thanks Downright for his staunch support and then makes the necessary arrangements for leaving Leaphigh to visit Leaplow, accompanied by People's Friend and Downright. While People's Friend secures a reliable chargé d'affaires (a disguised Leaplower) as his replacement and instructs him fully on his duties [in an exceedingly ironic passage, pp. 326-328] and then takes care to preserve his removable tail in pepper for possible later use, John, Poke, Downright, and Jack Coppers seek cargo for the *Walrus*. Downright recommends the buying of "opinions," available in quantity at a certain shop, and extensive purchases are made according to Downright's judgment of their likelihood of a brisk market in Leaplow. By the time the Negro cook is offered his choice, the shop's shelves are almost bare; the shopkeeper sells him at half price a packet labeled "Distinctive Opinions of the Republic of Leaplow," though Downright doubts that they will sell any better in Leaplow than they have in Leaphigh. In short order, all are aboard, including the cabin boy, whom Poke kicks to his heart's content for his effrontery; then sail is set for Leaplow.

Barely outside Leaphigh's territorial waters, the *Walrus* is boarded by Leaplowers, who test each one aboard with a given set of shibboleths and naturalize as citizens of Leaplow all except the second mate, who pronounces "altar" "halter." In rapid succession as the ship approaches

Leaplow, nominating committees from the three political parties in Leaplow come aboard and enlist legislative candidates: Goldencalf for the Horizontals, Poke for the Perpendiculars, and Bob Smut (unbeknownst to Poke) for the Tangents. Inquiry by John reveals that the only requirements for voting in Leaplow are that one be alive and that he want something; possession of property—or a "social stake"—is considered a distinct liability in effecting sound government.

Bivouac, the harbor city, boasts a Wide-path [Broadway] and houses which tower over the government buildings, in conformity with the principle that government is the servant of the people. The visitors soon discover that other than entirely favorable comments by outsiders on fixed objects such as houses, streets, and public buildings, poor though they may appear to be, are fiercely resented; on the other hand, slurs and aspersions may be freely cast at the residents themselves. The visitors' opinions respecting the place and the residents are immediately sought by a social pretender named Gilded Wriggle; Wriggle and his kind are loathed by Downright and his solid fellow citizens.

John and Poke diligently study the Leaplow constitution, and brief themselves and each other on their responsibilities as elected representatives. John admires the logic of the balance of powers among the Great Sachem, the Riddles, and the Bobees (of which body he is to be a member). As for Poke, he is equally bemused by the "allegory" of the balance of powers and by the agility required to execute gyration No. 3 of the gymnastics required of politicians. (They have succeeded in selling all the "opinions" they had bought in Leaphigh, with the cook's half-price purchase proving in the end most lucrative, as those opinions of Leaplow had been procured abroad!) The first legislative matter debated, "*Resolved, that the color which has hitherto been deemed to be black, is really white*" (p. 381), engages Poke for the Perpendiculars, John for the Horizontals, and Bob Smut for the Tangents. By means of cunning reasoning and innuendo, the upstart Bob succeeds in amending the resolution to read "*Resolved, that the color which has hitherto been deemed to be black, is really lead-color*" (p. 390). In the course of the debate, John discovers that the one document considered far too sacred to quote is the national constitution! The second matter, concerning reparations to be paid by another nation, Leapthrough, for destruction of 126 Leaplow ships sixty-three years previously, is finally settled by a humanitarian who, envisioning war as the outcome of each of the four solutions previously proposed, recommends that no legislative action at all be taken; his recommendation passes unanimously. John, discovering that the humanitarian has a real-estate development that will be ruined if war occurs, recognizes this ploy as an outgrowth of the social-stake principle, apparently at work in Leaplow.

Shortly after the legislature adjourns, Downright shows John and Poke a pamphlet from Leaphigh predicting to the day, hour, minute, and second a nine-year moral eclipse in Leaplow, a period in which moral principle will be overshadowed by selfish monetary interest. As John, Poke, and Downright discuss the implications of such an eclipse for the moral welfare of the monikins, John hears some plain talk from Downright about the fallacies of the social-stake system that proves only too true during the succeeding days. Those who were previously generous toward others and concerned for others' welfare become more and more self-centered, grasping, and devoted to the almighty dollar; principle is indeed eclipsed by interest. The legislative scene quickly reflects the change in emphasis, with harsh criticism directed against those who vote or speak without a declared personal motive; disinterested concern for public welfare is held highly suspect. Property fever rages among the monikins as it has been known to rage among men in England. The old standards of virtue give way to respect for cunning, deviousness, and trickery. Captain Poke, a man for whom thinking and reasoning on legislative matters becomes daily more difficult as he subsists on acorns, the Leaplowers' fare, rather than the pork to which he has long been accustomed, adopts the practice of many of his colleagues in taking his political guidelines from a "God-like" [sic]; the one occasion thereafter on which he votes according to his own conscience forces his resignation as a legislator, for he is accused of the basest of behaviors: voting according to principle, without a sign of vested interest. Judas People's Friend, who shocks John and Poke by tripping in his political gymnastics and consequently being shaved of all his hair and deprived of all but the merest stump of a tail, is, on the contrary, most optimistic when he looks most desolate: in Leaplow, he says, humility is everything as a means to promotion, and if he accounts himself as unworthy of even the lowest post, he can be assured of speedy appointment to a high one.

Such a confused state of affairs prompts John to further philosophical inquiry; but it leads Poke to think of more basic things, such as good roast pork. John returns to the quarters he shares with Poke to discover the appetizing scent of roasted meat; the man in him overcoming his respect for monikin abstention from meat, he accepts Poke's invitation and eats both flesh and bones. As he is looking around for more to eat, he sees a reproachful gaze, and suspicion grows in him: Poke has cooked and eaten Brigadier Downright, and he—John Goldencalf—has been party to the crime! In horror and indignation, John grasps Poke's throat to force him to disgorge the meat of their friend and rescuer. In turn, Poke throttles John in an effort at self-preservation, and John begins to feel faint and dizzy.

Little by little, his senses clear; he finds himself not in his lodgings in Bivouac but in his Paris hotel quarters. As he looks around, he finds all as he had left it on going to London to buy the *Walrus* for the polar voyage, with three significant exceptions: on a table lie many closely written sheets containing the account of the voyage and the visits to Leaphigh and Leaplow; on the floor lies a small ship, accurately rigged, named the *Walrus*; in the air there is a pervasive odor of roasted meat. Peering over the top of a trunk is the head of Dr. Reasono, still firmly fastened to the shoulders, with its owner still clad in his street-performance costume. Voices outside the room catch his attention, but the language spoken is not that of the monikins. In a moment, Dr. Etherington is standing in the doorway, relieved to be recognized, and full of apologies for causing such distress by his unkind letter—the letter Anna had indeed penned, but at her father's dictation.

John, aware now that his only really meaningful "social stake" is Anna Etherington, is told by the rector that he can see her on the morrow. As for Poke, he has been a faithful nurse to John, says the rector, and deserves nothing less than free passage home. John assures the stout-hearted Captain Poke that a ship will be fitted out to replace the lost *Debby and Dolly*, with its owner Captain Poke and its immediate destination Poke's beloved Stunin'ton. The four monkeys, clearly uncommon specimens, will be well provided for, as well. But Poke shows a curious disinclination to talk about the adventures he and John had shared, saying only that he has grown to know Anna very well during the "voyage" and counseling John not to talk about the "voyage" overmuch, especially to Anna.

John's reunion with Anna the following day is an emotional and satisfying one for both. Anna has repented a thousand times about the letter [presumably the cause of John's indisposition], and she eagerly returns John's repeated declarations of love. In no uncertain terms, John declares that he is abandoning all social stakes around the world, having learned that they are not at all as important as he had thought. Acting promptly on this declaration, John sells all his foreign investments—at a handsome profit—and buys, instead, three more boroughs. Shortly thereafter, Lord Pledge exercises his influence to have John elevated to the rank of viscount; John Goldencalf, Viscount Householder, thus becomes a peer of the realm. Meanwhile, John buys a residence overlooking St. James's Park, a location pleasing to Anna, and he and Anna are married.

Though the voyage—apparently only a product of delirium [recorded by whom, the author does not say]—is rarely mentioned between John and his beloved wife, even ten years later John is digesting and sharing with his colleagues the useful conclusions drawn from his experiences among the monikins. These conclusions he shares with the reader as a fitting climax to this allegorical sociopolitical novel.

Archbishop of Leaphigh, Lord Chatterino, Lady Chatterissa, Jack Coppers, Brigadier Aaron Downright, Rev. Dr. Etherington, Anna Etherington, Francis, John Goldencalf, Hightail, Sir Joseph Job, Baron Longbeard, Vigilance Lynx, Miss-Mrs. [sic] Norton, Judas People's Friend, Lord Pledge, Captain Noah Poke, Dr. Socrates Reasono, Bob Smut, Gilded Wriggle.

Le Mouchoir; an Autobiographical Romance, 1843.

Set in Paris and New York in the 1830s, this fable is narrated by a pocket handkerchief, an article which at that time was used more for show than for blow. It is, thus, distinguished for its beauty rather than for the function of ordinary handkerchiefs. It begins its autobiography by establishing its ancestry back through several generations of flax plants, starting in America and then moving to France when a large shipment of flaxseed was captured by a French privateer. Every flax plant and its linen offspring enjoy a special kind of clairvoyance which unites their perceptions with those of both their vegetable ancestors and their human associates. For this reason all pieces of linen are wiser and better informed than is generally supposed, and the observations of a sophisticated pocket handkerchief provide a most fitting vehicle for the broad social satire of the story.

Part of a bolt of fine cambric, the pocket handkerchief is to be purchased, while still in its undecorated state, by Adrienne de la Rocheaimard, the orphaned granddaughter of the Viscountess de la Rocheaimard. It is her intention to trim it with fine lace as a gift for the dauphine, who, some time after the restoration of the Bourbons, had arranged a small pension for the aged and widowed viscountess. The July Revolution of 1830 intervened, however, causing the deposition of Charles X and a termination of the pension. The old woman sells precious items from her trousseau to maintain herself and her granddaughter in very frugal circumstances, and Adrienne becomes a seamstress for a milliner. Sensing Adrienne's inexperience in the workaday world, the milliner exploits the girl ruthlessly. She pays the refined young noblewoman fifteen sous a day, less than she pays her other employees, even though she makes a greater profit from Adrienne's superior workmanship. When her grandmother falls ill, Adrienne spends all her remaining cash, twenty-eight francs, to purchase the piece of fine cambric, no longer to be used as a gift but to be sold for a profit. After each day's work for the milliner, Adrienne spends several hours of the night trimming the pocket handkerchief with precious antique lace. She is reduced to a diet of bread and water, though she manages to buy small quantities of wine for her dying grandparent. The old viscountess dies just as Adrienne finishes the exquisitely beautiful needlework. Having sold all of their other valuables in order to survive, Adrienne now sells the pocket hand-kerchief to get enough money to give her grandmother a decent burial. A commission agent, Désirée, pays her forty-five francs for the hand-kerchief and immediately resells it for a hundred francs to Colonel Silky, a Yankee purchaser (and smuggler) for the fashionable shop of Bobbinet and Gull. This is a New York business firm in which Silky owns a large interest.

In New York City the pocket handkerchief is purchased by Eudosia, daughter of Henry Halfacre, land speculator and flamboyant member of the nouveaux riches. Eudosia is fascinated by this bit of linen finery when she learns from Bobbinet that its price of $100 will exceed considerably that of the most expensive handkerchief hitherto sold in America. Her millionaire father feels it quite appropriate that Eudosia be indulged in this little venture in conspicuous consumption. Such a status symbol should expedite her acceptance among elite circles in the metropolis. Ironically, Eudosia, having now spent her allowance, cannot meet her three-dollar subscription payment due to the Widow's and Orphan's Society fund; so she asks her close friend Clara Caverly, daughter of a moderately successful lawyer, to take care of this obligation for her.

At the most fashionable ball of the season that night, Eudosia is the center of attention, all of the women present wishing to examine the country's most expensive pocket handkerchief. But at this most demon-strative moment of materialistic success, the Halfacres are toppled from their financial pinnacle, for this is the day in 1832 when President Jackson withdraws government deposits from the Bank of the United States. A momentary panic ensues during which creditors call for payment on their loans to speculators. Greatly overextended on credit, Henry Half-acre suddenly finds himself bankrupt. With a show of piety and humility, he sells his personal property to pay his creditors, but in reality he pays only those who are most influential and then places enough of his hard cash in the hands of his brother-in-law for safekeeping so that after the bankruptcy proceedings are completed, he will still have a competency. Under such circumstances he cannot, of course, flourish status symbols;

so the famous pocket handkerchief is sold back to Bobbinet—it is considered a gesture of noble sacrifice—for $50.

Within a day the linen narrator is purchased again for $100, this time by Julia Monson, daughter of an older, more financially secure family than the Halfacres. At home with her treasure, Julia shows it to her family and to young Betts Shoreham, a friend of the Monsons; but she has better taste than to mention its price. Shoreham, in whom Julia could be interested, is scornful of all possessions acquired for the purpose of prestige. His attitude becomes quite evident in his dismay that Mademoiselle Hennequin, French governess for the two younger Monson children, should be emotionally moved by the pocket handkerchief. Secretly in love with the genteel governess, Shoreham asks her why she is so affected by such an object. Her response disturbs him even more, for, pressed for an answer, she says it is envy that has brought tears to her eyes.

That evening, at another ball, the splendid handkerchief again enjoys flattering attention, but its owner fails to receive the particular attention which she seeks, that of Betts Shoreham. Betts spends all of his time with the French governess, who, because of her education and modest charm, is always invited to accompany the Monsons at such soirees. In an effort to draw Betts's attention to herself, Julia engages in exaggerated flirtation with an acquaintance named Tom Thurston. The Thurston/Monson and Shoreham/Hennequin romances provide the framework for the satire of the concluding episodes of the story.

When Betts proposes to Mademoiselle Hennequin, the governess demurs because of her poverty and her lowly position. Betts insists that however pertinent such distinctions might be in France, they are not applicable in America. After further discussion, the governess reveals that she is Adrienne de la Rocheaimard and recounts the history of her misfortunes and sufferings, all of which were painfully recalled, she says, by her first glimpse of Julia's lace-trimmed pocket handkerchief. This identification scene reveals not only Adrienne's aristocratic lineage but also—even more surprising—her relationship to Betts: they are third cousins! His great-grandmother had had the name Rocheaimard. Though Adrienne knew that there had been an American branch of the family, she had never learned the names or whereabouts of her New World kinsmen. Betts and Adrienne are soon married in a fine wedding at the Monson home. Betts purchases from Julia the pocket handkerchief which has meant so much in the life of his beloved, and Julia uses the money to buy the couple a wedding gift of equal market value.

Contrasting sharply with this happy romance is that of Julia and Tom.

A penniless fortune seeker who has already proposed to twenty-six heiresses, Tom mistakenly assumes that the heart of Julia has capitulated to his amorous advances. He is informed of his error not by Julia but by her father, and in an indirect way. When Tom asks for the hand of his daughter, Monson does not flatly refuse his request. Instead, he describes the financial arrangement he intends to make with Julia and the husband of her choice. He will settle upon the couple any sum up to $50,000 provided that the amount is matched before the marriage by the prospective bridegroom. The affair ends at once, but the farce is carried on mercilessly to its conclusion. Tom marries the daughter of a wealthy butcher whose business fails the day after the wedding. When the young opportunist fails in his attempt to have the marriage annulled, he commits the ultimate act of desperation: "Tom went to Texas" (p. 32).

Bobbinet, Clara Caverly, Adrienne de la Rocheaimard, Viscountess de la Rocheaimard, Désirée, Mrs. Eyelet, Mrs. Halfacre, Eudosia Halfacre, Henry Halfacre, Mrs. Leamington, Monson, Mrs. Monson, John Monson, Julia Monson, Honor O'Flagherty, Betts Shoreham, Silky, Tom Thurston, Mrs. Trotter, Mary Warren.

The Oak Openings; or, The Bee-Hunter, 1848.

Although the action of this Indian story turns on physical combat and the flight-and-pursuit motif, its theme is religious. The novel opens in July of 1812 on the partly wooded prairies of western Michigan known as "oak openings." Four men, all strangers to each other, meet in apparent amity and talk together. Two of these men are Indians: Elksfoot, an elderly Pottawattamie, and Pigeonswing, a young Chippewa. The other two are white men: Benjamin Boden, a bee-hunter and honey merchant from Pennsylvania, and Gershom Waring, an alcoholic trader from New England. In the story's first episode Boden shows his three new acquaintances the scientific method he practices for locating hives of wild bees. He uses simple triangulation, releasing two honey-laden bees at points 1,600 feet apart and then observing closely the direction of their respective flights; where their lines of flight intersect, there will be their hive.

After chopping down the dead oak tree containing several hundred pounds of honey, the men go to Ben Boden's log cabin for dinner. As they are smoking their pipes and talking about the possibility of another war between the Americans and the British, Pigeonswing startles his three companions with the announcement that the war has already started and that Fort Mackinaw has fallen to Canadian forces.

The next morning before breakfast, Pigeonswing draws Boden aside and warns him against Elksfoot, who, he claims, is in the pay of the

Canadian British. Then to prove his own pro-American position, the Chippewa takes from his tobacco pouch a letter which he is bearing from Detroit-based General Hull (Governor of the Michigan Territory) to Captain Heald, the officer who commands the small garrison at Chicago. After breakfast the two Indians depart, and Boden and Waring proceed by canoe to a point along the river near the felled bee tree in order to collect the honey. After driving off eight bears which are also interested in the honey, they accomplish their mission and start back down the Kalamazoo River to their cabins. Boden has decided to move back to the settlements until the British-American conflict has ended lest he be caught in the Indian hostilities that will inevitably erupt during such a war. He hires Waring to help him take out of the wilderness the large store of honey he has been accumulating for several months. As they are about to proceed to Whiskey Centre, the Waring shanty, they discover the shot and scalped body of Elksfoot propped in a sitting position against a tree, and it seems likely that the Pottawattamie died at the hands of the Chippewa just after the two Indians had left Boden's cabin that morning. As their heavily laden canoe floats down the river, Gershom Waring reveals how his drinking has brought him down in life from a fairly prosperous New England merchant to a frontier trader whose whole wealth now is two barrels of whiskey. He had heard that in the West soldiers and Indians were paying high prices for whiskey, so he had put all of his remaining funds in that commodity and come to western Michigan accompanied by two virtuous and loyal women, his wife, Dorothy (Dolly), and his sister, Margery (Blossom) Waring.

At Whiskey Centre—it is the name Waring gives to every house he lives in and a name used as an epithet for the man himself—Benjamin and Gershom are welcomed by the two women, who have spent five wakeful nights in fear of Indian attack. Their fears were warranted, for the women had seen on the river three canoes loaded with Indians. The men realize that the savages will probably return with the intention of taking all their scalps. Upon Boden's advice, they abandon the Waring cabin, hide all its contents in the nearby woods, and prepare to leave in two canoes between which the bee-hunter has divided his stock of honey. While Gershom is occupied with this work, Boden discovers and destroys his two kegs of whiskey in an effort to save the alcoholic from his greatest enemy. As they are near the river that evening, ready to depart, they observe the arrival of four canoe loads of Indians who land and proceed to the now deserted cabin. There they build a large fire, in the glow of which Boden is able to discern the figure of a captive tied to a tree. It is Pigeonswing. Boden circles the cabin carefully and cuts the withes binding the Chippewa while Margery, standing at a safe distance, focuses a shielded lantern in such a way as to provide a guide point for the bee-hunter but remain invisible to the Pottawattamies. All three escape the Pottawattamie camp.

Back at the riverbank, they find Gershom Waring dead drunk on some brandy found in Boden's personal belongings. The bee-hunter mans one canoe and Pigeonswing the other as they edge away into the deep water towing behind them the four canoes of the Pottawattamies. The little flotilla moves silently across the river and ties up on the opposite bank. Instead of moving away with all possible dispatch, Boden (for some unexplained reason) feels it necessary to reconnoiter the Pottawattamie camp. Landing the contents of one canoe, he uses it to approach the Indians quietly in the dark and tie up in a tall clump of wild rice near them. Observing the Pottawattamies behaving very strangely, Boden finally realizes that they are trying to account for the strong scent of alcohol which lingers around the spot where he had spilt some of Waring's whiskey when rolling the two kegs from the cabin. The bee-hunter's curiosity now makes him so careless that he is unaware that his canoe has come untied and is floating in to shore directly toward two sentinels. Making a virtue of what is now a necessity, Boden steps from his canoe and coolly greets the startled shore guards.

Ben now pretends to be a great white medicine man and indulges in elaborate mummery to distract the Indians sufficiently to permit his escape. He first impresses them with his power by means of the spyglass he uses in his trade. Having never seen such an instrument, the Indians are easily persuaded that its magnification or diminution, depending upon which end one looks through, is the result of magic. Boden then astounds his audience by informing them that they are close to the site of whiskey springs, hence the smell of liquor in the air. After he has a large fire built, which he makes dazzling by throwing into it chunks of resin, he utters some supposed incantations and leads the Indians to the spot where the kegs had burst against a rock as they were rolled down a steep bank. There he points out small pools of whiskey in the rocks, and his ruse is complete. Saying that he needs more resin from his canoe in order to continue his conjuration and show them where to dig for firewater, Boden leaps aboard his bark vessel and attempts to escape. To his consternation, he discovers that the Pottawattamies have been smart enough to remove all of his paddles. As he pushes his canoe once again into the bed of tall wild rice, he is pursued by several savage young swimmers. When a captive canoe, containing Margery and towed by two of the swimmers, passes alongside his hiding place, Boden steps into this second boat and beats off the two surprised Pottawattamies with the butt of his rifle. He and Margery, who had attempted to come to his aid, escape with both of the canoes and recross the river to join Gershom, Dolly, and Pigeonswing.

The size of their group is increased the following day by the arrival of three newcomers: Parson Amen, Corporal Flint, and Onoah (better known as Scalping Peter). The Rev. Mr. Amen, missionary to the western Indians, is an ardent advocate of the theory [popular at the time] that the red men of America are descendants of the "lost tribes" of Israel. Amen is accompanied on his travels by an old soldier, Corporal Flint. Onoah, the third stranger, a man of about fifty, is a more complex character than either of the whites. Despite the fact that his tribal origin is unknown—he is sometimes called Nameless, at other times Tribe-less—Onoah has great status among many tribes as a result of his persistent efforts to unite all Indians against the white settlers. Like Tecumseh, with whom he is compared, he entertains the hope that by united effort, the Indians can drive the European settlers from the whole North American continent. He now visits the Pottawattamie camp and soon returns with the promise that those Indians will not attack the white group if the latter will leave the warriors' canoes tied along the riverbank to be picked up at a later time.

Boden, the Warings, Pigeonswing, and the three newcomers decide to leave the area now; to confuse the Pottawattamies, they travel not down river toward Lake Michigan (seemingly the easiest escape route) but upstream toward its source. They come, after more than a week of travel, to Castle Meal (a corruption of the French *Château au Miel*, meaning Honey Castle), a cabin built by Ben Boden near a clearing (opening) known as Prairie Round. There the men set to work at once chopping trees and digging a trench in order to construct palisades around the cabin.

On two successive nights the inhabitants of Castle Meal are awakened by the sound of a mysterious horn. On the second night Ben's dog, Hive, leads the bee-hunter and Corporal Flint to the event announced by these strange horn blasts: a council on Prairie Round of fifty Indian chiefs from several different tribes. Boden and Flint conceal themselves near the edge of the clearing to observe the proceedings. They see the arrival of Parson Amen and Scalping Peter, who debate before the assembly the missionary's contention that the Indians are really Jews. They note also the arrival of a runner who brings the news that Detroit, as well as Chicago, has also fallen to the British. At this point a herd of deer bursts upon the scene pursued by a wolf pack. The Indians kill several of the deer and begin shooting the wolves, but not before one of the predators overruns the position of the whites and tangles with Hive in a noisy fight. The eavesdroppers are exposed; but Peter, for reasons of his own, protects them from any hostile act. After Boden, Flint, and Amen return to their palisaded cabin, Pigeonswing takes the bee-hunter aside and warns him to depart at once and alone if he values his life at all. Boden will not leave, however, without Margery; Margery, in turn, will not desert her brother and sister-in-law.

On the following morning Boden is requested by the council of chiefs to demonstrate his art of finding honey. Again the bee-hunter attempts to intimidate the Indians with his purportedly magical powers—will they dare attack a great medicine man?—and he pretends to communicate with the bees for the purpose of prophecy. Supposedly they tell him where their honey is stored, and they also inform him that a pack of bears is molesting the hive, though it is obvious to the reader that Boden has deduced these facts from observable evidence. During all this flummery, which actually achieves nothing by way of safeguarding the whites, Margery's conversation with Peter softens somewhat that fanatic's hatred for them. She admits the truth of several of the charges leveled against the encroaching settlers. As Boden distributes great quantities of honey among the Indians, Peter confers privately with Parson Amen, exacting from the missionary a promise to do all he can to persuade Boden and Margery to be married at once, this very day.

As the simple wedding rites are being performed by Parson Amen, the assembled chiefs discuss the time and method for the slaughter of the six Americans. Peter now takes the position that the bee-hunter and his squaw should be spared, but he is opposed by the opportunistic Ungque (better known as Weasel), an ambitious demagogue who has long resented Peter's power. In the debate that develops, each speaker uses the high rhetoric and figurative language often attributed to Indian orators. Feeling in the council favors Weasel's argument, and the meeting ends when Peter concedes victory to his opponent.

The group at Castle Meal sees nothing of any Indians until breakfast time the next morning, when the Chippewa returns with venison and ducks he has killed. Although Pigeonswing has not mingled with the other Indians, lest he be recognized by one of the Pottawattamies, he senses that a crisis is at hand, and he uses all of his limited English to persuade first Margery and then Boden of the absolute necessity of their immediate departure. Scalping Peter, too, who appears shortly afterwards, leaves no doubt about the imminence of disaster. Meditative and melancholy, he finally reveals to Boden the decision of the council to kill all of the whites. It is evident from his speech and behavior that Peter is experiencing a powerful inner turmoil. Margery and Boden he admires and wishes to save; Amen, Flint, and the Warings he still views as part of that invading force he has worked twenty years to exterminate.

Peter takes Parson Amen and Corporal Flint to Prairie Round, where the chiefs now have their followers around them, some three hundred Indians in all. When the two white men are completely surrounded, they are told their fate: immediate execution. The missionary now realizes that he has been mistaken about the intentions of Onoah, but with the fortitude of a martyr, he does not quail before the truth. He preaches to the assembled red men, and just before his death, he prays for his executioners. This Christian principle of returning good for evil Peter had often heard enunciated by Amen, but he had never considered it humanly possible. Witnessing it now in actual practice, he is profoundly moved. The execution of Amen and his attitude toward his executioners constitute a close parallel to the Crucifixion. Corporal Flint, on the other hand, remains a soldier to the last. Although disarmed, he seizes Weasel's tomahawk, brains its owner, and, slashing right and left, wounds six or seven others before he is subdued. Because of his bravery, the Indians decide to honor him with the opportunity to show how much torture he can stand. Bending two strong saplings to the ground, they tie the old soldier by the arms between the two. When the young trees are released, they will lift him from the ground, separating his shoulder sockets and causing excruciating pain. But the corporal never feels the intended agony, for just as the withes are cut to release the saplings, a rifle shot rings out and Flint is killed instantly by a bullet through the temple. The chiefs suppose that act was committed by one of their own number intent upon taking some private revenge; it is, instead, a coup de grâce from the rifle of Pigeonswing.

It is now noticed that Peter is missing, and the chiefs suppose that he has gone to fetch the remainder of the condemned whites. When he does not reappear, the Indians decide to attack Castle Meal and capture its defenders. Hive barks at them from within the building, but no human form is seen at the palisades or near the cabin. Flaming arrows set fire to the roof, but still no one appears from within the cabin. At last the Indians realize what has happened: their quarry has escaped. Peter rejoins the Indians now; but in the meantime, he has given the inhabitants of Castle Meal timely warning and has guided them a quarter of a mile farther upstream in canoes to a place where they can hide safely. He now suggests to the other chiefs that their intended victims must have taken the obvious route of escape and fled downstream.

Ben Boden, now firmly convinced that the Michigan Territory will be unsafe until the war ends, hopes to be able, in some way, to return to the settlements in Pennsylvania. After remaining hidden for three days and nights, he and his party feel that it is time that they move again. Inasmuch as Peter has not returned to them, there is growing doubt in the minds of Boden and Pigeonswing about his real intentions. Boden is reluctant to go farther upstream, for if they continue in an easterly direction, they will eventually have to cross most of the Michigan peninsula by land, a hazardous journey among hostile tribes. The Chippewa now suggests that they float downstream behind their pursuers until they reach Lake Michigan, and this is the course ultimately agreed upon by all. They travel by night and rest by day hidden in swamps that drain into the river. After five nights of such guarded travel, they hear Indians ashore talking among themselves, but the canoes of the fugitives pass through the vicinity in the dark without being detected. The following day the travelers, weary as they are, sleep but little. Pigeonswing leaves at once to scout the area for Pottawattamies. When Margery strays beyond the limits of their hiding place, she encounters Peter; the two talk at length of the conversion of Tribeless to Christianity after he had seen the martyrdom of Parson Amen. After they pray together, Margery teaches Peter the Lord's Prayer. In their religious fervor, they unfortunately become oblivious to danger until they realize that their presence has been discovered by two youthful Pottawattamies posted along the riverbank as lookouts. As the guards rush back to give the alarm to the chiefs camped at some distance upstream, Peter urges the whites to flee immediately downstream, their only hope now being to reach Lake Michigan well in advance of their pursuers. Peter leads the way in his own canoe; and at the mouth of the Kalamazoo River, he distracts the attention of two canoeloads of braves until his white friends are safely past them and on the open waters of Lake Michigan.

Moving well away from shore, they paddle northward aided by a fresh breeze from the south. To increase speed and reduce lateral drift, Boden lashes their two canoes together and then swings a small lugsail from each side of this double-hull vessel. After sailing steadily in this manner for two days and nights, they reach the Straits of Mackinac and turn southeastward into Lake Huron. They are soon met by Peter and Pigeonswing, who have tracked Bear's Meat and a band of Menominees across the Michigan peninsula to intercept the fugitives in Lake Huron. Abandoning their own makeshift canoe, the two Indians join their friends, one in each canoe; again Peter serves as guide. Avoiding several ambushes laid for them, they proceed from Lake Huron into Lake St.

Clair, and then, via the Detroit River, into Lake Erie. As the group approaches Erie, Pennsylvania, its destination for now, Peter and Pigeonswing bid their white friends farewell in order to return to their own territory. Boden gives them one of the canoes plus his rifle and most of his personal possessions.

The final chapter is not an integral part of the plot but rather a postlude to the action. The narrative method changes from that of omniscient observer to that of autobiographical commentator, and the coda is told from the author's point of view. It is thirty-six years later when the author visits Michigan (now a place of fertile farms and pastoral villages) to meet those characters of the novel who are still alive. He comes as a result of receiving from Ben Boden, now nearing seventy, a set of notes that constitute the memoirs of his life in the oak openings. The author meets the elderly Ben and Margery Boden, their daughter (an only child), and their two granddaughters. He is also introduced to Pigeonswing during the Chippewa's annual visit to the Boden homestead. Most impressive of all those he meets is Peter, completely Christianized and dressed in conventional clothes of the settlers. Now in his late eighties, Peter, though still illiterate, has spent the intervening years preaching the Gospel and witnessing in behalf of God's "Blessed Son, who pray for dem dat kill him" (p. 497).

Rev. Mr. Amen, Bear's Meat, Benjamin Boden, Bough of Oak, Crowsfeather, Elksfoot, Corporal Flint, Onoah, Mrs. Osborne, Dorothy Osborne, Margery Osborne, Pigeonswing, Thunder Cloud, Ungque, Dorothy Waring, Gershom Waring, Margery Waring, Wolfeye.

The Pathfinder; or, The Inland Sea, 1840.

[This is the third of the five Leather-Stocking Tales in relation to plot, the fourth in order of composition.]

Accompanied by her seaman uncle, Charles Cap, Mabel Dunham travels toward Fort Oswego, on Lake Ontario, to visit there her father, a sergeant major in the British 55th Regiment. They are guided through the wilderness by a Tuscarora (Iroquois) named Arrowhead, who is accompanied by his wife, Dew-of-June. En route they come upon the camp of Natty Bumppo (the guide and scout now known as Pathfinder) and his adopted brother Chingachgook (Great Serpent), both sent as additional protection for Mabel and Cap as the French and Indian War flares up sporadically along the northern edges of the British colonies. With the scout and his Delaware companion is their friend Jasper Western, a young freshwater sailor on the "inland sea" (Lake Ontario).

An opinionated, dogmatic "old salt," Cap appreciates only the ocean mariner's way of life. He scorns in supercilious manner both Pathfinder's forest and Jasper's freshwater lake. As the whole party proceeds on its way, the scout and his friend retaliate with a frontier-style practical joke: they take Cap over the falls of the Oswego River in a bark canoe. The fun ends quickly when they discover that they are beset by a band of Iroquois on the warpath. [Although historically the Six Nations of Iroquois were allied with the British cause, there were always renegades whose services could be bought; more important, there were northern groups of Iroquois-speaking Indians, notably the Hurons, who, living in the French territory, were traditionally pro-French. Natty refers to all Iroquois-speaking Indians as "Mingos."]

Greatly outnumbered by the Iroquois, the party bound for Fort Oswego uses every possible stratagem to escape its pursuers: decoy, camouflage, the superior canoe handling of Jasper Western, and the reliable marksmanship of Pathfinder. Although they manage to place the river between themselves and their foes—they on the west bank, the Indians on the east—they lose one of their two canoes. When this light vessel hangs up on a shoal, it affords the Iroquois a potential means of reaching the opposite shore. As Jasper and Chingachgook swim to the shoal to recover the canoe, under the cloak of darkness, they discover that several Iroquois are on the same mission. By a series of maneuvers, Jasper and Chingachgook, unidentified in the indifferent light, secure the canoe; but the last Iroquois who might obstruct their flight recognizes the ruse and locks himself in fierce struggle with the Delaware chief. As the two grapple in the water, Jasper, unable to aid his friend in the dark and fearful of being captured by the now alerted Iroquois, paddles the canoe to the west bank. All but Pathfinder feel that an effort should be made to rescue Chingachgook, but Natty, confident of his friend's prowess, insists on their next dash down the river toward Fort Oswego. They are rejoined a short distance downstream by Chingachgook, richer by three Iroquois scalps. By now several of the attackers have been killed, but Pathfinder's group has been reduced by two through the desertion of Arrowhead and Dew-of-June. While he was among the Iroquois, Chingachgook discovered from their conversation that Arrowhead had deliberately led them into an ambush. Under the cover of darkness the refugees at last reach the safety of Lake Ontario.

Sergeant Dunham discloses that one of the reasons for inviting his daughter to this frontier outpost is to have her married to his close friend Pathfinder. Natty himself has serious doubts that a refined girl accustomed to life in the settlements could accept an illiterate woodsman or be happy in the rude living conditions of the frontier. The sergeant will not, however, listen to such misgivings. Shortly after his discussion with Pathfinder, Sergeant Dunham is summoned by his commanding officer, Major Duncan, who speaks on behalf of Lieutenant David Muir, regimental quartermaster, for the hand of Mabel. Duncan is surprised to learn of her betrothal to Pathfinder. Later in the evening the major breaks the news to his thrice-married fellow officer, and the two share a bottle of wine as they reminisce in broad Scotch dialect of their boyhood together in the old country. None of these men is aware that Mabel's heart has been won by young Jasper Western.

At the request of several soldiers, Major Duncan announces that a shooting match will be held on the following day. After firing at a conventional bull's-eye target, those still in contention must drive a nail into a stump with their bullets. All but three of the marksmen are eliminated by this test: the boastful David Muir, Jasper Western, and Pathfinder. When Jasper tells Pathfinder that he wishes to win the grand prize, a silk calash, in order to present it to Mabel Dunham, the scout decides to let his friend win. In the final trial of skill each contestant in turn shoots at a potato tossed up into the air. Muir misses completely; Jasper punctures the center of the potato; and Pathfinder deliberately nicks the skin. After Mabel receives the calash from Jasper and the shooting match ends, Natty confides to the girl that he could have defeated Jasper if he had wished to do so. To substantiate this claim, he kills with a single bullet two seagulls circling above the lake at some distance from them. In appreciation of his generosity to Jasper and of his superior skill, Mabel gives Pathfinder a silver brooch as a memento of the occasion.

Major Duncan places Sergeant Dunham in charge of a unit to relieve a force stationed among the Thousand Islands to intercept French supplies coming to the area by way of the St. Lawrence River. The detachment is to travel in the *Scud,* a cutter-rigged vessel of forty tons burden, Jasper Western, Master. Pathfinder and Chingachgook are among the combatants selected to go; Mabel and Cap join the party by way of diversion from the routine of garrison life. Just before the *Scud* sails, the major receives an anonymous letter accusing Jasper of being a French spy. Although Sergeant Dunham defends Jasper's loyalty when he is first apprised of the accusation, he later becomes suspicious himself, largely because the young sailor speaks fluent French. Cap believes the accusation for equally specious reasons: he imagines that Jasper's navigational tactics are French, and his prejudice against all freshwater sailors causes him now to see treasonous intent in the young man's every motion. Pathfinder staunchly supports the fidelity of his young friend.

En route to the Thousand Islands the *Scud* overtakes a canoe paddled by the treacherous Arrowhead and his wife, Dew-of-June. The two Indians are captured but manage to escape when they pretend to be going to their canoe for blankets. After Cap blames Jasper for the loss of the two prisoners, Sergeant Dunham has both Jasper and the pilot arrested and sent below deck. Command of the *Scud* is now transferred to Cap, who condescends to sail such an irregular little bark on what he considers a pond. Without charts or bearings, however, he becomes hopelessly lost as they approach the St. Lawrence River and the Thousand Islands.

Although they are apparently close to their destination, they are suddenly driven westward by a heavy storm. They are swept past their starting point at Fort Oswego, and on toward Niagara and the end of the lake, held by the French. At one point they come within hailing distance of the *Montcalm*, a larger and better-armed French vessel. As they are about to be driven on the rocky shore, the baffled but stubbornly conceited Cap finally agrees to consult Jasper Western concerning means of saving the *Scud*. Brought up on deck, Jasper advises immediate anchoring, a move so unacceptable to Cap's saltwater training that he scoffs at it in high indignation. As a last resort, Dunham returns command of the vessel to Western, who confounds Cap even further by steering the *Scud* directly toward the steepest bluff, knowing that from it there must be an undertow, a current returning to the lake the water driven against the shore by the strong east wind. Locating such an undertow, Jasper knows that his anchors will hold and that he can ride out the storm in safety.

With its ground tackle holding, the *Scud* awaits a change in the wind in order to sail east again. Sergeant Dunham, Mabel, and Pathfinder go ashore in a canoe, the father's purpose being to provide the guide an appropriate time to propose to his daughter. This Pathfinder does in his untutored and backhanded way. Considering the difference in their ages—she is twenty, while he is in his mid-thirties—Mabel is surprised by Natty's proposal and equally surprised by the fact that her father had encouraged this suit. Refusal of Pathfinder's offer is made difficult for Mabel by the great respect and admiration she has for the man. Natty is so enamored of Mabel—this is his only active pursuit of a woman in the Leather-Stocking Tales—that he momentarily weeps at his rejection.

When the *Scud* sails east, its access to the garrison at Oswego is cut off by the *Montcalm*, which lies in wait just beyond the range of the fort's artillery. Outdistancing the French warship, Jasper finally eludes it completely among the Thousand Islands, where he threads his way easily to the secret British outpost. After the new contingent lands and the old embarks, the *Scud* sets sail again almost immediately for Oswego.

At this new island quarters, the thrice-married Muir continues to bore Mabel with his exaggerated but insincere gallantries. As Sergeant Dunham prepares to lead two boatloads of troops to intercept French supplies bound for Frontenac, he calls his daughter to him in order to discuss her future. He could die in battle happily, he tells her, if he knew that she were to wed Pathfinder. His reluctance to insist on her marrying the guide prompts Mabel to promise to do just that if Pathfinder should propose again.

Only six men, including the ineffectual Lieutenant Muir and Charles Cap, remain on Station Island after the raiding party leaves. Besides Mabel, supposedly only one other woman is present. She is Jennie, the wife of a soldier named Sandy. Mabel is surprised, therefore, to be visited on the following day by Dew-of-June, who urges her to sleep henceforth in the blockhouse. An Indian attack on the island is imminent, and June (as she is often called) has come to warn only Mabel; if the men are informed of the forthcoming strike, June says, her husband will kill her for having alerted his foe. June also reveals that Arrowhead wants Mabel for a second wife in his wigwam. After the Indian woman departs, Mabel finds a piece of red bunting tied to a tree, an obvious signal to someone. She takes the banner to Muir, who suggests that it resembles bunting he has seen aboard the *Scud*—a further intimation of treason on the part of Jasper. After Mabel has left him, however, Muir attaches the banner to a tree in an even more noticeable position than it had had earlier.

Some twenty Indians attack the island, led by Arrowhead and loosely supervised by the French Captain Sanglier. Corporal McNab, his three regular soldiers, and Jennie are all killed and scalped. Cap and Muir seem to have disappeared. Mabel and June retreat to the blockhouse and bar the heavy door. The logs of the blockhouse are still too green to burn easily, but actually neither Arrowhead nor Sanglier wants it destroyed. To set up a perfect ambush for the returning British troops, they wish to keep the scene completely unchanged. To achieve this end, they even prop up the bodies of the slain redcoats in likely postures.

Mabel and June sleep in the blockhouse safely throughout the night. On the following day, the Indians, threatening to storm the blockhouse, announce that Muir and Cap will be scalped unless Mabel surrenders the little fortress and its valuable supplies. Brought forward, Muir pleads with Mabel to capitulate; Cap urges her to resist. A stalemate develops when Mabel tells the besiegers that the rifle protruding from one of the loopholes is that of Pathfinder. Later in the day Mabel sees Chingachgook approaching the island by canoe, and she waves to him. At dusk she sends June to serve as lookout on the upper level of the blockhouse while she herself stands ready to unbar its door if Chingachgook should appear. To her great surprise, however, the person she admits proves to be not the Delaware but Pathfinder.

After the expedition sinks three boatloads of French supplies, Pathfinder and Chingachgook, traveling in their respective canoes, return to Station Island more quickly than do the heavier boats carrying troops. Detecting and avoiding the ambush, Natty hopes to be able to warn Dunham of the well-laid trap, but the sergeant and his troops arrive before any communication can reach them. They march blindly into the ambush and suffer heavy casualties. Sergeant Dunham, mortally wounded, staggers to the blockhouse door and is dragged inside by Pathfinder and Mabel. Cap, effecting his escape during the massacre, arrives safely at the log stronghold.

Muir now appears outside the blockhouse and tries, unsuccessfully, to persuade Pathfinder to surrender. The attack begins. The Indians fire into the blockhouse the single shell available for the howitzer captured the day before from the French. Although this blast causes some damage, the log walls remain impervious to the rifle balls that follow. Their next and expected stratagem is to attempt to set fire to the building. The flames from the burning brush heaped up against the front wall are easily extinguished by the water Cap pours on them from above, but not before their light has enabled Pathfinder to dispatch one of the enemy with a shot from his trusty rifle, Killdeer. This ends the attack for the night.

When the *Scud* arrives the next day, Jasper approaches with great caution, informed by Chingachgook, who is aboard, of the state of affairs on the island. Sweeping in close to shore, he tows away the two British boats and all of the canoes tied up to them, thus making escape for the Indians impossible. A shower of small shot from the *Scud's* howitzer, along with deadly fire from Killdeer and from Chingachgook's rifle, soon forces the enemy to request terms of surrender. With Lieutenant Muir interpreting for him, Captain Sanglier agrees to return all British prisoners (six of whom, besides Muir, have survived), to surrender all arms (including the knives and tomahawks of the Indians), and to depart at once. Jasper recovers the Indian boats and then, when they are loaded, tows them a mile to leeward of the island; to each boat he allows but one oar, an implement with which they can steer to the Canadian shore.

Of the enemy forces only Arrowhead, June, and Captain Sanglier remain as the French officer and Lieutenant Muir draw up and sign the documents of surrender. With both Sergeant Dunham and his next in command, Corporal McNab, dead, the quartermaster (who had not fired a shot or otherwise aided the British effort) at once takes command and claims credit for the victory. He promptly orders that Jasper Western be arrested again for treason. Even the cunning Arrowhead is outraged by Muir's duplicity. Before anyone can stop him, the Tuscarora stabs Muir to death and then slips away into the brush; he is trailed by Chingachgook, who soon returns with a bloody scalp. Jasper now appeals to Sanglier to identify his spy among the British forces. Sanglier points to Muir and then dumps from the dead man's purse a number of double-Louis coins, part of his espionage pay from the French. It is also revealed now that it was Muir who had written the anonymous letter to Major Duncan accusing Jasper of treason and that it was Muir who had betrayed to the French the exact location of the British outpost in the otherwise French-controlled Thousand Islands area.

While the affairs of war have been advancing thus rapidly, so have the affairs of the heart. Pathfinder unwittingly jolts Jasper when he discloses his intention of marrying Mabel, a step to be taken with the approval of her father. It is clear that the scout is totally oblivious to the affection felt by Jasper and Mabel for each other. The seaman controls his strong emotions and congratulates his friend as the person most worthy of wedding the beautiful and capable Mabel Dunham. As Sergeant Dunham is dying, he clasps Mabel's and what he thinks is Pathfinder's hands, symbolically uniting the couple. The male hand he clutches, however, is Jasper's rather than Natty's, but no one tells the sergeant of this error as he draws his last breath. Immediately after the death scene Jasper and Pathfinder again discuss the latter's forthcoming marriage to Mabel, and only now does the ingenuous woodsman discover that his friend too is desperately in love with the girl. The friendship between the two men is so strong that each defers to the other, and both suggest that they discuss their dilemma later.

After a delay of three days, the *Scud* is ready to return to Fort Oswego, and all are aboard except the love triangle and the grieving Dew-of-June. As the first three are about to paddle to the ship in canoes, Pathfinder insists on resolving the marriage problem. With remarkable steadiness and candor he reviews the relationships among the three and acknowledges that the only woman he has ever loved would be better matched with the younger and more-educated Jasper than with himself. So impressive is his magnanimity that Jasper and Mabel momentarily feel guilty for their unspoken but clearly recognized love for each other. With a tearful embrace, Mabel and Pathfinder bid each other farewell, after which the girl kneels to receive the blessing of the woodsman. The essential saintliness of Natty Bumppo is perhaps most apparent in this scene. As the young lovers embark for Fort Oswego, where they are to be married at once, Pathfinder remains on the island.

Finding June sorrowing over the grave of Arrowhead, Natty assures the forlorn woman of his understanding and friendship. Each day he brings her game which he has killed and cooked, but he maintains a proper relationship with the woman by sleeping on an adjacent island. After a month elapses and the falling leaves signal the end of the summer season, Chingachgook returns, and the three travel together to Fort Oswego. There Pathfinder talks for the last time with Jasper and Mabel as he visits them in their new log house. Leaving Dew-of-June with the Westerns, Pathfinder and Chingachgook disappear into the forest.

After living for a year on the shore of Lake Ontario, Jasper and Mabel move to New York City, where Jasper becomes a successful merchant. Over a period of several years, Mabel receives three large parcels of valuable furs, the sender unidentified, though she has no doubt that they are the gifts of Pathfinder. Once later in life, after the Revolution, she sees a renowned scout called Leather-Stocking gazing at her during a trip she is taking with her several sons along the Mohawk River. Although they do not speak or otherwise acknowledge each other, Mabel knows intuitively that this elderly figure is the Pathfinder she had known in her youth.

Anderson, Arrowhead, Nathaniel Bumppo (Pathfinder), Charles Cap, Chingachgook, Dew-of-June, Major Duncan, Mabel Dunham, Sergeant Thomas Dunham, Jennie, Corporal McNab, Lieutenant David Muir, Sandy, Captain Sanglier, Captain Jasper Western.

The Pilot: A Tale of the Sea, 1824.

An American frigate and her supporting schooner enter a shoal-filled bay off Northumberland (northeastern England) on a bleak day in December during the American Revolution. Their immediate purpose is to pick up from the rocky cliffs someone referred to at first simply as a pilot. There is a suggestion that he may be a very special pilot when Captain Munson, commander of the frigate, orders his first officer, Lieutenant Edward Griffith, to stand offshore in the ship's barge, filled with marines, while Lieutenant Richard Barnstable, commander of the schooner *Ariel*, goes ashore in a whaleboat with a handful of men to bring off the stranger. (Griffith, an educated man who received his commission directly, is the senior lieutenant; Barnstable, who ran away from school, worked his way up through the ranks.)

With Barnstable, as he goes ashore, is his trusty companion and first nautical mentor, the "old salt" and coxswain Tom Coffin, who carries with him everywhere the harpoon used during his whaling days. The most colorful figure in the novel, Long Tom—he is well over six feet tall—is a member of the most renowned family of American whalers, the Coffins of Nantucket. He himself had spent few hours of his life at Nantucket or on land anywhere.

"I was born on board a chebacco-man [a type of vessel used on the Newfoundland fishing banks], and never could see the use of more land than now and then a small island to raise a few vegetables and to dry your fish. I'm sure the sight of it always makes me feel uncomfortable unless we have the wind dead offshore" (p. 20).

Before Barnstable encounters and identifies the pilot, he is intercepted by Katherine Plowden, his intelligent and high-spirited fiancée, disguised as a man. Katherine and her cousin, Cecilia Howard, have been held virtual captives by the latter's uncle, Colonel Howard, a wealthy South Carolina Tory who retreated to England at the outbreak of the Revolution; guardian of both his niece and Katherine, he has, mindful of his obligation to protect them, compelled the girls to accompany him. Katherine will not agree to board the *Ariel* until her cousin (engaged to Edward Griffith) is also willing and able to leave England. Giving Barnstable a written description of their place of confinement and a code book to be used in signaling, Katherine disappears into the brush.

By the time that Barnstable is again on the deck of the *Ariel* and Griffith, accompanied by the pilot, is aboard the frigate, the sea heaves with a strong ground swell that threatens to drive the larger vessel ashore on the rocky coast. As they wait for a wind, their situation grows steadily more perilous, and Griffith thinks that nothing can now save them from destruction. When a tempest begins to blow, the strange pilot adds sail instead of reducing it and, with what seems to be miraculous skill, extricates the frigate from the shoals and carries it clear of the land. Known to no one, at this point, but Captain Munson, the pilot (he is sometimes called Mr. Gray but more often the Pilot, spelled now with a capital *P*), the man who saves the ship, is John Paul Jones, America's first naval hero.

Captain Munson now calls a meeting of his officers to plan an expedition ashore to capture some prominent Englishmen to be held as hostages. Griffith, placed in command of the landing party, is to be supported by twenty marines under Captain Manual. When Griffith objects to taking along Mr. Gray on such a difficult mission, the Pilot produces a paper and asks the lieutenant to examine it. We are not told the contents of the document, but it identifies for Griffith the man whom we later infer to be John Paul Jones. After the military plans are complete, Barnstable and Griffith, old friends, talk in private about their hopes of locating Katherine and Cecilia during the foray ashore. The invading force transfers to the *Ariel*, which can run in close enough to the beach to permit an easy landing in small boats.

The scene shifts now to St. Ruth's Abbey, an old, partly fortified mansion, which the elderly Colonel Howard had rented on his arrival in England. The Colonel drinks and talks with two friends: Christopher Dillon, attorney, a morose, self-centered, and malign man who seeks (with the encouragement of the Colonel) the hand of Cecilia Howard; and Captain Borroughcliffe, a recruiting officer and commander of a company of green troops guarding the Abbey. The gentlemen move to the ladies' apartment to take coffee, and there they engage in repartee with Katherine, Cecilia, and their older companion, Alice Dunscombe. The verbal exchange between Katherine and Colonel Howard is especially sharp as the two voice diametrically opposed views of the American Revolution. Cecilia, shy and retiring, says little; Alice, loyal to the Crown, has no cause to quarrel with her host.

The social hour is terminated by the announcement that three prowlers have been captured on the premises by the sentries. Recent raids by Americans (including the unnamed John Paul Jones) have made residents of the coastal area suspicious of unidentified strangers. Well might they be anxious about the trio just apprehended, for they are Jones himself, Edward Griffith, and Captain Manual, all disguised as common seamen. After questioning the men, Colonel Howard concludes that they are simply what they claim to be: unemployed deckhands looking for work. Dillon does not agree with this assessment and urges Borroughcliffe to keep the three under arrest. A compromise is reached whereby the men will be detained but will be housed in comfortable rooms in the Abbey rather than in the guardhouse. Dillon, pretending to depart for a fox hunt in the morning in another town, rides to a nearby British military base to report his suspicion that one of the three captives is Edward Griffith, an enemy officer. Colonel Howard and Captain Borroughcliffe resume their drinking after leaving the apartment of the ladies.

During the night the three women bribe the sentinel stationed outside the rooms of the captives and are permitted to talk with the Americans. Katherine and Cecilia promise to send with Griffith's breakfast means of escape. A more animated discussion develops between the Pilot and Alice Dunscombe, who was once betrothed to Jones and who still loves him despite her disapproval of his activities on behalf of the revolutionary cause. Like Colonel Howard, she thinks the American Revolution not only treasonous but also sacrilegious.

Still later, Captain Borroughcliffe, by now befuddled by too much wine, comes to Captain Manual's room to attempt to enlist the marine in the British army. Earlier he had detected in Manual the bearing and manner of a military man. When Borroughcliffe releases not only Manual but his two companions as well, the sentry, Peters, observing his officer's irresponsible condition, rushes to a window to call the sergeant of the guard. Before Peters can spread the alarm, however, Griffith wrenches from his hands his musket and floors the man with it. All three captives depart.

When the escape is discovered, soldiers are sent to scour the coastline for the men. Among the troops are a number of light dragoons who have come at the request of Christopher Dillon. The lawyer guides them to the coast where they see a small boat lying offshore, apparently waiting to pick up someone. While Cornet Fitzgerald and his cavalry search the bluffs that rise from the beaches, Dillon rides at a gallop to a nearby naval post and persuades the commander of the *Alacrity*, a cutter harbored there, to attempt to trap the schooner anchored farther out in the bay. This the captain of the cutter agrees to do, but he requires the unwilling Dillon to remain on board and serve as their guide to the location he has described.

While the Pilot, Griffith, and Manual are ashore reconnoitering, their return is awaited by Barnstable, Coffin, and several sailors in the *Ariel's* whaleboat, which they keep just outside the breaking surf. When their companions do not return and the second day's wait begins, the men in the open boat become so bored that they pass their time pursuing and eventually killing a large right whale. Tom Coffin is the principal performer in this melodramatic little episode. Before the whale turns belly up and dies, it tows the boat farther than it had been from the *Ariel;* thus when the British cutter bears down upon it, the Americans have a rigorous stint of rowing to reach the schooner. No sooner are they aboard than the *Ariel* is engaged in battle by the *Alacrity*. The cutter makes the mistake of not closing in at once on its prey, for the schooner has a long-range deck gun known as a Long Tom which is fired, quite appropriately, by Long Tom Coffin with deadly accuracy. By the time that the *Alacrity* pulls abreast of the *Ariel*, the former has already suffered heavy losses. Her commander's strategy now is not to resort to exchanging broadside for broadside with the *Ariel* but to board the schooner, and this he attempts to do. The boarders are repulsed; when Tom Coffin pins the English captain to the mast with a harpoon, the battle is over. Dillon, cringing with fear, is taken prisoner and held aboard the *Ariel*. After the dead and wounded are given due care, Barnstable again moves toward the shore where the Pilot, Griffith, and Manual are to be retrieved; but he flies a union jack above his own flag, pretending that the British have won the battle and are in possession of the schooner. Since the noise of the fight has probably brought spectators to the shore, this is the only strategy he can employ to approach the land without causing a general alarm that would eventually bring heavy warships after them.

After the trio of Americans escape from St. Ruth's Abbey, they proceed, under cover of darkness, about half a mile. There the Pilot informs his two companions that he must go apart by himself on secret business. Until he returns, Griffith, Manual, and the latter's twenty marines are to hide inside an old ruin. Manual foolishly insists on posting a sentinel, who soon challenges Captain Borroughcliffe and his troops. The sentinel is killed immediately, along with five of his comrades at arms; four more are seriously wounded, and Griffith is recaptured. The Americans have no real choice but to surrender. As the wounded are being treated, the grim scene is relieved by a comic episode. Colonel Howard, the old soldier, cannot remain inactive during all of this excitement, so he now appears on the scene shouting orders to *his* troops, Caesar and Pompey, two confused black slaves from St. Ruth's Abbey. The Colonel upbraids Griffith, son of an old friend, for his treason to the Crown. He also erroneously informs the lieutenant that the *Ariel* has been captured by the *Alacrity*. As he is talking, he is interrupted by the return of the Pilot, whom his two-man contingent charges quite ineffectually. The Pilot escapes.

When Griffith and his companions are many hours overdue at the shore, Barnstable returns to the *Ariel* convinced that they have been taken prisoner. He now promises Dillon his freedom if he will agree to go to the Abbey, accompanied by Long Tom Coffin, and have Griffith liberated in exchange. Dillon accepts this proposal at once, and Barnstable asks him for no other guarantee than the word of a gentleman. Leaving the *Ariel* in command of the youthful Midshipman Merry, Barnstable, Coffin, and Dillon go ashore in a whaleboat. Coffin and Dillon then proceed toward the Abbey; Barnstable, awaiting the return of Coffin and Griffith, lies offshore a few yards beyond the breakers. Knowing something of the dastardly character of Dillon, the reader is not surprised to discover his treachery at this point. He has Tom Coffin imprisoned, and he reveals to British authorities the truth about the recent naval engagement and the false colors now being flown by the *Ariel* and its captive ship, the *Alacrity*. Orders are issued for the capture of Barnstable, and a dispatch is sent to the commander of a shore battery to sink the *Ariel* at once.

Borroughcliffe, always looking for recruits, takes Tom Coffin to his quarters, feeds him, and tells him of the dismal prospect for the Americans, both those imprisoned at the Abbey and those still afloat. Then he suggests that the coxswain save himself from execution as a spy by joining the British army. Infuriated by such an insult, Tom overpowers Borroughcliffe and leaves him bound and gagged. He then recaptures Dillon at the entrance of the apartment of Katherine and Cecilia, who guide him back to the coast. The stereotyped old tar can navigate anywhere in the seven seas, but he cannot find his way over the two-mile stretch of land to the shore. Despite Dillon's pleas for mercy, he is led by the collar back to the sea and there thrown aboard the whaleboat. All hands now strain at the oars to reach the *Ariel* before either the impending storm or the shore battery can destroy her.

To move the schooner out of the shoal-filled bay and beyond the range of the powerful piece of coast artillery, they must sail against a strong northeast wind blowing out of the North Sea. Their progress is slow but steady until a direct hit carries away the main mast. Now unable to make any headway, they cut down the rest of the spars and rigging to reduce the surface exposed to the wind, and drop their anchors. The force of the wind and the drift of the water are so strong that their anchor hawsers are broken, and the *Ariel* is driven toward the rocks. Ordering his men into the whaleboat, Barnstable intends to go down with his ship. Long Tom grabs his commander from behind, throws him into the whaleboat, and in the same motion releases the boat's painter. Most of those in the whaleboat reach the sandy beach safely, but Christopher Dillon and Long Tom Coffin die, the former drowned when he tries to swim to shore, the latter going down with the wreck. When the storm subsides, the body of Dillon is washed ashore; that of Coffin is never found, the sea having apparently reclaimed its own.

As Barnstable and Merry lead their ten surviving seamen to the old ruin, where they are all to hide for the night, the two officers sight in the distance the sail of their frigate. Taking courage from the approach of such substantial support, they plan to persevere in their efforts to liberate Griffith. Merry relieves a passing pack peddler of his wares and, disguising himself appropriately, proceeds in the early evening to the Abbey in the role of the itinerant vender. His costume is convincing, but his ignorance about the merchandise he offers for sale betrays him before the sharp scrutiny of Captain Borroughcliffe, and now he too is taken prisoner.

While Katherine and Cecilia are walking in the garden, Katherine observes a signal from Barnstable spread on the wall of the ruin. By using their prearranged code they are able to apprise each other of the circumstances prevailing at their respective locations and to agree upon a time and place to meet. During this meeting Barnstable reveals to Katherine his plan to attack the Abbey that night, capture all its inhabitants, and convey them to the frigate. Knowing that Griffith, who has been well treated as a captive, will probably not concur entirely with his plan, Barnstable intends to supersede the authority of his superior. As a prisoner, Griffith, he reasons, has only nominal, not active, authority.

As the residents of the Abbey are leaving the dinner table, Barnstable and his seamen burst in upon them and declare them all prisoners. Captain Borroughcliffe calmly refuses to surrender, and with good reason: apprised of the American landing and knowing its limited strength, he has ordered the Abbey encircled with regular redcoats to trap the invaders. Redcoats appear now at the door and effectively close the trap. Alice Dunscombe moves courageously through the doorway to stand between the opposing forces and plead that there be no bloodshed. Suddenly, however, she grows speechless and immobile, staring straight ahead. What she sees is the Pilot, who has landed with a strong force of marines from the frigate and has completely surrounded the British troops.

As Barnstable predicted, he and Griffith now disagree about the procedure to be followed. So heated becomes their difference of opinion that they draw their swords and momentarily clash. At the sound of steel against steel, Katherine and Cecilia rush to the sides of their respective lovers and declare their willingness to accompany the men wherever they may go. At this critical point, the Pilot exerts his authority: ordering the combatants to desist, he announces that all present must move at once to the seashore. Not a soul is left behind lest he be the means of spreading the alarm to other British forces.

When they reach the shore, Griffith informs Borroughcliffe, much to the surprise of the recruiting officer, that once safe embarkation of the rest is assured, he and his redcoats will be released. The women, too, are free to stay or leave, as they wish; Alice Dunscombe declares her intention to remain in England. After the frigate's barge, commanded by Barnstable and carrying Colonel Howard and the two young women, departs, Alice and the Pilot, moving apart, bid each other farewell forever. Although she still feels affection for the man, she cannot overcome her nationalist and royalist conditioning sufficiently to accept him as a husband.

As the last boats are ready to be pushed off, the released Borroughcliffe, who feels that his hospitality and gentlemanly behavior have been abused, demands a duel first with the Pilot and then with Captain Manual. The Pilot simply ignores him, but Manual accepts the challenge.

The antagonists fire their pistols simultaneously, the redcoat receiving a wound in the leg and the marine a crease across his scalp. They shake hands cordially and part the best of friends as the boatswain's pipe signals the departure of the Americans.

The boats all move to the captured British cutter *Alacrity*, standing a few miles offshore under the command of David Boltrope, the sailing master [nautical housekeeper] of the frigate. Filled to capacity and towing a string of boats, the cutter heads for the open sea, where at dawn its lookouts sight the frigate. A short run brings the two vessels alongside of each other, and all but the cutter's crew are transferred to the larger ship. Captain Munson graciously welcomes Colonel Howard aboard and extending to him the hospitality befitting his rank, assigns to him and his wards the vessel's two staterooms. With less formal but more hearty greetings, he welcomes back the participants of the partially successful expedition ashore.

A ninety-gun ship of the line now comes in pursuit of the Americans, but the frigate outruns this heavy vessel before its large-calibre cannon can find the range. Not to be so easily outrun, however, are two British frigates that accompany the huge man-of-war. The first of these is disabled with well-timed broadsides, and the second is eventually eluded as the Pilot takes his ship through some dangerous shoals that the British do not dare attempt. Predictably, the success of the Americans was achieved at a price. A number of sailors were killed, including Captain Munson, who was carried overboard by a direct hit on the quarterdeck. Mortally wounded by that same shot are Boltrope, the sailing master, and Colonel Howard; after the battle, each expires in a protracted and pathetic death scene. The most urgent of Colonel Howard's last request is his wish to see the marriage of his niece to Griffith and his other ward to Barnstable. Striving to do his pledged duty in behalf of these girls, he wants to see them properly married before he dies. The wedding ceremonies are performed at once by the ship's chaplain.

Transferring command of the frigate to Barnstable, Griffith orders him to return to America at once. He himself takes command of the *Alacrity*, and, accompanied by his bride and the Pilot, sails for the coast of Holland, where he goes to keep his pledge to bury Colonel Howard in consecrated ground. While they are still well off the Dutch coast, the Pilot bids them farewell and goes his own way alone in a small skiff. The Griffiths never see him again.

Edward and Cecilia visit Paris before returning to their own country, where the lieutenant, promoted in rank, remains in the navy until peace is restored. Barnstable, after returning to Boston, is promoted also and given regular command of a warship. Temporarily out of the service after the war, he subsequently accepts a new commission to help develop the new United States Navy. Captain Manual, returning to the regular army and participating in the western campaigns of "Mad" Anthony Wayne, acquires sufficient military reputation to be placed in command of a fort on the St. Lawrence River. There he soon discovers that the commanding officer of the British base on the opposite side of the river is a one-legged officer named Major Borroughcliffe. These two old soldiers meet to carouse and enjoy each other's company in a hut maintained on the neutral ground of an island in the middle of the river. Returning to his duty one morning after a night of heavy drinking, Manual forgets the password and is shot by his own sentry. Borroughcliffe dies of a high fever brought on by the inroads he makes on a quarter-keg of Madeira while mourning for his friend.

The novel closes with a scene in the year 1792 in the Griffith home, where Edward reads a newspaper account of the death of John Paul Jones. After extolling to Cecilia the valor of one she had known as the Pilot, Edward indicates that great man, like all other mortals, had had his weakness, namely, an excessively romantic love of glory that required that his less honorable exploits be veiled in secrecy. Maintaining his promise to protect Jones's anonymity during the Northumbrian episode, Edward carefully removes the newspaper from the table and declines to tell even his beloved wife the identity of the Pilot.

Lieutenant Richard Barnstable, Ben, David Boltrope, Captain Borroughcliffe, Caesar, Tom Coffin, Christopher Dillon, Sergeant Drill, Alice Dunscombe, Cornet Fitzgerald, Gray, Lieutenant Edward Griffith, Cecilia Howard, Colonel George Howard, Jack Joker, John Paul Jones, Captain Manual, Midshipman Andrew Merry, Captain Munson, Nick, Peters, Katherine Plowden, Pompey, Sam, Lieutenant Somers, Tourniquet.

The Pioneers; or, The Sources of the Susquehanna, 1823.

[This is the fourth of the five Leather-Stocking Tales in relation to plot, the first in order of composition.]

Near sunset of Christmas Eve, 1793, Judge Marmaduke Temple and his daughter, Elizabeth, are approaching Templeton, a village of Central New York, in a sleigh driven by Agamemnon, a Negro slave. Elizabeth is returning home after four years spent in the city completing her education. When a deer, pursued by hounds, crosses their path, Judge Temple fires at it with his shotgun, but the animal continues to flee until two rifle shots bring it to earth. Natty Bumppo, an aged woodsman, and a youthful companion emerge from the place where they had been hiding to ambush the deer. Hoping to lay claim to at least part of the carcass, the Judge insists that at least one of his five buckshot must have struck the deer. Natty's young friend proves the Judge in error by pointing out four bullet holes in the tree behind which he had been hiding and a fifth bullet hole in his own arm. The ownership of the deer is all but forgotten as the Judge and Elizabeth, shocked at the mishap, persuade the reluctant youth, who goes by the name of Oliver Edwards, to return with them to Templeton for treatment of his wound.

The Temple estate through which the sleigh now passes had been earlier part of the property of a business partnership between Temple and Edward Effingham, both then young Pennsylvanians, the former a Quaker. The partnership had deliberately been concealed from Effingham's father, a retired British major who disliked Quakers and who eschewed, as a matter of professional principle, all mercantile connections. The Revolutionary War had separated the partners, with Effingham remaining loyal to England, Temple supporting the patriot cause, and the separation continued after the war when Effingham failed to reappear. Temple had then moved permanently to Central New York, where he had added to his extensive holdings by purchasing at low rates Loyalist lands that had been confiscated. The party soon comes within view of the Temple mansion, a large but architecturally dubious structure conceived by Richard Jones, the Judge's cousin and business manager, and erected by Hiram Doolittle, an erratic, incompetent builder and jack-of-all-trades.

The travelers are met by a welcoming party of Temple's friends in a second sleigh driven by Richard Jones. With Jones is Major Frederick (Fritz) Hartmann, an elderly German descendant of Palatines settled along the Mohawk River shortly after the reign of Queen Anne; he is a frequent guest at the Temple mansion. A second friend is Monsieur Le Quoi, a political refugee from the French island of Martinique, who operates a small general store at Templeton and, near the end of the novel, moves to Paris. Among the welcomers is also Mr. Grant, Episcopal minister and temporary rector of the newly constructed and still interdenominational St. Paul's Church. Jones's poor horsemanship almost causes his companions and himself to be thrown over a cliff, but the wounded Oliver Edwards, dashing forward from Temple's sleigh, saves the welcomers.

At the mansion two others welcome the Judge and Elizabeth: Remarkable Pettibone, the competent but presumptuous and disputatious housekeeper, and Ben Stubbs (called Ben Penguillan or Pump), the majordomo who still thinks and talks like the bluff British sailor he had been during much of his previous life. Oliver Edwards's wound is to be treated by Dr. Elnathan Todd, a Yankee pretender to more medical knowledge than he possesses. After the doctor makes an incision in the skin of Edwards's arm, the shot falls out unaided. Indian John, or John Mohegan (whose Indian name is Chingachgook, meaning Big Serpent), appears and proceeds to dress the wound quietly and efficiently. Oliver Edwards then leaves after insisting on his right to the carcass of the deer; Judge Temple acknowledges his claim but is baffled by the younger man's barely restrained hostility.

The Judge and his friends dine well at the mansion and then proceed to a Christmas Eve church service conducted by Rev. Mr. Grant. Afterwards the characters divide into three groups. Oliver Edwards and John Mohegan walk home with Rev. Mr. Grant, a widower, and his daughter Louisa, the latter the sole survivor of six children in the family. Oliver claims Delaware descent, a claim which the Grants take literally; his Indian lineage, however, is from his grandfather, an adopted member of the Delawares, who called him Fire-eater. Oliver condemns Temple for being unjust and rapacious, one whose sole objective is the acquisition of gold. Grant supposes that this enmity results from Temple's accidental wounding of the young man, but Oliver hints vaguely of some greater evil committed by the Judge. Meanwhile, the Judge and his friends gather at the Bold Dragoon Tavern, owned and operated by Captain Hollister, a Revolutionary War sergeant now commander of the local militia, and his good-natured, garrulous Irish wife, Betty. Having left the Grant residence, John Mohegan also joins the group and proceeds to become helplessly drunk. Amid the revelry of song and drink, melancholy notes are struck by Natty Bumppo's recollections of John as a powerful chief and of Fire-eater as the original white owner of the area. A third scene is set at the Temple mansion, where, after Elizabeth retires for the night, Remarkable Pettibone and Ben Pump, both comic characters, drink and quarrel in slapstick fashion.

The next morning Elizabeth presents Richard Jones with a Christmas present: a commission as sheriff secured for him by Judge Temple. The group from the mansion then proceeds to the annual Christmas-day turkey shoot. Abraham Freeborn (Brom), a free Negro, is the proprietor of this event, providing a large turkey to be won by the marksman who can hit its head at a distance of a hundred yards. Elizabeth chooses Natty as her champion at this contest and pays his entrance fee. After Billy Kirby, a boisterous woodchopper, and the injured Oliver fail to hit the bird, Natty kills it and presents it to Elizabeth, who, in turn, gives it to Oliver as a peace offering from her family. Oliver is then offered the job of private secretary to the Judge, the position held by Richard Jones before his appointment as sheriff. Both the Judge and Elizabeth are baffled by the impoverished Oliver's reluctance to accept such a fine offer. Richard Jones, jealous of Oliver, attributes his strange behavior to what he insists are the young man's half-breed origins. En route home to the cabin of Natty and John Mohegan, Oliver laments that he has agreed to live and work thereafter in the dwelling of his "greatest enemy."

At the end of April the citizens of Templeton organize, under Richard Jones's direction, to shoot pigeons migrating northward in great flocks that darken the sky. In the resulting mayhem thousands of birds are slain needlessly and wastefully. Natty Bumppo, after shooting the single bird he needs for food, leaves the scene uttering his condemnation of the sinful carnage, and afterwards Judge Temple acknowledges the error of his townsmen's ways. Soon after this a similar onslaught against Nature is made as part of Lake Otsego is seined and more fish are taken than can be consumed by the entire settlement. Again Natty inveighs against the waste, demonstrating the moral norm by spearing just the one fish that is needed at his cabin. The fishing ends in near tragedy as Ben Pump, coxswain of the seining bateau, falls overboard and almost drowns. Natty catches the old sailor's queue in the tines of his long fishing spear and pulls him to safety.

On the following day the Judge receives in a large shipment of mail a distressing letter from one Andrew Holt, an English lawyer. It bears the bad tidings of the loss at sea of someone close to the Judge, though the name of the person is not revealed to the reader. The Judge closets himself all day with his attorney, Dirck Van der School, and Richard Jones, the business at hand being too personal and confidential to permit the presence of Oliver Edwards.

Early in July Judge Temple and Richard Jones ride out to inspect what the latter has often claimed is the start of a silver mine. Elizabeth and Louisa walk in the woods after Elizabeth has superciliously rejected Oliver Edwards's offer to accompany them with a gun for protection. Oliver, thus rebuffed, visits briefly the cabin of Natty Bumppo and observes the hasty departure of Hiram Doolittle from the premises. An hour later, while Oliver, Natty, and John Mohegan are fishing together, they hear Natty's hounds, tied securely when Oliver left the cabin, baying a deer on the mountainside. When the deer enters the lake to escape the dogs, its nearness arouses the hunting instincts of Natty and Mohegan. Despite Oliver's repeated warnings that the deer season has not yet opened, the old men pursue and kill the deer in the water. It is then discovered that the buckskin thongs with which the dogs had been tied had not broken but had been cut by a knife; Hiram Doolittle is justly suspected of having committed this act of stealth. They later discover the padlocked door of the cabin has been tampered with. On their walk Elizabeth and Louisa, beset by a panther, are rescued from the beast by two shots from the rifle of Natty Bumppo.

Meanwhile, Richard Jones leads Judge Temple to sites which, he feels, will substantiate his claim that there are rich silver deposits in the area. They first visit a site at which Jotham Riddel, a shiftless Yankee employed by Jones, is prospecting on behalf of the Temple estate. Although Jotham insists that silver deposits are present, he can offer no tangible proof, and he evades questions about his rationale for digging there. The pair then proceed to an even more mysterious undertaking. By piecing together bits of circumstantial evidence, Jones has half persuaded Temple that Oliver and his two aged friends are secretly mining silver and smelting it at night in Natty's closely guarded cabin. He shows the Judge a nearby natural cave in which marks of excavation are clearly evident. Although no trace of ore is visible, the Judge is convinced that further investigation is warranted.

Hiram Doolittle, local justice of the peace, requests of Judge Temple a warrant to search the hut of Natty Bumppo for the remains of a deer allegedly shot out of season. However reluctant he is to intrude upon an old man who has saved his daughter's life, Judge Temple must, in all impartiality, honor the request, supported as it is by sworn testimony. Afraid to serve the warrant himself, Doolittle deputizes Billy Kirby and Jotham Riddel to assist him. After Natty hurls Doolittle a distance of twenty feet from his door rather than permit him to step across the threshold, he picks up his rifle and confronts Billy Kirby. Terrified at the sight of Natty's rifle, Doolittle and Riddel flee, whereupon Billy and Natty compromise and part as friends. Billy agrees to forgo entry into the cabin when Natty offers him the deer hide as evidence of having killed a deer illegally.

Though Judge Temple has insisted on enforcing the game law against Natty Bumppo, he agrees to let Elizabeth pay the fine, thus clearing the old hunter. When, however, he now learns of Natty's forcible resistance to the law and his menacing its agents, he rushes from his study to inform Elizabeth that Natty must be treated as a criminal and brought to trial. In his distress the Judge is unaware of the presence of Oliver Edwards, who has just been entreating Elizabeth to aid Natty in his difficulty with the law. Oliver exchanges heated words with the Judge and then bids Elizabeth farewell, saying that he is forthwith leaving his employment in the Temple household.

On the night before the regular session of the county court, presided over by Judge Temple, is to convene, Richard Jones, Sheriff, goes, with a number of deputies, to arrest Natty Bumppo for trial. To their great surprise, the group finds at the former site of Natty's cabin only a heap of smoldering embers. Unarmed, Natty appears out of the dark and surrenders himself. He had burned his home of many years rather than have it entered against his will.

At the trial Natty is arraigned on two charges: assault and battery against Hiram Doolittle, Justice of the Peace, and resistance to the execution of a search warrant. Acquitted of the first charge, he is found guilty of the second; and Judge Temple sentences him to one hour in public stocks, one month in jail, and a $100 fine. Quite out of order, Natty makes an ingenuous but touching plea for a lighter sentence, reminding the court that he had once provided food and shelter for Judge Temple and that recently he had saved the Judge's daughter from a panther. A further disruption of courtroom procedure is then made by Ben Pump, who offers all of his savings to buy Natty's freedom. Both Natty's and Ben's pleas are, correctly, ruled out of order.

When Natty is being placed in the stocks, Ben Pump feels so sorry for the disgrace put upon the old man that he takes his place by Natty and bids the constable lock them both there. Hiram Doolittle comes to the stocks to gloat over Natty's discomfort, but he passes so close to the prisoners that Ben Pump is enabled to grab him and pummel him badly before the sheriff can come to his rescue. Although Ben is Jones's favorite employee, the sheriff has no choice but to order the ex-sailor to be imprisoned for the night with Natty Bumppo.

That evening Judge Temple gives Elizabeth $200 to deliver to Natty. As Louisa and Elizabeth approach the jail to present this money to the old hunter, they meet Oliver Edwards driving a team of oxen in the same direction. Refusing to take the gold guineas, Natty does agree to accept on the following day a canister of gunpowder so that he can kill beavers to pay his own fine. He and his cell mate, Ben Pump, have cut through the wall to make their escape, so Elizabeth and Louisa leave quickly in order to avoid being party to a jailbreak. When a posse pursues Oliver and Natty, however, Elizabeth aids the fugitives. They abandon the ox cart Oliver has borrowed, sans permission, from Billy Kirby. Buried in the cart in straw is Ben Pump, too drunk to be helped to freedom. The owner finds Ben there and takes him, now asleep, to the place where Kirby is to chop wood the next day.

In the morning, Elizabeth and Louisa go to the store of Monsieur Le Quoi and buy the canister of powder promised Natty. Louisa, still shaken by the panther incident, refuses to go beyond the village limits, leaving Elizabeth to ascend Mt. Vision alone to meet the hunter at the appointed time and place. Near the summit she comes across John Mohegan clothed and decorated as if for some special occasion. Talking mainly of his imminent death, John seems to be on the verge of answering Elizabeth's repeated question about the identity of Oliver Edwards when they are engulfed in the thick smoke of a forest fire. Hearing John give a low and familiar call, Oliver Edwards rushes upon the scene.

Unable to stir to action the dying Indian, Oliver attempts to flee the fire-encircled summit with Elizabeth. All escape routes seem to be cut off by the flames, however, and the two prepare to die. At that moment, Natty comes crashing through the burning brush, hatless, hair and clothes singed, seeking Elizabeth. Hearing the canister explode, he thinks that she has been killed, but Elizabeth had earlier given the gunpowder to John Mohegan. His approach to death is hastened by the powder burns he suffers, but Natty Bumppo straps the Indian on his back and carries him out of the flames. Oliver and Elizabeth follow Natty to safety. The group is joined by Rev. Mr. Grant, who ineffectually tries to rouse Christian thoughts in the dying chief. After John's death, his body is carried to a nearby cave by Natty. As Oliver escorts Elizabeth to the highway, where voices of a rescue party can be heard, he promises her that the mystery of his identity will soon be removed.

Rumors in Templeton make of Natty and Oliver at once possessors of great quantities of gold and silver and dangerous criminals. Sheriff Jones organizes a posse, supported by Captain Hollister and his militia troops, to attack the outlaws' fortified cave. Natty Bumppo, joined by Ben Pump, holds off the fearful troops and their ludicrous commander with injury to none but Hiram Doolittle, who is nicked in the rump by a ball from Natty's rifle. After Judge Temple arrives to order a cessation of hostilities, Oliver Edwards, accompanied by Major Hartmann, appears and also forbids violence, promising that the cave and its contents will be yielded.

To the amazement of Judge Temple and the townsmen, Oliver Edwards and Major Hartmann carry from the cave on a rude chair a senile, white-haired figure. Oliver explains that this is his grandfather, Major Effingham (Fire-eater), the original owner of the land patent for that area. The Major's son, Edward Effingham, had stayed loyal to the Crown as a colonel during the Revolutionary War after placing all his property in trust with his business partner, Marmaduke Temple. Taking his son to

Nova Scotia, Edward had later moved to England; there he had secured a government position in the West Indies. En route to that new post, he had been lost at sea, with his only son assumed to have died in the same disaster, and thus Temple, never having met the Major and uncertain of his whereabouts, had lost contact with the Effinghams. Oliver, whose real name was Edward Oliver Effingham, had come when old enough to do so to what is now the United States and traced his grandfather to the cabin of Natty Bumppo, where the hunter (once the Major's servant) and John Mohegan cared for the old man in his senility.

Back at the Mansion, Judge Temple shows Oliver a copy of his will, drawn on the day, earlier that year, when news of Edward's death had reached Templeton. It bequeaths half his wealth to the heirs of Edward Effingham. Oliver and Judge Temple are now completely reconciled, and the Judge gives to the young man the hand of his daughter, Elizabeth. When, shortly afterwards, Monsieur Le Quoi arrives to make a chivalric but halfhearted proposal to Elizabeth, he is kindly but firmly refused. Le Quoi, again affluent, will soon move to Paris, abandoning his sugar plantation in Martinique.

Early in September Oliver and Elizabeth are married. Shortly after this happy event a sad one ensues: the death of Major Effingham. Natty Bumppo and Ben Pump are persuaded to return to jail to serve their sentences, but they are soon freed by a pardon from the governor of the state, a pardon quietly arranged through the good offices of Judge Temple. Oliver gives a farm to the Rev. Mr. Grant, and Judge Temple secures for him a "living" along the banks of the Hudson River, a more settled area, where Louisa can meet other young people of her social and educational level. One day in October Oliver and Elizabeth visit the graves of Major Effingham and John Mohegan to examine their newly erected tombstones. There they find Natty Bumppo preparing to leave Templeton, his pack, his rifle, and his dogs in readiness for a long journey. Despite repeated pleas by the young couple to spend his last days close to them, Natty takes his farewell and heads west, never again to be seen by them.

Agamemnon, Nathaniel Bumppo, Chingachgook [John Mohegan], Hiram Doolittle, Edward Oliver Effingham, Major Oliver Effingham, Abraham Freeborn, Rev. Mr. Grant, Louisa Grant, Major Frederick Hartmann, Captain Hollister, Betty Hollister, Richard Jones, Billy Kirby, Le Quoi, Chester Lippet, Remarkable Pettibone, Jared Ransom, Jotham Riddel, Benjamin Stubbs [Ben Pump], Elizabeth Temple, Judge Marmaduke Temple, Dr. Elnathan Todd, Dirck Van der School.

The Prairie: A Tale, 1827.

[This is the last of the five Leather-Stocking Tales in relation to plot, the third in order of composition.]

Deep in the heart of the newly acquired Louisiana Purchase, five hundred miles beyond the Mississippi River, a group of travelers in the year 1805 pushes yet farther westward over the prairie. Called "squatters" and equipped with covered wagons, livestock, farming implements, and household furnishings, they give every appearance of being ordinary settlers except for the fact they have bypassed the fertile river bottoms for the less productive Great Plains. This group is comprised of the rough, semiliterate Ishmael and Esther Bush, now in their fifties; their numerous children, including seven grown sons; Esther's brother, Abiram White; Ellen Wade, a niece, whose bearing bespeaks a more refined background; and Dr. Obed Bat, an eccentric naturalist. In search of a camping place for the night, they are suddenly confronted by a colossal figure who momentarily fills them with superstitious awe. It is Natty Bumppo, whose form, greatly magnified by an optical illusion, is outlined against the setting sun on the horizon. Once a hunter and scout but now reduced in his old age to trapping, Natty is almost as startled as the newcomers by the encounter. It has been months since the octogenarian has seen white people so far beyond the settlements. He leads the Bush party to a campsite which will provide for their basic needs: water, fuel, and fodder for the animals.

As he watches the camp being set up, Natty notices that one wagon is kept apart and treated with special care. When, innocently curious, he attempts to approach this vehicle and its attached tent, he is roughly pushed aside by Abiram White. At supper Natty answers the many questions about the area asked by his hosts and then takes his leave. Outside the encampment he is surprised to meet Ellen Wade walking alone. Their conversation is interrupted by the appearance of a third person. It is Paul Hover, Ellen's lover, who, unwelcome among the Bush party, has nevertheless followed the travelers unbeknownst to all but Ellen. A bee-hunter, Hover makes his living by gathering honey from the hives of wild bees. Natty and the young couple are hardly more than introduced to each other before all three are discovered and captured by a band of mounted Tetons of the Sioux (or Dahcotah) nation.

Threatening the captives with death if they raise an alarm, the Sioux chief, Mahtoree, crawls stealthily into the Bush camp where he turns loose all of the travelers' animals: beasts of burden, cattle, sheep, and even pigs. His followers then, with great whooping, drive them out upon the open prairie. When his guard grows careless, Natty manages to cut the rope tethering the Sioux horses, and they too run wild. As the Indians pursue both their own and Ishmael Bush's livestock, the three white captives make their escape, Ellen and Natty to return, separately, to the Bush camp and Paul Hover to his own secret hiding place nearby.

A comic interlude is provided in the first appearance of Obed Bat, physician by profession but avid naturalist by avocation. He has attached himself to the household of Ishmael Bush, where his zeal for gathering specimens of flora and fauna is tolerated in order to secure his medical services. Off by himself on a collecting expedition, Dr. Bat (or *Battius*, as he Latinizes his name) is unaware of the Indian raid on the Bush camp. He returns before dawn the following morning with news of great zoological interest: his discovery, during the night, of a fierce prairie monster as yet unclassified by scientists. The full light of day reveals the horrendous creature to be only his own ass (referred to, pedantically, as *Asinus Domesticus*), one of the animals released by the Sioux. (Throughout the novel are numerous incidents and discussions in which Dr. Bat's ostentatiously displayed scientific learning is the butt of humor. Sometimes his theoretical knowledge is compared unfavorably with Natty's woodcraft and common sense; sometimes it is shown to be less dependable than the instincts of Natty's dog, Hector.)

Without its horses, the Bush caravan is stranded and vulnerable to attack. Natty directs the group to a small hill that is defensible against even a large force of Indians. The strong sons of Ishmael pull the heavy wagons the three miles to this new location. Again Natty reveals his curiosity about the small wagon set apart from the rest of the vehicles, and again Abiram White expresses hostility toward the old man.

After this little wagon is placed atop the citadel, its contents are suddenly revealed as a young woman is seen to step from it and gaze momentarily at the plain below. Asa, the eldest Bush son, and Abiram White exchange harsh words about the unidentified female. Asa accuses his uncle of being a kidnapper, and Abiram retorts that in Kentucky rewards had been posted for the captured of Ishmael, Esther, Asa, and four of his brothers. Asa strikes Abiram, and Ishmael has to intervene to prevent further violence.

At the same moment, a few miles away, Paul Hover and Dr. Bat join Natty Bumppo in eating a buffalo hump, the choicest meat of the animal, which the old man has roasted. As the three talk, Dr. Bat's abstract learning and his pedantic parade of Latin terms are shown to be ridiculously removed from the realities of life. At the conclusion of their feast, Natty hears for five minutes a creature in the brush that is undetected by either of his guests; from Hector's behavior Natty infers that it is not a fierce beast, as Dr. Bat fears it is, but a human being. Emerging from the brush in answer to Paul Hover's challenge is Captain Duncan Uncas Middleton.

There ensues a recognition scene by means of which the novel is linked to the earlier Leather-Stocking Tales. The captain is identified as the grandson of Duncan Heyward and Alice Munro Heyward, romantic leads in *The Last of the Mohicans*, set more than forty years earlier in upstate New York. (It is the captain's middle name, Uncas, which provides Natty with the first clue of Middleton's ancestry; Natty had known the young man's namesake, Uncas, the titular hero of *The Last of the Mohicans*.) This chance meeting with a descendant of his former officer prompts Natty to recount his own part in the French and Indian War and in other military operations, a reminiscence quite natural to an old man and strategic, from the author's point of view, as a device for providing exposition both for this novel and for the series of novels which it concludes. Captain Middleton then gives the group an account of his reason for being in this remote area—a story not revealed to the reader until some time later.

The men of the Bush household go hunting on this day for game with which to feed everyone at their little citadel. All return at evening except Asa. Esther is concerned for her first child's welfare, and at breakfast the next morning she demands that they search for the boy. They find Asa dead, killed by a bullet bearing Natty Bumppo's insignia. After their first anguish subsides, the family buries Asa near the place of his murder.

During the absence of the other family adults, Ellen has been left to guard the children and the security of the Bush fortress. She is now called upon to carry out her command as four armed men approach: Natty, Paul Hover, Middleton, and Dr. Bat. Having shared their fragmentary information, these four have concluded that the inhabitant of the light wagon and the white tent is not the animal decoy that Bush pretends it to be but Inez Augustin Middleton, the abducted wife of Captain Middleton; they are attacking the Bush fortress to liberate Inez. Despite her love for Paul, Ellen feels committed to defend the citadel, and this she and the older Bush daughters prepare to do with loaded muskets and stone catapults. At the moment of confrontation, Inez comes forth from the white tent and appeals to both sides to avoid violence. Startled by this new presence suddenly among them—Bush had deceived his children about the occupant of the white tent—Phoebe Bush fires at Inez instead of at the attackers. Fearing Inez has been shot, Ellen abandons her command post and rushes to attend the supposedly wounded girl. During this moment of confusion, Paul and Middleton breach the defenses and enter the camp.

With the reunion of Middleton and his unharmed wife, the story of their marriage and separation is revealed. Inez's father, Don Augustin de Certavallos, a member of the Spanish gentry in Florida, had moved to Louisiana where he had remained during both its French and American ownership. There he had offered the courtesy of his hacienda to Captain Middleton, the young officer sent to command a small body of American troops in the newly acquired Louisiana Purchase. Some time later he also gave in marriage to Middleton his only child, Inez. Immediately after the wedding ceremony, Inez had been kidnapped by Abiram, by then part of the Bush caravan. Middleton, with a handful of soldiers, had pursued these fugitives from the law and had finally overtaken them.

After the capture of the citadel, Middleton, Inez, Paul, Ellen, Dr. Bat, and Natty seek refuge elsewhere. As they travel across the prairie, they come upon a Pawnee chief, Hard-Heart, scouting the location of his tribe's greatest foes, the Sioux. Beginning at this point, Natty Bumppo parallels the conflicting Pawnees and Sioux with the "good" (Delaware) and "bad" (Iroquois) Indians encountered in those of the Leather-Stocking Tales set earlier in time. Before riding off on his fine horse, Hard-Heart promises the travelers asylum in the Pawnee camp, but warns them that it lies at a great distance and will not be easily reached. Middleton's appointed place of rendezvous with his soldiers lies at an equally great distance.

The travelers soon find themselves in the path of a thunderous stampede of bison. Natty manages to split the herd by rushing fearlessly at the leading bulls, and Asinus (Dr. Bat's ass) widens the division by frightening the buffaloes with loud braying, a sound they had never heard before. The cause of the stampede is now revealed: a hunting party of Tetons. Natty goes forward to meet the Indians in order to pretend that he is alone, leaving his five companions hidden in the cover of a thicket. As he talks with Mahtoree, however, he is dismayed to observe his friends advancing across the open plains, preferring to be captured by the Sioux rather than by the Bush party, which has just entered the other side of the thicket.

Seeing Ishmael and his sons on foot and at a distance from their base, the Sioux decide to plunder the Bush camp. As the Indians pursue that purpose, followed by volleys of bullets from Bush rifles, Natty and the two young couples escape on Sioux horses. They soon overtake Dr. Bat, who had been allowed to flee on Asinus after Natty had persuaded the Indians that the white medicine man was possessed of potent super-natural powers.

In an effort to recapture or destroy the fugitives, the Tetons now set the prairie grass afire. After Natty saves the group from the flames by the well-known device of a backfire, they continue their flight. Among the charred prairie grass and brush they find the burned carcass of a horse and nearby the remains of a bison. When Paul and Natty lift the scorched hide of the beast, an Indian springs forth. It is, once again, the Pawnee chief, Hard-Heart. Unable to guide his terrified horse away from the inferno, Hard-Heart had saved his own life by crawling beneath the fresh hide of a buffalo. Still scouting the Sioux location, Hard-Heart has unhappy news for the fugitives: the Sioux and the Bushes have resolved their differences and have joined forces in pursuit of Natty and his companions. Hard-Heart informs them, however, that he had earlier dispatched an order back to his village to send him a force of Pawnee braves. In the continuing chase, the pursued, despite their various stratagems, are all finally captured by their pursuers.

Bush now demands of the Sioux the return of his property and the custody of the white prisoners. When he receives only the former, he moves a mile away, with his wagons and livestock, and there sets up his own temporary camp. Hard-Heart, who has in his time killed eighteen Sioux warriors, is led to a stake, there to be tortured to death. As the Sioux council members smoke their pipes and discuss the fate of their victim, Natty promises Hard-Heart to go to the Pawnee village, tell of the chief's death, secure there a sleek colt, and, returning, slaughter it on his grave so that he may ride comfortably in the Happy Hunting Ground.

The torture is delayed by a scene of domestic pathos. Mahtoree, impassioned by the beauty of the white women, wants Inez and Ellen to live henceforth in his tent, where they are presently held as prisoners. His youngest and most favored Indian wife, Tachechana (Skipping Fawn), pleads with him not to take these strangers as wives. When Mahtoree persists in his desire for them, Tachechana removes all of her jewelry and fine outer garments, places her infant son at the feet of Inez and Ellen, falls abject in the dust, and refuses to move. Again the torture is about to commence; again it is delayed, this time by an ancient chief who bears so many battle scars that he is known not by an Indian name but by an honorific given him by the French, *Le Balafré* (The Scarred Man). Exercising an old Indian privilege, he claims Hard-Heart as a son, one who will support him in his final years. Although such adoption would save his life, Hard-Heart, after paying his respects to *Le Balafré*, chooses to die as a Pawnee rather than live as a Sioux. As the torture is once again about to begin, Weucha, dastardly foil to the villainous but dignified Mahtoree, aims a tomahawk at Hard-Heart. Seizing the weapon, the Pawnee brains its owner with it, and then, having immobilized the spectators in mute astonishment, dashes to the nearby river and plunges into its waters. The timely arrival of Pawnee horsemen prevents his recapture.

As the superior force of Sioux engages the better-armed, better-mounted group of Pawnees, Mahtoree gives orders to an aged chief to issue knives to the older women of the band so that they may kill the bound prisoners, Hover, Middleton, and Bat. Natty cuts the rawhide thongs binding Hover and Middleton, but the circulation has not yet been restored to their limbs when the armed squaws advance upon them. The fortuitous braying of Asinus scatters the hags in fear, and the captives now prepare to defend themselves. At this critical point, another force enters the conflict. Ishmael Bush and his sons return, recapture the momentarily freed white prisoners, and carry them off to their own encampment.

Before the general conflict between Tetons and Pawnees begins, their leaders engage in single conflict on a low island in the middle of the river. Mounted and bearing lances and shields among their other equipment, they have some of the appearance of medieval knights representing their respective armies. When, after a protracted fight, Mahtoree is killed, his warriors fall upon the smaller Pawnee force. The Sioux are winning the battle until Ishmael deserts his recent allies and decimates their ranks with the deadly fire of Kentucky rifles. In the massacre that ensues, only a few of the Sioux escape with their lives.

On the following day, each of the prisoners is tried before a rude frontier court presided over by Ishmael Bush. His own conflicts with the law and his frequently stated abhorrence of legal procedures make Ishmael's new role an ironic one. He releases Inez and Middleton, as well as Ellen and Paul, to go their respective ways as they wish. Ellen, grateful for Ishmael's care since she had become an orphan, says she chooses to depart with Paul but only if she can do so with her uncle's blessing. This blessing is bestowed. Tachechana and Le Balafré he declares to be Hard-Heart's prisoners and thus beyond his jurisdiction. Dr. Bat is also released, but Natty Bumppo is detained and accused of the murder of Asa. Natty describes in detail the fight he had seen between Asa and Abiram White after White had shot his nephew in the back. Paul and Dr. Bat had also gone with Natty to give what medical care they could to Asa, but the boy was dead. Abiram's guilty behavior and attempt to flee condemn him of the murder as much as does Natty's testimony. Natty is released, and Abiram White is captured and bound. As unsympathetic a character as Ishmael Bush is in other respects, he has throughout these proceedings acted with a true sense of justice, dealing fairly both with his foes and with those close to him. With the trials now at an end, all but the members of the Bush family take their leave and depart in the direction of the Pawnee territory.

The Bush caravan now reverses its direction and heads back eastward toward more fertile land. At their first stop, Ishmael and Esther discuss their painful responsibility to punish the murderer of their firstborn child. Although Abiram is her brother, Esther agrees that he must die for his crime. Thinking at first that he should be shot, as Asa was, they finally arrive at a less bloody method of execution. They place the culprit on a narrow shelf of rock, several feet above the ground, beneath a dead willow tree. A rope around his neck is tied to a branch above his head. As long as he does not move, he will live; when he slips from the rock ledge, he will, in effect, hang himself. Although his arms are bound to his body at the elbows, his forearms are left free to hold a section of the Bible which Esther gives him to read during his last moments. "I forgive you my wrongs and leave you to your God," says Ishmael in parting.

Proceeding a mile farther eastward, the Bushes make camp for the night. In the west wind that rises with the moon that evening, Ishmael and Esther hear a long shriek and know that it is Abiram's death cry. The two return to the place of Abiram's execution and, after a brief prayer, give the corpse a proper burial.

After a brief rest at Hard-Heart's Pawnee village, the six whites (joined now by several of Middleton's soldiers) start downstream by boat toward the towns along the Mississippi River. Once out of sight of the village, however, Natty requests that he be landed on the riverbank again. Having lived so long in nature, he cannot spend his final days within the confines of the settlements. Paul Hover and Captain Middleton both offer him comfortable homes if he will go with them, but these offers he declines with courtesy and gratitude. He will accept nothing for his many services to the group except the gift or the loan of Middleton's pup as a comfort to himself and to Hector, neither of whom can live much longer. He sends with the travelers four pelts to be traded for traps which are to be sent to him in care of the Pawnee village. Then, after saying farewell and wishing Godspeed to each of his new friends, Natty pushes the boat back into the current of the river.

Natty returns to the Pawnee village to live with his adopted son, Hard-Heart. In the autumn of the following year, Captain Middleton visits the upper Missouri to carry out a government assignment. He is accompanied by Paul Hover and a small body of cavalry. From the point on that river nearest to the Pawnee village, they travel by horseback to renew their friendship with Natty and Hard-Heart. They arrive on the very day of Natty's death and find the whole Pawnee tribe assembled there to honor the old man in his final moments. With Hector (dead but carefully stuffed and preserved) between his feet, the trapper sits, facing the setting sun, in a large, rudely made reclining chair. After recognizing Middleton, and after making known his last wishes, Natty seems to lapse into unconsciousness. Suddenly, however, the old man jumps to his feet and shouts "Here!" responding to a call that only he can hear. His last word is uttered with his last breath, and the trapper is dead before friendly hands lower him again into his chair. After a brief eulogy by the equally old *Le Balafré*, the mourners disperse. Natty becomes in time a legend among the Plains Indians, and all visitors to the area are shown the simple stone (provided by Middleton) which marks the grave of a wise and just white man.

Don Augustin de Certevallos, *Le Balafré*, Dr. Obed Bat, Bohrecheena, Nathaniel Bumppo, Abner Bush, Asa Bush, Enoch Bush, Esther Bush, Hetty Bush, Ishmael Bush, Jesse Bush, Phoebe Bush, Hard-Heart, Paul Hover, Father Ignatius, Inesella, Mahhah, Mahtoree, Captain Duncan Uncas Middleton, Inez Augustin Middleton, Swooping Eagle, Tachechana, Tetao, Ellen Wade, Weucha, Abiram White.

Precaution: A Novel, 1820.

The entire focus of this novel rests on the determined though sometimes woefully mistaken efforts of three British families—the Moseleys, the Jarvises, and the Chattertons—to arrange suitable marriages for their respective sons and daughters. The bulk of the early-nineteenth-century action is therefore played out through dinners, social calls, visits to summer resorts, and development of various designs employed toward the end of matrimony. The "precaution" displayed by Mrs. Wilson in guiding her niece Emily Moseley through the treacherous shoals toward a sound Christian marriage furnishes the novel's title and indicates the author's moral and ethical position.

Initially, a spirited and good-humored discussion of the Jarvises, soon to occupy the neighboring Deanery, animates the dinner party hosted by Sir Edward Moseley and Lady Anne, a party including the couple's son John, their three marriageable daughters—Clara, Jane, and Emily—Sir Edward's widowed resident sister Mrs. Wilson (by agreement the spiritual and social mentor of Emily), the parish rector Rev. Dr. Ives and his wife and their son Francis, and Mr. and Mrs. Haughton and their daughter Lucy. Clara's future has already been determined: she is to wed Francis as soon as the young man has been assigned a parish. Thanks to

Sir Edward's timely retrenchment and rebuilding of his financial status, and to the good will of friends and relatives intending to make the Moseley children their heirs, marriages of the proper kind seem likely for the younger two daughters and for John, as well.

A slight accident at the gate of the Deanery, with minor injury to a Colonel Egerton, provides occasion for Rev. Dr. Ives's immediate visit to the Jarvises. His report on the new family prompts the Moseleys' call shortly thereafter, a call revealing that the Jarvis parents—the husband is a retired prosperous merchant—are pleasant enough, and that their daughters are pretty but somewhat lacking in polish. Colonel Egerton's lie, told to protect the Jarvises' absent son Harry, arouses Mrs. Wilson's doubts about the Colonel's strength of character, a point that fails to dampen the romantic interest Jane feels in the dashing gentleman; the eligibility of Harry is clouded by his quite evident hunting out of season, but his family's prosperity promises to outweigh that defect. A visit from a family favorite, Uncle Roderic Benfield—a wealthy eighty-year-old bachelor who delights in Emily—brightens the following days for the Moseleys.

During a subsequent dinner at the rectory attended by the Moseleys, the Jarvises, and Colonel Egerton, the Jarvises display their lack of refinement and the Colonel his want of principle, points noted by Mrs. Wilson for Emily's benefit. A curious interruption occurs after dinner: the arrival of a debilitated sixty-year-old man and his handsome twenty-five-year-old son, producing shock and grief among the Iveses and an early end to the conversation. Mrs. Jarvis's fruitless and ill-bred attempts to secure fuller information about the unidentified visitors, as well as the death of the elderly visitor during Francis's first sermon, increase suspense concerning the visitors, suspense given little relief by the newspaper notice merely naming the deceased "George Denbigh, Esq."

Interest in Colonel Egerton continues to draw Jane and Mrs. Moseley to the Jarvises', despite the latter family's obvious coarseness. At the same time, Clara's long-awaited marriage to Francis is made possible by the young rector's being offered the fine living at Bolton, adjacent to his father's parish; at the wedding, Colonel Egerton serves as groomsman in the absence of the Moseleys' handsome cousin Lord Chatterton. Mrs. Wilson, increasingly concerned about Jane's infatuation with the unprincipled Egerton, is unable to persuade Lady Moseley of the danger therein; Lady Anne is disposed to overlook the Colonel's obvious flaws in favor of his probable inheritance of a title and substantial income.

Shortly after the Ives wedding, Lady Chatterton and her son and two daughters arrive at the Moseleys' for a visit. Lord Chatterton stirs strong interest among all the marriageable girls, and Lady Chatterton herself sees in John Moseley a likely match for one of her daughters. Young George Denbigh, a guest of the Rev. Dr. Ives and his wife, also catches her attention, as he does indeed of both the other matchmaking mothers; his charms are not lost on Emily, who, under Mrs. Wilson's guidance, is prudent enough not to reveal her interest. Lady Chatterton's bait, first for John Moseley and next for Colonel Egerton, is her daughter Catherine's display of a shapely ankle, a bait to which neither man is drawn.

A visit of all the neighbors to Clara Ives in her new home offers John Moseley the opportunity to drive Grace Chatterton to the Bolton rectory; his favorable response to Grace's charms is cooled by Lady Chatterton's effort to push the match. Colonel Egerton and George Denbigh, also of the party at the rectory, appear discomfited by one another's presence, a fact marked only by Mrs. Wilson.

A fortnight later, the Haughtons give a ball for Lucy to which the Moseleys, the Jarvises, the Chattertons, their various guests, and a number of young military officers are invited. George Denbigh's immediate request that Emily give him the first dance, assented to by Emily, prompts an inquiry by Mrs. Wilson of Rev. Dr. Ives concerning the young man's character, but the rector's sound recommendation of Denbigh relieves Emily's mentor's anxiety. Both Emily and Mrs. Wilson are increasingly disturbed, however, about Jane's evident attachment to the artful Egerton, since each discerns his lack of principle.

At the Moseleys' dinner the evening following the ball, honoring the officers of the regiment stationed nearby (an event Denbigh declines to attend), Mrs. Wilson inquires of her respected friend Sir Herbert Nicholson concerning Denbigh's character and is further reassured about the young man's soundness. Lord Chatterton, after the guests leave, relates the refusal of Denbigh to duel with Captain Harry Jarvis over Emily's declining to dance the first dance with Jarvis and then accepting Denbigh's invitation to dance. All present are horrified at Jarvis's conduct and reconfirmed in their respect for Denbigh's character. Sir Edward Moseley's cautionary and offended conversation the following day with Mrs. Jarvis concerning the matter of the duel elicits an apology by Captain Jarvis (to avoid the threatened loss of six months' allowance!). Young Jarvis had that morning killed Captain Digby in a duel fought to avenge Digby's scornful toast to Jarvis at mess.

Lord Chatterton, hopelessly in love with Emily but heretofore without financial means, proposes to her on the strength of his appointment to a lucrative post in the patent office. Gently but firmly refused by Emily, he retires to weep, at which business he is encountered by the compassionate Denbigh, himself an undeclared suitor for Emily's hand. The two young men go together to London for a brief period, with Denbigh laying aside his interest in Emily out of respect for Chatterton.

Lady Chatterton, seeking more promising matrimonial prospects for Catherine yet unwilling to relinquish her hope of matching Grace with John Moseley, leaves Grace pointedly with Emily and goes with Catherine for a long-delayed visit some fifty miles distant. The embarrassed Grace and Emily, at Grace's suggestion, spend two weeks with Clara at the Bolton rectory. John, on the pretense of visiting Clara, goes to the rectory and takes Emily and Grace for an airing. Their way blocked by Denbigh's gig, they inquire into the circumstances: Denbigh has stopped to render aid to an impoverished family. John impulsively gives the family several guineas, in marked contrast to Denbigh's half-crown offering, a difference that troubles Emily. John's reckless driving prompts Denbigh to offer Emily a ride back to the rectory, leaving Grace to accompany John; en route, Denbigh gives Emily a sealed letter from Lord Chatterton urging her to place her affections with Denbigh (Denbigh is clearly unaware of the letter's contents). The following morning, Mrs. Wilson, Grace, and Emily, intent on visiting the stricken family at their temporary lodging, on arrival overhear Denbigh counsel the man to abandon liquor and attend to his family; Denbigh furnishes two letters to aid the family in resituating itself, an act of greater charity by far, Mrs. Wilson tells Emily, than the guineas bestowed by John the day before.

Just as John, under the influence of Denbigh's reading aloud of a moving poem on wedded love, is ready to state his affection for Grace, Lady Chatterton and Catherine return. Matrimonial prospects for the latter have failed to materialize; but Lady Chatterton, assuming that John has already declared his suit to Grace, displays her heavy-handed management and provokes John into disavowing any matrimonial intentions and promptly thereafter accompanying his uncle, Mr. Benfield, to the latter's home. Her hopes for both Grace and Catherine thus disappointed, Lady Chatterton takes her daughters home to London. As for Colonel Egerton, he promises to visit the Moseleys at the unfashionable resort near Benfield Lodge during their projected stay there.

Shortly after this, a presumably unloaded gun (loaded by the impulsive Captain Jarvis) playfully aimed by John at Emily in the Moseley arbor is discharged; Denbigh, seeing the danger and therefore placing himself between Emily and the gun, receives the shot himself. During his ensuing delirium, Denbigh repeatedly mentions Emily's name, but also repeats "poor deserted Marian" (p. 187), a reference puzzling to Emily, who devotedly attends him during his recovery, a period requiring a full month to complete.

The Earl of Bolton, on a visit to the Moseleys one day, reveals that the Earl of Pendennyss himself had urged the post of rector for Francis Ives to show his respect for Mrs. Wilson. (Mrs. Wilson's husband, spiritual mentor of Pendennyss during their military service, had extolled the Earl in his letters to his wife, and Mrs. Wilson, convinced of Pendennyss' integrity, welcomes every additional evidence of her paragon's virtue.) On the information that the Earl of Pendennyss will be visiting Bolton Castle soon, the Moseleys delay their holiday departure for Benfield Lodge as long as possible, to allow them the pleasure of meeting the Earl, but they receive his invitation hours too late to have the honor of his visit at Moseley Hall. The Moseleys, as well as most of their neighbors, depart for various summer resorts.

En route to Benfield Lodge, the Moseleys stop overnight at Moseley Arms, an inn managed by a former butler in the Moseley household, and learn that it has been recently patronized—by virtue of a display of the Moseley family arms—not only by the Duke of Derwent and Lord Chatterton, but by the Earl of Pendennyss himself, a matter of gratification to the entire family. Warmly greeted by Uncle Roderic Benfield, they find various modes of entertainment, including a visit to the public library, where John, Emily, and Jane encounter the elderly Spanish companion of a lovely young lady whom Emily and John had once helped and in whom John feels a romantic interest. Mrs. Wilson and Emily agree to visit the young lady—a Mrs. Julia Fitzgerald—at her cottage the following morning. On that occasion, John is left behind to entertain Denbigh, a welcome but unexpected guest at Benfield Lodge, and Jane remains to await the promised arrival of Colonel Egerton.

The lovely Spaniard proves a gracious hostess and agrees to accept John as a visitor, but no others—she allows only one other gentleman in England (unidentified) to visit her, and he himself has come but once. Clearly, the lady has had an unhappy past, one unrevealed on this first visit. After a number of calls, Mrs. Wilson and Emily one day find Mrs. Fitzgerald in tears, the recipient of a distressing letter from none other than Lord Pendennyss, to whom she claims she owes everything— "honor—comfort—religion—and even life itself" (p. 233). Too upset to talk further that day, she promises to reveal her life story the following day on their visit to her.

Meanwhile, Colonel Egerton, taking advantage of the flurry occasioned by the unexpected arrival at the summer resort of Mr. and Mrs. Jarvis and their daughters, goes walking with Jane and proposes to her;

the flattered, flustered girl refers him to her parents but confesses her love for him. Her parents are not surprised at Egerton's declaration but express the need to inquire further into his background before giving their consent. To Mrs. Wilson's surprise and concern, Mary Jarvis displays rudeness toward both Egerton and Jane, behavior that only Mrs. Wilson thinks to attribute either to jealousy or to some shortcoming in the Colonel himself. During the conversation, Emily mentions hearing further good word about Lord Pendennyss, an animated remark that, Mrs. Wilson notes, appears to make Denbigh uneasy and unwilling to hear more. Can the feeling prompting his reaction be envy? Mrs. Wilson is troubled at this evidence of a flaw in the young man's character. Invitations to a ball given for the resort residents and the officers of the frigates anchored nearby necessitate postponement of the visit to Mrs. Fitzgerald; Denbigh declines to attend, but the rest spend a pleasant evening, with Lord Henry Stapleton attentive to Emily, commendatory of Lord Pendennyss, and barely polite to Colonel Egerton. A conversation overheard by Mrs. Wilson concerning Colonel Egerton confirms her worst suspicions: the dissoluteness—a matter of public knowledge—of the suitor for Jane's hand. While Sir Edward is still pondering this bit of scandal, confided to him by Mrs. Wilson but vehemently denied by Colonel Egerton, it becomes apparent that Egerton has eloped with Mary (Polly) Egerton, unexpectedly recipient of a substantial inheritance. Jane, whose affections and pride are deeply wounded by this betrayal, can be comforted only by Emily; Jane's unhappy state serves to underline for Emily the need for precaution in determining the character of one's lover before placing one's affections.

The long-delayed visit to Mrs. Fitzgerald reveals that the young widow, the daughter and granddaughter of Protestant women married to committed Catholics, after a two-year confinement in a convent by her irate father in an attempt to break her will on the matter, had wed a Major Fitzgerald and was, after the battlefield death of her husband, placed in the care of a British officer for safe delivery to Fitzgerald's mother in England. En route, the officer had attempted to seduce her; she was rescued from this threatened indignity by the Earl of Pendennyss, who had thereafter provided for her welfare. The letter from the Earl that grieved her had reported that her father was still adamant in his rejection of her Protestant faith. A subsequent visit by Mrs. Wilson acquaints her with the fact that the proposed abuser of Mrs. Fitzgerald had entered her cottage on the day of the ball; from her maid's report, Mrs. Fitzgerald concludes that the abuser must have been Colonel Egerton. In any event, he had left his pocketbook behind in his hasty exit

and Mrs. Wilson agrees to return it to its owner at her earliest opportunity. On the way home, she examines the pocketbook and finds, to her
shock and horror, that it belongs instead to George Denbigh. She recalls,
then, the oddities in Denbigh's behavior that she has earlier noted, and
she determines to return the pocketbook to him publicly in order to
observe his reaction. He is indeed shocked to receive it, and even more
that Mrs. Wilson is the agent of its return. His response confirms Mrs.
Wilson's suspicions, and she resolves to protect Emily from the attentions of this reprehensible man.

Emily, deeply shocked by the revelation, refuses Denbigh's offer of his
hand, whereupon Denbigh leaves, a development startling to all but
Emily and Mrs. Wilson, who do not tell what they have found of his
presumed character. Both John Moseley and Peter Johnson go to London
(the latter at Uncle Roderic Benfield's direction) to implore Denbigh's
return. In the same carriage, en route to the city, are a foreign general
and Lord Henry Stapleton, both also—as it later proves—seeking Denbigh. They meet again at Denbigh's hotel in London. Denbigh declines
the invitation to return to Benfield Lodge and leaves his quarters without
notice. John, disconsolate, encounters Lord Chatterton, who takes him
to see Grace and to meet Catherine's prospective husband, an aging,
dissolute bachelor, Lord Herriefield; both John and Grace are horrified at
the match.

On a visit to Mrs. Fitzgerald, Mrs. Wilson and Emily meet the foreign
general John had seen in the carriage and at Denbigh's room in London.
He proves to be Julia's uncle, General Louis M'Carthy y Harrison, who
has come to try to persuade Julia to accept the Catholic faith, return to
Spain, and be reunited with her father, the Conde d'Alzada. Julia refuses
to renounce her faith, and after a day's visit, her uncle returns to Spain.

A sudden shift of scene reveals Lord Pendennyss and his sister Marian,
in seclusion in Wales, as Pendennyss is leaving to attend the wedding of
his kinsman, George Denbigh, to Lady Laura Eltringham, sister of Lord
Henry Stapleton; the wedding is also attended by the Duke of Derwent,
another kinsman. News of the wedding, confirmed by a notice in the
paper, stuns John Moseley and his family, who begin to wonder about the
character of their friend George Denbigh—and of his bride. Doubts also
arise in Lord Herriefield's mind about Catherine, his bride, as he observes
the high-handed management of Lady Chatterton in the affair of John
and Grace; these doubts sow the seeds of great unhappiness for
Catherine in her ill-considered marriage. During Lady Chatterton's
shopping trip with Lord Herriefield and the new Lady Herriefield, John
proposes to Grace and is accepted, a matter of rejoicing in all quarters, as
well as a comfort to the Moseleys in the light of Denbigh's defection.

The Jarvises, reconciled to their son-in-law—now a baronet, thanks to the death of his uncle, Sir Edgar Egerton—become the butt of humor as the Jarvis women become vulgarly proud of their new rank. Provoked by an embarrassing incident involving the placing of the Egerton arms on Mrs. Jarvis's carriage, Mr. Jarvis sends up a letter from his new borough and is awarded the title his colleagues have humorously attached to him: Sir Timothy, Baronet. The conceit of the Jarvis women causes a rift, also, between them and the Chattertons. Egerton, engrossed in gambling, spends little time with his new wife. As for Lord Herriefield, he has become suspicious of Kate's every move, and she finds her marriage not only bitter but unbearable.

The Moseleys' holiday at Bath is made difficult by the presence of Denbigh's and Egerton's wives and of Egerton himself. In addition, the Duke of Derwent, similar to Denbigh in his voice and in his attentions to Emily, and Lady Laura Denbigh—wife of Colonel George Denbigh— both provide reminders for Emily of her lost love; neither seems aware of her discomfiture, nor does Lady Harriet Denbigh, warmly attracted to Emily and enamored of Lord Chatterton. All join, however, in commending Pendennyss, a sentiment in which Emily can concur. Some diversion at Bath is afforded by the obvious efforts of Caroline Harris—the daughter of Sir William Harris—to secure as a husband the Marquis of Eltringham, an attempt foredoomed to failure. Jane and Emily are during this period drawn closer together through their common misfortune, though Emily's strong Christian upbringing and faith enable her to bear the loss more philosophically than can Jane, whose pride is wounded by the knowledge that she had bared her love to a man universally acknowledged as unworthy.

In response to a desperate plea from Catherine, who is now miserable in Lisbon with her abusive husband, her mother, Grace and John—now married—and Jane voyage to Portugal. Matters in the Herriefield household have so severely deteriorated that, after a short visit, John, Grace, and Jane leave for England; Lady Chatterton remains behind to try to bring about a separation between the pair without the loss to Catherine either of her new title or of her substantial allowance. En route home, Grace experiences a spiritual awakening through the agency of a fine young rector, Rev. Mr. Harland. The rector, having met Jane on the voyage to Portugal and having, by his brother's recent death, become an Irish peer, proposes to the lovely, lonely girl but is rejected.

Meanwhile, Emily is being courted at Bath by the Duke of Derwent, and Lady Harriet Denbigh is being wooed by Lord Chatterton. Caroline Harris, failing to catch Eltringham, attempts to capture Captain Jarvis by contributing money to help him buy into the British peerage, a device that, once made public, redounds to the disfavor of both. Emily refuses the hand of the Duke of Derwent, but Lady Harriet Denbigh accepts Lord Chatterton and they are engaged to be married. On the Moseleys' return to Moseley Hall, Rev. Dr. Ives is distressed to learn that Emily had refused George Denbigh's offer of marriage.

Again, a change of scene shows Lord Pendennyss and his beloved sister, Lady Marian, in Wales, in receipt of letters from the Duke of Derwent and from Lady Harriet reporting Emily's refusal of the Duke of Derwent and urging the Earl to court her himself, since she clearly seeks a man of principle and the Earl certainly meets that qualification. A letter from Mrs. Fitzgerald apprising him of her agreed return to her father without the requirement of her renunciation of her faith also extols Miss Emily Moseley.

Meanwhile, the Moseleys, planning to spend their first winter in London in eighteen years—now that Sir Edward's fortunes are mended—persuade Uncle Roderic Benfield and the good steward Peter Johnson to spend the winter with them. To Mrs. Wilson's and Emily's delight, the Earl of Pendennyss and his sister will also winter in London. Lord Chatterton and his bride Lady Harriet, John and Grace Moseley, Lady Laura, and all the other principals will brighten the season with their company.

During a visit of Mrs. Wilson and Emily to Lady Harriet Chatterton, an occasion on which Lady Harriet announces that Lord Pendennyss and his sister will be dinner guests, Denbigh enters and after a moment's stunned surprise reveals that he is actually the Earl of Pendennyss. Both Mrs. Wilson and Emily are overjoyed that Emily's affections have not been misplaced. A lengthy explanation, requiring nearly seven full chapters of the novel to unravel, reveals the complex interrelationships among the Earl of Pendennyss, the Duke of Derwent, and Colonel George Denbigh—not the George Denbigh who had courted Emily—the family history that almost included Isabel Ives (wife of the good Rev. Dr. Ives), the accidental and subsequently planned disguise of the Earl as plain George Denbigh (actually, one of his names) while he courted Emily, and the cause of the pocketbook's being found in Mrs. Fitzgerald's cottage (it was picked up by Egerton, who proved to be the attempted seducer of Julia). The occasions on which "Denbigh" appeared embarrassed, as well as the social events he eschewed, were those on which he feared his disguise would be penetrated. All, then, is explained to the relief and the satisfaction of Emily, Mrs. Wilson, and the reader.

Emily and Pendennyss, to the great delight of all who know them, are married, and spend their honeymoon in a little cottage outside London, after which Emily takes her place as the hostess of Annerdale House, Pendennyss's London palace. On the Earl's invitation, Mrs. Wilson is to live henceforth with him and Emily, an arrangement highly satisfying to all three. Marian, the Earl's only sister, loves Emily dearly, and Emily warmly returns her love.

Not long after their marriage, the Earl is called into service in the war against Napoleon, and Emily and Mrs. Wilson move from Annerdale House to the Deanery, now the property of the Earl, where the combined duties of homemaking and of socializing help to pass the difficult time of Pendennyss's absence. Pendennyss, in the course of his battleground experiences, saves the life of a wounded British officer, Egerton, who before dying confesses to him the whole of his sorry record; he was indeed the attempted seducer of Julia Fitzgerald, and her visitor on the occasion on which Denbigh's honor was compromised by the pocket-book.

On his safe return to England after Waterloo, Pendennyss and his wife resume their contented way among their friends, with the promise of a closer connection between Lady Marian and the Duke of Derwent, and with Jane, still single, as a reminder of the lack of precautionary inves-tigation into the character of one seemingly at ease before the world, and with the sage concluding agreement of Mrs. Wilson and Rev. Dr. Ives that "prevention is at all times better than cure" (p. 484).

Sir Owen Ap Rice, Roderic Benfield, Lord Bolton, Lady Chatterton, Catherine Chatterton, Grace Chatterton, Astley Cooper (Lord Chatterton), Sam Daniels, David, Thomas Davis, Mrs. Thomas Davis, Frederick Denbigh, George Denbigh, George Denbigh (Earl of Pendennyss), Colonel George Denbigh, Lady Harriet Denbigh, Marian Denbigh, Captain Horace Digby, Colonel Henry Egerton, Marquis of Eltringham, Julia Fitzgerald, Francis, Rev. Mr. Harland, Harmer, Caroline Harris, Sir William Harris, Haughton, Mrs. Haughton, Lucy Haughton, Lord Herriefield, Holt, Miss Howard, Humphreys, Rev. Dr. Ives, Francis Ives, Isabel Ives, Jackson, Captain Henry Jarvis, Mary Jarvis, Sarah Jarvis, Timothy Jarvis, Mrs. Timo-thy Jarvis, John, Peter Johnson, Jones, Lady Juliana, Donna Lorenza, General Louis M'Carthy y Harrison, Martin, Lady Anne Moseley, Clara Moseley, Sir Edward Moseley, Emily Moseley, Jane Moseley, John Moseley, Sir Herbert Nicholson, Saunders, Lord Henry Sta-pleton, Lady Laura Stapleton, Lady Sarah Stapleton, Lord William Stapleton, Stevenson, Tom, Miss Wigram, William (Jarvis servant), William (Moseley servant), Willis, Charlotte Wilson.

The Red Rover: A Tale, 1828.

In the opening chapter of exposition, devoted largely to colonial history (particularly that of Rhode Island), two minor characters serve as a comic chorus to set the stage for the subsequent action. The time is October, 1759, just after Quebec has fallen to the British, and the seaport of Newport, Rhode Island, has just finished celebrating the victory. Hector Homespun, a stereotype of the cowardly tailor, interprets for his rustic customer, Pardon Hopkins, the significance of the day's events. He then regales Pardon with accounts of the awesome and often uncanny exploits of a notorious pirate thought to be in the area. Both the pirate captain and his ship (with *Dolphin* as its real name) are known as "The Red Rover." Homespun also calls to the countryman's attention the strange behavior of and the mysterious aura surrounding a reputed slave ship that has been anchored offshore for several days.

Two groups of strangers have appeared in Providence: the crew of the supposed slave ship and a trio of seamen ostensibly seeking employment. The latter group is comprised of a young gentleman, known to his companions as Harry Wilder, and two middle-aged mariners, Dick Fid and a free black named Scipio Africanus. Still another stranger excites curiosity, a lone, green-clad man who claims to be a lawyer but who in fact is the Red Rover himself. To this stranger Homespun confides his suspicions that the reputed "slaver" in the outer harbor is the *Red Rover.* The suave Rover assures the gullible tailor of rewards, including knighthood, for his help in capturing the pirate, and then, after swearing Homespun to secrecy, agrees to meet him that night at 11 o'clock.

Harry Wilder and the disguised Rover encounter each other several times, each trying to identify the other without revealing his own identity. While the two are examining an old structure (apparently the ruins of a mill but thought by local residents to be an ancient military tower), they eavesdrop on the conversation of four women: young Gertrude Grayson; her governess, Mrs. Wyllys; her aunt, the widow of Admiral de Lacey; and Cassandra, a Negro servant. Mrs. de Lacey (née Grayson) is bidding farewell to her niece, who is preparing to rejoin her father, General Grayson, now a Carolina planter. Both men are amused by the widow's nautical malapropisms, the product of the late Admiral's twisted sense of humor: he had wittily mistaught his wife seamanship, with all its technical terminology, simply for his own entertainment.

Late that night Wilder and his two companions row out to the "slaver" to inquire about berths for themselves aboard the vessel. While awaiting an interview with its captain, Wilder notices being swung aboard on a boom a parcel which he recognizes as a human body. He is told that it is a drunken seaman being returned to his duty, but (as Wilder and the reader later learn) it is actually the bound and gagged Homespun, kidnapped and imprisoned aboard the *Red Rover* lest he alert his fellow townspeople about his suspicions about the "slave ship." Wilder also observes that the ship is very heavily armed, and that the captain's quarters, while displaying an exotic, oriental decor, are in some ways like an inner citadel. The captain turns out to be the green-clad "lawyer" Wilder had seen earlier that day, and it soon becomes apparent that he is also none other than the Red Rover himself. In their conversation Wilder and the Rover engage in subtle intellectual sparring and repartee, each trying to evaluate the character of the other. Each seems to be aware of the motivation of the other; Wilder is not surprised to find himself in the presence of the Rover, and the Rover, in turn, is not surprised that Wilder has come to him. Wilder agrees to become first mate aboard the vessel but insists that he return to the land for the rest of that night—if only to assure himself that he is trusted and that he is not a prisoner. Confident that he knows his man, the Rover believes Wilder's promise not to reveal the ship's true identity while ashore. Less confident about the discretion of Dick Fid and Scipio Africanus, however, he has them made too drunk to leave—excellent hostages just in case he has mistaken Wilder's intentions.

Wilder's real purpose for returning to shore is to warn Gertrude Grayson and Mrs. Wyllys not to take passage on the *Royal Caroline*. He cannot give his actual reason for this warning (that the ship will probably be followed and captured by the pirates), so he invents a number of defects in the ship and its rigging to suggest that it is an unsafe vessel. Twice he calls at the de Lacey mansion to warn the ladies of this peril, and twice he is gainsaid by one "Bob Bunt," seemingly an aged seaman but in reality one of the many masquerades of the Red Rover. In the debate that follows, the decision goes to Bob after he claims that he served for years under Admiral de Lacey. Later Wilder bribes Bob with a guinea to change his story about the *Royal Caroline,* and this Bob promises to do—a promise which he does not keep.

Wilder later meets Bob Bunt in a private room at the "Foul Anchor," an inn owned by a pious hypocrite named Honest Joe Joram. Intending to press Bob to carry out his agreement to dissuade the ladies from embarking on the *Royal Caroline,* Wilder becomes cautious when he senses that Bob and Joe Joram are collaborators in some sort of shady business. Later, while watching the *Royal Caroline* being readied for departure, Wilder is handed a letter by Roderick, the cabin boy of the *Red Rover*. The Rover informs him that Nicholas Nichols, captain of the *Royal Caroline,* has just broken a leg, and he orders Wilder to apply at once for his job.

The Rover's agents ashore will, says the letter, support his application. Boarding the ship, Wilder offers his services to its Newport agent, Mr. Bale, and, at length, secures the position but not before Honest Joe Joram has commended him with elaborate fictitious evidence of his nautical accomplishments. As the *Royal Caroline* is leaving the inner harbor, it becomes hopelessly entangled by an incompetent pilot in the ground tackle of the *Red Rover*. At this point, Wilder literally takes command of the *Royal Caroline*. Contrary to maritime law, he orders the pilot thrown into his boat to return to port. The new captain then gives orders necessary to separate the two ships; but by the time these maneuvers have been completed, the tide and wind are unfavorable for setting out to sea. There is no choice but to anchor the *Royal Caroline* offshore, parallel to the *Red Rover*.

A fishing skiff floats alongside the *Royal Caroline*, its sole occupant, Bob Bunt, only pretending to fish. He and Wilder quarrel quietly over Bob's failure to carry out his promise to warn the ladies against boarding the *Royal Caroline*. When Bob's deceit and villainy become too much for Wilder to tolerate, he orders one of his mates to capture the old man. A jolly boat pursues the skiff until it passes behind the *Red Rover* and then simply disappears. It has, obviously, been taken into the seemingly unmanned "slaver," for Bunt seems to be one of the pirate's men; but the superstitious crewmen of the jolly boat think he was spirited away by a different master, namely, the Devil.

It is not long after reaching the open sea before other ominous signs become apparent. The *Royal Caroline* is soon followed by a strange ship which it cannot outrun. Wilder alone is aware that this pursuer is the *Red Rover*. The crew concludes that it is a spectre ship sent after them by the Devil. In their terror they fuse into sinister association quite unrelated pieces of circumstantial evidence: the uncanny disappearance the day before of Bunt, the unexplained and inopportune accident that had disabled Captain Nichols, the uncommonly cool behavior of Wilder, whom none had seen or heard of before this voyage, the unaccountably heavy seas, and the eerie light on the water at night. Unable to outdistance his pursuer, Wilder turns back toward Newport only to be struck by a hurricane so furious that he is forced to have the masts cut away in order to keep the ship from capsizing. In the midst of this tempest, the mystery ship, without a sail showing or a soul aboard visible, glides past the disabled *Royal Caroline* at a distance of only one hundred feet. The image of the legendary ghost ship is now complete as far as the crew is concerned. Because the gale drives the *Red Rover* before it at a rate four times as fast as it does the heavier merchantman, Wilder prays aloud that it continue to blow until dawn. This is decisive evidence for Knighthead, the second mate, that their new captain is an agent of Hell leading them to destruction. He leads in mutiny a crew that needs little urging. Unable to take the ship's large launch without masts from which to swing it over the side, the mutineers escape in open boats, leaving aboard the doomed ship Wilder, Gertrude, Mrs. Wyllys, and Cassandra. When the ship sinks, however, the launch floats free and provides a means of survival for Wilder and the three women. Their need for this boat is of but short duration, however, for they are soon picked up by the *Dolphin.*

To divert the two ladies aboard the *Dolphin,* its master, Captain Heidegger, gives the order "To mischief!" There follows some horseplay, including the arrival of King Neptune to initiate new travelers in his realm; he is generously tipped a guinea apiece by Gertrude and her governess. The good-natured revelry soon degenerates into a confrontation of foretopmen and marines. When bloodshed seems imminent, Wilder steps between the two groups. The freebooters are too aroused, however, to obey the orders of a newcomer whose status is, to them, still in doubt; turning their fury now against him, they prepare to throw him overboard. The Rover, in the meantime, stands, Byron-like, lost in meditation and unaware of the violence until Mrs. Wyllys calls his attention to it. He immediately restores order to the ship and announces that Wilder is his second in command.

That evening, with peace restored to the *Dolphin,* the captain and Wilder discuss the hazards of piracy. Heidegger reveals why he had become a pirate. An American colonial in the British navy, he had challenged to a duel an officer who had slandered his native land. Having killed his antagonist, he decided to wage a one-man war against Great Britain rather than submit to a court martial whose sense of justice he distrusted. His piracy is thus rationalized as a form of patriotism. Had there been an American flag to which he could have given his allegiance, he tells Wilder, the world would never have seen the crimson pennant of the *Red Rover.*

Acquainted with ships, their rigging, and the composition of their crews, and aware that they are headed for the Caribbean, Mrs. Wyllys suspects the nature of the ship on which she and her young ward now find themselves. She interrogates closely Roderick, the cabin boy, but learns little from him about either the ship or its charismatic commander. She does discover, however, that Roderick is actually a woman, apparently the captain's mistress. She never reveals her discovery—nor does the narrator ever openly acknowledge Roderick's sex—but the reader infers the fact from Mrs. Wyllys' discharging Roderick from further duties in the ladies' cabin in order to protect the innocent Gertrude. Captain Heidegger, for his part, is equally curious about the real identity of his lieutenant, Harry Wilder, so to secure information about the young man, he quizzes Dick Fid about this old seaman's relationship to Wilder. Fid spins a lengthy yarn, marked by a rambling style and salty diction, about "Master Harry," as he calls Wilder. Twenty-four years earlier he and Scipio Africanus had found the child and a dying woman, apparently his mother, on a deserted and sinking vessel. They had saved the child, obviously of upperclass background; but both they and their naval officers had failed to locate the boy's family. Their only clue, providing no real evidence, was the name of the ship on which he was found, *Ark, of Lynnhaven.* Harry was therefore reared on shipboard, taught seamanship by Fid and Latin by the captain. Before Fid's story describes Wilder's adult years (of much more interest to Heidegger), it is interrupted by the cry "Sail, ho!"

The approaching ship, Heidegger discerns, is one with which Wilder, Fid, and Scipio are all familiar. Wilder admits that the stranger is the British cruiser on which they had sailed before joining the Rover, and he advises the captain to try to pass this formidable warship unnoticed. The advice cannot be acted upon, however, for Dick Fid lets loose a topsail—it is a deliberate signal—which reveals the position of the *Dolphin.* As they reconnoiter each other, both ships prepare for possible battle. When the Rover becomes aware that Wilder and his men are reluctant to participate in armed conflict against their former shipmates, he generously exempts them from this duty. (This is one of the many reflections of admirable qualities in Heidegger's character.) But there is no engagement at this time, for the Rover suddenly decides to fly British colors and pretend that his is a ship specially commissioned to hunt the *Red Rover!* So confident is Captain Heidegger of his own and his ship's disguise that he coolly goes aboard the cruiser *Dart* to visit with its commander, Captain Bignall. While on the *Dart,* Captain Heidegger calls himself "Captain Howard." In reading the names of the *Dart's* officers, he discovers one Henry Ark listed as Bignall's first lieutenant. When he is told that this young officer is on a mission so secret that it cannot be discussed, he realizes that his own second in command, Harry Wilder, is in fact this very Henry Ark.

Back on his own ship, the Rover accuses Wilder of treachery. Wilder acknowledges his special commission to destroy the Red Rover but claims that his admiration of Heidegger's personality has induced him to greater cooperation and less pursuit than he had intended. The admiration is mutual, and the Rover magnanimously frees Wilder to return to his position on the *Dart*. When Wilder insists that he cannot leave the two ladies behind on the *Dolphin*, Heidegger also agrees to free both of them as well as Dick Fid and Scipio Africanus.

Captain Bignall is astounded to see his own first officer coming aboard the *Dart* from the *Dolphin's* boat, but Wilder's explanation is delayed by an equally surprising discovery. The *Dart's* chaplain, old Dr. Merton, recognizes in Mrs. Wyllys the woman he had wed more than twenty years earlier to Paul de Lacey, British naval officer and son of the famous Admiral de Lacey. Since the girl's father had opposed the union, they had been wed secretly by Dr. Merton. Paul de Lacey then had died in battle before the couple could be reconciled with the bride's parent and before news of the marriage could be made public; thus the de Laceys had not known that their son had had a wife.

Apprised of the Rover's magnanimity toward Wilder and his chivalric behavior toward Gertrude Grayson and Mrs. Wyllys, Captain Bignall is persuaded to offer amnesty to the pirate in return for total surrender and the dismantling of his ship. Bignall also sends with Wilder, his emissary, an enumeration of the *Dart's* armament to convince Heidegger that the *Dolphin* could not survive a battle with the cruiser. When the Rover scornfully rejects the ultimatum, Roderick, the cabin boy, pleads with Wilder to withdraw Bignall's aggressive message and substitute for it an appeal to Heidegger's many admirable qualities. (It is apparent here now that Roderick is no ordinary cabin attendant; he speaks with fearless familiarity to the pirate, calling him "Walter.") After the failure of negotiations, the two ships soon engage in battle.

Through a combination of good fortune and superior seamanship the *Red Rover* defeats and captures the more heavily armed cruiser. Among many killed are Captain Bignall and Scipio Africanus, the latter trying, barehanded at the end, to protect Wilder from the vengeful pirates. The victors are determined to hang Wilder and Fid as traitors to their cause. Such are the terms of agreement under which the pirates have shipped aboard the *Red Rover* that its captain cannot deny them this vengeance. The execution is stayed momentarily as the dying Scipio is prayed for by the *Dart's* chaplain. Scipio calls the attention of the spectators to the dog collar worn on his arm, the collar of the dog found with the infant Wilder on the sinking *Ark*. An inscription on the collar reads "Neptune, the Property of Paul de Lacey." It is now manifest that Wilder is the son of Paul de Lacey and his secretly married wife, who still goes under the name of "Mrs. Wyllys." The latter now pleads so movingly for the life of her child that even the hardened freebooters are silenced momentarily; the Rover, moved again by his nobler qualities, takes this opportunity to declare all punitive proceedings postponed until the following morning.

When morning arrives, it reveals a different *Dart* from the one on which the had sun set. Heidegger has supervised during the night the replacement of its broken masts and spars and the repair of its sails so that it is once again seaworthy. Announcing to his crew on the *Red Rover* that he is terminating his agreement with them, he orders them ashore and has distributed among them all of his gold. Stunned and confused, the crew has no choice but to obey his orders, for he has had the nearby *Dart's* guns trained on his own decks. The gold is all theirs, he tells them, but the ship and its prisoners are his.

Turning over the *Dart* and the ladies to the care of Wilder, the Rover bids the new captain farewell. Shortly after the *Dart* sets sail for an American port, an explosion destroys the *Red Rover*. Those who view with field glasses the previous location of the pirate ship think that they see a small object on the surface of the sea, possibly a boat containing survivors, but the distance is so great that they soon lose sight of the object.

The last scene is set more than twenty years later in the Newport home of Captain Henry de Lacey (alias Harry Wilder) of the American Navy. He and Gertrude Grayson have now been married for many years and have a seventeen-year-old son, Paul. With them live Henry's mother and the aged Fid, the seaman now serving as the majordomo in the household. As the citizens of Newport are again celebrating a victory, this time the successful conclusion of the American Revolution, a mortally wounded American naval officer, accompanied by a grieving woman, is brought on a litter to the de Lacey home. The dying man is Heidegger, formerly the Red Rover, and his consort apparently the erstwhile "cabin boy," Roderick. Heidegger is now, at long last, recognized by the elderly Mrs. Paul de Lacey as the brother from whom she had been parted in childhood; he is thus also Henry de Lacey's uncle. In the battle of the colonies for independence Heidegger had finally found the cause he had always sought. With almost superhuman effort, he raises himself from the litter, unfurls an American flag which he has kept folded beneath his pillow, and with his last breath he shouts, "Wilder! We have triumphed!" (p. 522).

Scipio Africanus, Bale, Captain Bignall, Bob Brace, Cassandra, Admiral de Lacey, Henry de Lacey, Paul de Lacey, Dr. Dogma, Edward Earing, Richard Fid, General Grayson, Gertrude Grayson, Captain Walter Heidegger, Desire Homespun, Hector Homespun, Pardon Hopkins, Joe Joram, 'Keziah Joram, Judy, Francis Knighthead, Rev. Dr. Merton, Nab, Captain Nicholas Nichols, Jack Nightingale, Roderick, Mrs. Wyllys.

The Redskins; or, Indian and Injin: Being the Conclusion
   of the Littlepage Manuscripts, 1846.

[This is the concluding volume of a trilogy of which the first volume is
Satanstoe and the second is *The Chainbearer*.]

Early in the 1840s, Hugh Roger Littlepage, a bachelor of fifty-nine
commonly called Ro (the second son of Mordaunt and Ursula Malbone
Littlepage), and his nephew Hugh Roger Littlepage, twenty-five (son of
the deceased first son, Malbone, of Mordaunt and Ursula Littlepage),
resettled in Paris after extended travels in the Mideast, discuss at length
the changing customs of their home country, the United States, and
admit to a twinge of homesickness. Numerous letters and newspapers
awaiting them following their eighteen-month absence from Paris ac-
quaint the two men with the increased fervor of the anti-rent movement
in New York State, a movement that threatens the security of their own
property holdings. Every aspect of current life at home is reviewed
during the ensuing discussion—political, social, economic, philosophical,
and sentimental—and thus the background is provided for the action
that later takes place in the novel. Most of the significant characters of
the entire novel are introduced in the course of the two-day discussion,
interrupted only by the hours spent in sleep, and prompted by the tidings
found either in family or business letters or in the accumulated newspapers from home.

In view of the serious developments associated with the anti-rent
movement, the two decide to return home at once, incognito—there has
been violence against various landholders—sending their servants home
separately by way of England. On their arrival in New York City, the two
Littlepages, deliberately avoiding their own townhouses, go to the
quarters of Jack Dunning, Uncle Ro's agent, who acquaints them with
even more distressing details concerning the unrest. Jack Dunning also
informs them that Ursula Malbone Littlepage, Martha (Patt or Patty)
Littlepage, Henrietta Coldbrooke, and Anne Marston (the last two are
wards of Uncle Ro, as well as prospective wives for young Hugh) are all
presently at Ravensnest and thereby exposed to the risk of abuse by the
anti-renters. Hugh and his uncle assemble costumes, including wigs, and
adopt heavy German accents, disguises that not even family members
can penetrate; they retain the father/son name Davidson under which
they had booked for the transatlantic voyage, and each chooses a trade:
the uncle to be an immigrant trinket and watch peddler and the nephew
to play the hurdy-gurdy, accompanied by a monkey; the monkey is
discarded after a single day as being too much trouble. On the boat en
route to Albany, the two encounter Seneca Newcome (grandson of Jason

Newcome), and Uncle Ro sells "Squire Seneky" a watch at a low price in exchange for his help in locating a good market for the rest of the articles he has for sale; Newcome is completely deceived by their disguises. In Troy, they encounter the Rev. Mr. Warren and his daughter Mary, both of whom have heard of the "Germans" from Newcome; there, young Hugh first tries out his music in public and finds a warm response from the Warrens. Invited upstairs by the Warrens, Hugh is still with them when Opportunity Newcome (sister of Seneca Newcome) enters the public parlor. Fortunately, she fails to recognize young Hugh in his disguise—though she has known him for years—and carries on a mindless chatter and an affectation of French that cause Hugh and Mary to exchange amused glances.

On Seneca Newcome's arrival, all board the train for Saratoga, where the anti-rent conversation becomes heated. From Saratoga, Uncle Ro and Hugh go on alone to the inn at Mooseridge, where discussion of the anti-rent controversy is even more marked; greater sensibility and balance on the matter are evidenced here, an encouraging sign to Hugh as he listens to the temperate judgments of attorney Hubbard and mechanic Hall. From Mooseridge, the uncle and nephew approach Ravensnest, and after considerable debate decide to test their disguises first on black Jaap (Jacob Satanstoe) and Susquesus, the Onondago; Jaap has lost much of his recent memory, but Susquesus proves to be as observant as ever. During the "peddlers'" visit with Jaap and Susquesus, Ursula Malbone Littlepage (now eighty) and the young women staying with her—Hugh's sister Martha, Henrietta Coldbrooke, Anne Marston, and Mary Warren—stop by in the course of an airing by carriage, and Mary recognizes them as the "Germans" met in Troy. At Mary's request, Hugh plays a tune on the flute (an instrument on which he is highly accomplished), and the music is enjoyed by all; Ursula pays him a dollar and he kisses her hand, but his relatives do not recognize him. While Uncle Ro and Jaap see the ladies off, Susquesus asks why Hugh had not kissed his grandmother's face; he was the only one to penetrate the disguises. Young Hugh, surprised, urges Susquesus not to reveal his identity, explaining the danger from the anti-renters, or "Injins." (The irate tenants, intent upon gaining ownership of lands leased from the Littlepages, have adopted hoods and mock-Indian calico dresses and, styling themselves "Injins," have been committing abuses and depredations against the landlords and their property in this crude disguise.)

Uncle Ro and Hugh, deciding to maintain their disguises, next visit Tom Miller, manager of the Ravensnest farm and a steady sort. With Tom are two of his sons and two hired men; of the latter, one—Joshua

Brigham—is especially outspoken for anti-renters and against aristocrats and is finally sent about his business by Tom Miller. Further
discussion reveals that Tom recognizes a social "pecking order" in which
he himself participates by not allowing his daughter Kitty to associate
with the daughters of a man of poorer family. [A long author's commentary is introduced here on the subtleties of "aristocracy."] The conversation between young Hugh and Tom Miller is interrupted by the return of
Madam Littlepage's carriage. The women want to look again at the
peddler's trinkets, to which he quickly adds some high-quality watches
and other items bought in Europe as gifts for his wards. Mrs. Littlepage
buys a gold pencil for $15.00 and presents it to Mary Warren, and shortly
thereafter purchases a French-made watch and gives it to Mary, who
protests the extravagance but will accept the gift if her father approves.
Since Mary's father is to dine at Ravensnest that evening, Mrs. Littlepage
invites the two peddlers to have their dinner at the 'Nest also, an
invitation they eagerly accept. At the 'Nest, while they are all examining
Hugh's flute, Mrs. Littlepage realizes who the two "peddlers" must be,
and she draws young Hugh into a nearby parlor and asks him about her
conjecture. He confirms what she suspects: that he is her grandson and
that the peddler is her son. Some little furor is caused by Patt's desire for
a $100 gold chain—bought specifically for the girl young Hugh will
marry—but the discussion subsides as Mrs. Littlepage realizes that no
amount of money can buy that chain. The girls make other selections,
totaling $200; and the peddler and Mrs. Littlepage are left alone in the
room, ostensibly to conclude the business, but in truth to be together as
mother and son.

The two peddlers are served dinner immediately by John, the footman;
during the dinner, Hugh openly declares his strong attraction to Mary
Warren, a declaration displeasing to his uncle, who wants Hugh to marry
one of his two wards. Following the dinner, the footman returns, and the
three men talk at length about the anti-rent unrest. This conversation is
interrupted by Mrs. Littlepage, who sends John on an errand and then
arranges for Hugh and his sister, Patt (Martha), to talk undisturbed.
Following a tearful yet joyous reunion and much conversation, the two
are at last ready to join the rest of the company. Since the family dinner
hour is at hand, the peddlers leave, promising to come again. From
Ravensnest they go to Tom Miller's farm, to find Joshua Brigham more
distrustful than ever. Much talk ensues about anti-rent matters and
about aristocracy, talk in which Josh's intention to defraud Hugh Littlepage is made evident. By agreeing at the right moments, Hugh is
invited to become an Injin, an offer he accepts with alacrity. [A long

authorial intrusion here deals with the term "aristocratic."] Joshua leaves on an errand after this conversation; Hugh is certain, however, that he will see both Joshua and Tom Miller at the meeting the following day, a meeting featuring a paid lecturer.

Tom Miller provides the two peddlers with a dearborn [a one-horse wagon] and uses a two-horse wagon to transport his wife, his daughter, one of the hired men, and himself to the meeting. Hugh notes a dearborn standing before the rectory; obviously, the Rev. Mr. Warren plans also to attend the anti-rent meeting. As Hugh and his uncle drive through the woods, they are set upon by fifty Injins, hooded and in calico dress, who demand to know their business. "Selling watches" seems innocent e-nough, and many examine the watches while their leader, Streak o' Lightning, continues to question the peddlers. At the sound of a low whistle, all the Injins disappear into the woods just as the Rev. Mr. Warren's dearborn comes into sight. The rector and his daughter Mary stop because the peddlers' dearborn is blocking the road; a frank conver-sation concerning the meeting ensues, overheard by the hidden Injins, a conversation in which the peddlers, to protect both themselves and the rector, assume an anti-rent position quite disconcerting to the rector. While they are still talking, the Injins come whooping out of the woods. When the rector begins to warn them of the illegality of their attack, they put the rector and Uncle Ro into Tom Miller's dearborn and take the two with them to the meeting. The Rev. Mr. Warren asks Hugh to see Mary safely home and then to come along to the meeting. After the rest go down the road, Hugh reveals his identity to Mary, who is greatly reassured by this information but fearful for his safety. Nevertheless, the two proceed toward the meeting house, where they find the Rev. Mr. Warren talking with Seneca and Opportunity Newcome, and Uncle Ro engaged in peddling watches. All except the Injins go inside the meeting house. As soon as the Rev. Mr. Warren discerns that two ministers plan to dignify the meeting by prayer, he arises and takes Mary with him, followed quickly by Hugh, who assumes that Warren is ill. Mary having told him of Hugh's identity, he explains his reason for leaving the meeting so hastily: the participation of ministers in a flagrantly lawless undertaking. As soon as the opening prayers are concluded, the Rev. Mr. Warren, Mary, and Hugh re-enter the meeting house and listen to the two-hour impassioned, ill-informed, rabble-rousing speech. When a call is given for questions or comments, the mechanic Hall stands up and speaks calmly, literately, and sensibly about the falsehoods presented in the lecture. Popular disapproval of Hall's concluding remarks brings the Injins rushing in, and the audience scatters far and wide. Injins surround

Hall threateningly, but none dares to harm him. Hugh, detecting Seneca Newcome beneath one of the Injin costumes, approaches him and addresses him by name. Seneca, an attorney embarrassed to be thus detected, takes Hugh to the store which he and his brother own and treats him to a glass of strong whiskey that Hugh secretly spills; Hugh also sees an Injin enter the store and commandeer twenty yards of calico, to be charged to "Down Rent." Clearly, the Injins have begun to victimize their employers. A discussion between Uncle Ro and two of the Ravensnest tenants, Holmes and Tubbs, concerning the function of land-holders in the "old countries" follows, with an obvious failure of reason to prevail over wrath.

As Uncle Ro and Hugh are driving the dearborn back through the woods, they see two Injins commandeer the wagon behind them and drive it off; soon afterwards, they find Holmes and Tubbs walking, having lost their wagon to Injins in the same fashion. After listening for a few minutes to Holmes's woeful tale, Uncle Ro and Hugh drive on, expecting at any moment to be stopped by the Injins they see in ambush, but they are not halted.

At length they meet a band of genuine red Indians, in search of Susquesus—to pay homage to the noble Onondago on their way back home from Washington—and Uncle Hugh takes off his wig and intro-duces himself and Hugh, also unwigged, as the Littlepages known among the Indian band. When Uncle Ro says there are Injins in the woods, the real Indians hail them and, not being answered, pursue them, capturing only two: Joshua Brigham and Seneca Newcome, each of whom blames the other for this degrading capture, prompting a tooth-and-nail strug-gle between the two. Uncle Ro indicates to the red Indians the direction of Susquesus's wigwam; then he and Hugh hurry home, stopping only long enough to discover that the rector and his daughter have already left for Ravensnest for dinner.

Uncle Ro and Hugh are warmly welcomed at the 'Nest, and each dresses himself in his own proper clothes for dinner. Dinner and the following conversation are thoroughly enjoyed; meanwhile, watch is being kept for the arrival of the red Indians. On their arrival, they are courteously greeted and then allowed to examine the details of the fortress and environs that have been preserved in their oral history. They are to be sheltered in Herman Mordaunt's original farmhouse, with all necessities supplied. Susquesus is notified of the presence of the visitors so that he can greet them as becomes the noble man he is. Susquesus, appropriately garbed and painted, receives the compliments of his visitors, delivers a moving response, and accepts the tributes of the group's orator. Then the Indian band retires for the night, and the Littlepages and their household return to the 'Nest, having had the speeches interpreted by Manytongues.

That night when all others have apparently retired, Hugh sees a horseman riding toward Ravensnest on a little-used trail. Mary Warren also sees the rider, and hurries to the gate, where she and Hugh admit Opportunity Newcome. Opportunity warns Hugh privately that injury is planned against him; as she prepares to ride home, she indicates that fire is to be the method used. Hugh alerts the red Indians, who are eager for action. Meanwhile, Injins have climbed the cliff and set fire to the kitchen, an action detected by Mary and reported to Hugh. While Mary hurries to alert Uncle Ro and also Manytongues, Hugh discharges his rifle once, and then uses it to club one of the incendiaries, knocking him senseless; he then grapples with the second incendiary. The advantage of surprise yields to the enemy's superior strength and wrestling skill, and Mary returns just in time to save Hugh from being choked to death. Manytongues, accompanying Mary, secures the incendiaries while Hugh extinguishes the fire. Removal of the blackface disguises reveals the intruders as Joshua Brigham and Seneca Newcome. Grandmother Littlepage, hearing the noise, summons the family to her and elicits a full report. While they are still discussing the kitchen fire, they discover that a barn filled with hay has been set afire half a mile from the house. The redskins are stealthily creeping up on the Injins dancing around the flames; the Injins flee as soon as they discover the approach of the real Indians. The rest of the night passes quietly.

The family and their white guests attend Sunday morning services the next day, finding the Episcopal church crowded with non-Episcopalians, all resentful of Hugh's sitting in the family's canopied pew. Following the service, these outsiders hold a public meeting and approve a set of resolutions, previously drawn up, which is presented to Hugh as he and the younger members of his party walk home from church. At first refusing to accept the resolutions because of the peremptory manner in which they are presented by the three men delegated to deliver them, Hugh accepts them when politely requested to do so. The resolutions are read aloud by Hugh in a copse en route to the house; in the resolutions, strong objection is made to canopied pews and to a landlord's setting a barn afire so that he can accuse others of arson. Hugh is determined not to remove the canopy under pressure and to scotch the rumor he had set his own barn afire. On arrival at the 'Nest, Hugh is told that Opportunity Newcome awaits him; he hurries to the ravine where she is concealed and, hearing her plea for the release of Seneca, invites her to come openly to the 'Nest to appeal for her brother's release.

The following morning, Hugh is awakened by the news that his pew canopy has been moved and now covers the pigpen on Tom Miller's farm, news that amuses rather than angers him. Much discussion of the matter follows among the family and guests. The conversation reveals that in the last three weeks Seneca Newcome has proposed marriage to the three young ladies at the 'Nest, and has been refused by all three (all by means of letters); this discovery deeply angers Uncle Ro, who regards the proposals as sheer effrontery. The conversation is interrupted by word that the red Indians are to hold a closing ceremonial for Susquesus on the lawn below the piazza; benches are set up for the occasion, and plenty of tobacco is provided. All the family and guests have chairs on the lawn, and the servants are also allowed to watch the ceremonial. Both Susquesus and Jaap are elaborately dressed, and Susquesus is elegantly painted. On the arrival of the Indian guests, the pipe-smoking begins, with Jaap the only one refusing to relinquish the pipe until the tobacco has been all used. Eloquent speeches are given by Prairiefire and by Deersfoot, the latter addressing Jaap; Jaap's response is interrupted by the approach of two hundred Injins, first noted by old Jaap himself. All of the party at the 'Nest, as well as Susquesus, Jaap, and the visiting Indians, are moved to the piazza, and the fort is barricaded. Opportunity Newcome comes to warn Hugh of his danger, and she too is brought into the fort. As the Injins advance across the lawn, Mr. Warren is seen; when the Injins attempt to stop him, Mary, heedless of her own safety, runs out to meet him, and the Injins fall back, allowing Mary and her father to enter the fort. The ceremony continues, in full hearing of the Injins, with the last portion of Jaap's speech addressed to them and their shameful behavior. Prairiefire, in a dignified but moving speech, asks Susquesus to accompany them westward, to die among his own people; Susquesus, in response, honors but refuses the request, and then condemns the attitudes and practices of the Injins. Eaglesflight then tells the story of Susquesus's leaving his own tribe because the Delaware squaw he desired belonged to another warrior by virtue of capture and he would not break the Indian law governing this matter. The Injins, offended by this just comparison between Susquesus's honorable way and their own dishonorable one, rattle their muskets preparatory to attack, but restrain themselves on seeing the sheriff of the county appear on the piazza. For their own safety, Hugh puts Seneca Newcome and Joshua Brigham in the library; Opportunity finds them there, unbinds them, and leads them by a secret route to freedom. At the sheriff's order, the Injins disband and flee, an action scornfully observed by the visiting Indians. Susquesus speaks for the last time, counseling his visitors to do right and to keep the

Indian law. Then the visitors bid him farewell, thank their Ravensnest hosts, and leave with as little ceremony as they had come.

In a subsequent family discussion, Uncle Ro reveals that he is settling a sum of $50,000 on Mary Warren and that she will marry young Hugh Roger Littlepage; his hope that Hugh would marry Henrietta is satisfied in Henrietta's being courted and won by a colleague of Hugh, even as Anne was courted and won by another. Rejoicing at the news is evident except among the anti-renters, who consider Mary and Hugh's match unequal and therefore unsuitable. Injin activity no longer intrudes on Ravensnest, and the family members remain there in safety, with Hugh and Mary happily married.

> Barney, Big Thunder, Joshua Brigham, Peter Bunce, Henrietta Cold-brooke, Deersfoot, Jack Dunning, Eaglesflight, Flintyheart, Tim Hall, Onesiphorus Hayden, Hester, Demosthenes Hewlett, Holmes, Hubbard, Jacob, John, Hugh Roger Littlepage [uncle], Hugh Roger Littlepage [nephew], Martha Littlepage, Ursula Malbone Littlepage, Manytongues, Anne Marston, Harry Miller, Kitty Miller, Tom Miller, Mrs. Tom Miller, John Mowatt, Opportunity Newcome, Orson Newcome, Seneca Newcome, Peter, Prairiefire, Jacob Satanstoe, Betty Smith, John Smith, Streak o' Lightning, Susquesus, Pulaski Todd, Hezekiah Trott, Shabbakuk Tubbs, Rev. Mr. Warren, Mary Warren.

Satanstoe; or, The Littlepage Manuscripts: A Tale of the Colony, 1845.

[This is the first volume of a trilogy, succeeded by *The Chainbearer* and concluded by *The Redskins*.]

Cornelius (Corny) Littlepage, narrator and hero of the novel, born in 1737 at Satanstoe (a peninsula rumored formed by the print of Satan's toe) in New York, is of the minor landed gentry and is early made aware of the pronounced differences between New Yorkers and New Englanders in religion, philosophy, and social practices. A marked aversion for "Yankee" ways determines his family's choice of the college he attends after preparatory study under the Rev. Mr. Thomas Worden, the Episcopal rector, one more concerned with the form than with the spirit of his profession: at the age of fourteen, Corny sets off with his father for Nassau Hall (later Princeton), which has no Yankee "peculiarities." En route, they spend a night and a day at Aunt Jane Legge's home in New York, Corny's first visit to that city of 12,000. On an outing to view the arrival of the Patroon of Albany, Corny encounters a pretty little girl in whose defense he gives a bullying butcher's boy a sound thrashing approved by his guide, Pompey, one of his aunt's Negro slaves.

Corny's four years in college are pleasant and beneficial, and he returns home after graduation to the solid friendship he has always maintained with sturdy, honest Dirck Follock (Van Valkenburgh) and to the awkward but provocative presence of a Yankee schoolmaster, Jason Newcome, hired to replace the Rev. Mr. Worden. Corny and Jason differ on almost all points, chiefly in openness of manner and in value systems; Jason's Puritanical notions and actions are highly entertaining but rather disgusting to Corny.

Corny's first visit to New York as a young man, accompanied by Dirck, occurs when he is twenty, and produces two interesting pieces of information en route: that of the joint acquisition of 40,000 acres of Mohawk land by Corny's and Dirck's fathers, a tract to be located and surveyed by the sons the following spring, and that of the tender interest of Dirck in his seventeen-year-old second cousin Anneke Mordaunt, whose country home, Lilacsbush, they see in the distance. Further affirmation of Anneke's charms is furnished by the talkative Mrs. Light, innkeeper at whose place the two young men eat dinner, increasing Corny's interest and curiosity. Arriving in New York toward nightfall, the two stable their horses and go to stay with their respective relatives.

Early next morning, Corny hurries to meet Dirck for sightseeing before the Pinkster festivities begin. There he encounters Jason Newcome and relishes introducing him to "white wine" (buttermilk); Jason had expected rum. Jason joins Corny and Dirck in looking the town over and then in viewing Pinkster (Pentecost) merrymaking ("the great Saturnalia of the New York blacks" [p.69])—noises, dances, music, games—all genuinely African preservations. White children as well as young ladies of the upper classes accompany their black nurses or maids to enjoy the scene. Corny recognizes among them the seventeen-year-old whom he had once rescued; when Dirck addresses her as "cousin Anneke," Corny knows she must be Anneke Mordaunt. On introduction to Corny, Anneke is reminded by her old nurse that this is her young champion, and she greets him warmly. Jason, once introduced, joins Corny and Dirck in accompanying Anneke and her friend Mary Wallace to various Pinkster activities, including a visit to a caged lion. Anneke's scarlet shawl attracting the lion's attention, he snatches it and pulls her with it to the cage; Corny, seeing Anneke's danger, lifts her away bodily and sets her down at a safe distance from the lion. Anneke soon recovers her poise and thanks him for his prompt action. Dirck escorts Anneke home; Corny slips away from Jason and wanders by himself, admiring especially the bearing and uniform of the British soldiers. On returning to his aunt's house, Corny finds Herman Mordaunt, Anneke's father, awaiting him to thank him for the service to Anneke and to invite him to dinner immediately after Pinkster. Dinner guests include Bulstrode and Harris—two British military officers—several of Anneke's female friends, and Corny and Dirck; Corny is chosen by Anneke's father to lead her in to dinner, a feast and a good-humored event followed by amateur singing. A theater party follows, with a play presented by Bulstrode's brigade; the play, hugely successful, is followed by "The Beaux Strat- agem," entertainment fashionable in England but too coarse for An- neke's and Mary Wallace's tastes. Supper, toasts, and more singing conclude the evening.

Corny and Dirck leave New York a day or so later for Satanstoe, encountering Jason Newcome en route; he stops with them at the Mordaunts' home, Lilacsbush, for a late breakfast. Corny learns from his mother shortly after his arrival home that he and Anneke are themselves distantly related through his mother's family. In May, Corny and Dirck visit Lilacsbush overnight; in September Herman Mordaunt and Anneke visit Satanstoe for a day. Bulstrode's regiment has been moved to Albany to strengthen the colony's defenses against the French.

On March 1, 1758, Corny, Dirck, the Rev. Mr. Worden, and Jason Newcome set out for Albany, Worden to serve as army chaplain, Corny and Dirck to locate the 40,000-acre patent Mooseridge jointly owned by their fathers, and Jason for a reason known only to him. They go by sleigh, sending ahead with Jaap (Corny's slave) and other blacks three four-horse-drawn lumber sleighs loaded with supplies, chiefly flour and pork, to be sold, with the draft horses, to the army contractors. They keep away from the river, to ensure enough snow for their sleigh runners, and arrive in Albany after three days' travel. Herman Mordaunt and Anneke are to be in Albany for the summer—perhaps to keep Anneke near Bulstrode for a good marriage (Bulstrode is heir to a British title) as well as to tend to some business of Mordaunt's. Albany is an impressive town, old and dignified, second in size to New York, so all four men are handsomely dressed for their arrival at the capital. As their sleigh crosses the river into the city, Bulstrode and a sleighful of young girls, including Anneke Mordaunt, drive past. The Rev. Mr. Worden, afraid to trust a loaded carriage on the ice-coated river, walks across the river, soon running desperately to avoid being transported by a sleighful of strangers wishing to respect his Anglican dress, an act gaining him the sobriquet The Loping Dominie. The driver, Guert Ten Eyck, a daredevil of the upper class, apologizes when he learns the cause of the Rev. Mr. Worden's anxiety, and promises to visit them soon at the tavern where they are to stay.

As soon as they are housed, Corny and Dirck go sight-seeing, and encounter Guert Ten Eyck, who invites all four to join him and his friends at a supper party that night, an invitation accepted with alacrity. The Rev. Mr. Worden meets the Episcopal chaplain and is invited to preach the following Sunday, an opportunity he eagerly accepts. After dinner, Corny meets Guert Ten Eyck again, and Guert—learning Corny's wish to dispose of his produce and horses—drives a good bargain for the sale of the loaded sleighs, contents, horses, and all; Guert is honest but a slick dealer in horses. Guert proves to have fallen in love with Mary Wallace, Anneke's best friend, and posts himself in the street daily to watch for her. Anneke and Mary see Guert and Corny on the corner, and Anneke is obviously pleased to greet Corny. She is less pleased to see him a few moments later when, on Guert's suggestion, Corny sleds with him down the main street and, to avoid a collision, is upset into the snow; the carriage posing the obstacle is occupied by Anneke and Mary, who consider sledding sport for boys, not men.

Their supper has been stolen by pranksters, so Guert entices the Rev. Mr. Worden into distracting the kitchen maid by a sermon on honesty while they "recapture" their dinner from a nearby house. They succeed in snatching the dinner, which they eat with good appetite, and are toasting the ladies when a constable's entry on the scene proves the dinner to have been stolen from the house of Mayor Cuyler, that evening entertaining guests including Herman and Anneke Mordaunt and Mary Wallace. The offenders are pardoned, since Guert's tricks are well known and good humored, and they all dine again, on an even finer meal; Guert explains the visitors' innocence in the matter, and Anneke becomes less cold toward Corny. The Rev. Mr. Worden is dubious about continued friendship with the rapscallion Guert, but Corny intends to continue his association with the mischievous Dutchman.

During breakfast, at which Bulstrode is also a guest, Major Bulstrode reports Harris's account of feasting on a snatched dinner whose owners in turn had eaten on the mayor's dinner. Herman Mordaunt tells the whole story, quite amused by it, and Bulstrode's comment on the scapegrace Guert prompts Anneke to criticize Guert also. Corny and Bulstrode leave Anneke's house after the meal and walk to Bulstrode's quarters; en route, Corny learns that Bulstrode, with his father's reluctant permission, has asked Anneke's hand of her father but that Anneke has not yet consented to the marriage.

That afternoon, after Jaap's arrival with the entourage of supply-laden sleighs, Corny finds Guert and they go with the sleighs to the army contractor; again, Guert does the bargaining, making a fine profit for

Corny and Dirck. Afterwards, Corny visits Guert's spotless bachelor quarters and then goes for a ride with him in his smooth-riding sleigh drawn by two spirited black horses. They stop to introduce Corny to Madam Schuyler and find Anneke and Mary just leaving, after having dined there. Madam Schuyler greets Corny warmly both because she knows his mother and because Anneke has told her about his rescuing her from the lion. Madam Schuyler, fond of Guert, inquires about his team and thus furnishes an opportunity for Guert to invite Mary and Anneke to ride home in his sleigh. Anneke refuses, but Mary agrees to ask Anneke's father and, on his approval, to try the sleigh the following week.

A thaw having set in over the weekend, Corny learns that Guert will still take the party sleighing—on the river. Assured that the ice is thick enough, Herman Mordaunt consents, and they take his sleigh and Guert's on an excursion to Kinderhook, where they are welcomed— though not expected—for dinner with relatives of Mordaunt's after a safe and joyous ride. They stay, on the hostess's insistence, until 8 P.M. The evening is especially relished by Corny since Anneke en route has indicated no preference for Bulstrode, who feels himself superior to those in the colony. On the way home, they meet several sleigh drivers who call warnings about "Albany" and "the river," warnings disturbing to Mordaunt but discounted by Guert until suddenly the ice cracks behind them. On consultation, they continue toward Albany; Mordaunt places Anneke in Corny's care, since Herman is driving his own sleigh with his lady guest, Mrs. Bogart. Mordaunt's and Guert's parties are abruptly separated by a heaping up of ice floes; by dint of courage and persistence, Corny, Guert, and the girls reach an island with the sleigh. Accidentally, the two couples are separated; eventually, Guert and Mary reach Albany that night, while Corny and Anneke encounter Dirck (of Mordaunt's party), who leads them to Herman Mordaunt and the rest of the party, overnight guests of a kind farm couple who provide a wagon for their return to Albany. Guert has cut his horses free of their harness to swim ashore; Mordaunt's horses, still fastened to his sleigh, drown, though eventually both sleighs are recovered, as are Guert's horses. When Bulstrode thanks Corny for saving Anneke's life, Corny acknowledges that he too is courting Anneke; Bulstrode declares that Herman Mordaunt has accepted his suit, and Corny realizes that Mordaunt feels the matter is thus quite satisfactorily arranged.

A month later, half in sport, Corny, Guert, and the Rev. Mr. Worden disguise themselves and consult a fortune-teller, Madam Doortje. Ahead of them are Jason Newcome and Dirck Follock, and Madam Doortje appears knowledgeable about all five. She advises Jason to buy the mill seat at the cheap price he proposes; she tells Dirck he will never marry; she predicts that Beelzebub will overtake the Loping Dominie; she recommends that Guert accompany Corny into the bush, to allow Mary to discover her real feeling for him; she warns Corny to beware of "knights barrownights." Later, Guert reports the visit to Bulstrode, Anneke, Mary, and Herman Mordaunt, saying he will accompany Corny and Dirck into the bush. It develops that Mordaunt owns a large estate, Ravensnest, near the land owned by Littlepage and Van Valkenburgh, and that he and Anneke and Mary are going to spend the summer there to reassure their tenant farmers, uneasy because of the advances of the French into the colony. The only one displeased by this news is Bulstrode, who has been assigned a post near Ravensnest and had hoped to complete his suit of Anneke without Corny's competition.

Bulstrode's company is ordered north, and he comes for a last breakfast with the Mordaunts, Corny, Dirck, and Guert. Bulstrode shows deep regret at leaving the group and moves the ladies to tears with fond farewells. He and Corny part as friends, though competitors, and Corny decides not to urge his suit with Anneke at a time when the answer would be likely to be "No."

Ten days later, the Mordaunt party (including four black and three white servants as well as the principals) and Corny, Dirck, and Guert (with Jaap, Traverse the surveyor, two chainbearers, and two axe-men and Guert's black Pete) set off for their estates dressed for wilderness travel. The Rev. Mr. Worden and Jason Newcome, wearing their usual clothes, manage to secure a ride in a government carriage; Mordaunt's wagon carries Anneke and Mary, while the rest travel on foot. They halt during the first day at Madam Schuyler's for dinner, where they meet her nephew, Philip Schuyler, about Corny's age; with Philip, Corny discusses the traditional and understandable dislike between New Yorkers and Yankees. Corny talks briefly also with Lord Howe, favorably disposed toward Corny because of his heroism in the Hudson River sleighing episode.

For thirty miles, the combined parties travel by road due north; then they bear northeast toward Ravensnest and Mooseridge, with Anneke and Mary on horseback along the narrow trail, and the wagons, reloaded, following slowly behind. Corny and Guert, leading the party, find the Rev. Mr. Worden and Jason Newcome in a clearing playing cards, a matter highly embarrassing to the Puritanical Yankee. The entire group (including Worden and Newcome) moves onward to the scheduled overnight shelter, a log house, safely reached, and the scene of a fine pigeon supper.

The following morning, the group reaches the first clearing on Mordaunt's estate, and Mordaunt explains to Corny the tremendous expenditure in capital and patience needed to establish tenants on such wilderness property, the hard terms driven by the tenants, and the unlikelihood of the owner's turning any profit on his investment until the third generation. The main structure at Ravensnest, reached soon afterwards, is a well-fortified log building a hundred feet by fifty feet, plain but warm and secure.

After several days' stay at Ravensnest, Corny, Dirck, and Guert engage two Indians, Susquesus and Jumper, as hunters and messengers, and then go in search of Mooseridge. Aided by the surveyor's map and by Susquesus's forest skills, they locate the corner tree of Mooseridge; the party thereafter erect near a good spring a smaller log house with a riven-log door, as protection against intruders, and a [puncheon] floor. Traverse and his men divide the patent into thousand-acre squares, recording also a description of the soil, surface, and trees of each lot; Corny and Dirck record the details of the lot at Traverse's dictation, while Guert and the hunters keep the party supplied with meat, fowl, and fish, all members observing Sunday as a day without work. A letter brought from Mordaunt by runner expresses concern about increased military activities and questions the reliability of Susquesus, who has left his own tribe to live with the Mohawks. Corny learns from Susquesus only that the Onondaga (his tribe) are not after scalps this season. Susquesus's disappearance a few days later stirs Corny's doubts about the Indian's loyalty.

Corny, Dirck, and Guert visit Ravensnest for two or three days, finding Anneke and Mary safe and in good spirits; Mordaunt returns with the men to Mooseridge and spends two or three days examining that estate. The Rev. Mr. Worden has left to join the army as chaplain, and Jason Newcome has driven a hard bargain with Mordaunt for the mill seat. Susquesus returns, having ascertained that the French and the English will soon be fighting, and urges Corny, Dirck, and Guert to follow their intention of joining the English forces as colonials. After a dispute—won by Susquesus—about the merit of going by way of Ravensnest to battle (such a route would cause too much delay), the three and Jaap set off for Lake George, led by Susquesus. Guert's brash attempt to lead the group by compass and sight turns them in exactly the opposite direction, so Susquesus resumes his post as competent guide. Abercrombie's 16,000 troops have embarked when the group arrives at the lake, but Susquesus locates a canoe and takes them directly to Lord Howe's ship; Howe invites them to join his advance brigade rather than

Bulstrode's, situated in the middle, and they accept, whereupon Susquesus leaves the group. Corny and Howe talk briefly of the dangers
ahead, the last personal word Corny has with Howe.

A landing is effected; a brief and successful skirmishing follows, and
the English-led troops pursue the fleeing French and their Indian allies,
with the British troops in the two center columns and the provincials
either in the two flanking columns or left behind to guard the flotilla of
1,025 boats. Howe is killed in the first serious encounter, and Guert—
fiercely loyal to Howe—assumes temporary leadership, pursuing the
French to their intrenchments. Retreat becomes necesssary, made difficult by attack by a party of Indians; but Jaap by quick thinking preserves
his white comrades by knocking down three Indians while Guert, Dirck,
and Corny are reloading. Dirck's shooting the fourth Huron through the
heart drives the rest of the marauders away while Guert covers the
party's retreat. After Abercrombie encamps, Corny and his party locate
and join Bulstrode's brigade, welcomed warmly for their fine service with
the advance forces; all mourn the loss of Howe, the genius and soul of the
British forces, and all doubt the success of the army against the French in
his absence. The attack on Fort Ticonderoga ordered by Abercrombie
fails because it is undertaken with insufficiently heavy armament; and a
general retreat begins, with the entire flotilla returning to the embarkation point on Lake George after a loss of 548 dead and 1,356 injured.
Bulstrode is wounded in the leg, and Billings is killed. While debating his
own party's best move, Corny is soundlessly approached by Susquesus,
who leads them to his well-concealed canoe. Jaap's Huron prisoner,
Muss, is released by Corny, who finds Jaap rope-beating him before he
sets him free. After the party has returned safely to its starting point,
Susquesus warns them that Muss will take revenge for his beating by
scalping as many settlers as he can find; he urges Corny to go first to
Mooseridge to warn the surveyors before he goes to Ravensnest, and the
party follows Susquesus's counsel.

They arrive without incident at Mooseridge. Apparently the surveyor
and his helpers are camping out at some distance, for everything is in
order in the log house. Susquesus, suspicious, sets out to reconnoiter,
followed by Corny; Susquesus detects signs of Huron visitors and finally
convinces Corny of their presence. On conference, all—whites, blacks,
and the two Indians—decide to barricade themselves that night in the log
house. At two o'clock in the morning, Susquesus awakens Corny and
leads him outside. Following a human cry, they find Pete, suspended
from a spring trap made of two saplings, dead and scalped. Susquesus and
Corny, after determining that the Huron party was a small one—three or

four—report the melancholy news of Pete's death to the rest, who vow
vengeance. Jaap buries Pete's body, and Guert prays over it. After
breakfast, they set out to warn the surveying party, en route finding and
burying Sam, one of their hunters, knifed and scalped; Guert prays and
pronounces a brief, heartfelt sermon at his grave. At last Susquesus finds
Traverse, his two chainbearers, and the hunter Tom, shot and scalped,
but propped up as if alive; the four are buried carefully but without
ceremony, since Susquesus's diligent examination of footprints has
revealed that at least a dozen Hurons had taken part in the killings. They
return cautiously to the log house and are eating when Jumper comes
from Ravensnest with letters from Anneke, Mary, and Herman Mordaunt urging them to take shelter in that fortified place, for many
Indians' trails have been seen. They leave at once for Ravensnest, led by
Susquesus and Jumper apart from the frequented path, to avoid detec-
tion by the enemy. Seeing forty Hurons eating around a campfire in the
ravine Mordaunt has told Dirck to use as an approach to the fortress,
they decide to surprise the enemy, take revenge for the scalpings, and
then rush for the gate, each man responsible for his own safety. They
succeed in their purpose and all are afterwards secure inside the fortress.
Mordaunt, inquiring about Traverse and his helpers, learns the news of
their grisly murder. Since Bulstrode has now arrived and wishes to see
Corny, Corny goes to the injured major's room. The two men talk of
their respective prospects for winning Anneke's hand, and Bulstrode
advises Corny to use to its fullest his present advantage as Anneke's
defender, since Bulstrode plans to capitalize on his battle wound. On
leaving Bulstrode's room, Corny finds Anneke alone, restates his love for
her, and is told that she loves him and has no feeling for Bulstrode. On
Guert's suit of Mary, Anneke has no word; Guert himself tells Corny
afterwards that Mary has refused him again.

   Mordaunt and his men guard the fortress throughout the night; all
men are awakened well before dawn, to expect attack. The Hurons have
painstakingly prepared to set the fort on fire, a project Susquesus
detects. All agree to wait until the fire has actually been started before
action is taken against the enemy; when Guert sees that the incendiary is
Muss himself, he shoots at him, an act precipitating the Huron's war
whoop and much shouting among the enemy. Anneke summons Corny
and tells him her father agrees to her marrying Corny rather than
Bulstrode. Thus heartened, Corny joins the others in defending the
fortress against attack by the Hurons: first, he goes outside to examine
the fire and returns to warn Mordaunt to apply water from the lookout
point above it; next, he goes out with Susquesus to rescue the party led

by Guert intended to drive off the Hurons gathered below the fort. His efforts are supported by a charge led by Mordaunt, and most of them safely reenter the gate; Guert and Jaap are missing, and Jumper and two settlers—Gilbert Davis and Moses Mudge—are dead and scalped. Suspecting that Jaap and Guert are captives of the Hurons, Mordaunt sends Susquesus as a messenger, to offer to ransom the two captives. In the subsequent parleying, Muss declares that Jaap must be killed and scalped for his beating of Muss; Guert will be killed and scalped unless two "chiefs" and two "common men" or four common men or two common men and all of Ravensnest are exchanged for him, terms unacceptable to Mordaunt. Jaap, determined not to die, manages to steal an Indian's knife and cut both his bonds and Guert's while Corny is being permitted to give Guert a message: that Mary Wallace loves him. Jaap and Guert seize rifles from their guards and attack the Indians fiercely; the Indians flee before the combined forces from Ravensnest, but a last stray shot mortally wounds Guert. Mary tends Guert lovingly through his last hours, and joins the Rev. Mr. Worden in the prayers Guert asks in his behalf; Guert dies in Mary's arms. The young Dutchman's body is taken by Corny and Dirck to Albany for burial. After the funeral, Corny and Dirck go by boat toward New York; Dirck rejoins his family, and Corny, after a brief visit with his aunt and uncle Legge, goes home to Satanstoe. After his full recounting of the Ticonderoga campaign and of the Ravensnest events, Corny is questioned by his mother about the Mordaunts; after teasing her a bit, he announces to her joy that he has won Anneke.

The Mordaunts return to Lilacsbush in September; Corny, invited to come for late breakfast, goes the preceding evening with the romantic notion of watching Anneke from a distance. He encounters Bulstrode, who acknowledges himself bested in the courting of Anneke and attributes his own loss to his having offended Anneke by playing Scrub in the bawdy entertainment presented by his brigade at the theater party in New York. Corny overhears Mary telling Anneke that she will remain forever the widow of Guert, whose proposal she should have accepted. Corny and Anneke are married early in October; Bulstrode remains a bachelor all his life but maintains correspondence with the Littlepages, a matter left to Anneke's and Corny's son Mordaunt to include in the ongoing family narrative.

General [James] Abercrombie, Captain Billings, Mrs. Bogart, Major Henry Bulstrode, Caesar, Cato, Mayor Cuyler, David, Gilbert Davis, Doortje, Mother Doortje, Hugh Gaine, Ensign Tom Harris, Major Joe Hight, Lord Viscount Howe, Katrinke, Captain Charles Lee, Legge, Jane Legge, Mrs. Light, Madam Littlepage, Cornelius

Littlepage, Major Evans Littlepage, Captain Hugh Roger Littlepage,
Mari, Anna Cornelia Mordaunt, Herman Mordaunt, Moses Mudge,
Musquerusque [Muss], Jason Newcome, Major Nicholas Oothout,
Petrus, Pompey, Quissquiss, Major Rogers, Sam, Jacob Satanstoe,
Madam Schuyler, Philip Schuyler, Silvy, Susquesus, Guert Ten
Eyck, Tom, Traverse, Mrs. Van der Heyden, Jeremiah Van
Rensselaer, Colonel Abraham Van Valkenburgh, Dirck Van Valken-
burgh, Mary Wallace, Rev. Mr. Thomas Worden.

The Sea Lions; or, The Lost Sealers, 1849.

The novel begins on a Sunday in September, 1819, at Oyster Pond
(Oyster Point), Southold township of Suffolk County in the northeast
corner of Long Island. It is an area separated from the New England coast
by that narrow strip of water known as Long Island Sound, and the
inhabitants are as often of Yankee origins as they are of native New York
stock. Deacon Pratt, in whose house the action commences, is a stereotype of the Yankee as he was often viewed in that period by citizens of
neighboring states: seemingly pious but in reality hypocritical, materialistic, and grasping. A man of considerable affluence, the Deacon
affects humility and practices frugality. Guardian and benefactor of an
orphaned niece, Mary Pratt, he keeps careful records of all expenditures
made on her behalf with the expectation of reimbursement from her
future husband. In his grotesque way Pratt personifies that avarice,
together with its destructive effect, which constitutes one of the primary
themes of the novel.

On this particular Sunday the Deacon does not remain at church—
"meeting house," he and the Calvinist community call it—for the afternoon service but instead hurries home on urgent business. His concern
centers on an ailing superannuated seaman, Thomas Daggett, who had
been set ashore at Oyster Pond several weeks earlier by an incoming
vessel bound for New York City. Housed at the nearby cottage of the
widow Betsy White, Daggett has grown steadily weaker until now his
death seems imminent. Penniless and possessed of only an old sea chest
of personal belongings, the seaman has prompted succor for himself by
exploiting Deacon Pratt's cupidity. He confides to the Deacon that charts
in his chest show the locations of two great treasures: an uncharted
breeding ground for seals in the Antarctic, and a cache of pirate gold on a
tiny key in the West Indies. As Daggett's health deteriorates day by day,
Pratt visits the old man more frequently and presses him more zealously
for the precise locations of these treasures. Prudence dictates that
Daggett withhold this information, and he tells Pratt he has taken an

oath not to divulge the position of these sites until after the sealing season of 1820. Daggett's account has sufficient credibility, however, to induce Pratt to purchase a newly built schooner (christened *Sea Lion*), commission as its captain young Roswell Gardiner, and finance a sealing expedition to the South Polar Seas.

When Thomas Daggett dies in the night, after a protracted and wearying discussion of these two treasures, Pratt pays for his funeral services, gives the Widow White ten dollars for her nursing care, and then triumphantly carries home the sea chest containing Daggett's two valuable maps. As he had expected, Pratt finds the seal island and the Caribbean key marked on the charts, with the exact latitudes and longitudes written in the margins. After copying this information in his notebook, Pratt proceeds to expunge both sets of marks from these two documents.

The next day the Deacon, Mary, Roswell Gardiner, and the Rev. Mr. Whittle are having dinner at the Pratt residence when a stranger appears. He is a nephew of the deceased seaman, a young captain named Jason Daggett, who has come from Martha's Vineyard to visit his ailing kinsman. When informed that his uncle has died, Captain Daggett reimburses Pratt the ten dollars paid to the Widow White and then demands his uncle's sea chest. Hastily examining the two charts that it contains, the Martha's Vineyarder is disappointed not to discover on them the notations he had expected to secure. Much to the alarm of Deacon Pratt, the visitor now reveals that Thomas Daggett had confided to several people his possession of charts showing the locations of sealing grounds and buried gold, and that these reports had reached the large Daggett family of Martha's Vineyard. Suspecting that the charts have been tampered with, Captain Daggett next visits at some length with Widow White, from whom he learns of Pratt's frequent and fervent discussions with his uncle. Keeping his own counsel in the matter, Captain Daggett leaves Oyster Pond without the specific information he came seeking but with the firm conviction that his uncle's accounts of treasure were more than mere yarns spun by an old seaman.

A rival ship, also named *Sea Lion*, is being outfitted at Martha's Vineyard under the direction of Captain Jason Daggett. Its agents delay the sailing of Pratt's schooner by confusing Gardiner's job applicants with the misinformation that the sealer named *Sea Lion* will sail from Holmes' Hole on Martha's Vineyard rather than from Oyster Pond, Long Island. To determine the degree of Gardiner's readiness to sail, Daggett sends a spy aboard the Oyster Pond vessel. He is Daggett's second mate, Watson, who pretends to be seeking employment but who refuses to sign a contract.

Before sailing, Captain Gardiner confers privately with both Deacon Pratt and his niece. Swearing his young captain to secrecy, Pratt reveals to him the locations of the seal island and the Caribbean key on which the pirate gold is buried. Roswell's conversation with Mary is much longer as they discuss (obviously not for the first time) the one barrier to their future marriage: their religious differences. Roswell cannot accept the concept of Christ's divinity; Mary cannot, she says, marry a man who allows his reason to keep him from faith in the Trinity. Although they love each other, they part without resolving this issue. Their controversy introduces the second major theme of the novel: unitarian versus trinitarian Christianity.

Some forty miles out of her home port, the *Sea Lion* of Oyster Pond is joined by the *Sea Lion* of Martha's Vineyard under the command of Captain Jason Daggett. The second vessel is an exact replica of Pratt's schooner—the same design, tonnage, and rigging; even their sea-lion figureheads have been carved by the same Boston wood sculptor. Soon the two ships are caught up in a heavy storm from the east which drives them landward to within sight of offshore breakers. When Gardiner loses his masts and then discovers that his anchors are not holding, he feels certain that the ship and all aboard her will be lost. When the storm abates, almost miraculously, Gardiner exclaims, "God is with us! . . . blessed forever be his holy name!" To this a voice adds, "And that of his only and *true* Son" (p. 152). Thus does an old mariner named Stephen Stimson become the spokesman for trinitarian Christianity aboard ship as Mary Pratt has been ashore.

Daggett and his crew assist in installing temporary "jury masts" on the Oyster Pond *Sea Lion*, and they refuse to accept the "salvage" payments to which they are legally entitled for recovering from the sea Gardiner's detached spars, sails, and rigging. When the Oyster Point ship docks at Beaufort, North Carolina, to replace its masts, its twin from Martha's Vineyard also lands. Having faced and then escaped destruction together, Daggett tells Gardiner, the two vessels should henceforth accompany each other. Knowing the loss in profit that the Vineyarders may incur by this delay, Gardiner is touched by their apparent sense of fellowship and generosity. He does not understand Daggett's true motive: keeping the Long Islanders under constant surveillance with a view toward claiming at least part of the treasures they seek. (Throughout the tempest and its aftermath, the reader is frequently introduced to nautical operations, shipboard equipment, and seamen's lingo. Sometimes these items are mentioned only in passing; occasionally they become the subjects of brief interpolated essays.)

When the twin ships sight a school of spermaceti whales, off the coast of Brazil, they at once lower boats and give chase. Gardiner harpoons a giant spermaceti bull and Daggett later strikes a smaller one. As the two boats are being towed some distance by the wounded whales, their lines cross, causing the Vineyarders' shaft to be pulled out of the smaller "fish" and then caught in the jaws of the larger one. After the great bull, exhausted, surfaces, both Gardiner and Daggett drive their lances into its vitals; when it is dead, both captains mount its carcass to claim title to the rich prize. Although Daggett knows that he has no legal claim to the whale—Gardiner's "irons" were "fast" in the creature before his own line had become entangled—he pushes his claim just short of the point of physical combat. It is a ploy, however. By conceding at the last minute to Gardiner's claim, he can again appear to be extending generosity and camaraderie, as he had, he reminds Gardiner, while aiding the Oyster Ponders after the storm off North Carolina. While Gardiner's crew is cutting up the blubber and "trying out" the valuable oil—it nets more than $4,000 for Deacon Pratt—the Vineyarders kill some whale calves and thus enjoy some profit from the venture. But Daggett has won a great victory, for the ingenuous Gardiner now feels doubly indebted and conscience smitten by his wish to elude such a chivalrous rival. His dilemma is evident in the two letters that he mails from Rio de Janeiro, one to Deacon Pratt and one to Mary.

When they reach Cape Horn, Daggett gives the promontory and its islands a wide berth, swerving well to the east. With the guidance of Stephen Stimson, who has rounded the Horn eleven times, Gardiner anchors his ship in a protected cove within the Cape islands. On the fourth day Gardiner and Stimson, going ashore on a high, rocky island, see the *Sea Lion* of Martha's Vineyard passing the Cape, apparently searching for its consort, and then, not finding her, sailing away due south. Once the Vineyarder is out of sight, the Oyster Pond schooner leaves its snug anchorage and sets its course south-southwest for its destination in the Antarctic Ocean. Six days later, after passing several icebergs, they discover the island Thomas Daggett had described, its beaches covered with sea lions, sea elephants, and other aquatic mammals.

The business of sealing now begins. Sea lions are killed and skinned, and their pelts cured. Sea elephants, some nearly thirty feet in length, are taken and the oil rendered from their carcasses. Great care is exercised to avoid alarming the great herds of animals that gather on the shores of the island. On the twenty-third day, a Sunday, Stephen Stimson, the old boat steerer, requests Captain Gardiner to declare a Sabbath, a day of rest.

Although Gardiner disagrees with Stimson's religious position, he realizes that from a more practical point of view, allowing a free day for the
men might be a wise move. Stimson and Gardiner later start to climb a
nearby peak when they see, at some distance, the *Sea Lion* of Martha's
Vineyard jammed in an ice floe. After a day's hard work by both crews,
the Vineyard ship is freed from the ice, guided to the cove where
Gardiner's sealing operations are being conducted, and, by nightfall, tied
up alongside its twin from Oyster Pond.

A month later, again on a Sunday, Captain Gardiner, Captain Daggett,
and Stimson climb to the top of the highest peak and view the sterile
valley below. Their reveries as they gaze on this wasteland reflect well
their respective preoccupations. Daggett's mind is on sealing and the
probable profits of the voyage; Gardiner dreams of Mary Pratt; Stimson's thoughts are lost in religious meditation. During their descent,
Daggett declines the aid of a safety line, slips on the snow, and plunges to
the base of the mountain. He suffers a broken leg and has to be carried
back to the sealing camp.

Macy, Daggett's first mate, now takes command of the Vineyarders'
fur and oil procurement. Ignoring Gardiner's practice of killing only as
many animals per day as they can process, Macy leads a ferocious
onslaught on the sea lions and sea elephants, taking more than they had
on any previous day. The result is exactly what Gardiner had predicted:
the herds are frightened, and only a few return to the island each day
thereafter. When March arrives and the Vineyard ship is still only half
full, Daggett uses all his wiles to play upon Gardiner's sympathy and
persuade him to remain until their cargo is complete. Gardiner, whose
hold has been filled for some time, agrees to remain for another twenty
days, the latest date on which they could hope to thread their way among
the ice floes before the Antarctic winter closes in and makes all travel
impossible. When twenty days have passed, Gardiner gives orders to his
crew to weigh anchor and start the homeward voyage. With a rebellious
mate and a leg not fully recovered, Daggett reluctantly but wisely decides
to leave with him.

There are ominous indications, however, that they may have waited
too long. Their course is blocked by towering icebergs among which they
maneuver their craft with utmost care. [The fearsome and sublime
seascapes are based in part on accounts of exploring expeditions of the
1830s, especially the one led by Lieutenant Charles Wilkes which spent a
winter jammed in the ice near the Antarctic Circle.] After a short run, the
Sea Lion of Martha's Vineyard is "pinched" between two icebergs and
damaged too severely to permit any further progress. Again playing on

Gardiner's sense of compassion and loyalty, Daggett persuades the younger captain to return with him to their sealing camp and help repair the damaged schooner. This Gardiner does, although another precious two weeks are lost in the endeavor. By then, it is too late to leave: they are trapped in the ice.

There is no choice now but to prepare to winter in the Antarctic. Both crews move into the processing shed, a cabin belonging to Deacon Pratt which Gardiner had dismantled, carried aboard his ship, and rebuilt on the island. Stimson, who had earlier survived a winter on Cape Horn, provides invaluable advice to the two captains. He directs the insulating of the cabin, the rationing of the scant supply of wood for fuel, and the hardening of the men (via daily baths in ice water) against extreme cold. It soon becomes evident that securing fuel in that treeless area will be the most pressing problem. The wrecked Vineyard schooner would seem to be the most logical source of wood, but Daggett reacts strongly against this idea. In fact, he and his men are so alarmed at the suggestion that they withdraw from the cabin and move to the wreck in order to protect it. As the winter intensifies, however, each group runs out of fuel and is forced to start burning its own ship, piece by piece, beginning with the upper works and deck planking. Just how severe the weather becomes is made dramatically clear by the loss of Macy and a fellow crewman, both frozen while returning to the wreck after visiting the cabin.

Throughout the long nights Gardiner and the devout boat steerer, Stimson, read from the Scriptures and discuss religion. Gardiner digs from his duffel the marked copy of the Bible Mary Pratt had given him just before his departure from Oyster Pond. Observing with fascination the many strange climatic phenomena of an Antarctic winter, Gardiner slowly comes to the realization that his reason can account for them only to a certain point. Beyond that point one simply accepts on faith that there is some causative pattern. Although he still does not believe in the doctrine of the Trinity, he now recognizes that he does depend upon faith in many matters as little subject to rational proof as the divinity of Christ. His religious orientation has thus begun to change.

One night in the depth of winter Gardiner and Stimson hear a distant cry for help. Concluding that the Vineyarders must be in trouble, they make their way toward the wreck and find along the path Joe, the Negro cook, almost frozen to death. He had been the third man sent for help; the first two were later found dead. Revived with brandy and hot coffee, Joe describes the disaster that has befallen the men on the wreck. Their fire had died during the night, and their tinder had been misplaced. After hours of effort to kindle a fire, some had crept into their bunks and the others had yielded to the cold. A rescue mission, led by Gardiner and Stimson, finally manages to reach the wreck, where only Daggett and a young ship carpenter named Lee are still alive. Both Daggett's hands and feet, however, are badly frozen. Gardiner becomes aware of how low the temperature must be when he observes that all of the mercury has contracted into the ball of the thermometer and that ordinarily combustible fuel will not easily ignite even in the direct flame of their lantern. The two survivors are taken back to the cabin, they and Joe now being all that remain of the fifteen men who shipped aboard the *Sea Lion* of Martha's Vineyard.

When rain signals the beginning of spring and some thawing occurs, reconstruction of the *Sea Lion* of Oyster Pond begins. The wreck is used as the source of needed timbers and planking. Daggett, dying of gangrene in his frostbitten hands and feet, offers no objection to this use of his vessel. The death of Daggett serves as an object lesson to Gardiner that of all idols men worship, the most objectionable is that of self.

As the spring progresses and the field ice around the island starts to break up, the *Sea Lion* of Oyster Pond finally commences its return voyage. After stopping briefly at Rio de Janeiro twenty days later, to sell some of its oil and buy badly needed provisions, it travels another twenty days to reach the Caribbean key on which pirate gold was said to be buried. Although a month is spent on that islet searching out the landmarks indicated on the chart and triangulating on the treasure (one hundred and forty-three gold doubloons worth sixteen dollars apiece), we are given none of the details of this operation.

Age, disease, and worry over his supposedly lost ship had led Deacon Pratt to his last illness. On the day that he dies, in April of 1821, the strangely altered *Sea Lion* of Oyster Point sails into the harbor, and its captain wastes no time in reporting to its owner. Mary, who nurses her ailing uncle, is distressed that his last thoughts should be on material wealth. Besides its considerable earnings from oil, the schooner has brought back a cargo of seal fur worth $20,000. Not satisfied with such a bountiful return on his investment, Pratt impatiently demands news of the pirate treasure. Drawing his last breath, the Deacon clutches the bag of gold that Gardiner hands him and dies.

Numerous relatives of Deacon Pratt, including a previously unmentioned brother and sister, gather to lay claim to his property. Mary produces a "letter" from the Deacon addressed to Gardiner. When opened, this "letter" proves to be Deacon Pratt's will, correctly drawn up, and duly witnessed. Except for a horse, a mirror, and a pincushion left to his brother, his sister, and a cousin, respectively, the Deacon has be-

queathed all of his wealth to his niece, Mary, and has named Gardiner
executor of the estate.

Learning from Gardiner even before he enters the sickroom of the
dying Deacon that her lover had been converted to trinitarian Christianity, Mary agrees to marry him at once. After their wedding, they
spend some little time settling the estate of the late Ichabod Pratt,
suitably rewarding Stimson and other members of Gardiner's crew, and
distributing the pirate gold—scruple forbids their keeping it themselves—and other money to survivors of the Vineyarders lost in the
Antarctic. Their responsibilities fulfilled, Mary, fearful that Gardiner
may again hear the call of the sea, persuades her husband to move to
western New York State and there invest in the booming flour industry.
It has been a long road that has led Roswell Gardiner from the role of
unitarian sea captain to that of conservative trinitarian businessman.

Baiting Joe, Squire Craft, Betsey Daggett, Captain Jason Daggett,
Thomas Daggett, Bartlett Davidson, Jake Davis, Hiram Flint, Pri-
mus Floyd, Captain Roswell Gardiner, Timothy Green, Sylvester
Havens, Philip Hazard, Jenkins, Jim, Joe, Lee, Cato Livingston, Macy,
Catherine Martin, Arcularius Mott, Peter Mount, Ichabod Pratt, Job
Pratt, Mary Pratt, Dr. Sage, Sam, Joshua Short, Smith, Robert
Smith, Stephen Stimson, Widow Stone, Jane Thomas, Nathan
Thompson, Marcus Todd, Watson, David Weeks, Betsy White, Rev.
Mr. Whittle.

The Spy: A Tale of the Neutral Ground, 1821.

The time is October, 1780, and the place, Westchester County, New
York, the so-called "Neutral Ground" during the Revolutionary War. It is
neutral only in being the no man's land between the British forces in and
around New York City and the Continental Army which holds most of
the Hudson River Valley and upstate New York. The Wharton family is
divided in its sympathies during the War of Independence, the son,
Henry, being a British officer, and the elder daughter, Sarah, remaining
loyal to the crown, while her sister, Frances, is outspoken in the cause of
her country. Their father, Mr. Wharton, with many close friends on both
sides of the conflict, strives to remain impartial. He feels that his
uncommitted position can better be maintained outside the metropolis,
and he has, therefore, moved his family to its summer home, known as
"The Locusts." With them comes Miss Jeanette Peyton, Virginia-born
aunt and governess to the girls since the death of their mother.

Late in the afternoon of a rainy, autumnal day, two strangers seek
shelter and accommodations for the night at The Locusts. Unknown at

first to each other, as they are to Mr. Wharton and his daughters, the travelers are George Washington, clad in mufti and using the name Mr. Harper, and Captain Henry Wharton, so thoroughly disguised that even his own family cannot immediately identify him. Washington is personally reconnoitering the area. Henry, at the risk of being detected and captured as a spy, has managed to evade Continental pickets for a brief visit to his home.

Early the next morning a third visitor arrives at The Locusts, the Yankee pack peddler, Harvey Birch, who, with his father and their housekeeper, Katy Haynes, lives in a small house nearby. Using the cover of his former occupation, Harvey is in reality now a spy and counterspy in the service of Washington, and the two men silently recognize each other at once. After selling some yard goods to the ladies, Harvey withdraws from the family and its guests, who are still at breakfast. To the astonishment of all at the table, Mr. Harper, who has penetrated Henry's disguise after viewing his portrait on the wall, addresses him as Captain Wharton and assures the young man that he will not be betrayed.

On the third day Harper resumes his travels, but as he leaves, he warns Henry of his extremely dangerous situation and promises to aid him (in return for the succor he has enjoyed at The Locusts) if the young man should fall into trouble. Since none present but Harvey Birch knows the identity of Harper, the words of the parting guest are not, at this time, taken very seriously. Immediately after his departure, however, Harvey Birch repeatedly urges Henry to shorten his visit, warning him to beware a tall Virginian with a bushy beard. Although he does confess to some uneasiness, Henry decides to remain at home one night longer.

As the Wharton family sit at breakfast the following morning, they observe the approach of a small body of cavalry led by a tall, bewhiskered man, one Captain John Lawton, they later learn, of the Virginia Dragoons. The troops first surround the home of Harvey Birch, hoping to capture and hang the peddler as a British spy. Not finding Harvey at home, they proceed to The Locusts. Although Henry has hastily resumed his masquerade, his disguise is futile. At first alarmed at this exposure of Henry, they are soon relieved when they learn that the commanding officer of the Dragoons is Major Peyton Dunwoodie, an old friend of the family, a former classmate of Henry, and, more recently, the fiancé of Frances. When Dunwoodie learns the identity of the British officer, he faces a grave dilemma between his love for Frances and his sense of duty to his country. The conflict between love and loyalty in the novel becomes even more involved when the Virginia Dragoons are attacked by a company of British troops led by Colonel Wellmere, a suitor for the hand of Sarah Wharton. Henry escapes to join Wellmere's forces (which include some Hessian mercenaries), but when the Americans prevail, both he and Wellmere are captured. The dead and injured are not numerous, but among the latter are Henry Wharton and John Lawton, suffering only minor cuts, and Captain George Singleton, a seriously wounded Virginia Dragoon. Only because it may be necessary in order to save the life of his companion at arms, Dunwoodie sends for the dragoon's sister, Isabella Singleton, to come and nurse her brother; to the reader it is evident from the reticence with which he takes this action that Major Dunwoodie has had an unpleasant association with Isabella which he does not care to renew.

After the defeated British forces withdraw to a waiting ship on the Hudson River, the Continental cavalry rides back at dusk toward its camp. When, en route, they come upon the pack peddler, Captain Lawton shouts to his horsemen, "Harvey Birch! Take him, dead or alive!" (p. 131). Fifty pistol shots ring out, and several dragoons, led by Lawton, charge upon their intended victim. In despair at such barbarous intentions on the part of the very forces he secretly serves, Harvey remarks bitterly, "Hunted like a beast of the forest!" (p. 131). But when Lawton's horse falls over the prostrate form of the peddler, sending itself and its rider crashing to the ground, Birch takes heart and, almost miraculously, makes his escape. Lawton, badly shaken by the fall, goes to The Locusts to have his bruised body examined for broken bones by the doctor attending George Singleton there, the comic and grotesque military surgeon, Archibald Sitgreaves.

After eluding the dragoons, Harvey Birch rushes home to his mortally ill father, Johnny Birch, who has been attended by the greedy housekeeper, Katy Haynes. Caesar Thompson, a Negro slave from the Wharton household, is also lending his aid. Harvey's final conversation with his dying father is rudely interrupted by a band of Skinners, rapacious irregulars who are commissioned to forage for the patriot forces, but who misuse their authority and plunder the countryside for their own profit. They intend to loot the peddler's stock of merchandise, extort from him his accumulated gold, and then deliver Harvey himself to the American command for the reward posted for his capture. Harvey willingly reveals where his money is hidden in order to buy a few last moments with his expiring parent. In the agony of death, the elder Birch, wrapped in a sheet, staggers from the bedroom to give his final blessing to his son. Terrified at what they believe to be the ghost of Mr. Birch, Katy and Caesar bolt from the cottage closely followed by the Skinners.

After the funeral of Johnny Birch, attended by Captain Wharton, Mr.

Wharton, and other neighbors, Harvey sells his house for an unfairly low price to an opportunistic speculator. As he bids farewell to Katy Haynes, his faithful housekeeper and would-be wife (to whom he leaves the contents of the building), he is again apprehended by the band of ruthless Skinners. As they carry off the unfortunate peddler for a reward of fifty guineas, they burn his former home to the ground. Deprived of family, home, wealth, and now even freedom, Harvey is playing a role that makes him an outcast for whom (as he tells Katy) "all places are now alike, and all faces equally strange" (p. 202).

Having viewed the funeral of Mr. Birch from her window, Frances Wharton, feeling melancholy, decides to make a courtesy call at the suite of Isabella Singleton, who now lives at The Locusts while she nurses her wounded brother. There she discovers (what the reader has inferred) that the passionate Isabella is madly in love with her own fiancé, Peyton Dunwoodie. At the same moment, Isabella's quick sensibilities detect Frances's love for the major, and the two girls collapse tearfully in each other's arms.

Near the village of Four Corners, where the Virginia Dragoons are stationed, a tavern has been hastily established in a deserted house by the enterprising camp follower Elizabeth (Betty) Flanagan. The singing and drinking of the cavalry officers there is interrupted by the arrival of the Skinner band delivering Harvey Birch to the American regulars. The American guerrillas receive not only their reward of fifty guineas but also thirty-nine lashes apiece, a Mosaic measure of punishment ordered by Captain Lawton for acts of burning, looting, and murder. In the meantime, Dunwoodie has condemned Harvey to be hanged in the morning for espionage activity on behalf of the British. Declaring that Washington would not have treated him so, Harvey takes from a tin container hung from his neck a slip of paper which he starts to hand to Dunwoodie. Then, changing his mind, he declares that he knew in advance the conditions of his service and will not now forfeit them to save his life. Before anyone can restrain him, he quickly swallows the paper.

Confined to a small room in the "Hotel Flanagan," as the officers jestingly call Betty's tavern, Harvey tries, unsuccessfully, to gain his freedom by bribing Sergeant Hollister. During the night Harvey makes his escape in some of the clothes of Betty Flanagan, easily passing the sentries with his imitation of the woman's well-known Irish brogue. With the same convincing reproduction of Betty's dialect, he frightens an encampment of Skinners in the nearby woods by pretending to be leading the much-feared Lawton to their place of bivouac. Later, perched on a rock ledge above the path, he intercepts Major Dunwoodie, strolling in the woods after a sleepless night, and threatens to shoot with a Skinner musket the military judge who had just condemned him to death. Claiming approval for his acts from a higher authority, Harvey warns Dunwoodie to double his guard and strengthen his patrols lest imminent danger harm those he loves. Then, discharging the musket into the air, he throws the empty weapon at the feet of the astonished dragoon and disappears before the smoke clears.

Doubting his own senses, Dunwoodie returns to his camp where he finds pre-dawn preparations being made for the execution of Harvey Birch. Leading his men to Harvey's closely guarded cell, he finds (to the amazement of Sergeant Hollister and the guards) the room occupied not by Harvey but by Betty Flanagan. After the confusion subsides, Sergeant Hollister, once assured of Betty's sympathetic ear, interprets the whole event in religious terms: What had seemed the peddler had been Satan, and the apparent Skinners who had delivered him to the dragoons had been Satan's imps; the Evil One had come in the form of Birch and departed in the form of Betty. Not entirely convinced by this explanation, Mrs. Flanagan offers no objection but encourages the matrimonial relationship she has long sought with Hollister, the old military comrade of her dead husband, Michael. The legend of Harvey Birch, however, has here assumed supernatural dimension, and even the commanding officer of the Virginia Dragoons accords the peddler a measure of awesome respect by following his advice to reinforce his pickets.

Remembering also Harvey's warning to guard more closely those he loves, Dunwoodie rides rapidly to The Locusts. He arrives as Henry Wharton is being transferred to his newly ordered detention at American headquarters. Finding Frances sobbing by the road where she has viewed her brother's departure, Dunwoodie tries to console her with an assurance that he will intercede with Washington himself on Henry's behalf. The girl's grief is motivated in part, however, by another cause: her conviction Dunwoodie has deceived her in his declaration of love. Obviously thinking of Isabella Singleton, Frances says that she is resigned to his marrying a more high-spirited girl than herself. Her jealous suspicion has been deepened by Dunwoodie's absence from The Locusts in recent days. His engagement to Frances now suddenly and inexplicably broken, Dunwoodie rides off in despair to his command post.

Later while Lawton and Dr. Sitgreaves ride slowly toward The Locusts to visit Singleton, they are halted momentarily when a stone rolls from a cliff into their path. Attached to the stone is a note warning the travelers that they are foolishly exposing themselves to more dangerous weapons than stones. Lawton recognizes the wisdom of what must be the warning of Harvey Birch and for once, however grudgingly, speaks in praise of the peddler.

At The Locusts they find that the wedding of Colonel Wellmere and Sarah Wharton is about to take place, but the ceremony has been delayed for want of a ring for the bride. Dr. Sitgreaves offers a ring formerly belonging to his sister, Anna, and Caesar is dispatched to Hotel Flanagan to secure it. There Caesar enjoys a drink and listens briefly to the continuing discussion of Sergeant Hollister and Betty as to whether Harvey Birch is a fiend or a mortal man. From nowhere Harvey suddenly appears and informs Hollister that he and his dragoons are urgently needed by Captain Lawton at The Locusts. Again Hollister thinks Harvey the devil himself, but urged by Betty to answer the summons, the sergeant assembles his troops and departs.

When Caesar returns with the wedding ring, the wedding ceremony begins. It is suddenly halted, however, by the arrival of Harvey Birch, who accuses Colonel Wellmere of bigamy. Sarah, observing Wellmere's consternation and realizing that the charge against him is true, collapses. To defend Sarah's honor, Captain Lawton challenges Wellmere to a duel, but the combat is halted by a company of Skinners who wish to kill Lawton in a less ceremonious way. Failing to kill or capture Lawton, the Skinners proceed to plunder The Locusts and set it afire. Before the building is completely consumed by the flames, all occupants are evacuated, the last being the now deranged Sarah, who is rescued, after the roof collapses, by the ubiquitous Harvey Birch. Although exhausted and defenseless, Birch is not taken prisoner by Lawton, who admires the peddler's heroic behavior and chivalric attitude.

The residents and guests of The Locusts are now moved to Four Corners, there to be housed in Hotel Flanagan. As Captain Lawton is working to make these quarters suitable to accommodate the Whartons, he is fired upon by a Skinner, but the bullet intended for him strikes Isabella Singleton, mortally wounding the girl. As she lies dying, she confesses to Frances that her love for Peyton Dunwoodie had never been returned, that he had never by word or act manifested amorous interest in her.

After the burial of Isabella, the Whartons are summoned to an American base farther north, at Fishkill, to serve as witnesses at the military court trying Henry for espionage. At the trial, presided over by Colonel Singleton, Henry acknowledges traveling in disguise behind the American lines to visit his father. The judges seem inclined to attribute his indiscretion to filial devotion rather than to espionage activity until

Frances mentions his contact with Harvey Birch. Since it is generally accepted as a fact that Henry is in the employ of Sir Henry Clinton, the British commanding officer in the area, testimony as to Henry's contact with the peddler is damning evidence. The unfavorable verdict is based upon guilt by association.

Awaiting execution in the morning, Henry clings to the hope of an eleventh-hour pardon from George Washington. This last hope disappears, however, when a messenger arrives bearing a statement from the commander-in-chief which approves of the military court's decision. As the anguished Wharton family discusses Henry's fate, Frances mentions the promise of Mr. Harper to aid them if he can ever do so. When Major Dunwoodie hears the account of Harper's obligation to the Wharton family, he (knowing but not disclosing the true identity of Harper) insists that a pardon from Washington is still possible. He then sets out to locate Mr. Harper, but he returns disappointed several hours later.

At the jail cell where Henry is to spend his last night, a Yankee preacher appears to minister to the spiritual needs of the condemned man. It is Harvey Birch in disguise. Ordering Henry and Caesar to exchange clothing, Harvey fits Henry with black mask and wig sufficiently convincing to allow him to deceive the guards. Caesar, wearing white gloves and Henry's clothes, is left, head buried in his hands, in the cell. Harvey and Henry barely pass the last sentinel before the ruse is detected, an alarm raised, and pursuit begun. Once in the woods, the refugees abandon their horses and proceed on foot.

Hoping to be able to aid her brother in some way, Frances goes to a hut of Harvey's in the nearby hills. There, to her surprise, she finds Mr. Harper, who reassures her that he will keep his promise to help Henry. When Harvey and Henry reach the hut, Harper steps behind a curtain and into the cave that it hides, but not before he tells Frances to insist that the fugitives continue their flight at once. Astonished to find Frances in such a desolate place, Henry wishes to conduct her safely back to the settlement. As the brother and sister talk, Harvey silently steps into the cave to confer with Mr. Harper. When he returns, Harvey, as well as Frances, urges Henry to continue the retreat from the area. After the departure of the fugitives, Mr. Harper returns, guides Frances back to the plain below, gives her a paternal blessing, and, locating his horse, rides away. Her intuitive sense of Harper's high status is corroborated a few minutes later when she sees him ride by accompanied by servants and protected by a strong cavalry guard.

Back at the Continental camp Frances delivers to Dunwoodie the sealed letter her brother had sent to the major. The missive requests that

Dunwoodie and Frances be married at once. Dunwoodie feels that his first duty is to recapture Henry and then somehow secure for him a pardon from Washington. However, he does take time (crucial time) for the wedding ceremony. Then, before he can pursue Harvey and Henry, a message from Washington arrives ordering him to special duty immediately at Croton and indicating that the escape of the English spy is not important.

Harvey conducts Henry to the bank of the Hudson River, where a British ship awaits. As soon as he sees Henry picked up by a boat from the vessel, Harvey starts back, now accompanied by an unwelcome Skinner separated from his band and afraid to travel through enemy territory alone. Overtaken by a group of Cow-boys, British guerrillas and foragers, the two men receive different treatment. Birch is set free when he shows his pass from Sir Henry Clinton; by arrangement with Washington, Harvey has pretended to be a British spy in order to be able to move freely in enemy territory. The Skinner the Cow-boys coolly hang.

New duties for the Virginia Dragoons require their support of a poorly trained Continental infantry unit. Hard pressed by British regulars, the American forces are rallied by Captain Lawton, who impetuously tries to lead them across an open plain. Man and horse are easy targets, and both are killed in a fusillade of musket fire. Major Dunwoodie commits a similar indiscretion when, motivated by vengeance, he leads the remaining dragoons in an attack on the retreating redcoats. The wound he receives keeps him from duty for the remainder of the fall and winter. Accompanied by his bride, Dunwoodie (now promoted to lieutenant colonel) visits his Virginia estate during his convalescence.

In September of 1781 Harvey Birch is summoned to the presence of General Washington, who, after thanking and congratulating the spy for his many dangerous espionage missions, offers him one hundred doubloons. It is not nearly enough, Washington says, but it is all that the new country can afford. Despite Washington's repeated urging, Harvey refuses the gold; his service, he insists, was purely patriotic. Washington reminds the peddler that he must go to his grave with the stigma of having been a British agent during the Revolution. As both spy and counterspy he has acquired vital information which, if revealed, could, even in future years, endanger the lives of many men on both sides of the conflict. Although Washington will never be able to acknowledge him publicly, he pledges his friendship to Harvey and promises assistance if it is ever needed. He also gives Harvey a written statement of his appreciation, whereupon the two men shake hands and bid each other farewell.

Thirty-three years later, in July of 1814, young Captain Wharton

Dunwoodie (son of Peyton and Frances) and Lieutenant Tom Mason, Jr., rest momentarily during a lull in battle near Niagara during the War of 1812. An old man bearing a light pack listens with great interest to their reminiscences about the Wharton family, its friends, and its servants. When the captain mentions his mother, the aged stranger comments, to the surprise of his two young listeners, that she was an angel. Before any explanation can be made or the conversation continued, a British artillery barrage sweeps the field, wounding Mason and killing the old man. Captain Dunwoodie removes from the hands of the corpse a small tin box containing a note which reads as follows:

> Circumstances of political importance, which involve the lives and fortunes of many, have hitherto kept secret what this paper now reveals. Harvey has for years been a faithful and unrequited servant of his country. Though man does not, may God reward him for his conduct.
>
> Geo. Washington (p. 463)

Harvey Birch, Johnny Birch, Major Peyton Dunwoodie, Captain Wharton Dunwoodie, Elizabeth Flanagan, Katharine Haynes, Sergeant Hollister, Captain John Lawton, Lieutenant Tom Mason, Lieutenant Tom Mason, Jr., Jeanette Peyton, Cornet Shipwith, Captain George Singleton, Isabella Singleton, Dr. Archibald Sitgreaves, Caesar Thompson, Dinah Thompson, General George Washington, Colonel Wellmere, Wharton, Frances Wharton, Captain Henry Wharton, Sarah Wharton.

The Two Admirals: A Tale, 1842.

The novel opens not with the main action (naval warfare during the Jacobite rebellion of 1745) but with the subplot: the inheritance of the Wychecombe baronetcy and its estate. The Wychecombe holdings on the Devonshire coast date back to the late Middle Ages, but the title is of more recent origin, having been conferred upon Sir Michael Wychecombe in 1611 by James I. The incumbent during much of the novel is Sir Wycherly Wychecombe, sixth baronet, eighty-four years old and now, as the last of his four brothers lies dying, without legitimate heir. Sir Wycherly is the oldest of five brothers, three of whom have died, and the fourth, Lord Thomas Wychecombe (baron and judge), dies at the opening of the tale. As far as Sir Wycherly can determine, his brothers all remained bachelors, like himself, though Thomas had had three natural sons by his housekeeper, Martha Dodd. Always legalistic in his thinking, the judge on his deathbed strongly urges his brother not to bequeath his estate to Tom, the eldest of his own illegitimate sons. There is some question in the baronet's mind as to whether his youngest brother, Gregory, might have wed and left heirs; but Gregory, a naval lieutenant, had departed almost fifty years ago and had not been heard of again. The dying Thomas suggests to Sir Wycherly that the fairest move would be to will his property to Sir Reginald Wychecombe of Hertfordshire, the present head of the family line descended from Sir Michael's younger brother. A "half-blood" relative has better right to the estate, he insists, than a *filius nullius*, a term the judge does not explain to the baronet before he expires.

Shortly before this a young American sailor had been brought to the baronet's estate by naval surgeons. The youth was a Virginian who, surprisingly, also bore the name Wycherly Wychecombe. Critically wounded in a sea battle, he had been made a lieutenant for heroism during the engagement, but there was doubt that he would survive to enjoy this promotion. Sir Wycherly had provided care for the young man, though, and he has fully recovered by the time he first appears in the novel. This scene occurs early on a July morning in 1745 as Lieutenant Wychecombe gathers flowers along a sea cliff for Mildred Dutton, daughter of Frank Dutton, an alcoholic petty officer who attends a small signal station there. Beautiful but also resourceful and courageous, Mildred lowers a rope to young Wycherly when, leaning out too far, he falls from the cliff to a ledge some six fathoms below. During the rescue Frank Dutton is incapacitated by nervous tremors and Sir Wycherly, who happens to ride up at the moment, is too feeble to be of any real assistance. Afterwards, as the three men and Mildred gaze out to sea, they see a number of warships approaching the roadstead serviced by Dutton's signal station. It is the fleet of Vice Admiral Sir Gervaise Oakes, whose second in command is Rear Admiral Richard Bluewater—the titular heroes of the book. The two emissaries who come ashore from the lead vessel identify themselves as none other than Oakes himself and his secretary, Atwood. The baronet quickly and graciously extends to these two officers the hospitality of his home, Wychecombe Hall.

Before retiring to the Hall, the admiral sends Lieutenant Wychecombe to intercept the mail coach with important dispatches to the Admiralty. Soon after arriving at the manor, Oakes is joined by Bluewater, his lifelong friend and, at times, almost his alter ego. They differ only in their politics, Oakes being a Whig, Bluewater a Tory with strong Jacobite sympathies—a matter of little moment ordinarily. It takes on unusual significance, however, when Lieutenant Wychecombe returns with the news that Charles Edward Stuart, the "Young Pretender," has landed in

Scotland from his exile in France. After making a few pro-Jacobite observations, Bluewater turns his attention to his charming dinner companion, Mildred Dutton. Because of the great disparity in their ages—he is fifty-four, she nineteen—their repartee is not flirtatious in the usual sense of that word. With a vague feeling that he has somehow known the girl for a long while, Bluewater enjoys her refined manner and refreshing wit.

As the dinner ends and the ladies leave the table, both Mildred and her mother recognize that Frank Dutton is growing drunk from over-indulgence in port wine. It is the story of their lives. Dutton had been a naval lieutenant when he married Martha Ray, a girl who, though of lowly origins, had grown up in genteel circumstances after Lady Wilmeter had made her the companion of her own daughters. The couple had disappeared from their home area for twenty years, during which time Frank had been court-martialed for drunkenness while on duty and had been demoted to the noncommissioned rank of sailing master. Taking to drink even more heavily after that, he had proceeded to ruin his health as well as his fortune, and the minor post he now held had been secured for him through the influence of Lady Wilmeter's son, the present Lord Wilmeter. Mildred's education and aristocratic bearing derive entirely from her long-suffering mother.

The two admirals each receive mail brought by special courier. Besides operational orders from the Admiralty, there are personal communications. Bluewater receives an announcement that he has been made a Knight of the Bath. Inasmuch as the letter containing this information was postmarked after the date on which the Young Pretender had returned to Great Britain, it is obvious that the honor extended to Bluewater is an effort to secure his loyalty to George II during the imminent uprising. He also receives from a prominent member of court an underhanded ploy which both admirals see through at once and resent. Bluewater's correspondent warns him to be vigilant to prevent any effort Oakes might make to desert King George and deliver the fleet into the hands of Bonnie Prince Charlie! Knowing the closeness of the two admirals, and knowing that Bluewater would probably show the letter to his friend, the sender had intended in this sly way to remind the solidly Hanoverian Oakes of the rear admiral's known Jacobite predilection.

Although the two admirals and Lieutenant Wychecombe soon excuse themselves from the post-dinner drinking, Sir Wycherly continues to carouse with three of his guests: Dutton, Vicar Rotherham, and Tom, the natural son of the late Lord Thomas Wychecombe. All too aware of

Dutton's weakness for alcohol, his wife and daughter wait with apprehension in an antechamber where they are joined first by Lieutenant Wychecombe and then by Admiral Bluewater. The latter finally recognizes Mrs. Dutton and surmises he now knows why Mildred had looked so familiar to him. Years before, Bluewater, serving with the panel who had court-martialed Frank Dutton, had been torn between his duty and his sympathy for the wife and infant daughter of the accused man. The three now talk frankly about the alcoholism lying behind Dutton's downfall and subsequent degeneracy. A shout from the revelers in the dining room is now heard as Sir Wycherly collapses with a stroke. When Dutton locates his wife and daughter, he is too much the worse from wine to notice Bluewater's presence in the room. He speaks abusively to both women, threatens Mildred, and crassly orders her to snare a husband—either Tom or Lieutenant Wychecombe. Mortified by such coarse treatment in public, Mildred rushes, weeping, into the arms of the admiral. Although Dutton apologizes to his superior officer for his behavior, he has revealed all too clearly his true character.

The stricken baronet, put to bed, requests that Vicar Rotherham, Sir Gervaise, and the latter's secretary remain in his room after all others have departed. Tom demands the right, as heir apparent, to remain but is removed at the patient's orders. Rather incoherently the failing baronet tries to indicate that he wishes his property to be inherited by Sir Reginald Wychecombe of Hertfordshire and not by the illegitimate Tom, whom he refers to several times as *nullius*, a legal expression which no one present (including the baronet) understands completely. His auditors take careful note of all he says, however, including this incomplete Latin term.

Admiral Bluewater escorts Mildred and her mother home in the coach that has been standing by to take him to the seashore. In private conversation with Mildred, after they arrive at the sailing master's cottage, Bluewater warns the girl against Tom, about whom he knows nothing but whom he intuitively distrusts. The admiral then takes a waiting boat back to his own flagship, the *Caesar*, having long made it a practice not to sleep ashore. The following morning he draws up his will, leaving all of his property to Mildred Dutton, and has three of the *Caesar's* officers witness the instrument. When he returns to Wychecombe Hall later that day, he takes with him a very young midshipman, a cousin once removed, named Lord Geoffrey Cleveland. The admiral is startled at dinner that evening by the striking resemblance between Geoffrey and Mildred Dutton.

Shortly after Bluewater reaches Wychecombe Hall the announcement is made of the arrival of Sir Reginald Wychecombe, whose presence has been asked by the dying baronet. Before the group enters the sickroom, Sir Reginald takes Oakes aside and explains that he himself is not in the direct bloodline to inherit the title and that young Tom is illegitimate, having no legal claim to either the title or the property. Shortly thereafter Sir Wycherly revives sufficiently to attempt once again to dictate his will. The bulk of his property he leaves to Sir Reginald; £3,000 goes to Mildred Dutton; generous bequests are made to his four principal servants; but only £50 is assigned to Tom Wycherly. Lieutenant Wycherly Wychecombe respectfully refuses to accept the £1,000 which the baronet wishes to give him, declining to accept money from one who had spoken ill of his native Virginia. He does, however, accept the signet ring which the old man takes from his finger and hands to him. To the lieutenant's surprise, the coat of arms on the ring matches exactly that of his own signet ring and of the Virginia branch of the Wychecombe family. As the baronet is about to sign the will, Tom, stepping forward, objects to the whole proceeding and calls upon all present to bear witness to his objection. Sir Wycherly, angered by this presumption, orders Tom from the room, but the emotion and effort are too much for his condition, and he dies before he can place his name on the document.

Tom now feels certain enough of succeeding to the title and to the estate of Wychecombe to begin referring to himself as Sir Thomas. He carries in his pocket a forged wedding certificate to prove that his father and Martha Dodd had been legally wed, though Sir Reginald has a sworn affidavit to the contrary signed by Martha. His claim is quickly challenged by what the two admirals and Sir Reginald consider to be a stronger claim. Lieutenant Wycherly Wychecombe produces papers to show that he is the legitimate heir of Sir Wycherly: he is the oldest grandson of Gregory Wychecombe, the late baronet's youngest brother, thought dead for decades. Gregory had struck a senior lieutenant and had been condemned to death by a naval court. Because neither his adversary nor the captain of his ship, the *Sappho,* had wished to see him executed, he had been allowed to jump ship and swim to a nearby island in the West Indies. Thence he had gone to Virginia where he had later wed a wealthy woman, Jane Beverly. His son, Wycherly, had preceded him in death; Gregory had then become the guardian of Wycherly's son, named Wycherly. Before his grandson had left Virginia to join the Royal Navy, Gregory had had made certified copies of the vital family documents and advised Wycherly to carry these with him to England. The young sailor had never sought English relatives partly because he had had doubts about a connection with Sir Wycherly before receiving the baronet's ring, partly because the old man had scorned those born in America, partly because he had supposed there were legitimate English heirs to the baronetcy. The two admirals, Sir Reginald, and several others who hear his story concur that by entail he is the true heir to both the title and the estate of the late baronet. The courts, they feel, will sustain his claims.

Word reaches Sir Gervaise that the French Atlantic fleet under the command of the Comte de Vervillin has finally left its base, and Oakes determines to engage it as soon as possible. The French force numbers thirteen capital ships to eleven of the British, but this fact does not deter Oakes in his intention to do battle with the enemy. As usual, he will lead the van and Admiral Bluewater will bring up the rear squadron. Although he knows Bluewater's strong Jacobite sympathies, and although it seems likely that the French naval force will support Charles Edward Stuart's bid for the English throne, Oakes is confident that his junior admiral will not fail to support him once he attacks the Comte de Vervillin's flotilla.

Oakes sails with his squadron of six ships and orders Bluewater to follow within a few hours with his squadron of five. As he waits to depart, Bluewater is approached by Sir Reginald, a much more active Jacobite than the admiral himself. He solicits Bluewater's support for the Stuart cause, suggesting that he could best serve his legitimate prince by defecting with his ships to the French allies of the Young Pretender. Although shocked by the proposal for such treachery, Bluewater is sorely beset by temptation, as if the devil himself had set bait before him in its most inviting form. In his troubled state of mind, he makes no definite commitment to Sir Reginald as he boards a launch to go to his waiting flagship. With him goes Lieutenant Wycherly Wychecombe, the new (seventh) baronet of Wychecombe.

As a wind of gale proportions arises, Admiral Oakes directs his squadron of ships into position for engaging the French fleet. With six "ships of the line" plus three smaller supporting vessels he will, at the outset, be opposing a force of nineteen vessels, thirteen of them heavy warships. He expects, however, that before the battle continues very long, Bluewater will bring up the second squadron in his support. In the initial brief encounter the British demast the French admiral's flagship, the *Foudroyant*, capture the *Victoire*, and knock out of action the *Scipio*, which, subsequently, is also captured. Heavy seas now intervene to halt the action temporarily, but they do not halt the *Druid*, a swift frigate from Bluewater's squadron, which now comes up alongside the *Plantagenet*, Oakes's flagship. The wind howls too loudly to permit vocal communication, and the waves run too high to allow a boat to pass from one ship to the other. On a light line thrown from the frigate to the *Plantagenet* Lieutenant Wychecombe is hauled aboard the flagship in a most unconventional manner. He bears a sealed letter from Bluewater to Oakes in which the rear admiral asks his superior officer to delay attacking the French for twenty-four hours; within that time Bluewater will decide whether or not to shift his allegiance to the Young Pretender. It is obvious that the rear admiral is undergoing anguished introspection as he tries to determine where his higher duty lies.

Trusting that his closest friend will never desert him in a life-and-death battle, Oakes regroups his ships in order to attack as soon as the storm abates. Each of the other five two-deckers in his squadron passes in review alongside the *Plantagenet*, its captain reporting to the admiral and, in turn, receiving his orders, his compliments, his criticism. Throughout these maneuvers and the deadly conflict that follows, the reader is given not only a close view of shipboard life and esprit de corps on individual vessels but also a panoramic picture of the dynamics and interaction of whole fleets of ships. Oakes's squadron performs most effectively but is badly outnumbered for the first three hours of the battle. Belatedly, the rear squadron joins forces with the van, and the British gain a major victory. As might be expected, the losses on both sides are heavy; but quite unexpectedly, one of the casualties is Admiral Bluewater, who suffers a mortal wound. (The fact that he was shot while *boarding* a French ship—hardly work for an admiral!—suggests an effort to compensate for his previous indecision and his tardy appearance on the scene of battle.)

The triumphant if battered fleet returns to the anchorage off the shore of the Wychecombe estate, now the property of the Virginian who is the seventh baronet of Wychecombe. Bluewater is taken to the Dutton cottage, where he is attended by naval surgeons and nursed by Mildred and her mother. A tent is set up nearby to serve as temporary headquarters for Vice Admiral Oakes as the death of his closest friend approaches.

Admiral Oakes and Captain Greenly, commander of the *Plantagenet*, decide that there is some information which must be imparted to Bluewater while he is still mentally competent to alter his will if he so wishes. Unbeknownst to the admiral, his long-dead younger brother, Colonel John Bluewater, had secretly wed Agnes Hedworth, sister of the Duchess of Glamorgan (Lord Geoffrey Cleveland's mother). The marriage had been secret because Agnes's guardian uncle had felt that an unpropertied army officer was beneath her. Greenly declares that both he and Captain Blakely, commander of the *Elizabeth*, had witnessed the wedding ceremony, and now Greenly is concerned lest there might have been some issue from this union. This account by Captain Greenly is interrupted by the smashing of a bowl dropped from the nerveless fingers of Mrs. Dutton. After recovering from her shock, Mrs. Dutton reveals that a year after the date given for the marriage by Captain Greenly, Agnes Hedworth had delivered a child in the Dutton home, to which she had come in the extremity of her need for assistance. Agnes had died shortly after the birth of a daughter, and Mrs. Dutton had taken the infant to replace her own child, whom she had recently lost. Inasmuch as Agnes had never mentioned the name of the baby's father, Mrs. Dutton had assumed that the child was illegitimate. When Frank Dutton had returned from a lengthy cruise, brutal and hopelessly alcoholic, his wife had decided against revealing to him that Mildred was not actually their own daughter. In fact, she had never revealed this to anyone until now that Greenly's story verified Mildred's legitimacy. Admiral Bluewater is delighted, knowing now that the girl to whom he willed his property is actually his niece. He also understands now why Mildred and Lord Geoffrey Cleveland look so much alike: they are first cousins. Admiral Bluewater's last wish is to see his young kinswoman and the new Sir Wycherly Wychecombe married, and the wedding ceremony is performed a few hours later in his room. He dies near sunrise the following morning in the presence of only his lifelong companion, Gervaise Oakes.

The new Sir Wycherly Wychecombe and his wife spend most of their time at the family plantation in Virginia, there building a suitable mansion for themselves and the three children born to them: Wycherly, Mildred, and Agnes. Twenty-five years later, while the family is in England, they visit the tomb of Rear Admiral Bluewater in Westminster Abbey. There they find Sir Gervaise Oakes, retired as full admiral but now, at eighty, quite senile, his memory almost completely gone. He is attended by the faithful steward Galleygo and by Geoffrey Cleveland, now the Duke of Glamorgan. Galleygo and Sir Wycherly try to reawaken Sir Gervaise's memory of his old friend Richard Bluewater, but it is Geoffrey who finally succeeds in doing so. After Sir Gervaise realizes where he is and why he is there, he asks pardon of the others while he kneels to pray. When they raise the old man from his knees and place him in a chair, they discover that Admiral Sir Gervaise Oakes has died performing his orisons.

Ben Barrel, Captain Blakely, Captain Thomas Blewet, Lord Bluewater, Mildred Bluewater, Rear Admiral Richard Bluewater, Lieutenant Bluff, Jack Brown, Lieutenant Bunting, Lieutenant Bury, Comte de Chelincourt, Lord Geoffrey Cleveland, Captain Comtant, Lieu-

tenant Cornet, Lieutenant Daly, David, Captain Denham, Vicomte
des Prez, Martha Dodd, Captain Drinkwater, Frank Dutton, Martha
Ray Dutton, Captain Foley, Furlong, David Galleygo, Duchess of
Glamorgan, Jack Glass, Captain Goodfellow, Greenleaf, Captain
Greenly, Agnes Hedworth, Larder, Locker, Sandy McYarn,
Magrath, Lord Morganic, Ned, Vice Admiral Sir Gervaise Oakes,
Captain O'Neil, Captain Parker, Record, Richard, Rev. Mr. Roth-
erham, Soundings, Tom Sponge, Captain Sterling, Captain Stowel,
Lieutenant Tom, Comte de Vervillin, Sam Wade, Lieutenant
Williamson, Agnes Wychecombe, Mildred Wychecombe, Sir Reg-
inald Wychecombe, Lord Thomas Wychecombe, Thomas Wy-
checombe, Sir Wycherly Wychecombe, Wycherly Wychecombe,
Lieutenant Wycherly Wychecombe, Wycherly Wychecombe [son of
the lieutenant], Sam Yoke.

The Water-Witch; or, The Skimmer of the Seas, 1830.

On a June morning in the early 1710s Myndert Van Beverout, a
prosperous fur merchant and alderman of New York City, is intercepted
on the street by Lord Cornbury, former governor of the colony of New
York but now fallen in disgrace from that high position. Having lived
beyond his means (both legal and illegal!), the viscount has incurred
heavy debts, and his creditors have had him imprisoned. As a member of
the aristocracy and a relative of Queen Anne, he is allowed special
privileges, among them his freedom during the night and early morning.
After flattering the alderman, a sturdy burgher of Dutch extraction,
Cornbury asks him for a loan of £2,000. His request is quickly refused by
the shrewd merchant. That Lord Cornbury is meant to represent those
profligate and rejected English peers too often appointed to high posts in
the colonies becomes apparent in the language applied to him. In the
narration his name is regularly preceded by such adjectives as *depraved,
degenerate,* and *dissolute.*

Proceeding on his way, the alderman calls at the city residence of Oloff
Van Staats, the young Patroon of Kinderhook. Strong and reliable, but
phlegmatic in disposition, taciturn in manner, the patroon is the stereotyped Dutchman of the comic stage of nineteenth-century America.
Bound for Lust in Rust, Van Beverout's villa on the Jersey coast, the two
men board a ferry where they are, through prearrangement, joined by
Alida de Barbérie, the merchant's orphaned nineteen-year-old niece. The
girl's vivacity and capriciousness are derived, according to her uncle,
from her Huguenot father. Van Beverout approves of Van Staats's
interest in Alida, but has advised him that he must press his claim more

warmly than he has so far done in his halfhearted (almost static) suit for the girl's hand. For her part, Alida is obviously more favorably inclined to the overtures of Cornelius Van Cuyler Ludlow, captain of Her Majesty's cruiser *Coquette.*

While still in the harbor, the ferry is hailed, and another passenger comes aboard, a tall, athletic seaman whose clothes are distinguished by a colorful India shawl. Coolly taking the helm from the captain, the newcomer asks for recent maritime news in the area. The captain knows none except for repeated reports of the appearance in nearby waters of a mysterious ship known as the *Water-Witch* and commanded by a notorious rover identified only as "The Skimmer of the Seas." As the ferry comes abreast of the *Coquette,* it is saluted by Captain Ludlow, who extends personal greetings to Alderman Van Beverout and Alida. The aggressive seaman now asks Ludlow if there is a berth to be filled aboard the cruiser, but when he is told that there is indeed a place for him, he scornfully declines the offer. As the vessels part, the warship lowers three boats, two of which pursue the ferry to capture the audacious seaman with the India shawl. Skillfully maneuvering the ferry through some treacherous, shoal-filled waters, the stranger brings the boat safely to the landing on Staten Island and then disappears ashore. He is not at all intimidated, however; and when Captain Ludlow himself lands, the bold fellow, now identified as Tom Tiller, seeks out the naval officer and, with only slight deference to the latter's rank, again inquires about a berth on the *Coquette.* He might, he tells Ludlow, join the crew of the cruiser if he is permitted, without any obligation, to inspect the ship. Swallowing his pride, Ludlow decides to humor this presumptuous stranger and agrees to his unusual terms. In the meantime, Van Beverout and his group move on to Rust in Lust in the alderman's own periagua [a flat-bottomed, two-masted boat with little or no decking].

That evening Alida is unexpectedly visited in her apartment at Lust in Rust by Captain Ludlow. A letter, supposedly from Alida, had prompted this intrusion; written in a woman's hand and bearing the forged signature of Alida, the letter had been substituted by Tiller for a missive by Alida herself. Alida had not invited the captain to her rooms, and as soon as Ludlow discovers the mistake, he leaves at once. Myndert Van Beverout enters his niece's quarters, extinguishes the large bright candles, and gives Alida a small lamp instead. As soon as he leaves, Alida lights the candles again and stands gazing out toward the water, expecting to see Ludlow's launch returning to the *Coquette,* anchored offshore at a distance. Instead, she sees a graceful, bare-masted brigantine float in noiselessly on the tide and anchor close to the villa. Only a few minutes elapse before someone vaults onto the balcony and enters her room. It is one Master Seadrift, agent of a smuggler, who has landed with a load of contraband for Van Beverout. His cue for landing was the bright lights in Alida's rooms, rooms unoccupied on those earlier occasions when Van Beverout had signaled him ashore. Seadrift is dressed somewhat like Tom Tiller, in bright India cloth, but his manner is more gentle, his speech more refined.

Alida leaves the room when the alderman enters to deal with the free-trader, but Seadrift insists that she return before showing samples of his wares. When the girl reappears, her uncle decides to have her examine Seadrift's samples while he himself goes to the wharf to inspect the bales of goods being unloaded from the brigantine. Although she is fascinated by the fine fabrics and exotic merchandise, Alida cannot help wondering if these goods are illicit. All her doubts are removed when Ludlow reenters, by way of the balcony, and warns her that they are contraband smuggled into the country by the Skimmer of the Seas. Ludlow knows whereof he speaks, for both he and the crew of his launch are prisoners of the Skimmer, all captured by men from the brigantine *Water-Witch* under the direction of Tom Tiller.

While Van Beverout and Van Staats are at breakfast the following morning, they are apprised of two pieces of bad news. François, the elderly French valet, announces that Alida is missing from her quarters, and Euclid, a slave, arrives from the city to report that one of the alderman's prize Belgian geldings has died. As the merchant addresses the two bearers of bad tidings in alternate sentences, the reader cannot help wondering which of his losses he feels more keenly. Van Beverout and his guest assume that Alida has eloped with Ludlow until the Captain himself, now freed, arrives and is clearly shocked to learn of the girl's disappearance. They can only conclude that she is aboard the *Water-Witch*, drawn there by the seductive manner of Seadrift. Seemingly, there are now three suitors for the hand of Alida, though the ardor of both the captain and the patroon is dampened by the moral implications of her latest caprice.

Van Beverout, Van Staats, and Ludlow send word to the *Water-Witch* requesting a conference with Seadrift (whom Ludlow identifies with the legendary Skimmer of the Seas). Tom Tiller comes ashore for the three men, takes them to the brig, and declaring that there is aboard neither armament nor contraband, invites Ludlow to inspect the hold of the ship. Although Tiller boasts of the speed of the trim, tall-masted ship, he attributes her safety to her namesake, the green-clad female figurehead with a malign smile. Suggestions of sorcery are associated with this figurehead, several images of which subsequently appear at critical moments. She holds an open book, on the metal pages of which are inscribed in enamel cryptic commentaries on life, some of them quotations from literature. A species of sortilege is practiced regularly by the crew and now by the guests, each supplicant for advice or prophecy opening the metal leaves at random with a long wooden wand and supposedly receiving his answer on the exposed page. Although Ludlow scoffs at this mummery, it is part of the mystique of this strange vessel which many people (including a majority of Ludlow's own crew) suspect to be a "flyer," a supernatural ship akin to the "Flying Dutchman."

As they await their audience with the Skimmer, the visitors are impressed by the luxurious appointments of the brigantine's cabin, especially its leather-upholstered furniture. They are pleasantly surprised by other unexpected effects: a guitar-accompanied song by the captain before his appearance, and a ten-year-old-cabin boy, Zephyr, with delicate features and expensive attire. The conference itself is unproductive, and Alida's whereabouts remain a mystery.

What could not be achieved by words is now attempted by force as the *Coquette* prepares to capture the *Water-Witch*. Restraint is required, however, for the possibility that Alida is actually aboard the brig precludes use of the cruiser's cannons. A boarding party in the cruiser's launch approaches the unmoved brig, but a heavy squall forces it to return to the *Coquette*. In the few minutes required to secure the safety of the cruiser and its launch, the *Water-Witch* disappears. On the next evening the free-trader is sighted offshore, and a similar pursuit-and-escape episode occurs. Darkness intervenes as the cruiser bears down upon its prey, but the Skimmer obligingly mounts a lantern on the figurehead. Guided by this light, the *Coquette* quietly moves to the brig's position, and the sailors cast their grappling irons to lash the two ships together, but the metal hooks strike only the surface of the sea. (Ludlow discovers on the following day a tub containing a lantern and a replica of the brig's figurehead, the decoy that had misled the crew.) The sailors are all certain that the *Water-Witch* is truly what her name indicates. In the middle of the night Ludlow, hearing indistinct noises across the water, senses that the *Water-Witch* is nearby mocking him in the dark. He lowers four boats, each to search in a different direction. When his own boat comes upon what he thinks is the *Water-Witch* and his men board it successfully, he finds, to his great embarrassment, that it is not the elusive brigantine but the *Stately Pine*, a small coastal freighter. Back aboard the cruiser, the members of his boat crew conclude they had indeed boarded the *Water-Witch* but enchantment had altered her appearance so that they could not recognize her.

On the succeeding day the chase continues, and twice the cruiser comes close to capturing its quarry only to lose it at the last moment. During the second of these abortive efforts, the doughty Patroon of Kinderhook actually throws himself over the brig's gunwales, but the *Water-Witch*, gathering speed, pulls away from the boarding boats with Van Staats a captive.

When Ludlow and Van Beverout return to Lust in Rust, they find Alida there. Before explanations can be made, Seadrift arrives with another packet of silks for Alida to examine. Even more engaging and exotic than his wares are the subjects of his conversation as he discusses romantic sites in Europe and the historical events which have enriched them with cultural significance. Ludlow leaves to secure Seadrift's skiff, a move which enables him later to capture the Skimmer and carry him to the *Coquette* as a prisoner. Under cover of darkness, Ludlow and Bob Yarn row to the *Water-Witch* to set her adrift in the light wind and ground her on the nearby beach. At the instant Ludlow's knife touches the anchor cable, the hawser emits a flash, the green figurehead suddenly glows in the dark, and the people of the brig are alerted.

As if to add insult to the injury of her naval suitor, Alida, accompanied by Van Beverout, comes aboard the *Coquette* to visit the captive Seadrift. Ludlow now stations armed boats for the night at all points of egress from the cove where the *Water-Witch* is anchored. With the land on one side of the brig, the cruiser on the other, and the latter's boats sealing off all routes of escape, the *Water-Witch* seems trapped. Soon Tom Tiller comes alongside and requests a parley with Ludlow. To Ludlow's surprise, Tiller's concern is less about the plight of the brig than about the welfare and comfort of Seadrift. When he learns that Alida and Van Beverout have come aboard the *Coquette*, Tiller seems relieved and soon departs. It is apparent by now that there are more mysteries connected with the *Water-Witch* than the questionable nature of her trading operations and the uncanny way in which she eludes pursuers. Of all the central characters, only Ludlow is as unenlightened as the reader about these matters.

The scene shifts to New York City and the place of business of one Carnaby, a grocer. Whether an agent of Tom Tiller or of Lord Cornbury, Carnaby is the intermediary who brings these two together for a meeting. The seaman pays Cornbury a sizable amount of gold to use his waning influence to secure a light sentence for Seadrift if he is brought to trial. When their conference ends, cannon fire is heard in the harbor as the *Coquette* closes in on the *Water-Witch*. Once Tiller is aboard, the brig makes another spectacular escape, coming within fifty feet of the cruiser on one tack in order to do so. It now becomes apparent that Tiller rather than Seadrift is the Skimmer of the Seas.

Ludlow goes to sea in pursuit of the free-trader without stopping to pick up the seventy members of his crew stationed in boats. He is thus caught dangerously shorthanded when he encounters not the unarmed trader but a French warship. Going to the cabin, Ludlow asks Van Beverout and Seadrift to command batteries of guns against their common enemy. The alderman agrees with alacrity and during the ensuing battle distinguishes himself. Seadrift declines, claiming inexperience at work of that nature. He actually seems quite effeminate as he chooses to stay below to comfort Alida during the naval engagement. After the British guns cripple the French ship, Ludlow prepares to board and capture the enemy vessel, but when another French cruiser appears, he is forced to change his tactics and flee shoreward for protection.

Quite unobserved by the *Coquette*'s lookouts, Tom Tiller comes aboard from a small skiff to warn Ludlow that the crews of the two French warships are planning some sort of attack on the British vessel. His prediction is verified when a swarm of French boats, with greatly superior manpower, attacks and boards the *Coquette*. Despite their dogged resistance, the British are about to be overwhelmed when two boatloads of reinforcements arrive from the *Water-Witch* and turn the tide of battle. In a short while the French withdraw with heavy losses, but the British victory is illusory, for a serious fire has developed in the *Coquette's* hold during the struggle. When the fire is clearly out of control, the Skimmer's boats take off most of the crew. Many of the remainder, fearful of the inevitable explosion of the ship's magazine, row off in the launch before the central characters can get aboard that boat. As the cruiser is being consumed by flames, Ludlow and Tiller shoot away her masts for the wood needed to build some sort of makeshift raft. This they accomplish just moments before the *Coquette* explodes in a fiery blast and sinks into the sea.

The situation of the castaways is most precarious. The masts and spars which constitute their rafts are lashed together only with the rope and cordage of the rigging. The first heavy sea will wrench them apart. One sailor is lost to a school of sharks. The crews of the two French ships, having witnessed from a distance the destruction of the *Coquette*, now arrive and search for survivors, but the raft has too low a profile in the water to be seen by them. Several hours later the castaways are picked up by the *Water-Witch*.

Back at Lust in Rust Tom Tiller and Van Beverout are closeted in a lengthy interview which clarifies for the reader much of the tangle of relationships. The alderman has been carrying on business with the *Water-Witch* for more than twenty years, beginning with Tiller's predecessor and benefactor (not his father, as the merchant had supposed). That predecessor had had a daughter whom Van Beverout had fallen in love with and lived with briefly in a common-law marriage; although he had intended to marry her legally, he had been unable to do so right away without jeopardizing his own career. Whatever were his good intentions toward the girl, they went unrealized, for she had died abroad. Van Beverout had not known that before her death she had borne him a daughter, Eudora, who had been protected and cared for by Tom Tiller as his own sister. Seadrift is that Eudora masquerading as a man. The alderman had known for several years that Seadrift was a woman, but he had mistakenly believed that she was, as Tiller claimed, the Skimmer's sister. (Knowing Seadrift's sex, Van Beverout had not been as disturbed as either Ludlow or Staats about his niece's recent association with that person.) The revelation of Eudora's identity is as great a surprise to her as it is to Van Beverout, for she had grown up thinking she was Tiller's sister.

After a tearful recognition scene between father and daughter, Tiller informs them of a suitor for Eudora's hand. The Patroon of Kinderhook, aware he would never win Alida, had become interested in Eudora while he was a prisoner on the *Water-Witch*. Persuaded that her virtue has been preserved unstained, despite her life aboard ship, Van Staats now wishes to marry Eudora. Emotionally agitated for the first time in the novel, Tiller tells Van Beverout that they would both be doing their duty on Eudora's behalf by having her married so advantageously. The girl herself, confused by her new status and her recently revealed identity, demurs. She will live ashore, she says, only if Zephyr will remain with her. When the cabin boy chooses to return to the *Water-Witch,* Eudora throws herself into the arms of Tiller and passionately declares her love for the Skimmer. Before either Van Staats or Van Beverout can stop him, Tiller whisks Eudora and Zephyr into his skiff and rows to the waiting brigantine, which departs at once with the tide. Knowing that his name will be prominent in the news following the sea battle and the loss of the *Coquette,* Tiller recognizes the impossibility of remaining in the area any longer. Accordingly, the *Water-Witch* vanishes, never again to be seen in this part of the world.

The subsequent marriage of the two conventional romantic leads, Ludlow and Alida, is relegated to two short sentences; the focus then returns to the titular hero, the Skimmer of the Seas, and his young bride. Although Tom Tiller is a smuggler and hence an outlaw, he remains a memorable and sympathetic character partly because he is colorful, courageous, and generous, and partly because the laws he breaks are repressive regulations which hamper the development of free trade in America.

Alida de Barbérie, Bonnie, Brutus, Carnaby, Bob Cleet, Coil, Lord Cornbury, Cupid, Dinah, Diomede, Dumont, Erasmus, Euclid, François, Hopper, Captain Cornelius Van Cuyler Ludlow, Lieutenant Luff, Phyllis, Reef, Rogerson, Captain Thomas Tiller, Ben Trysail, Eudora Van Beverout, Myndert Van Beverout, Oloff Van Staats, Robert Yarn, Zephyr.

The Ways of the Hour: A Tale, 1850.

In this sociological novel, Cooper's last full-length fictional work, the author evidences his concern about "the ways of the hour": lack of principle as shown in easy divorce, financial independence of women, and flagrant abuse of justice by elected judges, incompetent jurors, culpable lawyers, and an irresponsible press; an unreasoning worship of mass opinion; and failure to pursue the truth beneath the trappings of appearance. The vehicle for exploring the sociological theme is a mid-1840s murder trial assuming the pattern of a murder mystery, a "whodunit," complete with aliases, cloak-and-dagger schemes, a "revived" corpse, a missing treasure, a series of "jailbreaks," bribery, and a madwoman.

An innocent question concerning the wording of a dinner toast prompts Thomas Dunscomb, Cooper's spokesman, to deny his young legal apprentices' idealistic notion that the United States Constitution is the "palladium of our civil and religious liberties" (p. 14). This breakfast-table conversation in the opening scene introduces Dunscomb, a respected New York City lawyer and somewhat cynical sixty-year-old bachelor, and his orphaned niece Sarah Wilmeter and nephew John (Jack) Wilmeter. Present at the table also is Michael (Mike) Millington, friend and colleague of Jack, apprentice—as is Jack—of Dunscomb, and suitor of twenty-year-old Sarah, the naive observer. Their earnest discussion, well under way, is interrupted by the arrival of Dr. Edward McBrain, the family doctor, long-term friend of Dunscomb, and the good-natured object of Dunscomb's jibes for his upcoming marriage (his third) at the age of sixty to the charming Widow Anna Updyke.

McBrain, perturbed by his preliminary findings on an inquest to which he has been summoned as consultant by the coroner in adjoining Duke's (sic) County, reports the major features of what appears to be a clear instance of arson, robbery, and murder. A house fire in the county seat, Biberry, has produced several arresting but apparently related elements:

the discovery of the charred remains of two people, presumably Peter and Dorothy Goodwin, the disappearance of a German woman working there for her board, the theft of a stocking containing a substantial amount of money, and the rescue—with all her belongings intact—of a beautiful young boarder, Mary Monson. McBrain, prepared to examine the Goodwins' skeletons, finds instead the remains of two females, with their skulls fractured; moreover, from her behavior, he is convinced that the young boarder is using an alias. Concerned for the fate of the fascinating young lady in the face of strong circumstantial evidence, McBrain urges his attorney friend to attend the formal inquest that afternoon in Biberry.

Dunscomb, accompanied by John and Michael, goes by carriage with McBrain to assess the situation, still not determined to become involved in the case himself. Coroner Sanford's callous treatment of Mary Monson as a suspect rather than as a witness prompts Dunscomb to defend the friendless young woman. He is allowed to consult privately for an hour with Mary but is unable to learn anything about his client except her name—admittedly an alias—and the already-established circumstances of the case. The two return to the inquest to discover that McBrain's identification of both skeletons as females has been flatly contradicted by the county doctors called to examine the remains; all are persuaded that, since Goodwins' house had burned, the remains must be those of the owner and his wife, who had been almost exactly the same height. On the basis of testimony by a number of women that Mary Monson has in her purse a curious coin formerly seen among those hoarded in avaricious Mrs. Goodwin's stocking treasury—a twenty-dollar gold piece Mary claims to have given to the deceased—and on suspicion aroused by Mary's refusal to provide the solicited personal information about herself, Mary Monson finally stands accused of the first-degree murder of Peter Goodwin.

Leaving John and Michael to provide for Mary Monson's comfort and to assemble evidence toward a brief, Dunscomb returns to other cases in the city. The sheriff's wife, Mrs. Gott, convinced of Mary's innocence, makes her jail accommodations not only comfortable but elegant, furnishing the quarters under Mary's direction and at Mary's expense. John's frequent conversations with Mary—always through the jail grate—lead to his infatuation with the beautiful stranger. Michael and John amass between them considerable material toward a brief; in their various interviews to achieve this end, they become painfully aware that public opinion runs strongly against their client, with new fuel added daily by the countless rumors and by incendiary, irresponsible newspaper reporting of the case. Mary, seeking a maidservant, welcomes John's suggestion of Swiss Marie Moulin, formerly Sarah's maid. Marie, told that Mary claims to have known her in Europe, accepts the job; the maid's promise to inform Sarah of Mary's real identity is not kept, for Marie becomes loyal solely to Mary Monson and honors her wish for secrecy. All that John is able to learn concerning Mary is her clearly superior social rank, indicated by Marie's addressing her simply as "Mademoiselle."

The scene changes now to Dunscomb's New York office, where Squire Timms—a coarse but aspiring Duke's County lawyer whom Dunscomb has retained as an assistant in the Monson case—reports to Dunscomb but not to the reader the results of his assiduous efforts in their client's behalf. Various shady techniques countenanced by this country lawyer, including "horse-shedding" and "pillowing" [influencing of witnesses and jurors by agents' apparently innocent talk in the horse-sheds and in shared rooms at night], are distasteful to Dunscomb but are obviously effective in Biberry. The current of popular opinion, Timms says, has set even more strongly against Mary following her hiring of a maid to serve her in jail; he solicits and receives an additional $500 for "expenses" in countering this reaction of plain folks against what appears to be an aristocratic display.

Timms, back again in the county seat, pursues the leads provided by John and Michael. In addition, he spends his client's money where it will buy the greatest benefits for her cause among newspaper readers and among gossipmongers. Mary's strong-willed insistence on playing her harp (a sacred instrument) and her piano in her jail quarters, as well as her refusal to gratify the curiosity of the vulgar by displaying herself at the window, arouse more ill will among Biberry residents, however, than can be offset by Timms's most ambitious efforts in her behalf. Investigation persuades John and Timms that Sarah Burton, neighbor of the Goodwins, knows more about the case than she is willing to reveal. Mrs. Gott and John are more firmly convinced of Mary's innocence than is Timms, who thus far is working for Mary's money rather than for Mary.

The scene changes to the home of the Widow Anna Updyke, where excitement concerning the McBrain-Updyke wedding runs high. Sarah and the widow's daughter, Anna, nineteen years old, share their concern about John's infatuation with Mary; they had hoped he would marry Anna. Following the McBrains' wedding, the two girls spend a week at Rattletrap, Dunscomb's country home, to which Timms, Dunscomb, Michael, and John come to continue their work on the brief. Timms reveals that Mary has by "mother wit" initiated several clever schemes in her own behalf, devices not revealed either to Dunscomb or to the reader. While the two older lawyers are closeted for hours concerning the case, the lovers Michael and Sarah go off together, leaving John to rediscover the charms of the modest and winning Anna, a welcome contrast to the increasingly distasteful cunning and conniving John has detected in Mary Monson. John suspects—through Marie's slip of the tongue in addressing Mary as "Madame"—that Mary is in fact a married woman. His concern for Mary's perilous situation continues, however, and Anna's affection for John prompts her to console the prisoner; in addition to her warmhearted sympathy, Anna is motivated by a curiosity about Mary's identity never satisfied by Marie.

Further danger to Mary's cause develops in the hiring by Jesse Davis, nephew and heir of Peter Goodwin, of a clever country lawyer nick-named "Saucy" Williams to ensure Mary's conviction. Maintaining that Mary's plentiful supply of money must have come from Mrs. Goodwin's purloined stocking hoard, Jesse initiates a savage campaign against the accused woman. Meanwhile, Timms is falling in love with his client, a condition clearly evident to all concerned, providing an interesting counterbalance to the lively rumor that Dunscomb himself, working without fee, is working literally "for love."

In view of all these reports, Dunscomb drives to Biberry to visit Mary, accompanied by Anna Updyke. Mrs. Horton, landlady at Biberry's best tavern, greets Dunscomb and his companion warmly and, in a burst of good feeling, confides something that she and her husband, Daniel Horton, have kept secret for twelve years: Peter Goodwin had been so greatly addicted to mint juleps that many times the couple had hidden him away for several days in a "ward" at the inn to protect him from his shrewish wife's anger. This piece of information proves valuable to Dunscomb. Timms, arriving shortly afterwards, is distraught because Mary still refuses to divulge any of her past—a factor that has hampered her case from the very start—and because she seems entirely without anxiety concerning the outcome of a case plainly about to cost her her life. Dunscomb, commenting sourly on Timms's infatuation with his client, probes for further details on the local scene and learns that the Burtons, formerly willing to talk to Timms, have apparently moved to the side of the prosecution.

Mrs. Gott, still sympathetic to Mary, urges Dunscomb to persuade Mary to court popular favor by showing herself at the jail window, a move he does not support. He does endeavor to make clear to the confident prisoner her perilous situation, whereupon she assures him that she knows popular opinion is against her, since she has heard people discussing the case on her nightly walks through the village! Dunscomb is stunned by this revelation, and is further horrified to discover that Timms is aware of Mary's excursions away from jail. Her exhilarated, cunning expression as she describes both these illegal forays and her ingenious schemes set afoot makes Dunscomb apprehensive about her sanity. But Mary's composure and lovely smile so quickly follow these evidences of a diseased imagination that the lawyer scarcely knows how to deal with his unusual client. Suddenly, to Mary's surprise, he announces the presence of Anna Updyke, who is of Mary's own social class and is thus able to console her in her loneliness. Mary welcomes this source of comfort, and Dunscomb, assured that Mrs. Gott will house Anna comfortably, returns to the city.

As Dunscomb, at work in his office one evening, turns again to the brief, following an interruption by McBrain's coachman, Stephen Hoof, he is startled by the entry of Mary and Anna. The two have come by carriage after dark from Biberry to show him a letter from Timms to Mary beginning with a marriage proposal and continuing with a strong recommendation that she abscond. Astounded both by the letter and by this new proof of Mary's rashness, Dunscomb accedes to her request that she be allowed to nap for an hour before their return and that Anna be taken to visit her mother. Certain that Mary will have left before he returns to his office, Dunscomb accompanies Anna to the McBrains' and waits during her visit, to see her back safely. He overhears Anna's inadvertent mention of *Mrs.* Monson, arousing Dunscomb's suspicion that the obviously wealthy young woman may have sought inconspicuous housing in Biberry to hide from her husband, a violation of the proper respect for matrimonial bonds that the conservative lawyer deplores. The two girls return in good time to Biberry.

A lengthy authorial comment—one of many in the novel—on the quality of judges, jurors, lawyers, and witnesses in Duke's County (representative of the agents of justice throughout the republic) precedes the description of Mary's arraignment. The discussion that occurs in the courtroom before the arraignment reveals the malpractice and chicanery that have made a mockery of the trial-by-jury system; even before an official arraignment, the "outdoor"—or outside-the-courtroom—influences brought to bear on both jury and witnesses have deprived the accused of a fair trial. In the absence of the District Attorney, busy on a case elsewhere, the arraignment is postponed until the following day, and the session is adjourned. That evening, Williams, on the instruction of his client Jesse Davis, comes to Dunscomb and offers to withdraw himself and his damaging evidence from the Monson case in exchange for a "return" of $5000 of the money assumed stolen from the missing stocking by Mary Monson. Dunscomb, largely to gain time, conveys this offer to Mary, who indignantly refuses it on the grounds that she cannot "return" money she has not taken. For the first time, Dunscomb detects signs of insanity in his client; her spirited comments following her refusal convince him that if she is not a lunatic, she has a malevolent insight as well as cunning. Her mention of his early relationship with a Mary Millington and her knowledge of his family affairs mystify him. Who she herself is remains a mystery.

Rumors about the accused increase: that she is the wife of a Frenchman, that she has a streak of insanity, that she is independently wealthy, that she is in hiding from her husband. These and other bits of gossip, swollen out of proportion by news-hungry reporters, bode ill for her acquittal. Dunscomb and Michael, moreover, sense that there is an unsettling truth about this particular cluster of rumors. A repetition of Williams's offer to withdraw, with a "return" of $5000 still the condition, is refused by Mary, confident of her own innocence. A sudden fit of weeping is succeeded by an unnatural air of self-control assumed by the puzzling woman.

Mary is duly arraigned, the jury is empaneled with surprisingly little difficulty for a capital trial, and the court is adjourned for dinner. Dunscomb and Michael Millington then confer privately on a matter not revealed either to the other principals or to the reader, and Michael departs at once via horseback on a clearly urgent mission. Dunscomb then somberly reveals to John his own past, in which a Mary Millington had jilted him for a richer man. Mary Millington, Dunscomb believes, was the maternal grandmother of Mildred Millington (alias Mary Monson), who has, indeed, left her husband, a French viscount, and is afflicted by insanity. (Mildred Millington's daughter had married a cousin, Frank Millington, and in that way Mildred is distantly related to Michael Millington.) Moreover, Dunscomb considers Mary capable of the crime for which she is standing trial. During the hasty dinner that follows this conversation, Dunscomb and McBrain discuss a noisy, troublesome neighbor in their wing at the inn, a man either drunk or idiotic, but the two friends have not yet lodged a complaint about him to Mrs. Horton. The landlady herself, stopping to inquire after their comfort, insists that Mary will be acquitted—she has learned it in a dream, she says—but Dunscomb is far from sanguine.

Mary remains calm during the prosecution's opening speech, which cites largely circumstantial evidence and centers the attack on the curious gold coin found in Mary's purse. A series of state's witnesses, self-assured and ready to testify, one by one lose their credibility under Dunscomb's skillful cross-questioning: one cannot prove which of the two skeletons is that of Peter Goodwin; another cannot positively identify the stolen stocking. But the circumstantial evidence has already done the damage intended by the prosecution. At Dunscomb's request, the court is adjourned for that day.

During the evening, the noisy neighbor furtively enters Mrs. McBrain's quarters at the inn, where Dunscomb, McBrain and his wife, and Sarah are desultorily playing whist, and reveals that he knows—and Mary Monson knows—who set Goodwins' house on fire and who has the stolen gold. His frequent fearful mention of Mary Monson suggests connivance, but the man's comments are discounted by Dunscomb as the ravings of an idiot, and the man, hearing footsteps down the hall, disappears as slyly as he had come. Elsewhere at the inn, in two private and locked parlors, the coarser elements of the trial-related group, chiefly the country lawyers, are drinking, gambling, and discussing the case, a revolting scene vividly described and closing with Williams's reminding Timms that the lovesick attorney cannot marry a woman who has been hanged. Among the rumors widely circulated within the group is one identifying Mary Monson as the stool-pigeon of a New York City criminal gang.

At the jail, meanwhile, Anna, more fully taken into Mary's confidence than is any of the other principals, attempts to persuade Mary to use the "other means" (not identified for the reader) to gain an acquittal. Mary in her proudly negative response displays the same mad, cunning look that had distressed John and Dunscomb earlier; as before, this look is succeeded by a softer one that eases Anna's alarm. As soon as Anna leaves, escorted by Dr. McBrain to join her mother, Timms is admitted to the cell. During the ensuing conversation, it becomes obvious that Mary herself had started the rumors revealing her marriage and hinting her connection with a New York gang: she is stimulated by her own case, involved in buying rumormongers and in testing the susceptibility of the public to gossip. Once again she refuses Williams's offer to retire from the prosecution, determined to win acquittal on the merits of the case itself.

Court is reconvened the next morning, and Samuel Burton, initially a strong witness for the prosecution, loses his credibility under Dunscomb's cross-examination, chiefly on the matters of the corpses' identities and of Peter Goodwin's intemperance. The witnessing of Burton's three unmarried sisters—that the notched gold coin found in Mary's purse had frequently been displayed by Dolly Goodwin—cannot be shaken, however, and the evidence appears to trouble Mary herself. Mrs. Burton, called next, is even more convincing in her testimony against the accused, though she trembles as she testifies. Court is adjourned for the night, before Dunscomb's cross-examination of Sarah Burton, on the grounds that the witness is fatigued. Reactions to the day's events vary; Mrs. Gott is encouraged, Anna is confident, and Mary is curiously dejected. After a brief visit with Anna and Sarah, during which Mary appears to recover her steadiness and confidence of victory, she kisses the girls and bids them good night. Then she sends for Dunscomb, to whom she communicates facts—not revealed to the reader—that largely remove her lawyer's doubt of her innocence and increase his confidence in the outcome of the case. Still, he awaits anxiously the return of Michael from his errand of locating the husband of Mary Monson and of confirming her suspected identity as Mildred Millington; testimony from these sources would allow Dunscomb, if all else failed, to enter a plea of insanity for his client.

The following day, Dunscomb's cross-examination of Sarah Burton produces uncertainty in the witness, but she maintains her position throughout. Dr. McBrain's testimony that the charred skeletons are those of two females is this time upheld by several other doctors, leaving the case dependent on the notched gold coin. Michael Millington still has not returned from his mission, and Dunscomb lacks grounds for pro- longing the court's decision any further. The summing up of the case by both sides and the judge's charge to the jury make clear that the evidence, apart from the notched coin, is circumstantial. While the jury is in retirement to arrive at a decision, Mary, Anna, and Sarah talk quietly together, and Mary startles her friends by indicating her suspicion of Sarah Burton as guilty of exchanging two nearly identical gold coins while the contents of Mary's purse were being examined by the women.

When the jury announces—to the stunned surprise of nearly all in attendance—that it has found Mary Monson guilty of murdering Peter Goodwin, Mary takes the stand herself to deplore the injustice of conviction on insufficient grounds, a charge unsettling to both judge and jury. Her statement is less shocking, however, than the sudden ap- pearance—following the pronouncement by the judge of her punish- ment of death by hanging—of Peter Goodwin himself, led into the courtroom by Mrs. Horton. The supposedly murdered man had been housed at the inn—Dunscomb's noisy and intrusive "mad" neighbor— and is produced now to demonstrate the mockery of justice that had marked Mary Monson's trial. Even Dunscomb is caught by surprise at this development, one that Mary had planned to introduce after her acquittal but now finds imperative to prevent her unwarranted execution.

To avoid total disgrace, the court hastily empanels a jury to try Mary first on the charge of murdering Dorothy Goodwin and then on the charge of committing arson. After a brief period, Mary herself requests and is granted permission to question Sarah Burton, then on the witness stand, warning her in the name of God to answer truthfully. Mrs. Burton, heretofore considered the most reliable among the witnesses for the prosecution, admits that she had entered Goodwins' house before the skeletons were removed, unlocked the bureau drawer and stolen the stocking and its contents, and subsequently substituted the notched gold piece for the unnotched one in Mary's purse while the purse was being passed from hand to hand. Moreover, she acknowledges that the house had not been set afire by any person but had flared from a faulty flue that had twice before caused a fire in the Goodwins' house. The burned garret floor had allowed the plow stored right above the Goodwins' bed to fall on the heads of Dorothy Goodwin and her German servant Jette—sleeping in the same bed in the absence from home of Peter Goodwin; Moses Steen, who had removed the plowshare to recover the skeletons, would testify that the share had come to rest on the victims' foreheads, fracturing their skulls. Subsequent questioning reveals that Mary had seen Sarah Burton entering the house and stealing the stocking, as well as substituting the notched coin for the perfect one. While representatives of the court are sent to Sarah's house to fetch the stocking from her bureau drawer, for which she furnishes the key, the District Attorney agrees to an acquittal on the murder charge and the dismissal of the arson charge; the jury acquits the accused without even leaving the jury box, and Mary Monson is free.

After notice in the newspapers about the reversal of the accused's situation, the case is abandoned by reporters as no longer newsworthy, and the rumors die as quickly as the news. Sarah Burton, guilty of theft, is not prosecuted; ironically, the innocent have proved to be most in danger of the law. And, it develops, a person deemed qualifiedly insane—as Mary Monson proves to be—had been the only one able to penetrate the veil of appearances sufficiently to arrive at the truth, an unfortunate commentary on the state of justice in a republic.

Michael Millington returns just as the court adjourns, and reports in private conference with Dunscomb that, as suspected, Mary Monson is indeed Mildred Millington by birth and Madame de Larocheforte by marriage, that her insanity is recognized by her intimate friends, and that she had lodged with the Goodwins to avoid her husband and thus escape the intolerable marriage into which she had entered. The wedding of Michael and Sarah Wilmeter is celebrated soon after the trial's ending, and Dunscomb selects that occasion to announce his determination to retire from legal practice within a year; he names Michael and John as his law partners. The marriage of Anna Updyke and John Wilmeter follows in due course. Timms is finally persuaded that Mary Monson—now Mildred Millington—would not marry him even if she were legally free to do so; and Mildred, with Dunscomb's help, arrives at a quasi-divorce settlement with her husband, the viscount, who returns to France content with a share of Mildred's substantial fortune and will trouble her no more. Mildred gradually recovers most of her reason; for her own protection, however, she remains under the supervision of Dunscomb and of the Millingtons, her distant relatives, lest she fall further victim to "the ways of the hour."

Peter Bacon, Peter Bailey, Brookes, Miss Burton, Miss Burton, Miss Burton [three unmarried sisters], Samuel Burton, Sarah Burton, Dr. Coe, Crooks, Jesse Davis, Thomas Dunscomb, Garth, Dorothy Goodwin, Peter Goodwin, Gott, Mrs. Gott, Green, Hatfield, Hicks, Stephen Hoof, Nancy Horton, Hubbs [Sam Tongue], Jette, Johnson, Mrs. Jones, Ira Kingsland, Gabriel Jules Vincent Jean Baptiste de Larocheforte, Daniel Lord, Dr. Edward McBrain, Marvin, Michael Millington, Mildred Millington [Mary Monson], Marie Moulin, Peter, Abigail Pope, Jane Pope, Robert Robinson, Sanford, Scipio, Dr. Short, Timms, Peter Titus, Ira Truman, Widow Anna Updyke, Anna Updyke, Jonas Wattles, Frank Williams, John Wilmeter, Sarah Wilmeter, George Wood, Wright.

The Wept of Wish-Ton-Wish: A Tale, 1829.

Set in the seventeenth century on frontier land later to become part of Connecticut, *The Wept of Wish-Ton-Wish* is a fairly realistic story of the early American wilderness experience. Captain Mark Heathcote, a widower now for more than twenty years, decides (for religious reasons never fully particularized) to leave the Massachusetts Bay Colony and resettle in a fertile valley of the Connecticut Territory, not far from Fort Hartford. The new settlement is called Wish-Ton-Wish, a name which, the author claims, is the Indian term for whippoorwill. [Doubt has been cast on Cooper's translation of the word, but this disagreement is unimportant here, for the name has no bearing on the action of the novel.] A sturdy, resolute Puritan who had served in the English civil war, Captain Heathcote has also the more humble Christian qualities of forgiveness for evildoers and submission to the will of God. When his wife (his junior by some twenty years) had died in childbirth on the very day the Heathcotes had landed in the New World, the captain had overcome his grief enough to christen the baby boy with the meaningful name of Content. Now that he feels compelled to resettle, late in life, he does so without bitterness or rancor. With him go a considerable household including his son and the latter's wife, Ruth Harding Heathcote, a girl with many of the qualities required of a good wife and a good mother on the frontier.

As several years pass, Wish-Ton-Wish grows and prospers. Content Heathcote takes over more and more of the responsibility for the management of the settlement while his aging father remains the moral guide of the little community. The old Puritan is known and respected for his sense of justice and his hospitality toward all men. He had paid the Indians a fair price for his land—a rare virtue among English settlers—and he made a point of turning no stranger from his door.

The first action occurs on a day when Whittal Ring, a half-witted boy, rounds up a drove of colts he has been pasturing, and young Mark, Content's son, brings his flock back to the fold missing one of its thirty-seven sheep. An elderly and somewhat bedraggled stranger rides up to Wish-Ton-Wish (still an uncommon event at that remote site) and is welcomed by the captain to bed and board. At the conclusion of the evening meal, the unidentified guest shows his pistols and knives to young Mark, who, at fourteen, is fascinated by such weapons. In the middle of this demonstration, Whittal Ring observes on the haft of one knife what is unmistakably a tuft of the distinctive wool of the missing sheep; being a simpleton, the boy blurts out his discovery in no uncertain terms. After a few awkward moments, Captain Heathcote signals for everyone but the stranger to leave the room, and then he carries on a long, private conversation with his guest. When there is no longer the sound of voices in the dining room, Content, concerned about his father's safety, returns and finds, to his amazement, that the stranger has vanished. Still more odd than the disappearance of their guest is the order now given to Content to go at once to a designated place in the forest and bring home what he finds there.

At the specified location Content discovers the carcass of the missing sheep. An even greater surprise awaits him when he returns to the gate of the palisades encircling the homestead and hears his wife report that during his absence she has seen an Indian. Since there have been no red men in the area for some time, Content wonders if Ruth only imagined that she saw a savage. When Content and two of his men investigate, however, they do indeed find an Indian, a youth of fifteen, whom they capture, confine in the blockhouse, and hope to convert to the white man's civilization. But after six months of kindness and patience on the part of his instructors (primarily Ruth and Captain Heathcote) the boy seems to remain quite unchanged. It is the unidentified stranger who, on repeated brief visits to the settlement, seems to establish the greatest bond of sympathy with the young Indian.

In the meantime, four special agents of Charles II arrive in pursuit of a regicide (one of those responsible for the execution of Charles I) known to have fled to the New World after the Restoration. They arrive at Wish-Ton-Wish with a search warrant to inspect all buildings in the settlement, for they have had a report that the wanted man is being shielded by Captain Heathcote. Arrogant, rude, and worldly, these agents of the "merry monarch" provide a sharp contrast to the Puritans and their spiritual orientation. After a thorough search of Wish-Ton-Wish, the investigators grudgingly acknowledge their error in suspecting the Heathcotes and ride away to hunt their quarry elsewhere. It becomes evident to the reader that the strange guest occasionally found at Wish-Ton-Wish is the regicide sought. It is clear too that Captain Heathcote knows the man's identity, though the rest of the family does not, and that the captain is aiding him if not actually housing him.

After half a year of captivity, the Indian youth is finally trusted enough to be permitted to go on a deer hunt with the men of the village. The boy is Conanchet [Canonchet], son of the recently killed Miantonimoh, chief of the Narragansetts, but for some time yet his real name will be unknown to the settlers. They call him Miantonimoh because he resembles the late chief and because he once emotionally exclaims "Miantonimoh!" when he hears the settlers discussing his father. The hunt is successful, but Conanchet takes advantage of this opportunity to escape into the forest, where he eludes all pursuit.

At the conclusion of the expedition, Eben Dudley, doughtiest of all the frontiersmen at Wish-Ton-Wish, recounts an event that had startled him that day, an experience which reveals both his own superstition and the general willingness of the Puritans to believe in signs and omens from the invisible world. A ghostly deer had vanished, and the stranger to whom the wild animal had seemingly led Dudley had talked of troubled times ahead. At the moment of their sudden meeting (almost collision) on the narrow path, a single peal of thunder was heard, though the sky was clear and the weather was calm. When several of the women report having heard that same lone thunderclap at precisely the same time, it is generally taken to be an ominous sign. Without even permitting Eben to conclude his story, Captain Heathcote immediately raises a prayer for the protection of the community. In the midst of the prayer, a conch horn blown twice at the palisade gate startles everyone with its eerie sound. Responding to the urgent horn blasts, the guards are surprised to find at the postern gate their former, still unidentified guest and with him Conanchet. Captain Heathcote and the stranger are immediately closeted again in private conversation.

Just as the two older men rejoin the others, two blasts are blown on a conch horn, apparently the horn that hangs at all times outside the stockade gate. When Content and two others go to the gate, however, they find no one there. Posted inside the gate to watch for intruders, the powerful Eben Dudley, detecting no one, grows drowsy and falls asleep; he is aroused to his duty by his shrewish sweetheart, Faith Ring, who knows well both the strengths and weaknesses of her beloved. When Dudley returns to Captain Heathcote at the appointed hour, he reports having seen nothing unusual, but even as he is speaking, more eerie notes from a conch horn fill the night air. As Eben Dudley and the stranger (now called Submission) are sent outside the palisade wall to scout the area, repeated horn blasts are heard. Since no one is visible outside the gate, the two men conclude that the sounds have supernatural origins. They are presently disabused of this notion, however, as a horde of whooping savages rush at them from behind trees and stumps. In a rain of arrows the two scouts dive for the hitherto secret doorway in the wall through which they had emerged a few minutes earlier. When Conanchet is sent out, shortly afterwards, to ask the unidentified savages their reason for molesting a friendly settlement, he returns with a bundle of arrows wrapped in the skin of a rattlesnake, a well-known Indian sign for relentless warfare.

The attack is not long delayed. The Indians begin by setting fire to the wheat stacks in the fields and later, after several scale the stockade, to the outbuildings. Greatly outnumbered by several hundred savages, the settlers are slowly forced to retreat to their last defensive stronghold, the blockhouse. Under a steady shower of arrows and bullets, the besieged settlers dash in great confusion for this log structure, which most of them reach safely. Among those lost (though perhaps still alive) are Ruth Heathcote, a child of seven or eight, and Whittal Ring. Ring had been wounded while carrying a child——it turned out to be Martha, little Ruth's adopted sister—to the door of the blockhouse, and he is last seen being dragged away by two Indians. What has become of Ruth, child of Content and Ruth Harding Heathcote, is unknown; it is Ruth who is thenceforth referred to as the "wept" of Wish-Ton-Wish. Even the blockhouse does not offer certain security, for its roof is soon ignited by

heat from the buildings burning all around it. Despite their efforts to
quench the flames, the whole fortress is eventually consumed by fire.

By the following morning all of the Indians but Conanchet have left;
after this young man gazes meditatively for a while at the smoldering
ruins, he too departs from the valley of Wish-Ton-Wish. A couple of
hours later a number of survivors crawl from the well shaft sunk deep
beneath the blockhouse. Old Mark Heathcote, having lost so much,
including his only grandchild, is still able to accept his lot as the will of
God and offer up praise; although most of his followers are mute with
awe at his resolute faith, Content and Ruth, his wife, manage to add a
few words to the captain's thanksgiving. The old Puritan wants no
revenge; instead, he forgives the savages because of their ignorance. He
dispatches Reuben Ring and a young companion to solicit aid from the
nearest settlement. The rest unite their energies to construct a temporary shelter against the cold weather of early spring by roofing the stone
basement of the blockhouse with pine boughs. When these makeshift
living arrangements have been completed, Submission says that he must
again depart lest the agents of Charles II discover him if he lingers longer.

Again many years elapse in the action, and the story is renewed as the
last quarter of the seventeenth century begins. Wish-Ton-Wish, more
like the phoenix than the whippoorwill, has risen from its own ashes and
has been enlarged to accommodate forty families. While Eben Dudley
(now titled Ensign) and Reuben Ring (now holding the rank of sergeant)
are on guard duty, they capture an unusual Narragansett, one with
painted face above his blanket robe but white shins protruding beneath
it. After his face has been washed, this man proves to be Whittal Ring
almost completely converted to Indian ways. He denounces palefaces,
recites Indian accounts of injustices they have committed against the red
men, and boasts that soon he will be honored as a brave in his tribe. Faith,
his sister (now married to Eben Dudley), talks at length with Whittal
several times in the hope of achieving two ends: first, to redeem her
unfortunate brother from savagery, and second, to extract from him
some word about the long-lost little Ruth.

For some time now the child's mother has suffered a physical decline as
she continues to grieve for the loss of her daughter, and many efforts
have been made to determine if a white girl is held captive among any of
the neighboring Indian tribes. Content has traveled even among the
Iroquois of New York in his attempts to locate little Ruth. The feelings of
the parents are at times ambivalent. They both wish and do not wish to
find their daughter; it would be bad enough to learn that she was dead
but perhaps worse to discover that she was alive, Indianized, and mated

to a savage spouse. She would now be a young woman of seventeen or eighteen.

In 1675 Indians are again on the warpath, as Metacom (better known as "King Philip") attempts to organize all the red men of New England in a mighty effort to annihilate the English settlers. When the Narragansetts (whose hunting grounds extend all the way to the ocean) begin to cooperate with Metacom's conspiracy, they are attacked by a large army of aroused settlers; in a serious defeat at Pettyquamscott, they lose more than a thousand warriors. Conanchet, now their sachem, moves his people out of their villages, which are vulnerable to attack, and into the deep forest. This precaution taken, he commences systematic raids on English settlements, among them such important places as Andover, Groton, Warwick, and Weymouth. Again a powerful colonial force is raised; Content, now a captain like his venerable father, is directed by the governor to lead a contingent of troops from Wish-Ton-Wish. Content does not refuse this duty, but he prefers any course short of violence to deal with the Indian problem.

After the hasty arrival and departure of the governor's messenger on a Sabbath morning, the people of Wish-Ton-Wish gather in their new church for services conducted by their newly arrived minister, the Rev. Mr. Meek Wolfe. In the middle of their worship, a loud call to arms rings out as a large body of Indians—Narragansetts under Conanchet, Wampanoags under Metacom—falls upon the settlement without warning. As in the Indian attack ten years earlier, the defenders, though again outnumbered, put up a stubborn resistance to the invasion. That third of the white forces led by Content and Submission—the old regicide again arrives at a timely moment—is overwhelmed, and all its survivors are captured, among them the members of the Heathcote family. As these captives are about to be tortured and killed, Conanchet is shocked to discover that they are apparently reincarnations of people he had seen destroyed ten years earlier. The Narragansett and Metacom confer apart about this awesome development. When they question the captives, they are told by the honest Captain Mark that he and many of his followers had escaped the fire by retreating into the iron-covered well under the burning blockhouse. Metacom now assumes that Conanchet will have no further scruples about dispatching the prisoners at once, but he does not understand the inner conflict being experienced by his Narragansett counterpart. When Conanchet again postpones the execution, Metacom departs in disgust, taking with him his Wampanoag warriors.

Moved by seeing the Heathcote family again, Conanchet calls Narra-mattah, his wife, to his side. The beautiful blonde-haired, blue-eyed squaw who appears is young Ruth Heathcote. She is confused and distressed when Conanchet informs her that she is not really a Narragansett but the child of the captive white family, taken away when he had thought her family dead. In a recognition scene filled with emotion—even the stoical Conanchet is moved to tears—mother and daughter are reunited. Shortly afterwards Conanchet withdraws his forces from Wish-Ton-Wish, much to the dismay of the Narragansetts, who cannot understand why their chief thus leaves a hard-fought battle that he is winning. Conanchet himself returns to the area, just long enough to visit Submission at the old man's hideout on a rocky crag in the forest. He leaves with the regicide a bundle to be delivered to his Narra-mattah, a blanketed bundle that is later discovered to contain their infant son.

During family prayers that day Captain Mark offers thanks that Wish-Ton-Wish has not been destroyed this time. Required to attend these prayers, Narra-mattah is little moved by them. Nor is she at all responsive to her mother's efforts to revive in her memory the images of her childhood in the Heathcote household. During Ruth's attempt to communicate with her long-lost daughter, young Mark arrives with the beaded blanket pack left at Submission's hut by Conanchet. Narra-mattah takes the bundle, unwraps from its folds the infant son of Conanchet and herself, and proudly holds up the child for Ruth's approval. The entire family is shocked at the sight of the child, and Ruth's response is not as warm as Narra-mattah had hoped it would be. Aware of her daughter's disappointment, Ruth struggles bravely to show enthusiasm for her unexpected grandson, and manages to demonstrate love and sympathy for both her daughter and the infant boy.

This trying family scene is interrupted by a deputation of four prominent colonists who have come to confer with Captain Content Heathcote. A Wampanoag prisoner, one Mohtucket, has agreed to betray Metacom and Conanchet to the English, and the deputation (the Rev. Mr. Meek Wolfe, Dr. Ergot, Eben Dudley, and Reuben Ring) advises Content to avail himself of this opportunity to kill the two Indian leaders. Opposed to further bloodshed and cognizant of Conanchet's change toward more humane sentiments, Content at first rejects this proposal. His position becomes less tenable, however, when a scalped and mangled corpse is brought into his presence. It is the body of the official messenger who had come that morning to warn the community of a possible Indian attack. Notwithstanding this reminder of Indian ferocity, Content does not agree to lead the proposed punitive expedition.

While Meek Wolfe and his collaborators seek elsewhere for support for their plan, a more peaceable approach to the Indian problem is taken by Submission. Long the friend of Conanchet, despite their having been on opposite sides in battle, the old Puritan convinces the Narragansett sachem that a bloodless solution is possible. The two set out together to find Metacom in order to persuade this most powerful chief to adopt a more conciliatory attitude in his dealings with the white settlers. After long and arduous travel through the forest, they reach the Wampanoag camp, where Metacom, though dubious about their mission, welcomes the visitors into his wigwam. As they begin their discussion, Mohtucket races into the camp purportedly with news of some kind for Metacom. The chief is scornful toward this ne'er-do-well straggler who has never proved himself in battle, and he quickly points out that the scalp which Mohtucket now proudly displays has a bullet hole in it, evidence that Mohtucket (who has no gun) had not killed the one he had scalped. As Mohtucket begins to remonstrate, a volley of musket fire rings out and three Wampanoags fall dead. A force led by Meek Wolfe and accompanied by official observers from the governor's office has arrived. Inasmuch as both Mohtucket and the musket fire have entered the camp from the same direction, Metacom correctly deduces Mohtucket has revealed the position of the Wampanoag campsite to the English. He kills the traitor on the spot and then proceeds to extricate himself and his people from the trap.

Conanchet and Submission also flee, running downstream in a small brook to leave no trail. They are pursued, however, not only by colonists, whom they might elude, but also by the Mohican and Pequot allies of the settlers. Once aware that red men are tracking them, Conanchet realizes that the elderly Submission will never be able to escape by flight, if, indeed, he himself will now be able to do so. He therefore hides Submission in the top of a leafy tree and, departing, makes broad marks on the ground to give the impression two men had passed that way. This effort to protect Submission costs Conanchet those fatal few minutes that might have saved his own life. After a long chase Conanchet is captured by several swift young Mohicans and brought before their chief, Uncas. This Uncas is the son of the Uncas—there was a lengthy dynasty of Mohican chiefs so named—who had earlier dealt a devastating defeat to the Narragansetts, killing their leader, Miantonimoh. He is, thus, Conanchet's greatest enemy. The Mohican delivers his captive into the hands of the English to be tried; the settlers, under Meek Wolfe's urging, condemn Conanchet to death and then return him to the Mohicans for execution. Conanchet requests a day's reprieve in order to visit his wife and child, giving his word of honor to return for his execution. Knowing that so great a chief could not violate Indian ethics on a point of honor, Uncas quickly grants this request.

Conanchet proceeds to Wept-Ton-Wish, where, with the aid of Whittal Ring, he releases Narra-mattah and leads her into the forest. The chief, his wife, their son, and Whittal Ring (who carries the baby in his pack) travel during most of their last day together so that Conanchet can honor the terms of his reprieve. Back within the prescribed time, he places himself in the hands of the Mohicans. He is now ready for death and will accept neither assistance nor sympathy. He rejects Meek Wolfe's attempt to convert him to Christianity. He also refuses Eben Dudley's offer of a pardon if he and his Narragansetts will bury the hatchet and make peace with the Mohicans. Having resisted these two efforts to make him forsake his Indian values, he overcomes the third and final temptation: indulgence in sentiment toward his wife and child. Telling Narra-mattah that they will meet again on the happy hunting ground, he orders her to return to her people and there raise their son. Struck down by his two executioners, Conanchet dies with the fortitude and dignity appropriate for an Indian leader, his last words being "Mohican, I die before my heart is soft" (p. 461). There is an obvious dimension of irony in the execution of Conanchet, for regardless of how stoically the Narragansett dies, he had softened considerably, returning good for evil, while the Christian leader, Meek Wolfe, has played a vengeful role, returning evil for good.

Narra-mattah now sits stunned with grief by the body of her dead husband. It is there that her parents find her when they arrive shortly afterwards, guided to the spot by Submission. As her heart begins to fail, Narra-mattah regresses to early childhood, talking and praying with her mother as she had done years earlier. But when she gazes at the dead Conanchet, she is suspended in bewilderment between past and present, between Indian and white cultures; thus she dies. Although Content Heathcote lives on for almost half a century longer, his wife, Ruth, dies within a few months of grief for her child, the "wept" of Wish-Ton-Wish.

In the closing pages of the novel, the narrator comments on the history of Wish-Ton-Wish from a nineteenth-century point of view. In accounting for the fortunes of the characters and their descendants since 1675, he suggests that there have been many alterations in life in Connecticut since the time of the central action. One change is symbolized in the name of the latest clergyman, Meek Lamb, a descendant of Meek Wolfe.

Annawon, Charity, Conanchet [Canonchet], Eben Dudley, Dr. Ergot, Hallam, Content Heathcote, Captain Mark Heathcote, Mark Heathcote, Martha Heathcote, Ruth Heathcote, Ruth Harding

Heathcote, Hiram, Meek Lamb, Metacom , Mohtucket, Abundance
Ring, Faith Ring, Reuben Ring, Whittal Ring, Submission, Uncas,
Meek Wolfe, Wompawisset.

The Wing-and-Wing; or, Le Feu-Follet, 1842.

In August of 1799 an unidentified lugger [a small ship with squarish,
slant-topped sails] approaches Portoferraio, the principal city on the
island of Elba, six miles off the coast of Tuscany in the Tyrrhenian Sea.
The lugger sails into the harbor "wing-and-wing," that is, with a sail
protruding from each side, and it is from this arrangement of rigging that
the vessel acquires its pseudonym. With northern Italy overrun by
French forces, and with the Mediterranean now a central scene of the
Napoleonic Wars, any strange vessel in the area is a cause for concern.
Vito Viti, magistrate at Portoferraio, queries Tommaso Tonti, an ancient
mariner, about the nationality of the lugger, but the wise old man defers
judgment until the stranger unfurls the union jack of Great Britain. With
the crowd of Elbans observing the lugger is Ghita—no one present
knows or is concerned about her last name—a bright girl of eighteen who
was recently left by her uncle to board at a local inn. Although it is
observed only by the narrator, Ghita reveals a personal interest in the
lugger, signs of anxiety, even alarm, appearing on her face as a coast
artillery crew fires a warning shot over the vessel's bow.

After clearing himself and his ship with port officials, the captain of the
lugger reports to Vito Viti and then with this magistrate proceeds to pay
his respect to the deputy governor, Andrea Barrofaldi. The captain gives
his name as Jack Smith; he pronounces it *Jacques Smeet*, revealing to the
reader, though not to his Italian auditors, that he is not English but
French. The papers of the *Wing-and Wing* are in order and appear genuine.
About the ship itself there lingers some doubt. Is not the lugger a type of
vessel peculiarly French and Spanish rather than English? Captain Smees
(as the Italians call him) acknowledges this fact but claims that he, his
crew, and the vessel all come from the isle of Guernsey, once French and
still retaining many French customs and practices even after centuries of
British rule. Barrofaldi, a scholar of sorts who fancies himself for his
knowledge of foreign lands, quizzes Captain Smith about the politics,
religion, and language of England. Smith's superficial acquaintance with
English life is sufficent to satisfy most of the deputy governor's curiosity.
He invites both Vito Viti and Smith to dine with him.

After he leaves his official hosts, Captain Smith is intercepted by
Ghita. That the two are in love becomes apparent at once. Ghita is
concerned about the great risk run by Raoul Yvard (the captain's real

name) in bringing his vessel—its real name is *Feu-Follet*, French for Jack-o'-Lantern—into an enemy port, for the lugger is a French privateer. Raoul Yvard has come to Elba specifically to see Ghita, whom he wishes to marry. They had met when Raoul rescued Ghita and her guardian uncle (keeper of a watchtower on the Italian coast) from captivity and slavery in the hands of Algerine corsairs. Although she loves the young mariner, Ghita cannot marry him, she feels, so long as he (like many other French revolutionaries) disavows orthodox Christianity in favor of deism. Knowing that they may be observed together, they part with an understanding that they will meet again soon.

Meanwhile, Vito Viti and Andrea Barrofaldi have had renewed doubts about the strange ship which goes under the unusual name *Wing-and-Wing*. They call at the tavern of Benedetta Galapo, a coquettish widow but a shrewd businesswoman, to talk again with Tommaso Tonti about the lugger. This conversation has just begun when two strangers enter the tavern and order wine. One is Ithuel Bolt of the *Wing-and-Wing* and the other a Genoese named Filippo, a companion who serves as interpreter. Although the conversation of Bolt tells the magistrate and the deputy governor little about the *Wing-and-Wing*, it reveals a good deal about Bolt himself. Ithuel Bolt is a tall, angular New Hampshire Yankee, a jack-of-all-trades, who became a seaman at the age of thirty. He was soon impressed into service in the British navy by a shorthanded royal frigate; Bolt has, as a result, come to hate Great Britain and all things British. When the suspicious Barrofaldi asks him why he continues to serve on a British ship when escape would be so easy, Bolt reminds him of the distance to America and of the fact that Atlantic shipping is dominated by the British. What Bolt does not tell his Italian audience is that he has in fact escaped, along with Raoul Yvard, and has, in vengeance, joined the crew of the French privateer *Feu-Follet*. Some of the ambivalent character of this embittered New Englander is illustrated by his indignation at being offered a bribe for information about the *Feu-Follet*, followed immediately thereafter by his delight in smuggling ashore and selling three kegs of contraband tobacco.

Misgivings about the nationality and intentions of the *Wing-and-Wing* (*Ving-y-Ving*, the Italians call it) continue to grow in Portoferraio. When a British frigate, *Proserpine*, appears, Yvard, playing his assumed role of Captain Smith, pretends to be pleased. As the frigate, distrusting the deliberately confusing signals hoisted by Ithuel Bolt, bears down upon the lugger, Yvard tells Vito Viti that he fears the frigate is actually a French vessel flying false colors. Yvard now offers, with seeming self-sacrifice, to lead the enemy warship away from Portoferraio, even though the *Wing-and-Wing* might be destroyed in the resulting chase. Still flying British colors, Yvard not only escapes the *Proserpine* but also becomes a local hero in the process.

That evening, after dark, Ghita again meets Raoul and informs him that she and her uncle are seeking passage back to the mainland. She hopes that Raoul will offer to transport them in the *Feu-Follet*, for Ghita's primary purpose is to remove Raoul from the danger of being detected as an enemy at Elba. So confident is Yvard of his successful deception in Portoferraio, however, that he remains anchored in the harbor even after his two passengers are aboard, planning to depart in the morning. Meanwhile the *Proserpine*, lying a league offshore, sends Lieutenant Edward Griffin to Elba in order to apprise the authorities there of the real identity of Captain Smith and his *Wing-and-Wing*. With some difficulty Griffin persuades Vito Viti and Andrea Barrofaldi that the lugger is the French privateer *Feu-Follet* and her master none other than the notorious Raoul Yvard. The deputy governor offers to sink the lugger at dawn with fire from heavy shore batteries, but Griffin dissuades him from this course of action with the information that Captain Cuffe of the *Proserpine* wishes to capture the *Feu-Follet* intact. When Griffin signals to the *Proserpine* with a prearranged code of lights, the communication is upset by Ithuel Bolt, who, ascertaining the presence of the frigate nearby, releases two flare rockets. The *Feu-Follet* again escapes, much to the amazement of Captain Cuffe.

Cuffe and his officers now devise an elaborate ruse to capture the privateer. Renting a felucca [a small Mediterranean vessel with triangular sails set obliquely to the mast], they load it with marines and fly above it a British flag. The *Proserpine* then shows French colors and pretends to pursue the felucca. Boats from the *Proserpine* close in on the pretended prey, and the ruse is carried so far as to have the frigate's launch and the felucca exchange carronade fire. As both felucca and boats are drifting toward the lugger, Ithuel Bolt correctly analyzes the British stratagem; but Raoul is deceived until the boat crews, overtaking the decoy, make the fatal mistake of giving, in typical British fashion, three hearty cheers. The alerted Raoul fires a broadside into the felucca, killing or wounding twenty-two of those aboard. When the British abandon this small ship and pull for the shore, Raoul and Ithuel board the vessel and set it afire. They might also capture or kill all hands in the boats, but Raoul's sense of chivalry, strengthened by Ghita's pleas to be merciful, precludes such action. He has already inflicted heavy losses on the British.

The chase has not ended, however, for after recovering its boats, the *Proserpine* continues the pursuit. Coming closer than Yvard realizes, the frigate fires a broadside which does substantial damage to the lugger's rigging. Instead of trying to flee, thus crippled, in open water, Raoul reduces sail to protect his damaged spars and heads into the estuary of the Galo River on the shore of Corsica, a French island, while the frigate stands a couple of miles offshore. During the night, the British attempt to burn the *Feu-Follet* at her anchorage. Capturing a local felucca loaded with naval stores, including tar, several British sailors, pretending to be coastal traders, pass close to the lugger. Tying to the *Feu-Follet's* anchor cable, they set fire to the felucca and then flee in a small boat. Yvard and three of his ablest men climb aboard the burning felucca and separate the two vessels before the flames can spread to the lugger. So great is the conflagration that the British mistakenly suppose that their objective has been achieved. Their rejoicing lasts until the following day when they land at Portoferraio and discover that the *Feu-Follet* has passed that city during the morning.

Where the lugger, its two passengers, and its gallant commander have gone neither the authorities at Portoferraio nor the British officers know. The reader finds them at Naples just an hour before a gruesome episode, the execution of the historical Admiral Francesco Caraccioli [Caracciolo] for treason. Ghita and her uncle, Carlos Giuntotardi, have come on a most unusual mission but one that is understandable in the light of their family history. Admiral Francesco Caraccioli [Caracciolo], a Neapolitan, had a natural son of the same name who, against his father's wishes, had wed a commoner, the sister of Carlos Giuntotardi. To them had been born a daughter, Ghita. On her parents' death, Ghita had been reared by her uncle, a devout, monkish man who earned his living by serving as keeper of a set of watchtowers on Monte Argentaro. The admiral had rejected his disobedient son and had never learned of the existence of his granddaughter. Now that he is about to die, that granddaughter wishes to acknowledge him, pray for him in his moment of ignominy, and receive his blessing. To achieve these ends, Ghita, accompanied by her uncle, petitions the British admiral, Lord Horatio Nelson, who is now in military command of Naples. [Caracciolo is being executed for disloyalty to his king, Ferdinand IV of Naples, during that monarch's temporary dethronement by French forces. Great Britain and her allies had restored Ferdinand, and now Admiral Nelson, principal military power in the area, was carrying out, with marked distaste, the execution ordered by the Neapolitan courts.]

Ghita gains an audience with Lord Nelson to plead for the life of the grandfather she has never seen or at least for permission to visit the condemned man. Since the British admiral speaks no Italian, the pleas are presented to Nelson's unnamed mistress [Lady Emma Hamilton, wife of Sir William Hamilton, British ambassador to Naples]. Ghita is given no hope for her grandfather's life, but Nelson's mistress provides her with a note which will give her access to the old man's prison cell on a nearby English ship. Ghita's interest is filial and devout; in their brief interview, her primary wish is for the eternal salvation of her grandfather. As she and her uncle prepare to leave the ship from which Admiral Caraccioli [Caracciolo] will be hanged in a few minutes, they are picked up by Raoul Yvard effectively disguised as a Neapolitan boatman. Besides her grief for her grandfather, Ghita feels additional anxiety that Raoul Yvard is again risking his life, walking right into the lion's mouth, in order to be near her and serve her.

Her apprehension is all too soon justified. Rowing out into the Bay of Naples with Ghita and her uncle, Raoul meets Ithuel Bolt, disguised as an Italian fisherman, at a prearranged place. Bolt picks them up in the *Feu-Follet's* yawl, and they head for St. Agata, on the Cape of Sorrento, where Ghita and her uncle are to visit the latter's sister. The yawl is hailed by the *Proserpine* with a query as to whether they have seen a lugger in the vicinity. Raoul could most easily answer in the negative, but hoping to mislead the British about the *Feu-Follet's* location, he indicates that he has indeed seen such a ship. Taken aboard the frigate, Raoul is recognized by Vito Viti and Andrea Barrofaldi, who had attended Cuffe to Naples, and shortly afterwards, one of the midshipmen identifies Ithuel Bolt as a former crew member who had deserted the ship. The two men of the *Feu-Follet* are now in the hands of their worst enemies. Ghita and Carlos Giuntotardi, also taken aboard, are treated courteously and given the best staterooms on the frigate.

Admiral Nelson orders a court-martial to try Raoul Yvard as a French spy and Ithuel Bolt as a deserter. Officers appointed to this military court soon arrive from other British ships in the Bay of Naples. Bolt refuses to testify, claiming that he is an American and has the right to freedom despite his being impressed into British service. The court is no more successful, at first, in its case against Yvard, for none of the witnesses can prove that the prisoner is actually Raoul Yvard. All present feel quite certain that he is indeed Raoul Yvard, but the prosecution's two chief witnesses, Viti and Barrofaldi, admit that they have never heard the man refer to himself by any name other than "Captain Smees." Finally they question Ghita; ingenuous and honest, she positively identifies the man as Raoul Yvard. She is unaware that her testimony may condemn her lover to death. Yvard is convicted of being a spy for appearing in disguise among British ships at Naples, and Admiral Nelson approves of his

execution the following day. Bolt is ordered back to duty after Captain
Cuffe suffers some qualms of conscience about hanging for desertion an
impressed seaman who may well be, as he claims he is, a citizen of
another country. Furthermore, as he says, his ship is shorthanded!

Cuffe and his officers experience a reversal of feeling toward Raoul
Yvard as they come to know him better. He demonstrates dignity,
courtesy, and a high sense of honor as he refuses to trade his lugger for
his life. The fact that he was captured because love had led him into
danger earns him still further sympathy. In short, no one aboard the
Proserpine now wishes to see him executed, though the admiral's orders
are to hang him that day between sunrise and sunset. Captain Cuffe
dispatches Jack Clinch, master mate, to locate Nelson with a request for a
reprieve. Throughout the day there is no response from the admiral's
headquarters; as sunset nears, there is no sign of Clinch, and the tension
mounts. Finally the noose is fastened around the prisoner's neck before
three spaced rounds of cannon fire signal the last-minute reprieve.

The reprieved Frenchman is now visited by his two Elban acquaintances (who still call him Sir Smees), Vito Viti and Andrea. The deputy
governor had in sport been pretending to Viti his belief in the theory of
subjective idealism enunciated by the English philosopher Bishop
Berkeley. The magistrate, taking his old friend seriously, is outraged at
this offense to Catholic sensibility. After an exchange of social amenities
with Yvard and some brief discussion of a general nature, the two Italians
resume their philosophical argument. It grows louder and louder, and
soon a cluster of amused British officers gather outside the stateroom
door to enjoy the verbal fireworks. As Raoul Yvard leans back against an
open porthole, he hears Ithuel Bolt whisper directions for him to slide
back through the port and drop quietly into the departing boat of Ghita
and her uncle as they begin to row ashore. The boat is the yawl of the *Feu-
Follet*. Ithuel has arranged this maneuver with Ghita and Giuntotardi,
hoping that in this way, under the cover of darkness, they may escape.
Though considering the chances of success slight, Raoul follows Ithuel's
instructions.

The yawl moves past the stern of the ship and heads for the shore, but
while they are still within earshot of the frigate, a boat drops into the
water in pursuit. Lieutenant Yelverton, the first officer to be apprised of
the escape, assumes that Yvard has simply jumped overboard, so he has
lowered a boat and has circled the ship to pick up the swimmer. Then,
spotting the yawl, he starts in pursuit toward the shore of Sorrento. The
yawl veers off course and eludes Yelverton's gig as other boats from the
frigate now fan out in different directions. Suddenly, from shoreward of

their own position, those in the yawl are hailed. It is Clinch returning from his mission to Nelson for Yvard's reprieve. The refugees are talking with Clinch, at a comfortable distance, when Yelverton's gig hails Clinch. It becomes obvious Clinch had not been talking with residents of the area but with Bolt and Yvard, and so the chase continues. The rowers in the yawl have no real chance of outrunning the well-manned cutter and gig, but they are most unexpectedly saved by Ghita's uncle, who is at the tiller of the yawl. He steers the boat through a small natural arch in the Sorrentine escarpment, an opening that only a native could find in the dark. This is the only occasion in the novel when Carlos Giuntotardi is sufficiently drawn from his religious preoccupations to take effective action in the real world.

Raoul lands with Ghita and Carlos, who will walk to the home of their relative at nearby St. Agata. Giuntotardi walks on ahead, and the two young lovers bid each other farewell. Notwithstanding her love for Raoul, Ghita rejects (as she has been doing for some time) his proposal of marriage. Her devotion to a specifically Christian God will not permit her marriage to a deist. Raoul returns to the yawl, greatly depressed, and he and Ithuel row out into the Bay of Naples, where they are soon picked up by the *Feu-Follet* and her anxious crew. After a joyous reunion of old shipmates, the lugger is directed toward open sea. Almost immediately, however, they are hailed in English from a small boat. It is Clinch, whom they capture but release after he is dined, wined, and thanked by Yvard for securing from Nelson the reprieve that had saved the Frenchman's life.

After releasing Clinch and his boat crew, Yvard again heads for the open sea, but he holds that course only as long as the British cutter remains in view. Then, reversing his direction, he sails back to Sorrento and St. Agata, purportedly to capture some British ship as prize in the morning but actually to see Ghita again. He thus perseveres in his role of passion's fool. Most of the men of the *Feu-Follet*, including her captain, now turn in for some badly needed sleep. But the watch and the lieutenant on the quarterdeck are also exhausted; as they doze at their respective posts, the lugger runs aground on one of the Islands of the Sirens, just below the bluff on which St. Agata stands. Realizing that his dereliction of duty may cause the loss of the lugger and the death or capture of all her crew, the delinquent lieutenant commits suicide by hurling himself into the surf that boils around the island.

Raoul Yvard sends Ithuel Bolt in an armed boat to capture an approaching felucca while he himself directs the work to dislodge the lugger from its rocky berth. The felucca is captured and brought alongside the *Feu-*

Follet, but the crew of the small boat has fled ashore at the approach of the armed privateersmen. Raoul, knowing that these escaped seamen will quickly give the alarm that will bring his enemies down upon him, works diligently to extricate the *Feu-Follet*, lightening his ship by landing on the islet all but a few basic supplies. By dawn the lugger is free, but with daylight come eight British boats, the whole fleet having been alerted to the location of the stranded *Feu-Follet*. Both the lugger and the captive felucca are anchored to repel the attack. Two of the *Feu-Follet's* guns are mounted on the deck of the felucca, four are kept aboard the lugger itself, and the remaining four are set up behind the stones of a ruin on the nearest islet. To Raoul's great surprise, Ghita and her uncle row out to their anchorage at this critical moment to be present during the forthcoming battle. Ignoring Raoul's pleas that she return at once to the safety of the shore, Ghita refuses to leave.

The first British onslaught is repulsed with heavy losses, thirty-three of the attackers being killed and still more wounded. Regrouping his boats, Sir Frederick Dashwood, commanding the expedition, hurls them all against the rocky islet and overruns the central position of the defense. The French make a determined stand, but the sheer weight of superior numbers prevails. Sir Frederick himself is killed, and Raoul Yvard is mortally wounded. The latter orders his first lieutenant, Jules Pintard, to flee in the *Feu-Follet* and save that noble ship. Both the lugger and the felucca (commanded by Bolt) run for the open sea. The felucca soon outruns the British ships, and for a while the lugger seems to be doing the same. She moves even more swiftly than before because most of her ballast had been removed while she was being freed from the rocks. Her lightness proves to be a liability, however, when she encounters strong sirocco winds. When a heavy squall strikes the French vessel, and the *Proserpine*, coming within range, starts to fire at her, she capsizes. By the time the weather clears, a few minutes later, the *Feu-Follet* has disappeared, sunk with all hands aboard. Nothing but one of her flags is found, identifiable by the wing-and-wing emblem it bears.

At the conclusion of the battle, all surviving British forces return to their ships except for Lieutenant Winchester and a small detachment of men who remain to bury the dead of both sides. Ghita, her uncle, and a French surgeon remain to attend the dying Raoul Yvard. The men soon retire for the night, and Ghita keeps her vigil with her beloved. Raoul is less reluctant to die now than he was while he still had hopes of marrying Ghita. Gazing at the stars and speculating about their creation, Raoul passes imperceptibly from one world to the next, and it is some time before Ghita realizes that he has actually died. He is buried in consecrated ground at St. Agata, his funeral attended by many residents of the town plus several British officers who have come to pay their last respects to this gallant foe.

Ghita lives with her uncle until his death and then retires to a convent for the remainder of her days. Several of the British officers receive promotions for their respective roles in the destruction of the *Feu-Follet*. Some years later Ithuel Bolt returns to America with a sizable sum of money about which he does not care to talk. There he "gets religion," becomes known generally as Deacon Bolt, and devotes his time to the abolition and temperance causes.

Annunziate, Antoine, Andrea Barrofaldi, Benoit, Ithuel Bolt, Ben Brown, Daniele Bruno, Admiral Francesco Caraccioli [Caracciolo], Ghita Caraccioli [Caracciolo], Catfall, Jack Clinch, Captain Richard Cuffe, Sir Frederick Dashwood, Filippo, Benedetta Galapo, Carlos Giuntotardi, Lieutenant Edward Griffin, [Lady Emma Hamilton, active but never named in novel], Jacques, Josef, Captain Lyon, Lieutenant Archy McBean, Medford, Lord Horatio Nelson, Lieutenant O'Leary, Pietro, Lieutenant Jules Pintard, Midshipman Roller, Lieutenant Spriggs, Lieutenant Stothard, Strand, Tim, Tommaso Tonti, Vito Viti, Lieutenant Winchester, Lieutenant Yelverton, Captain Raoul Yvard.

Wyandotté; or, The Hutted Knoll, 1843.

The action of this novel is set in central New York near Unadilla Creek, a tributary to the headwaters of the Susquehanna River. There, in what was then (1765) frontier country, the British Captain Hugh Willoughby has just taken possession of a 7,000-acre patent. His first move toward settling his holdings is to drain a 400-acre beaver pond and establish a farm on the rich alluvial soil of its bottom. In the center of the pond there had been a rocky island rising forty feet above the water, and on this eminence the captain builds first some huts—hence the "Hutted Knoll"— and later a large house. (Both the building and its site are known as the Hutted Knoll and Beaver Manor.) Although their daughters, Beulah and Maud (adopted), remain in school at Albany, and their son, Robert, serves in the army, Captain Hugh and his wife, Wilhelmina, move to this new home with a number of workers, some slaves, some regular employees. Among the latter are Joel Strides, a selfish and calculating Connecticut Yankee, Michael O'Hearn, a comic Irishman recently arrived from County Leitrim, and Saucy Nick, an outcast Tuscarora who had introduced Captain Willoughby to the area. Not so much servant as member of the household is the Rev. Mr. Jedediah Woods, former chaplain of the retired captain's infantry company.

During the ten years that elapse before the narrative resumes in 1775, the captain's central holdings have been converted into a productive estate. Beulah and Maud, now young ladies, have completed their schooling and live at the Hutted Knoll with their parents. One morning in May the family sees Nick approaching on a trot, his first appearance at the Knoll in more than two years. He comes to announce the arrival of the captain's son, Major Robert Willoughby, home on leave. After Nick has received the jug of rum owed to the bearer of good tidings, and after Robert and the family have joyfully reunited, the son reveals news of interest to all. First there is a family matter, namely, the death of Sir Harry Willoughby, whose baronetcy now devolves upon his cousin, the captain. Although the old soldier is not at all interested in the title—what function would it serve on the frontier?—his wife and daughters point out that at some future date it might be useful to Bob. As the Willoughbys discuss this development, another conversation is carried on apart by Michael O'Hearn and Saucy Nick over the latter's jug of liquor. The Tuscarora tells the Irishman that during his absence he had been on a warpath and had taken three scalps. As he drinks more, Nick also reveals his repressed hatred for the captain, who, during his days of military duty, had thrice horsewhipped the Indian for infractions of army discipline.

Far more important news than the death of Sir Harry is the information that the Revolutionary War has begun, that blood has already been shed, and that there is a very strong current of rebellion running throughout the American colonies. Bob reports specifically on the Battle of Lexington in which, he reluctantly admits, the British forces suffered three hundred casualties, he himself being slightly wounded in the engagement. Captain Willoughby, shocked by the ominous nature of this news, begins at once to fortify the Knoll with stockade and trenches against Indian hostilities that may erupt in the wake of civil strife. Like many other families of the time, the Willoughbys are divided in their sentiments about the conflict between England and her colonies, the captain slightly pro-patriot but determined to take a neutral position, Beulah strongly pro-patriot, and Mrs. Willoughby, Robert, and Maud loyalist.

Another domestic dilemma arises from some apparent bad feeling between Robert and Maud. As she has grown into womanhood, Maud has fallen in love with Robert, their relationship, she feels, no longer being that of affectionate siblings. Since she is an adopted daughter of the Willoughbys and there is no consanguinity, there is no bar, theoretically, to their sexual attraction. In reality, however, there is indeed a great obstacle: the failure of everyone, including Bob, to recognize Maud's mature womanly love for the young man. In vain does she hint of this in various ways. She has of late been signing her letters to Bob simply with the name Maud, not Maud Willoughby. Bob wonders why. Woven into the fine silken sash she has made him is the name Maud Meredith, Meredith having been her actual surname. With incredible denseness Bob asks if she has had a quarrel with his parents or has been otherwise alienated from the family! Since female propriety of the day forbids her from being so forward as to declare her love, she is most frustrated. For the modern reader the misunderstanding becomes quite farcical when Mrs. Willoughby, in all maternal solicitude, brings together her two seemingly disaffected children and probes for some explanation of their differences. It is only when departing from the Hutted Knoll that Bob, observing Maud wave to him from her window, wonders momentarily about the girl's intentions.

Beulah's love life is fraught with no such social or psychological complexities. She has been for some time courted by Evert Beekman, owner of a patent a few miles away, and when war breaks out, both families agree that their marriage should take place at once. They are wedded in the church on the Willoughby estate, the service being performed by the Rev. Mr. Woods. The newlyweds continue their honeymoon until Nick returns from his trip (on which he had guided Bob back to his regiment) with news of the deadly Battle of Bunker Hill. Then Evert, a colonel in the Continental army, forces himself to leave his bride and hasten to American headquarters.

In November the family follows its usual practice of moving to the city for the coldest part of the winter. Instead of going to New York City this year, they choose Albany as a place less likely to be disturbed by the war. Colonel Beekman visits them there for several weeks in order to be with his beloved Beulah. Maud is courted by several eligible young men in Albany society, but she takes no interest in any of them, much to her parents' concern.

In April of 1776 the family returns to the Hutted Knoll, where life continues much the same, with no indication at first that the nation is convulsed in civil war. For some time the only threat to tranquillity at the settlement is the machination of the overseer, Joel Strides. He and a handful of other Yankees hope to benefit from the war by exploiting their employers, the Willoughbys. Joel has tried previously to betray Bob to patriot forces along the Mohawk River. Now he strives to represent the Willoughbys as strongly Tory, his purpose being to have their holdings confiscated so that they may then be acquired by himself and his friends. Under Strides's coaching a Committee of Safety is formed among the employees and tenants, supposedly for the purpose of self-protection but in reality simply for furthering their own interests.

When danger does finally beset the Hutted Knoll, protection is provided by Captain Willoughby and a small number of faithful retainers, not by the Committee of Safety. While Maud is walking in the woods, late in September of 1776, she hears a shout of alarm and then observes a rush of settlers to the stockade. A few minutes later she discovers the cause of the alarm: the approach of seventy to eighty Indians. Although her first impulse is to run for home, Maud quickly realizes that her safest recourse is silent immobility. She is, nevertheless, soon discovered, not by Indians but by Major Bob, home on leave again and this time disguised in the garb of a hunter. The two talk quietly until Michael O'Hearn and Joel Strides are dispatched to locate and rescue Maud. Not trusting the Yankee overseer, Bob sends Maud to meet the two men but remains hidden himself in the woods until nightfall. When he does finally rejoin the family, Bob tells them of the Declaration of Independence and of George Washington's masterly evacuation of New York City. His primary purpose in returning at this time is to bring his father a commission from General Howe reactivating him in the British army, but Bob finds Captain Willoughby growing more and more sympathetic to the rebel cause.

The Indians camped outside the stockade are not immediately hostile, though several are in war paint. One appears bearing a white flag of truce and carries on a brief parley with the captain. He claims that his people are on a peaceful mission, traveling to the Hudson River to discover for themselves why the American English are fighting the British English. Not deceived by this story, the captain deems it prudent to pretend to accept it, and in a show of good will, he provides the Indians with rations of meat and meal. When, shortly afterwards, the captain and Bob scout the encampment of the besieging force, they become convinced that it is made up largely of white men disguised as Indians. (It is later discovered that twenty-seven of the party are real Indians, mostly Mohawks and Oneidas, the remainder being whites masquerading as savages.)

After an exchange of musket fire (a single volley from each side), there is a lull in hostilities. Aware that something is unusual about this confrontation, Captain Willoughby decides to send a delegation to determine the real purpose of the invaders. He appoints Joel Strides to undertake this mission. The wily overseer, who has by now penetrated Bob's disguise, agrees to make this contact with the enemy if the newly arrived stranger will accompany him. Bob accepts this condition before his father can refuse it, and the two men depart at once for the hostile camp. When they disappear and do not return for several hours, the Rev. Mr. Woods, trusting to the savages' reputed respect for religious leaders, dons his white surplice, proceeds to the hostile camp, and tries to ascertain what has become of the two negotiators. Woods himself fails to return, however. Much later Joel Strides comes back to the Hutted Knoll alone and reports that they are beset by a fierce band of patriot partisans who have captured as hostages both the British Major Willoughby and the Anglican chaplain, Woods.

The only fierce person visible, however, is Nick, who now reappears at the Knoll transformed from the begging, alcoholic hanger-on to Wyandotté, the proud Tuscarora chief he had been in youth. He indignantly refuses the dollar offered to him and warns Captain Willoughby not to speak again of the floggings inflicted on his alter ego Nick. The captain decides to detain Wyandotté and places him in a bedroom guarded by Michael O'Hearn. Unadaptable to military discipline, Mike releases his captive and travels with him to talk with the imprisoned Major Willoughby. When he returns to the Knoll, Mike brings news of the younger Willoughby's well-being. He also bears a silver snuffbox which he delivers secretly to Maud. It contains a lock of her hair, and the girl reads correctly its symbolic message: Robert loves her.

The reader, enlightened by the omniscient narrator, learns as fact what Captain Willoughby can only suspect to be the case: that Joel Strides is a collaborator of the enemy to whom he has given the major. This becomes more apparent to those within the fortified manor house that night when Sergeant Joyce discovers that Joel Strides and all but one of his fellow Yankees have deserted, abandoning their cabins, taking along their families, and bearing with them all of their firearms. The defending force is now reduced to five men capable of performing guard duty: Captain Willoughby, his old comrade-at-arms Sergeant Joyce, a Scottish mason named Jamie Allen, the garrulous but goodhearted Michael O'Hearn, and the faithful but frightened slave Pliny the Younger. These five watch throughout the tense night, but the expected predawn attack, a regular feature of Indian warfare, does not occur. When daylight returns, the weary defenders are astonished to discover that all of the deserters have returned and are working at their usual occupations (plowing, gardening, chopping wood) as if nothing had happened.

Baffled by the strange behavior of his employees, Captain Willoughby determines to leave the Knoll secretly with his four loyal supporters and attempt to liberate his son. En route, he learns from Wyandotté, who intercepts them, that the prisoner is being held in a log lean-to buttery attached to the log cabin of Daniel, the Yankee miller. The Tuscarora guides them past the real and make-believe Indians who lounge about their camp in indolent fashion. Leaving his four men on guard just yards from the lean-to, the captain proceeds cautiously with Wyandotté through a dense thicket toward the makeshift jail. Nick soon returns, but not the captain. After waiting dutifully for a whole hour, Sergeant Joyce decides to leave his station to investigate. He fears that the excitement may have caused his commanding officer to suffer a "fit" [stroke]. He finds the captain leaning against the buttery dead, killed not by a fit but by a knife wound in his heart.

Stunned by this blow, the sergeant and his men carry the body back to the edge of the Willoughby estate, but there none can muster the courage to inform the women of the disaster. Wyandotté volunteers to perform this painful duty, but as he heads for the Hutted Knoll he slows down from a trot to a walk to a standstill. The reader now comes to appreciate more fully the complexity of this Indian character. Not only is his personality split between the lowly, subservient Nick and the proud, masterful Wyandotté, but it is further divided by ambivalence of feeling toward the Willoughby family. Toward the captain he has borne resentment for thirty years, since his first flogging by that officer. Biding his time, he has taken vengeance at last by killing the captain; ferocity and savage satisfaction mark his features as he wipes the blood clots from his knife. Toward Wilhelmina Willoughby he has felt only affection ever since the woman cured him of a virulent disease, and as he prepares to break the bad news to the widow and her daughters, his face softens into kindness and a trace of sadness.

It is Maud who orders the barred door opened to the Tuscarora when he appears at the Knoll, and it is Maud whom he apprises of the captain's death. Fond of Maud, he introduces his bitter news by insisting that the captain was not her father; the Indian had been present when her real father, Major Meredith, had been shot in the French and Indian War. Then, to counterbalance the shock of the death of one she loves, he offers to save from possible death another whom she loves, Robert, if she will accompany him to the major's place of imprisonment. Wyandotté knows that Maud trusts him and knows too that she can, in turn, persuade Robert to trust him in this delicate undertaking; he also knows intuitively what no one else has recognized: that Maud and Bob love each other.

Liberated from the buttery, the major is almost immediately pursued by a howling horde of real and pretended Indians. As he and Maud, guided by Wyandotté, make their circuitous way back to the Knoll, there is a final though only momentary failure of communication between them. Although their mutual love is now avowed openly, Maud's countenance reflects not joy but anguish. The contretemps is resolved as Maud breaks down and reveals the tragic news of the captain's death. After Bob recovers from the first impact of this loss, the three push on for home and enter the palisaded yard just as their pursuers come within musket range and commence firing.

Resentful about Bob's escape, the mixed red and white force now launches its long-awaited attack on the Knoll. With a total of only thirteen supporters, counting some of the female slaves, Bob makes good the defense of the house against the initial onslaught. During the temporary lull that follows, he rushes inside to pay respect to his dead father and to console his mother. Greater even than his grief for his father is that which he experiences when his gaze turns to his mother. Her sanity has snapped, and she is obviously raving mad. Beulah is distraught, Maud is deep in prayer, and Nick is trying to console the incoherent widow. The deep pathos of this scene is suddenly shattered by pandemonium as screaming savages pour into the house. Strides and his accomplices have pried from its hinges the main gate, allowing the Mohawks and Oneidas easy access to the building. Wyandotté behaves heroically as he fights to protect the life of Maud and the scalps of Mrs. Willoughby, dead from an apparent heart attack, and Beulah, killed by a stray bullet. Despite their stalwart stand, the outnumbered defenders are in danger of complete annihilation until the timely arrival of Colonel Beekman with a company of fifty Continental regulars. Hearing of the unauthorized movement of some self-appointed guerrillas toward the Knoll, he had started to its relief when he had met the Rev. Mr. Woods, who made clear to him the urgency of the situation. By forced marches his corps has arrived barely in time to rescue the garrison from slaughter. As it is, only Beulah, Jamie Allen, and Bess (the Negro woman usually called Great Smash) die from enemy action. As Beekman's troops quickly restore order, most of the Indians and guerrillas flee. A dozen cannot choose but to remain, four of them dead and the remainder seriously wounded; among the dead is Strides's friend Daniel.

After the funerals of Captain Hugh, Wilhelmina, and Beulah, the Hutted Knoll is closed. Robert and Maud are married and move to New York City after Beekman has arranged for the exchange of the major for a Continental prisoner held by the British. Young Willoughby now purchases a lieutenant colonelcy and assumes the baronetcy to which he has fallen heir. With this rank and title he is able to request and secure duty outside his native land for the duration of the war. He and Maud make their permanent home in England.

Nineteen years later, in 1795, Lieutenant General Sir Robert Willoughby and his lady visit America, their main objective being a pilgrimage to their old home in upstate New York. They arrive at the Hutted Knoll and walk through the rooms of the deserted house indulging in reminiscence of their years spent here at the family homestead. They then walk to the graves of their loved ones and find there Michael O'Hearn and Wyandotté (both aged markedly) and the Rev. Mr. Woods. After honoring the dead and renewing old friendships, Robert is apprised by the Rev. Mr. Woods that Nick, now Christian, has confessed having murdered Captain Willoughby. The chief places a tomahawk in the hands of the general, bows his head in resignation, and directs him to take vengeance for his father's death. Though saddened by the news of Nick's treachery, Robert forgives him his crime against man and urges him to make his peace with God. Overcome with emotion, the old chief dies of " . . . an incurable affection of the heart" (p. 521). The novel closes with Robert's evaluation of the Tuscarora's life. It serves as a paradoxical but fitting epitaph for the titular hero:

"As for Wyandotté, he lived according to his habits and intelligence, and happily died under the conviction of conscience directed by the light of divine grace. . . . He never forgot a favor or forgave an injury" (pp. 522-523).

Jamie Allen, Colonel Evert Beekman, Evert Beekman, Bess, Blodget, Daniel, Desdemona, Farrel, Sergeant Joyce, Mari, General Meredith, Maud Meredith, Michael O'Hearn, Pliny the Elder, Pliny the Younger, Joel Strides, Lyddy Strides, Phoebe Strides, Beulah Willoughby, Captain Hugh Willoughby, Major (later Lieutenant General) Robert Willoughby, Wilhelmina Willoughby, Rev. Mr. Jedediah Woods, Wyandotté.

CHARACTERS

CHARACTERS

Abbott, Bianca-Alzuma-Ann. *Home as Found.* Daughter of Mrs. Abbott, who pronounces the child's name *Byansy-Alzumy-Ann.*

Abbott, Orlando Furioso. *Home as Found.* Eldest son of Mrs. Abbott.

Abbott, Rinaldo-Rinaldini-Timothy. *Home as Found.* Son of Mrs. Abbott.

Abbott, Roger-Demetrius-Benjamin. *Home as Found.* Son of Mrs. Abbott.

Abbott, Widow-Bewitched. *Home as Found.* Hypocrite, gossip, and general busybody, she spends her time and energy making trouble for others.

Abdallah. *Mercedes of Castile.* See Boabdil.

Abercrombie [-y], [James]. *Satanstoe.* An historical figure, he is commander of the British and colonial forces attacking Fort Ticonderoga.

Admiral, The. *Mercedes of Castile.* See Colon, Christoval.

Africanus, Scipio. *The Red Rover.* Free black seaman, longtime companion of Richard Fid.

Agamemnon. *The Pioneers.* Negro slave in the household of Judge Temple.

Albrecht of Viederbach. *The Heidenmauer.* A knight of St. John (also called Knight of Rhodes), he is a cousin of Count Emich Leininger. Although a very worldly person, he is invited to Hartenburg Castle with the hope that his title will lend an air of religious respectability to the depredations of the Count of Hartenburg.

Alfonso. *Mercedes of Castile.* Half brother of Henry IV and brother of Isabella, he dies shortly after his accession to power; mentioned.

Alfonso, Don. *Mercedes of Castile.* Later Alfonso V, this historical figure is the second man to whom Isabella is betrothed; mentioned.

Allen. *Lionel Lincoln.* An American waterfront guard, he captures Cecil Dynevor and her party en route to Cambridge.

Allen, Jamie. *Wyandotté.* A Scottish immigrant, he is a mason employed on the Willoughby patent. He is killed during an Indian attack on the Hutted Knoll.

Alonso, Don. *Mercedes of Castile.* Portuguese husband of the Princess Royal of Castile, he dies in 1491 a bridegroom; mentioned.

Alonso de Carbajal, Don. *Mercedes of Castile.* Ambassador to Castile; mentioned.

Altieri, Annunziata. *The Headsman*. The deceased mother of Gaetano
   Grimaldi's illegitimate son Bartolomeo Contini (alias Maso); men-
   tioned.
Alzada, Conde D'. *Precaution*. Aged father of Julia Fitzgerald; mentioned.
Amen, Rev. Mr. *The Oak Openings*. Ingenuous but devout missionary to
   the Indians, he dies a Christian martyr. He is usually called Parson
   Amen.
Anchorite of the Cedars. *The Heidenmauer*. Epithet for Baron Odo von
   Rittenstein while he lives as a hermit among the ruins near the
   Heidenmauer.
Anderson. *The Pathfinder*. Crewman aboard the *Scud*.
André, [John]. *The Spy*. An historical figure, he was the British major
   captured as a spy and hanged by the American command in 1780;
   mentioned.
Angiolina. *The Headsman*. The deceased mother of Gaetano Grimaldi's son
   Gaetano Grimaldi (alias Sigismund Steinbach); mentioned.
Annawon. *The Wept of Wish-Ton-Wish*. Wampanoag brave who participates
   in the second attack on Wish-Ton-Wish.
Annette. *Home as Found*. French seamstress and chambermaid at the
   Wigwam.
Annual, Mrs. *Home as Found*. Pseudonym of a member of the New York
   City literati.
Annunziate. *The Wing-and-Wing*. Female fruit seller at Portoferraio, Is-
   land of Elba.
Anselmo, Ferdinand. *The Bravo*. Carmelite monk who is the spiritual
   adviser of Violetta Tiepolo.
Anson, George. *The Two Admirals*. Schoolboy friend of the titular heroes
   of the novel; mentioned.
Antoin [sic]. *Afloat and Ashore*. Cabin boy on the French ship *Pauline*.
Antoine. *The Wing-and-Wing*. Old seaman on the *Feu-Follet*.
Antonio. "Imagination." Code name for Edward Stanley.
Ap Rice, Sir Owen. *Precaution*. Neighbor of the Earl of Pendennyss in
   Wales.
Archbishop of Leaphigh. *The Monikins*. Benign head of the ecclesiastical
   establishment in Leaphigh.
Archer. *Jack Tier*. Midshipman on the U.S. cruiser *Poughkeepsie*.
Ark, Henry. *The Red Rover*. Name given to infant Henry de Lacey many
   years before his real identity is established.
Arnolph, Father. *The Heidenmauer*. Prior and spiritual leader of the Abbey
   of Limburg, he is the most consistently devout and benign Bene-
   dictine in the novel.

Arrowhead. *The Pathfinder.* Tuscarora (Iroquois) Indian who at first pretends to support the British cause but is soon discovered to be in the employ of the French. He is killed by Chingachgook.

Assheton, John. *Home as Found.* Name temporarily taken by John Effingham.

Assheton, Paul. *Home as Found.* Mistakenly thought to be the name of Paul Effingham.

Augustin de Certevallos, Don. *The Prairie.* Spanish grandee in the Louisiana territory, father of Inez Augustin Middleton.

Bacon, Peter. *The Ways of the Hour.* A witness testifying at the inquest and at Mary Monson's first trial.

Bailey, Peter. *The Ways of the Hour.* Ninth juror empaneled for Mary Monson's first trial.

Baiting Joe. *The Sea Lions.* Alcoholic and garrulous old fisherman at Oyster Point.

Le Balafré. *The Prairie.* Venerable Teton Sioux chief who attempts to adopt as son the captive Hard-Heart.

Bale. *The Red Rover.* Agent for the *Royal Caroline* at Newport, Rhode Island.

Bale. *Home as Found.* Merchant on Wall Street.

Ballesteros, Diego de. *Mercedes of Castile.* Queen Isabella's page at the time of Christoval Colon's return from the first voyage to the Indies; mentioned.

Balthazar. *The Headsman.* The hereditary executioner (headsman) of the canton of Berne; husband of Marguerite; father of Christine; adoptive father of Gaetano Grimaldi the younger (alias Sigismund Steinbach); also called Herr Müller.

Baptiste. *The Headsman.* Greedy owner of the *Winkelried;* drowned during a storm on Lake Leman (Geneva).

Barbérie, Alida de. *The Water-Witch.* Of partly Huguenot extraction, she is the orphaned niece and ward of Myndert Van Beverout. The female romantic lead, she marries (on the last page of the novel) Captain Ludlow.

Barclay. *Afloat and Ashore.* A half-pay colonel, he is British consul in New York City.

Barlow. *Jack Tier.* Crewman on the *Molly Swash.*

Barney. *The Redskins.* Irish footman and servant of Jack Dunning.

Barnstable, Richard. *The Pilot.* A lieutenant and later captain in the U.S. Navy, he has come up through the ranks. He marries the capricious, intelligent Katherine Plowden.

Barnwell. *Satanstoe*. Colonial military officer in Tuscarora expedition; mentioned.

Barrel, Ben. *The Two Admirals*. A quartermaster on the British warship *Plantagenet*.

Barrofaldi, Andrea. *The Wing-and-Wing*. Deputy governor at Portoferraio, Island of Elba.

Bartolo. *The Headsman*. See Contini, Bartolomeo.

Bartolomeo. *The Bravo*. Gondolier who participates in the regatta.

Bat, Dr. Obed. *The Prairie*. Physician and pedantic naturalist attached to the Bush caravan. He prefers to Latinize his last name to *Battius*.

Battista, Father. *The Bravo*. Venetian priest.

Bayard. *The Chainbearer*. Deceased owner of the Hickories, an estate near Lilacsbush; ancestor of Priscilla and Tom Bayard; mentioned.

Bayard, Priscilla. *The Chainbearer*. Sister of Thomas Bayard, former schoolmate of Ursula Malbone, friend of Katrinke Littlepage, and eventually wife of Francis Malbone; often called Pris.

Bayard, Thomas. *The Chainbearer*. Brother of Priscilla Bayard, and suitor and eventually husband of Katrinke Littlepage.

Bear's Meat. *The Oak Openings*. A Menominee chief.

Beekman, Evert. *Wyandotté*. A colonel in the Continental army, he marries Beulah Willoughby.

Beekman, Evert. *Wyandotté*. Infant son of Colonel Evert Beekman and Beulah Willoughby.

Ben. *The Pilot*. An American sailor.

Benfield, Roderic. *Precaution*. Aged, garrulous uncle of Lady Anne Moseley, he is a good-natured bachelor of considerable fortune.

Benoit. *The Wing-and-Wing*. Quartermaster on the *Feu-Follet*.

Benson. *Satanstoe*. Young man interested in Anneke Mordaunt; mentioned.

Beppo. *The Bravo*. Wine merchant, competitor of Tommaso Torti.

Bess. *Wyandotté*. Negro slave at the Hutted Knoll, she is the wife of Pliny the Younger. She is slain and scalped during an Indian attack. She is known by the sobriquet Great Smash.

Betts, Robert. *The Crater*. Old salt who teaches Mark Woolston seamanship, he survives shipwreck with Mark on a crater reef. He later becomes a wealthy citizen of a colony built around that same reef.

Beverly, Jane. *The Two Admirals*. Wife of Gregory Wychecombe; mentioned.

Big Pine. *The Deerslayer*. Huron epithet for Henry March.

Big Serpent. *The Deerslayer, The Last of the Mohicans, The Pathfinder, The Pioneers*. The Indian whose native name is Chingachgook. Big Serpent is said to be the English translation of Chingachgook.

Big Thunder. *The Redskins.* Pseudonym for an unidentified "Injin," or disguised anti-renter.

Bigelow. *The Crater.* Shipwright recruited by Mark Woolston at Panama, he becomes captain of one of the colony's ships.

Bigelow, Teresa. *The Crater.* Spanish wife of Bigelow the shipwright.

Bignall. *The Red Rover.* Captain of the British cruiser *Dart.*

Bill. *Jack Tier.* Crewman on the *Molly Swash.*

Billings. *Satanstoe.* A British captain in Henry Bulstrode's company.

Billings, Diogenes. *Miles Wallingford.* Black cook on the *Dawn.*

Birch, Abigail. *The Spy.* Deceased sister of Harvey Birch; mentioned.

Birch, Chester. *The Spy.* Deceased brother of Harvey Birch; mentioned.

Birch, Harvey. *The Spy.* Yankee pack peddler who serves as Washington's most trusted espionage agent, he is the titular hero of the novel.

Birch, Johnny. *The Spy.* The father of Harvey Birch.

Bitts, Richard. *The Two Admirals.* Butler at Wychecombe Hall, employed by elderly Sir Wycherly Wychecombe; mentioned.

Black Billy. *Lionel Lincoln.* Nickname for the British general William Howe.

Blackbird. *The Oak Openings.* Indian chief among the forces that captured Chicago from the Americans during the War of 1812; mentioned.

Blakely. *The Two Admirals.* Captain of the British warship *Elizabeth.*

Blanche of Aragon. *Mercedes of Castile.* First wife of Henry IV of Castile; mentioned.

Blewet, Thomas. *The Two Admirals.* Captain of the British frigate *Druid.*

Blodget. *Wyandotté.* A young Rhode Islander employed on the Willoughby estate, he is the only Yankee who remains loyal to the family during an Indian uprising.

Bloomfield. *Home as Found.* A nonentity, he is the husband of a prominent New York socialite.

Bloomfield, Mrs. *Home as Found.* Witty and vivacious socialite in New York City.

Blossom. *The Oak Openings.* Nickname of Margery Waring.

Bluewater, Lord. *The Two Admirals.* Only male relative of same surname who survives Rear Admiral Richard Bluewater.

Bluewater, John. *The Two Admirals.* Younger brother of Rear Admiral Richard Bluewater, he was a colonel killed in action. He was secretly married to Agnes Hedworth by whom he had a daughter, Mildred, whom he never saw; mentioned.

Bluewater, Mildred. *The Two Admirals.* Long thought to be the daughter of Frank and Martha Dutton, she is known throughout most of the novel as Mildred Dutton. She is actually the daughter of Colonel John Bluewater and Agnes Hedworth Bluewater. The female romantic lead, she marries the Virginian Wycherly Wychecombe, seventh baronet of Wychecombe.

Bluewater, Richard. *The Two Admirals.* Rear admiral, second in command in Sir Gervaise Oakes's fleet, he is one of the two titular heroes of the novel.

Bluff. *The Two Admirals.* First lieutenant on the British warship *Caesar.*

Blunt, Paul. *Homeward Bound, Home as Found.* One of several names used by Paul Effingham.

Boabdil. *Mercedes of Castile.* Last of the Moorish kings in Spain, this historical figure surrenders Granada to Spanish forces; also called Abdallah.

Bobadilla, Beatriz de. *Mercedes of Castile.* Close friend and companion of Isabella, this historical figure marries Don Andres de Cabrera and eventually becomes Marquesa (Marchioness) de Moya; high-principled guardian of Mercedes de Valverde and aunt of Luis de Bobadilla, the two romantic principals of the novel; also called Marquesa de Moya.

Bobadilla, Don Luis de. *Mercedes of Castile.* Young male romantic lead in the novel; truant nephew of Beatriz de Bobadilla and later husband of Mercedes de Valverde, he is given seeming historicity by his use of the sobriquet Pedro Gutierrez [a gentleman volunteer close to Columbus and serving on the *Santa Maria*]; also called Conde de Llera, Pedro de Muños, and Pedro (Pero) Gutierrez.

Bobbinet. *Le Mouchoir.* Part owner of a fashionable shop in New York City.

Boden, Benjamin. *The Oak Openings.* A bee-hunter on the frontier, he is the protagonist and male romantic lead in the novel.

Bogart, Mrs. *Satanstoe.* Friend of Herman Mordaunt who accompanies the ill-fated sleighing party.

Bogert. *The Chainbearer.* Captain of a sloop on the Hudson River.

Bohrecheena. *The Prairie.* Aged Teton Sioux chief.

Bolt, Ithuel. *The Wing-and-Wing.* Yankee seaman impressed by British, he escapes and joins the crew of the French privateer *Feu-Follet.*

Bolton, Lord. *Precaution.* An earl, owner of a large estate near Moseley Hall, and a cousin of the Earl of Pendennyss.

Boltrope, David. *The Pilot.* Sailing master on an American frigate during the Revolution, he is killed at sea during a naval battle.

Bonifacius. *The Heidenmauer.* See Wilhelm of Venloo.

Bonnie. *The Water-Witch.* Black male slave who is Myndert Van Beverout's caretaker at Lust in Rust.

Borroughcliffe. *The Pilot.* Captain and later major in the British army, he is a hearty and convivial old soldier. He dies from excessive drinking while mourning the loss of a friend.

Bough of Oak. *The Oak Openings.* Indian chief whose tribe is not identified.

Bounding Boy. *The Deerslayer.* Young Huron brave.

Bounding Elk. *The Last of the Mohicans.* Indian epithet for Uncas.

Bourdon. *The Oak Openings.* A French word meaning *drone*, it is, inappropriately, the nickname by which Benjamin Boden is most frequently called.

Bourrit, Herr. *The Headsman.* The châtelain of Sion, in Upper Valais; serves as the official judge in the trial of those accused of the murder of Jacques Colis; also called Signor Castellano and Podestà.

Bowater, Mrs. *Wyandotté.* Daughter of Sir Harry Willoughby, she inherits his estate; mentioned.

Brace, Bob. *The Red Rover.* First of the seamen on the *Royal Caroline* to conclude that the ship has been beset by demonic forces.

Brackett, Miss. *Home as Found.* New York City socialite.

Bradfort, Margaret. *Afloat and Ashore.* A cousin of Rev. Mr. Hardinge, she leaves her vast fortune to that rector's daughter, Lucy.

Bradstreet. *Satanstoe.* General in command of the British commissariat; mentioned.

Bragg, Aristabulus. *Home as Found.* Yankee attorney and jack-of-all-trades, he manages the estate of Edward Effingham. He marries the French chambermaid Annette.

Briarthorn. *The Deerslayer.* See Yocommo.

Brigham, Joshua. *The Redskins.* Blustery hired man on Ravensnest farm; outspoken supporter of anti-renters.

Brigham, Sarah. *Afloat and Ashore.* Wife of Wallace Mortimer Brigham.

Brigham, Wallace Mortimer. *Afloat and Ashore.* A resident of Salem, Massachusetts, this gossipy, name-dropping Yankee is a passenger on the *Dawn* during a voyage to Bordeaux.

Bright. *The Crater.* Crewman of the shipwrecked *Rancocus*, he is a captive of Waally until he escapes to join the colony of Mark Woolston.

Brom. *The Pioneers.* Nickname of Abraham Freeborn.

Bromley, Mary. *The Crater.* Young confidante and bridesmaid of Bridget Yardley.

Bronte. *The Wing-and-Wing.* Epithet for Admiral Horatio Nelson after Ferdinand IV of Naples made him Duke of Bronte, a province in Sicily.

Brookes. *The Ways of the Hour.* A neighbor of Mrs. Gott.

Brooks. *Homeward Bound.* Athletic young seaman of the *Montauk*, he is killed in battle with Arabs.

Brown, Ben. *The Wing-and-Wing*. Foretopman on the British frigate *Proserpine*.

Brown, Bill. *The Crater*. Ship carpenter on the *Rancocus*, he is held captive by Waally before escaping to join Mark Woolston's colony.

Brown, Jack. *The Two Admirals*. Sailor on the *Plantagenet*.

Bruno, Daniele. *The Wing-and-Wing*. Crony of Tommaso Tonti.

Brush, David. *The Two Admirals*. Valet at Wychecombe Hall, employed by elderly Sir Wycherly Wychecombe; mentioned.

Brutus. *The Water-Witch*. Black slave of Myndert Van Beverout.

Brutus. *Home as Found*. Pseudonym of a member of the New York City literati.

Brutus, Julius. *Home as Found*. Pseudonym of a member of the New York City literati.

Brutus, Lucius Junius. *Home as Found*. Pseudonym of a member of the New York City literati.

Budd, Mrs. *Jack Tier*. Foolish, somewhat senile aunt of Rose Budd, she drowns when thrown overboard from the yawl of the *Molly Swash*.

Budd, Rose. *Jack Tier*. Orphaned niece of Mrs. Budd, she is the female romantic lead who marries Henry (Harry) Mulford.

Bulstrode, Lady. *Satanstoe*. Mother of Major Henry Bulstrode; mentioned.

Bulstrode, Sir Harry. *Satanstoe*. Major Bulstrode's gouty, asthmatic father, resident of England; mentioned.

Bulstrode, Henry. *Satanstoe, The Chainbearer*. British major (later Sir Henry), he is a friend of the Mordaunt family. He courts Anneke Mordaunt but remains a bachelor.

Bumgrum, Ordeal. *Home as Found*. Child of a neighbor of Mrs. Abbott.

Bumppo, Nathaniel (Natty). *The Deerslayer, The Last of the Mohicans, The Pathfinder, The Pioneers, The Prairie*. Protagonist of all five of these Leather-Stocking Tales. An illiterate white man, he was adopted in youth by the Delawares and becomes sworn "brother" of Chingachgook. An unselfish man, he spends his life in service to others.

Bunce, Peter. *The Redskins*. A tenant at Ravensnest.

Bunt, Bob. *The Red Rover*. Wily old sailor, one of the many masquerades of the Red Rover.

Bunting. *The Two Admirals*. Lieutenant who serves as signal officer for Vice Admiral Sir Gervaise Oakes, he is killed in action.

Burgoyne, [John]. *Lionel Lincoln*. An historical general, he was a prominent British leader at the siege of Boston during the Revolution.

Burton, Miss. *The Ways of the Hour*. Eldest sister of Samuel Burton and witness in the first Mary Monson trial.

Burton, Miss. *The Ways of the Hour.* Second sister of Samuel Burton and witness in the first Mary Monson trial.

Burton, Miss. *The Ways of the Hour.* Third sister of Samuel Burton and witness in the first Mary Monson trial.

Burton, Samuel. *The Ways of the Hour.* Witness in the first Mary Monson trial.

Burton, Sarah. *The Ways of the Hour.* Taciturn, guilt-ridden witness questioned by Mary Monson following the latter's conviction for murder.

Bury. *The Two Admirals.* First lieutenant on the British warship *Plantagenet.*

Bush, Abner. *The Prairie.* Son of Ishmael and Esther Bush.

Bush, Asa. *The Prairie.* Oldest son of Ishmael and Esther Bush, he is murdered by his uncle.

Bush, Enoch. *The Prairie.* Son of Ishmael and Esther Bush.

Bush, Esther (Hetty). *The Prairie.* Wife of Ishmael Bush.

Bush, Hetty, *The Prairie.* Daughter of Ishmael and Esther Bush.

Bush, Ishmael. *The Prairie.* A "squatter" from Kentucky and Tennessee, he is the head of a large family of settlers well beyond the frontier in the Louisiana Purchase.

Bush, Jesse. *The Prairie.* Son of Ishmael and Esther Bush.

Butterfield. *The Ways of the Hour.* Participant in a lawsuit; mentioned.

Buzz, Ben. *The Oak Openings.* Nickname for Benjamin Boden.

Buzzing Ben. *The Oak Openings.* Nickname for Benjamin Boden.

Byng, John. *The Two Admirals.* Schoolboy friend of the titular heroes of the novel; mentioned.

Cabrera, Don Andres de. *Mercedes of Castile.* A waggish noble and friend of Ferdinand of Aragon, he weds Beatriz de Bobadilla and eventually becomes Marquis of Moya; also called Nuñez.

Caesar. *The Pilot.* Negro slave in the household of Colonel Howard.

Caesar. *Satanstoe.* Negro slave of Mrs. Jane Legge.

Calatrava, Master of. *Mercedes of Castile.* See Giron, Don Pedro.

Caonabo. *Mercedes of Castile.* Historical Carib chieftain feared by the Haitians, he vainly attempts to capture Ozema as a wife during Luis de Bobadilla's visit to Mattinao.

Cap, Charles. *The Pathfinder.* A stereotyped "old salt," he is scornful of the freshwater seamanship of the Great Lakes. He is the brother-in-law of Sergeant Dunham and the uncle of Mabel Dunham.

Caraccioli [Caracciolo], Francesco. *The Wing-and-Wing.* Historical Neapolitan admiral and statesman convicted of treason by a Neapolitan court and executed by Admiral Horatio Nelson.

Caraccioli [Caracciolo], Ghita. *The Wing-and-Wing*. Granddaughter of Admiral Caracciolo and fiancée of Raoul Yvard.

Cardonnel, Lady. *Lionel Lincoln*. Title inherited by Cecil Dynevor.

Cardonnel, Lord. *Lionel Lincoln*. Relative of Cecil Dynevor; mentioned.

Carlos, Don. *Mercedes of Castile*. First prince to whom Isabella is betrothed; mentioned.

Carnaby. *The Water-Witch*. New York City grocer who is the liaison between Thomas Tiller and Lord Cornbury.

Carrascal, Father Pedro de. *Mercedes of Castile*. Respected friar and former teacher of Luis de Bobadilla.

Cassandra. *The Red Rover*. Black servant of Gertrude Grayson.

Castellano, Signor. *The Headsman*. See Bourrit, Herr.

Catamount. *The Deerslayer*. Huron warrior who wishes to marry the captive Wah-ta-Wah.

Catfall. *The Wing-and-Wing*. Captain of the forecastle on the British frigate *Proserpine*.

Catholic Queen. *Mercedes of Castile*. See Isabella.

Cato. *Lionel Lincoln*. Black slave of Priscilla Lechmere.

Cato. *Satanstoe*. Herman Mordaunt's longtime slave.

Caverly, Clara. *Le Mouchoir*. Friend of Eudosia Halfacre.

Le Cerf Agile. *The Last of the Mohicans*. See Bounding Elk.

Chainbearer. *The Chainbearer*. See Coejemans, Andries.

Charity. *The Wept of Wish-Ton-Wish*. Maidservant in Heathcote household.

Charlton. *The Crater*. A merchant who joins Mark Woolston's colony.

Chatterino, Lord. *The Monikins*. The younger of the two male monkeys (monikins) met by John Goldencalf in Paris; a young nobleman in Leaphigh society.

Chatterissa, Lady. *The Monikins*. The younger of the two female monkeys (monikins) met by John Goldencalf in Paris, she eventually marries Lord Chatterino.

Chatterton, Lady. *Precaution*. Widow of a baron, she is the domineering mother of Astley (Lord Chatterton), Grace, and Catherine.

Chatterton, Lord. *Precaution*. See Cooper, Astley.

Chatterton, Catherine. *Precaution*. Older daughter of Lady Chatterton, she marries Lord Herriefield; also called Kate and Lady Herriefield.

Chatterton, Grace. *Precaution*. Younger daughter of Lady Chatterton and confidante of Emily Moseley, she weds John Moseley.

Chatterton, Lady [Harriet]. *Precaution*. See Denbigh, Lady Harriet.

Chatterton, Kate. *Precaution*. See Chatterton, Catherine.

Chélincourt, Comte de. *The Two Admirals*. Captain of the French warship *Scipio*.

Chingachgook. *The Deerslayer.* Sworn "brother" of Natty Bumppo and chief of the Mohicans, a tribe of the Delaware nation. He is the husband of Wah-ta-Wah and the father of Uncas. *The Last of the Mohicans.* Scout, with Natty Bumppo, for British during French and Indian Wars and father of the titular hero, Uncas. *The Pathfinder.* Scout, with Natty Bumppo, for American forces on the Niagara Frontier during the Revolutionary War. *The Pioneers.* Alcoholic and pathetic old Indian now known as John Mohegan. He dies near the end of this novel.

Christine. *The Headsman.* Daughter of Balthazar and Marguerite, and the bride renounced by Jacques Colis at the revels in Vévey.

Clawbonny, Chloe. *Afloat and Ashore, Miles Wallingford.* Slave girl (later freed) who is the personal servant of Grace Wallingford. She marries Neb Clawbonny.

Clawbonny, Cupid. *Miles Wallingford.* Slave (later freed) second husband of Venus Clawbonny.

Clawbonny, Dido. *Afloat and Ashore.* Slave (later freed) who serves as cook at Clawbonny.

Clawbonny, Hector. *Miles Wallingford.* Son of the slaves (later freed) Neb and Chloe Clawbonny.

Clawbonny, Hiram. *Afloat and Ashore.* Slave (later freed) who is in charge of the farm work at Clawbonny.

Clawbonny, Nebuchadnezzar (Neb). *Afloat and Ashore, Miles Wallingford.* Slave (later freed) who goes to sea with the protagonist, Miles Wallingford. He is one of Miles's closest friends.

Clawbonny, Pompey. *Afloat and Ashore.* Grandfather of Nebuchadnezzar (Neb) Clawbonny.

Clawbonny, Romeo. *Miles Wallingford.* Aged slave (later freed) house servant at Clawbonny.

Clawbonny, Venus. *Miles Wallingford.* Slave (later freed) housekeeper at Clawbonny.

Clawbonny, Vulcan. *Miles Wallingford.* Slave (later freed) who is a blacksmith at Clawbonny and the adjacent villages.

Cleet, Bob. *The Water-Witch.* Sailor on the *Coquette.*

Clements. *Miles Wallingford.* Lieutenant on the British frigate *Briton.*

Clench, Ben. *Jack Tier.* Boatswain of the *Molly Swash.*

Cleveland, Lord Geoffrey. *The Two Admirals.* A very young midshipman during the main action of the novel, he subsequently becomes the Duke of Glamorgan.

Clinch, Jack. *The Wing-and-Wing.* Master mate on the British frigate *Proserpine,* he was later promoted to the rank of lieutenant.

Clinton, Sir Henry. *The Spy, Lionel Lincoln.* An historical figure, he was one of the British generals responsible for the evacuation of Boston; subsequently British commander in New York City.

Coca, Father Alonso de. *Mercedes of Castile.* Young Isabella's priest and counselor.

Coe, Dr. *The Ways of the Hour.* Country doctor who testifies at the inquest.

Coejemans, Andries. *The Chainbearer.* A captain during the Revolution, he later becomes a surveyor and is often called Chainbearer. He is the guardian of his niece Ursula Malbone. He is killed by Aaron Timberman.

Le Coeur-dur. The Last of the Mohicans. See Hard Heart.

Coffin, Tom. *The Pilot.* A Nantucket whaler in the navy during the Revolution, he is a stereotype of the "old salt."

Coil. *The Water-Witch.* Seaman on the *Water-Witch.*

Coldbrooke [or Colebrooke], Henrietta. *The Redskins.* A ward of Hugh Roger Littlepage the elder; independently wealthy; marries a friend of Hugh Roger Littlepage the younger.

Colis, Jacques. *The Headsman.* The intended husband of Christine at the revels in Vévey; renounces Christine as bride; murdered by Conrad and Pippo.

Colombo, Christoforo. *Mercedes of Castile.* See Colon, Christoval.

Colon, Christoval. *Mercedes of Castile.* A Genoese historical figure whose determination to reach Cathay by sailing west provides the impetus for the novel; devout Christian, idealist, and superb navigator; also called Christopher Columbus, The Admiral, and Christoforo Colombo.

[Colon], Diego. *Mercedes of Castile.* An historical figure who is the legitimate son of Christoval Colon, a widower; mentioned.

[Colon], Fernando (Ferdinand). *Mercedes of Castile.* An historical figure who is the illegitimate son of Christoval Colon by Beatriz Enriquez; mentioned.

Columbus, Christopher. *Mercedes of Castile.* See Colon, Christoval.

Commodore. *Home as Found.* Eccentric septuagenarian who devotes his time to fishing on Otsego Lake.

Comtant. *The Two Admirals.* Captain of the French warship *Victoire.*

Conanchet [Canonchet]. *The Wept of Wish-Ton-Wish.* An historical figure, he succeeds his father, Miantonimoh, as sachem of the Narragansetts. He is killed in a battle with the English and their Pequot-Mohican allies. In the novel he marries the captive English girl who is the "wept" of Wish-Ton-Wish.

Conrad. *The Headsman.* Hypocritical pilgrim en route to Rome; Pippo's confederate in the murder of Jacques Colis.

Contini, Bartolomeo. *The Headsman*. The illegitimate son of Gaetano Grimaldi; a dealer in contraband; emergency captain of storm-beset *Winkelried;* usually called Maso, but also called *Il Maledetto*, San Tommaso, Tommaso Santi, and Bartolo.

Cooper, Astley. *Precaution*. Titled Lord Chatterton, he is the son of Lady Chatterton and brother of Grace and Catherine, and weds Lady Harriet Denbigh.

Coppers, Jack. *The Monikins*. Negro cook aboard the *Walrus;* knighted in Leaphigh.

Le Corbeau Rouge. The Deerslayer. See Red Crow.

Cork, Samuel. *The Two Admirals*. Cook at Wychecombe Hall, employed by elderly Sir Wycherly Wychecombe; mentioned.

Cornbury, Viscount. *The Water-Witch*. Former royal governor of the colony of New York and a distant relative of Queen Anne, he is in debtors' prison at the time of the novel.

Cornet. *The Two Admirals*. Lieutenant who serves as signal officer for Rear Admiral Richard Bluewater.

County of Fair-villain. *The Two Admirals*. Galleygo's mispronunciation of *Comte de Vervillin*.

Craft. *The Sea Lions*. Lawyer who draws up Deacon Pratt's will, he is called Squire.

Craig. *The Deerslayer*. British lieutenant.

Craig, Jimmy. *Lionel Lincoln*. Friend of Captain Polwarth; mentioned.

Crooks. *The Ways of the Hour*. Attorney in Duke's County.

Crowsfeather. *The Oak Openings*. The supreme chief of the Pottawattamies.

Crutchely. *The Crater*. Alcoholic master of the *Rancocus*, he runs his ship aground on reefs in the Pacific and is swept overboard to his death.

Cuffe, Richard. *The Wing-and-Wing*. Captain of the British frigate *Proserpine*.

Cunning Fox. *The Last of the Mohicans*. Indian honorific for Magua.

Cuno, Father. *The Heidenmauer*. Benedictine monk at the Abbey of Limburg.

Cupid. *The Water-Witch*. Black slave of Oloff Van Staats.

Cuyler. *Satanstoe*. Mayor of Albany.

D.O.V.E. *Home as Found*. Pseudonym of a member of the New York City literati.

Daggett, Betsey. *The Sea Lions*. Wife of Captain Jason Daggett.

Daggett, Jason. *The Sea Lions*. Captain of the *Sea Lion* of Martha's Vineyard.

Daggett, Thomas. *Miles Wallingford*. Distant relative of John Wallingford and the administrator of his estate.

Daggett, Thomas. *The Sea Lions*. Dying seaman, uncle of Jason Daggett, who discloses to Deacon Pratt the locations of a sealing site and a buried treasure.

Le Daim-Mose. The Deerslayer. See Moose.

Dale. *Afloat and Ashore*. Captain of the *U.S.S. Ganges*.

Daly. *The Two Admirals*. First lieutenant on the British warship *Achilles*.

Dama. *Mercedes of Castile*. Friend of Inez Peraza and witness to the visibility of land west of the Canary Islands.

Danforth, Agnes. *Lionel Lincoln*. The great-niece of Priscilla Lechmere, she is the friend and confidante of the female romantic lead, Cecil Dynevor. She is one of the few pro-patriot characters in the novel.

Daniel. *Wyandotté*. Miller on the Willoughby estate, he plots with Joel Strides against his employer. He is killed attacking the Hutted Knoll.

Daniels, Sam. *Precaution*. Innkeeper of the Dun Cow inn, a competitor of Moseley Arms.

Dashwood, Sir Frederick. *The Wing-and-Wing*. Baronet who commands the British frigate *Terpsichore*.

David. *Precaution*. Servant of Roderic Benfield.

David. *The Two Admirals*. Porter at Wychecombe Hall, employed by elderly Sir Wycherly Wychecombe.

David. *Satanstoe*. The old chainbearer with Corny Littlepage's party; killed and scalped by Hurons.

Davidson, Bartlett. *The Sea Lions*. Seaman on the *Sea Lion* of Oyster Point.

Davidson, Davy. *The Ways of the Hour*. Cited as an example of one who, reputed to be only moderately wealthy, dies very wealthy; mentioned.

Davidson, Peter. *The Ways of the Hour*. Resident of Biberry; mentioned.

Davis, Gilbert. *Satanstoe*. Tenant at Ravensnest killed and scalped by Hurons.

Davis, Jake. *The Sea Lions*. Resident of Oyster Point and crony of Baiting Joe.

Davis, Jesse. *The Ways of the Hour*. Nephew and heir of Peter Goodwin, he retains Frank Williams as prosecuting attorney in the Mary Monson trials.

Davis, Robert. *Homeward Bound*. Newly wed bridegroom aboard the *Montauk*, he is sought for alleged debts.

Davis, Mrs. Robert. *Homeward Bound*. Newly wed bride aboard the *Montauk*.

Davis, Thomas. *Precaution.* Discharged alcoholic gardener advised and aided by George Denbigh (Earl of Pendennyss).

Davis, Mrs. Thomas. *Precaution.* Wife of Thomas Davis and mother of his four children.

de Blonay, Roger (Sire). *The Headsman, The Redskins.* An old friend of Melchior de Willading, he is host for the Willading party near Vévey; mentioned in *The Redskins.*

de la Rocheaimard, Viscountess. *Le Mouchoir.* Grandmother of Adrienne de la Rocheaimard, the female romantic lead.

de la Rocheaimard, Adrienne. *Le Mouchoir.* Member of the noble family of de la Rocheaimard, she is the maker and final owner of a famous pocket handkerchief. The female romantic lead, she marries Betts Shoreham.

de Lacey. *The Red Rover.* Grandfather of Henry de Lacey and deceased husband of the Widow de Lacey, he was an admiral.

de Lacey, Widow. *The Red Rover.* Relict of Admiral de Lacey who, for humorous purposes, mistaught her nautical jargon. She is the aunt of Gertrude Grayson.

de Lacey, Henry. *The Red Rover.* Grandson of Admiral de Lacey and son of Paul de Lacey and Mrs. Wyllys, he is the romantic male lead in the novel. He uses the aliases Henry Ark and Harry Wilder.

de Lacey, Paul. *The Red Rover.* Dead before the novel commences, he was the father of Henry de Lacey.

de Willading, Adelheid. *The Headsman.* The sole surviving child of the Baron de Willading, she marries Gaetano Grimaldi the younger (alias Sigismund Steinbach).

de Willading, Melchior (Baron). *The Headsman.* A lifelong friend of Signor Gaetano Grimaldi and the father of Adelheid, he is rescued from drowning by Gaetano the younger (alias Sigismund Steinbach).

Deersfoot. *The Redskins.* One of the Indian band honoring Susquesus.

Deerslayer. *The Deerslayer.* Epithet given by Indians to the youthful Natty Bumppo.

Delafield, Seymour. "Heart." Suave, attractive, and wealthy young man about town, he marries Maria Osgood after being rejected by the protagonist, Charlotte Henley.

Denbigh, Duke Francis. *Precaution.* Deceased eldest brother of General Frederick Denbigh; mentioned.

Denbigh, Francis (Frank). *Precaution.* Deceased elder son of General Frederick and Lady Margaret Denbigh; mentioned.

Denbigh, Frederick. *Precaution.* A deceased general who was the grandfather of George Denbigh, Earl of Pendennyss; mentioned.

Denbigh, Frederick. *Precaution*. Duke of Derwent and brother of Lady Harriet Denbigh, he first courts Emily Moseley and later wooes Lady Marian Denbigh.

Denbigh, George. *Precaution*. Deceased younger brother of Duke Francis Denbigh; mentioned.

Denbigh, George [the elder]. *Precaution*. Younger son of General Frederick and Lady Margaret Denbigh, husband of Lady Marian Lumley, and father of George Denbigh (the Earl of Pendennyss) and Lady Marian Denbigh, he dies early in the novel.

Denbigh, George. *Precaution*. The Earl of Pendennyss. Male romantic lead in the novel, he is the only son of George Denbigh and Lady Marian Denbigh; he weds Emily Moseley; also called Lumley, Lord Lumley, and Lord Pendennyss.

Denbigh, George. *Precaution*. A colonel in the army, he is a cousin of the Earl of Pendennyss and the Duke of Derwent. He marries Lady Laura Stapleton.

Denbigh, Lady Harriet. *Precaution*. Sister of Frederick Denbigh (Duke of Derwent) and cousin of George Denbigh (Earl of Pendennyss) and Lady Marian Denbigh, she is courted and won by Astley Cooper (Lord Chatterton) and is thereafter called Lady Chatterton.

Denbigh, Lady Margaret. *Precaution*. Deceased wife of General Frederick Denbigh, mother of Francis and George Denbigh, and grandmother of George Denbigh (Earl of Pendennyss); mentioned.

Denbigh, Marian. *Precaution*. Reclusive devoted sister of George Denbigh (Earl of Pendennyss), she is wooed by Frederick Denbigh, Duke of Derwent; usually called Lady Marian.

Denham. *The Two Admirals*. Captain of the British warship *Chloe* during the action of the novel; in later years he received a peerage and the rank of rear admiral.

Dent, Sir Digby. *Lionel Lincoln*. British officer; mentioned.

Dermond, Lord Harry. *Miles Wallingford*. Captain of the British frigate *Speedy*.

Derwent, Duke of. *Precaution*. See Denbigh, Frederick.

des Prez, Vicomte. *The Two Admirals*. Officer in command of the rear squadron of the French fleet engaged by the titular heroes of the novel.

Desdemona (Mony). *Wyandotté*. Negro slave in the household of Captain Willoughby, she is manumitted after his death. She is also called Little Smash.

Désirée. *Le Mouchoir*. A Parisian commission agent.

Dew-of-June. *The Pathfinder*. Wife of the Tuscarora Arrowhead.

Dickey. *Home as Found.* Apprentice boy at Templeton.

Dickinson. *The Crater.* Crewman of the shipwrecked *Rancocus*, he is held captive by Waally until he escapes to join Mark Woolston's colony.

Dickon. *The Pioneers.* Nickname which Judge Temple uses for his cousin, Richard Jones.

Dido. *The Crater.* Wife of Socrates, she is a slave owned by Bridget Yardley.

Diego. *Mercedes of Castile.* Presumptuous but good-natured young soldier and member of the guard at Saragossa, capital of Aragon.

Dietrich. *The Heidenmauer.* A blacksmith of Deurckheim, he is Heinrich Frey's lieutenant in the attack on the Abbey of Limburg.

Digby, Horace. *Precaution.* A captain in the army, he is killed in a duel by his comrade, Captain Harry Jarvis.

Digges. *Afloat and Ashore.* Captain of the *Tigris*, the vessel on which the *John's* shipwrecked crew works its way home.

Diggins. *Miles Wallingford.* Alcoholic master's mate on the British frigate *Speedy*.

Dighton, Stephen. *The Crater.* Quaker leader who immigrates to Mark Woolston's colony.

Dillon, Christopher. *The Pilot.* Lawyer and American Tory, he returns to England during the Revolution. He is the villain of the novel: morose, malign, and completely self-centered.

Dinah. *The Water-Witch.* Black slave, maidservant of Alida de Barbérie.

Diomede. *The Water-Witch.* Black slave of Myndert Van Beverout.

Dipper. *Afloat and Ashore.* An Indian with whom the crew of the *Crisis* trades on the Canadian Pacific coast.

Dobbs, John. *The Monikins.* Upright steward of John Goldencalf's Householder estate.

Dodd, Martha. *The Two Admirals.* Housekeeper for Lord Thomas Wychecombe, she bears him three illegitimate sons.

Dodge, Steadfast. *Homeward Bound, Home as Found.* Yankee journalist of questionable character, he is editor of the *Active Inquirer*.

Dogma, Dr. *The Red Rover.* Clergyman at Newport.

Doolittle, Hiram. *The Pioneers.* Yankee carpenter, amateur architect and lawyer, and Justice of the Peace employed in various capacities by Richard Jones. He is flattered by the townspeople with the honorific Squire.

Doortje. *Satanstoe.* Kitchen maid in Mayor Cuyler's home in Albany.

Doortje, Mother. *Satanstoe.* Self-styled fortuneteller in Albany.

Downright, Aaron. *The Monikins.* Titled "Brigadier," he attends Judas People's Friend and aids John Goldencalf and Poke in Leaplow.

Doyle. *Lionel Lincoln.* Sergeant in the Royal Irish Grenadiers.

Drewett, Mrs. *Afloat and Ashore, Miles Wallingford.* Mother of Andrew, Caroline, and Helen Drewett.

Drewett, Andrew. *Afloat and Ashore, Miles Wallingford.* Unsuccessful suitor of Lucy Hardinge.

Drewett, Caroline. *Miles Wallingford.* Sister of Andrew Drewett.

Drewett, Helen. *Miles Wallingford.* Sister of Andrew Drewett.

Drill. *The Pilot.* A sergeant in the British army.

Drinkwater. *The Two Admirals.* Captain of the British warship *Dover* during the main action of the novel, he is subsequently drowned at sea during a storm.

Driven Snow. *The Wept of Wish-Ton-Wish.* Indian epithet for Ruth Heathcote.

Drooping Lily. *The Deerslayer.* Indian sobriquet for Hetty Hutter.

Ducie, Charles. *Homeward Bound, Home as Found.* A cousin of Paul Effingham, he is captain of the British cruiser *Foam.*

Dudley, Eben. *The Wept of Wish-Ton-Wish.* A doughty Indian fighter, he attains the rank of ensign. He marries Faith Ring.

Dumont, Pierre. *The Headsman.* An experienced mountain guide; led the de Willading party through the Great St. Bernard pass to Italy.

Dumont de la Rocheforte, Chevalier. *The Water-Witch.* Captain of the French cruiser *La Belle Fontange,* he is killed by musket fire from a British boarding party.

Duncan of Lundie. *The Pathfinder.* Scottish major who commands the British 55th Regiment, stationed at Fort Oswego on Lake Ontario.

Dunham, Bridget. *The Pathfinder.* Deceased wife of Sergeant Dunham and mother of Mabel Dunham; mentioned.

Dunham, Mabel. *The Pathfinder.* Daughter of Sergeant Dunham, she is betrothed to Pathfinder but later marries Jasper Western.

Dunham, Thomas. *The Pathfinder.* Sergeant major of the 55th Regiment, stationed at Fort Oswego on Lake Ontario. He is killed at a French and Indian ambush on one of the Thousand Islands.

Dunks. *The Crater.* Enterprising settler in Mark Woolston's colony.

Dunning, Jack. *The Redskins.* Agent in New York for Hugh Roger Littlepage the elder.

Dunscomb, Thomas. *The Ways of the Hour.* Respected New York City lawyer who defends Mary Monson in her two murder trials.

Dunscombe, Alice. *The Pilot.* Although once betrothed to John Paul Jones and still in love with him, this modest English woman parts with him forever after his commitment to the cause of the colonies during the American Revolution. She serves as governess to

Katherine Plowden and Cecilia Howard in the household of Colonel Howard.

Dunwoodie, Peyton. *The Spy*. Commanding officer (major) of Virginia Dragoons and the male romantic lead in the novel. Years after the main action, he attains the rank of general.

Dunwoodie, Wharton. *The Spy*. Captain, son of Major (ultimately General) Dunwoodie and Frances Wharton Dunwoodie, he serves in the War of 1812.

Dutton, Frank. *The Two Admirals*. Alcoholic lieutenant demoted to sailing master, he is long thought to be the father of Mildred Bluewater.

Dutton, Martha Ray. *The Two Admirals*. Wife of Frank Dutton and long thought by most people (including her husband) to be the mother of Mildred Bluewater.

Dutton, Mildred. *The Two Admirals*. See Bluewater, Mildred.

Dynevor. *Lionel Lincoln*. A deceased British colonel, he was the father of Cecil Dynevor; mentioned.

Dynevor, Agnes Lechmere. *Lionel Lincoln*. Deceased mother of Cecil Dynevor, she was the daughter of John and Priscilla Lechmere; mentioned.

Dynevor, Cecil. *Lionel Lincoln*. The female romantic lead, she marries Lionel Lincoln. She is the granddaughter of Priscilla Lechmere.

Eagle. *The Pioneers*. Delaware nickname for Colonel Edward Effingham.

Eaglesflight. *The Redskins*. Indian orator visiting Susquesus.

Earing, Edward. *The Red Rover*. First mate on the *Royal Caroline*.

Eau-douce. *The Pathfinder*. French for "Sweet Water," epithet applied to Jasper Western.

Eckford, Henry. *The Sea Lions*. Famous American ship builder of the early nineteenth century; mentioned.

Edmeston. *Wyandotté*. Holder of a patent on the frontier near that of Captain Willoughby; mentioned.

Edson. *Home as Found*. New York City socialite.

Edwards. *The Crater*. Crewman of the shipwrecked *Rancocus*, he is a captive of Waally until he escapes to join the colony of Mark Woolston.

Edwards, Oliver. *The Pioneers*. Name assumed by young Edward Oliver Effingham.

Effingham, Edward. *The Pioneers*. Son of Major Oliver Effingham, early business partner of Marmaduke Temple, and a Loyalist colonel during the Revolution. Separated from Temple during the War and dead before the action of the novel commences, he left a confused legacy for his son, Edward Oliver, to identify and inherit.

Effingham, Edward. *Homeward Bound, Home as Found.* Wealthy and refined widower, he is the father of Eve Effingham.

Effingham, Edward Oliver. *The Pioneers.* The son of Colonel Edward Effingham and the grandson of Major Oliver Effingham, he is orphaned, later impoverished and temporarily dispossessed by the displacements of war. After repossessing his family fortune, he marries Elizabeth Temple.

Effingham, Eve. *Homeward Bound, Home as Found.* A romantic female lead in both novels, she is the daughter of Edward Effingham and finally the wife of Paul Effingham.

Effingham, John. *Homeward Bound, Home as Found.* The supposedly bachelor cousin of Edward Effingham, he is ultimately revealed to be the father of Paul Effingham. He is well educated, aloof, and often sardonic.

Effingham, Oliver. *The Pioneers.* British career officer (major) and pioneer settler who held the original land "patent" at the source of the Susquehanna River, in central New York. Father of Edward and grandfather of Edward Oliver Effingham, he was an early employer of Leather-Stocking. He is senile at the time of the novel.

Effingham, Paul. *Homeward Bound, Home as Found.* Before he is identified as the son of John Effingham, he is known by the surnames Blunt, Powis, and Assheton. The principal male romantic lead in both novels, he marries Eve Effingham.

Egerton, Lady. *Precaution.* See Jarvis, Mary.

Egerton, Henry. *Precaution.* Profligate nephew of Sir Edgar Egerton, he wooes Jane Moseley but elopes with Mary Jarvis. A baronet in civilian life and a colonel in the army, he dies at the Battle of Waterloo.

Elksfoot. *The Oak Openings.* Elderly Pottawattamie, he is killed and scalped by Pigeonswing.

Eltringham, Marquis of. *Precaution.* Brother of Lord Henry Stapleton and Lady Laura Stapleton and mock suitor of Caroline Harris.

Emery, Benoit. *The Headsman.* A peasant of Vaudois; regular donor to the Bernardine convent.

Emmerson. "Imagination." An affluent attorney in New York City, he is the brother of Margaret Emmerson and the father of Katherine Emmerson; mentioned.

Emmerson, Katherine. "Imagination." Cousin of the protagonist, Julia Warren.

Emmerson, Margaret. "Imagination." Aunt and guardian of the protagonist, Julia Warren.

Enrico. *The Bravo.* A gondolier who participates in the regatta.

Enrico. *The Bravo.* Otherwise unidentified senator serving in the Council of Three.

Enriquez, Don. *Mercedes of Castile.* See Henry IV.

Enriquez, Beatriz. *Mercedes of Castile.* An historical figure [Beatriz Enriquez de Harana], she is the mother of Ferdinand, the (illegitimate) second son of Christoval Colon; mentioned.

Erasmus. *The Water-Witch.* Black slave of Myndert Van Beverout.

Ergot, Dr. *The Wept of Wish-Ton-Wish.* Physician among the later settlers to come to Wish-Ton-Wish.

Estaban, Don. *Jack Tier.* Don Juan Montefalderon's Spanish name for Stephen Spike.

Etherington, Rev. Dr. *The Monikins.* Anglican rector, father of Anna and guardian of John Goldencalf.

Etherington, Mrs. *The Monikins.* Deceased wife of Rev. Dr. Etherington; mentioned.

Etherington, Anna. *The Monikins.* The only daughter of the widower Rev. Dr. Etherington and childhood companion of John Goldencalf, she eventually marries the young man.

Etienne. *The Headsman.* One of the muleteers accompanying the de Willading party through the Alps to Italy.

Euclid. *The Water-Witch.* Black slave of Myndert Van Beverout.

Eyelet, Mrs. *Le Mouchoir.* New York City socialite.

Farrel. *Wyandotté.* Personal servant of Robert Willoughby.

Ferdinand. *Mercedes of Castile.* Prince of Aragon and King of Sicily, this cold, calculating historical figure weds Isabella of Castile and, after his father's death, becomes Ferdinand II of Aragon and Ferdinand IV of Castile; also called Don Fernando.

Ferguson, Robert. *Afloat and Ashore.* Captain of the *Dundee,* a Scottish vessel which rescues Moses Marble from the sea.

Fernando, Don. *Mercedes of Castile.* See Ferdinand.

Ferreras. *Mercedes of Castile.* Officer careless with the funds of Ferdinand's entourage to Valladolid; mentioned.

Fid, Richard. *The Red Rover.* Fatherly retainer of Henry de Lacey and longtime companion of Scipio Africanus.

Filippo. *The Wing-and-Wing.* Genoese who serves as interpreter for Ithuel Bolt.

Fire-eater. *The Pioneers.* Epithet of the Indians for Major Oliver Effingham.

Fitzgerald. *Precaution*. Deceased husband of Julia Fitzgerald; mentioned.

Fitzgerald. *The Pilot*. A cornet in charge of a company of British dragoons.

Fitzgerald, Julia. *Precaution*. Beautiful widow of Major Fitzgerald, daughter of Conde d' Alzada, and friend of Charlotte Wilson and the younger Moseleys, she is materially aided by the Earl of Pendennyss.

Flanagan, Elizabeth (Betty). *The Spy*. Camp follower with heavy Irish accent who serves meals and drinks (as well as washes clothes) for the Virginia Dragoons. *The Pioneers*. Garrulous wife of Captain Hollister.

Flanagan, Michael. *The Spy*. First husband of Elizabeth Flanagan; mentioned.

Flint. *The Oak Openings*. Old corporal who accompanies Parson Amen, missionary to the Indians.

Flint, Hiram. *The Sea Lions*. Seaman on the *Sea Lion* of Oyster Point.

Flinty-Heart. *The Pathfinder*. Pathfinder's nickname for the French Captain Sanglier.

Flintyheart. *The Redskins*. An Iowa Indian chief visiting Susquesus.

Floating Tom. *The Deerslayer*. Nickname for Thomas Hovey (alias Hutter).

Florinda. *The Bravo*. Governess and chaperon of Violetta Tiepolo.

Florio. *Home as Found*. Pseudonym of a member of the New York City literati.

Flower of the Woods. *Wyandotté*. Wyandotté's epithet for Maud Meredith.

Floyd, Primus. *The Sea Lions*. Black cabin boy on the *Sea Lion* of Oyster Point.

Foley. *The Two Admirals*. Captain of the British warship *Thunderer* during the main action of the novel, he subsequently attains the rank of rear admiral.

Follock. *Satanstoe, The Chainbearer*. See Van Valkenburgh, Abraham.

Follock, Brom. *Afloat and Ashore*. Shortened, colloquial form of the name Abraham Van Valtenberg.

Follock, 'Brom. *Satanstoe, The Chainbearer*. See Van Valkenburgh, Abraham.

Follock, Dirck. *Satanstoe, The Chainbearer*. See Van Valkenburgh, Dirck.

Fonda. *Wyandotté*. Owner of a patent near that of Captain Willoughby; mentioned.

Fonseca [Don Juan de]. *Mercedes of Castile*. An historical figure, he is seen by Christoval Colon as an enemy to his cause at the Castilian court following the Admiral's first successful voyage to the Indies.

Foote, Mrs. John. *Afloat and Ashore*. New York City socialite mentioned by the Brighams.

Fordham, Francis (Frank). *Satanstoe*. Law student toasted by Mary Wallace; mentioned.

Francis. *Precaution.* Servant of Charlotte Wilson.

Francis. *The Monikins.* Butler in the Etherington household.

François. *The Water-Witch.* Elderly French valet, he is the personal servant of Alida de Barbérie.

Freeborn, Abraham. *The Pioneers.* Free Negro who conducts the annual Christmas-day turkey shoot.

Frey, Heinrich. *The Heidenmauer.* Burgomaster of Deurckheim.

Frey, Meta. *The Heidenmauer.* Daughter of Heinrich Frey, she is the female romantic lead who marries Berchthold Hintermayer.

Frey, Ulricke Hailzinger. *The Heidenmauer.* Wife of Heinrich Frey and mother of Meta, she is one of the strongest characters in the novel.

Friedrich, Duke. *The Heidenmauer.* Elector of Saxony, he does not appear in person in the novel, but his political fortunes affect the attitudes and behavior of subjects in his area.

Friedrich, Gisela. *The Heidenmauer.* Daughter of Karl Friedrich, she marries Gottlob Frinck.

Friedrich, Karl. *The Heidenmauer.* Warden at Count Emich Leininger's Castle of Hartenburg.

Frinck, Gottlob. *The Heidenmauer.* Cowherd for Count Emich Leininger, he is also a close friend of Berchthold Hintermayer, whom, at the end of the novel, he succeeds as the count's forester.

Frontoni, Jacopo. *The Bravo.* Titular hero of the novel, he is a scapegoat for the crimes of the Venetian senate.

Frontoni, Ricardo or Francesco. *The Bravo.* Political prisoner, he is the father of Jacopo Frontoni. The author calls him by both first names.

Fuller. "The Lake Gun." A curious traveler who visits Seneca Lake to investigate the legendary "Lake Gun" and "Wandering Jew."

Fun. *Home as Found.* Pseudonym of a member of the New York City literati.

Furlong. *The Two Admirals.* Attorney for Sir Wycherly Wychecombe, elderly baronet.

Gaine, Hugh. *Satanstoe.* Innkeeper of the Crown and Bible tavern in New York City.

Galapo, Benedetta. *The Wing-and-Wing.* Coquettish widow who operates a tavern at Portoferraio, Island of Elba.

Galleygo, David. *The Two Admirals.* Steward of Vice Admiral Sir Gervaise Oakes on his flagship, *Plantagenet.*

Gallios. *Miles Wallingford*. Captain of the French privateer *Pollison*.

Gamut, David. *The Last of the Mohicans*. Yankee instructor in sacred music, especially psalmody, he is at once devout and comic.

Le Garçon qui Bondi. *The Deerslayer*. See Bounding Boy.

Gardiner, Lyon. *The Sea Lions*. Prominent ancestor of Roswell Gardiner.

Gardiner, Roswell. *The Sea Lions*. Captain of the *Sea Lion* of Oyster Point, he marries Mary Pratt.

Garret. *The Redskins*. Deceased black servant of Jack Dunning; mentioned; normally called Garry.

Garry. *The Redskins*. See Garret.

Garth. *The Ways of the Hour*. District Attorney, prosecutor in the Mary Monson trials.

Gelsomina. *The Bravo*. Daughter of the prison keeper, she is the fiancée of Jacopo Frontoni. She goes insane at the execution of Jacopo.

Giacomo. *The Headsman*. Mentioned as innkeeper at Aoste, Italy.

Giorgio. *The Bravo*. Gondolier, assistant to Gino Monaldi.

Giraud, Antoine. *The Headsman*. The impersonator of Silenus at the revels in Vévey.

Girolamo, Father. *The Headsman*. The monk who cared for Bartolomeo during the latter's youth; on his deathbed he witnessed that Bartolomeo Contini (alias Maso) was fathered by Signor Gaetano Grimaldi.

Giron, Don Pedro. *Mercedes of Castile*. Third suitor for Isabella's hand; deceased at the time of the novel; also called Master of Calatrava and Pachecho.

Giulio. *The Bravo*. Otherwise unidentified senator who serves on the Council of Three.

Giuntotardi, Carlos. *The Wing-and-Wing*. Uncle of Ghita Caraccioli [Caracciolo], he is by trade a keeper of watchtowers on the Italian coast.

Glamorgan, Duchess of. *The Two Admirals*. Older sister of Agnes Hedworth and mother of Lord Geoffrey Cleveland. She is referred to simply as Duchess, no given name being cited.

Glass, Jack. *The Two Admirals*. A quartermaster on the *Plantagenet*, he is killed in action.

Goldencalf, Betsey. *The Monikins*. A foundling adopted by Thomas Goldencalf's master and married by Thomas Goldencalf, she is the mother of the narrator; she dies shortly after the narrator's birth.

Goldencalf, John. *The Monikins*. Only son of Thomas and Betsey Goldencalf and male romantic lead in the novel, he marries Anna Etherington.

Goldencalf, Thomas. *The Monikins*. A foundling apprenticed early to a merchant, he is the wealthy, mercenary father of John Goldencalf, the narrator; he dies early in the novel.

Goodfellow. *The Two Admirals*. Captain of the British warship *Warspite* during the main action of the novel, he subsequently attains the rank of rear admiral.

Goodwin, Dolly. *The Ways of the Hour*. See Goodwin, Dorothy.

Goodwin, Dorothy. *The Ways of the Hour*. Wife of Peter Goodwin, this avaricious woman dies when her house burns; also called Dolly.

Goodwin, Peter. *The Ways of the Hour*. Confirmed alcoholic for whose presumed murder Mary Monson is first tried.

Gordo, José. *Mercedes of Castile*. Seaman, Portuguese by birth but in the service of Spain; informs Colon of the Portuguese plan to intercept his westbound fleet near Ferro, in the Canary Islands.

Gosford, Earl of. *Precaution*. Esteemed friend and colleague of Roderic Benfield; frequently mentioned.

Gott. *The Ways of the Hour*. Sheriff of Duke's County.

Gott, Mrs. *The Ways of the Hour*. Compassionate wife of the Duke's County sheriff and jailor of Mary Monson.

Grab. *Homeward Bound*. English bailiff who boards the *Montauk* at Portsmouth in search of a debtor.

Gracie, Archibald. *Afloat and Ashore*. New York City businessman; mentioned.

Gradenigo, Alessandro. *The Bravo*. Senator, member of the Council of Three, he is the state-appointed guardian of Violetta Tiepolo. The last two honors are removed during the action of the novel.

Gradenigo, Giacomo. *The Bravo*. Reckless and dissolute son of Senator Alessandro Gradenigo. He is sent to the provinces for ten years for plotting against the life of Don Camillo Monforte.

Graham. *The Deerslayer*. British military surgeon.

Graham, Jeannie. *The Pathfinder*. Deceased first wife of Lieutenant David Muir; mentioned.

Grant, Rev. Mr. *The Pioneers*. Episcopal clergyman and temporary rector of St. Paul's Church. A permanent position for him in the Hudson River Valley is arranged by Judge Temple.

Grant, Louisa. *The Pioneers*. Daughter of the Rev. Mr. Grant and confidante of Elizabeth Temple.

Graves, [Lord Thomas]. *Lionel Lincoln*. An historical figure, he was the British admiral who evacuated royal troops from Boston during the Revolution.

Gray. *The Pilot*. Referred to usually as the Pilot, he is in reality John Paul Jones.

Gray. *Home as Found*. Pseudonym of a member of the New York City literati.

Grayson. *The Red Rover*. A British general, he is the brother of the Widow de Lacey and the father of Gertrude Grayson; mentioned.

Grayson, Gertrude. *The Red Rover*. Daughter of General Grayson, she eventually marries young Henry de Lacey.

Great Sachem. *The Monikins*. Elected administrator in the balance-of-powers government of Leaplow; mentioned.

Great Smash. *Wyandotté*. Nickname for Bess.

Green. *Homeward Bound*. Agent of the British firm from which Henry Sandon absconded with £40,000 of government funds.

Green. *The Ways of the Hour*. Attorney in Duke's County.

Green, Timothy. *The Sea Lions*. Second mate of the *Sea Lion* of Oyster Point.

Greene. *Afloat and Ashore*. Neighbor of Mrs. Bradfort; mentioned by the gossiping Brighams.

Greenleaf. *The Two Admirals*. Surgeon on the British warship *Achilles*.

Greenly. *The Two Admirals*. Captain of Vice Admiral Sir Gervaise Oakes's flagship, *Plantagenet*.

Greisenbach. *The Redskins*. Name assumed by Uncle Ro (Hugh Roger Littlepage the elder) in talking with Tom Miller; part of Littlepage's disguise as a German watch peddler.

Gridley, Dickey [Richard]. *Lionel Lincoln*. Chief military engineer in the Continental army; mentioned.

Griffin, Dick. *The Monikins*. Son of Sir Harry Griffin and friend of Anna Etherington; mentioned.

Griffin, Edward. *The Wing-and-Wing*. Second lieutenant on the British frigate *Proserpine*.

Griffin, Sir Harry. *The Monikins*. Class-conscious baronet who dies early in the novel; mentioned.

Griffin, Sir Harry [the younger]. *The Monikins*. Oldest son of Sir Harry Griffin; on succeeding to his father's title, he proposes to Anna Etherington but is refused.

Griffith, Edward. *The Pilot*. Lieutenant and later captain in the U.S. Navy, he is an educated man of means. He marries Cecilia Howard.

Grimaldi, Gaetano (Signor). *The Headsman*. Illustrious Doge of Genoa; lifelong friend of Melchior de Willading; widower of the unhappy Angiolina; father of Bartolomeo Contini (alias Maso) and Gaetano Grimaldi (alias Sigismund Steinbach).

Grimaldi, Gaetano [the younger]. *The Headsman*. Legitimate son of Signor Gaetano Grimaldi and Angiolina, he is abducted in infancy, is adopted by Balthazar and named Sigismund Steinbach, marries

Adelheid de Willading, and is eventually identified as the son of the Doge of Genoa.

Le Gros Serpent. *The Last of the Mohicans*. See Big Serpent.

Gross, Abijah. *Home as Found*. New York City socialite.

Guacanagari. *Mercedes of Castile*. An historical figure, he is the benevolent Great Cacique, the "king of kings," of Haiti to whom lesser caciques such as Mattinao pay tribute.

Guienne, Mons. de. *Mercedes of Castile*. Brother of King Louis of France and fourth suitor for Isabella's hand; mentioned.

Guinea. *The Red Rover*. Nickname of Scipio Africanus.

Gull. *Le Mouchoir*. Business partner of Bobbinet and Colonel Silky; mentioned.

Gutierrez, Pedro (Pero). *Mercedes of Castile*. See Bobadilla, Don Luis de.

Guzman, Mercedes de. *Mercedes of Castile*. Deceased mother of Mercedes de Valverde; mentioned.

Hale [Nathan]. *The Spy*. American spy (captain) captured and hanged, without trial, in 1776; mentioned.

Halfacre, Mrs. *Le Mouchoir*. Wife of millionaire speculator Henry Halfacre.

Halfacre, Eudosia. *Le Mouchoir*. Daughter in a nouveau riche family, she is one of the five people who, at different times, own the title character.

Halfacre, Henry. *Le Mouchoir*. Millionaire speculator in New York, he is, until his bankruptcy, a prominent member of the nouveaux riches.

Hall, Tim. *The Redskins*. Mechanic; rational, respected tenant at Ravensnest.

Hallam. *The Wept of Wish-Ton-Wish*. Agent of Charles II searching for regicides in the American colonies.

[Hamilton, Lady Emma]. *The Wing-and-Wing*. Mistress of Admiral Horatio Nelson, and wife of Sir William Hamilton, she plays an important role in the novel but is never mentioned by name.

Hamilton, Sir William. *The Wing-and-Wing*. Ambassador to Naples and husband of Lady Emma Hamilton, Admiral Nelson's mistress; mentioned.

Hammer. *Home as Found*. Broker on the New York Stock Exchange.

Handlead. *Homeward Bound*. English pilot who sails the *Montauk* out of Portsmouth.

Hard Heart. *The Last of the Mohicans*. Prominent chief among the Northern Delawares.

Hard-Heart. *The Prairie*. Pawnee chief who cares for Natty Bumppo in his last days.

Harding, John. *The Wept of Wish-Ton-Wish.* Father of Ruth Harding Heath-
    cote; mentioned.
Hardinge, Rev. Mr. *Afloat and Ashore, Miles Wallingford.* Rector of St.
    Michael's Episcopal Church, he is the father of Lucy and Rupert
    Hardinge.
Hardinge, Lucy. *Afloat and Ashore, Miles Wallingford.* Daughter of Rev. Mr.
    Hardinge and sister of Rupert Hardinge, she marries the protago-
    nist of the two novels, Miles Wallingford.
Hardinge, Rupert. *Afloat and Ashore, Miles Wallingford.* Son of Rev. Mr.
    Hardinge and brother of Lucy Hardinge, he is a self-centered and
    dastardly person.
Harland, Rev. Mr. *Precaution.* Young rector, shipboard companion of Lady
    Chatterton, John, Grace, and Emily Moseley, he wooes Jane
    Moseley but is rejected; he becomes Lord Harland (Count, of the
    Irish peerage) prior to his courtship.
Harmer. *Precaution.* In military service with George Denbigh (Earl of
    Pendennyss), he later becomes the Earl's personal attendant.
Harper. *The Spy.* Alias used by George Washington.
Harris. *Afloat and Ashore.* Crewman of the *Crisis* who is killed during a
    French attack.
Harris. *The Crater.* Crewman of the shipwrecked *Rancocus,* he is held
    captive by Waally until he escapes to join Mark Woolston's colony.
Harris, Caroline. *Precaution.* Showy daughter and pampered only child of
    Sir William Harris; subject of ridicule for her fruitless attempts to
    secure a husband from among the British peers.
Harris, Tom. *Satanstoe.* A young ensign, he is the friend of Anneke
    Mordaunt.
Harris, Sir William. *Precaution.* Owner of the Deanery, he is the wealthy,
    indulgent father of Caroline Harris.
Harrison, Richard. *Miles Wallingford.* Miles Wallingford's attorney in New
    York City.
Harry. *Precaution.* Gamekeeper of the Earl of Gosford; mentioned.
Hartmann, Frederick (Fritz). *The Pioneers.* Elderly descendant of German
    refugees who settled the Mohawk Valley during the reign of
    Queen Anne, he is a periodic guest at the mansion of Judge
    Temple. In his youth he knew Major Oliver Effingham and held
    the same military rank.
Hatfield. *The Ways of the Hour.* A country trader rejected by the defense as a
    juror in the first Mary Monson trial.
Haughton. *Precaution.* Good-natured, prosperous neighbor of the
    Moseleys and friend of Rev. Dr. Ives, he is the father of Lucy
    Haughton.

Haughton, Mrs. *Precaution*. Wife of Mr. Haughton and mother of Lucy.

Haughton, Lucy. *Precaution*. Good-natured only child of Mr. and Mrs. Haughton.

Havens, Sylvester. *The Sea Lions*. Seaman of the *Sea Lion* of Oyster Point.

Hawker, Mrs. *Home as Found*. Gracious elderly socialite in New York City.

Hawkeye. *The Deerslayer, The Last of the Mohicans, The Pioneers*. Indian epithet for Natty Bumppo.

Hayden, Onesiphorus. *The Redskins*. Chairman of the anti-renters' Sunday public meeting approving a set of resolutions submitted to young Hugh Roger Littlepage.

Haynes, Katharine (Katy). *The Spy*. Housekeeper for years for the Birch family and would-be wife of Harvey Birch, she later is employed in the Wharton and Dunwoodie households.

Hazard, Philip. *The Sea Lions*. First mate on the *Sea Lion* of Oyster Point.

Hazleton. *The Chainbearer*. A colonel in the British artillery, he is the great-uncle of Priscilla and Thomas Bayard; mentioned.

Hazleton, Priscilla. *The Chainbearer*. Great-aunt and godmother of Priscilla and Thomas Bayard; mentioned.

Heald. *The Oak Openings*. Captain in command of the American forces in Chicago at the time of its surrender to the British during the War of 1812.

Heath, [William]. *The Spy*. An historical figure, he is the commanding general in the Highlands area above the Hudson River; mentioned.

Heathcote. *Satanstoe*. An acquaintance of Captain Hugh Littlepage; mentioned.

Heathcote, Content. *The Wept of Wish-Ton-Wish*. The only child of Captain Mark Heathcote, he succeeds his father as leader at Wish-Ton-Wish and also attains the rank of captain. He is the father of the captive girl who becomes the "wept" of Wish-Ton-Wish.

Heathcote, Mark. *The Wept of Wish-Ton-Wish*. Formerly a captain in the army of Cromwell, he is a Puritan leader who, with his family and followers, left Massachusetts Bay Colony to resettle for a second time in the Connecticut Territory.

Heathcote, Mark. *The Wept of Wish-Ton-Wish*. Grandson of Captain Mark Heathcote and son of Content and Ruth Harding Heathcote, he marries Martha, the adopted child of his parents.

Heathcote, Martha. *The Wept of Wish-Ton-Wish*. An orphan, she is adopted at an early age by Content and Ruth Harding Heathcote. She marries their son, Mark.

Heathcote, Ruth. *The Wept of Wish-Ton-Wish*. Daughter of Content and

Ruth Harding Heathcote, she is referred to as the "wept" of Wish-Ton-Wish after her captivity by the Narragansetts. She is married to the Narragansett sachem, Conanchet, to whom she bears a son. Her Indian name is Narra-mattah.

Heathcote, Ruth Harding. *The Wept of Wish-Ton-Wish.* Married to Content Heathcote at the beginning of the novel, she is the mother of Ruth, the "wept" of Wish-Ton-Wish.

Heaton, John. *The Crater.* A physician married to Anne Woolston, he becomes a member of Mark Woolston's colony in the Pacific.

Hedworth, Agnes. *The Two Admirals.* Mother of Mildred Bluewater, sister of the Duchess of Glamorgan, and wife (by secret marriage) of John Bluewater, she is a key to much of the novel though dead years before the central action; mentioned frequently.

Heidegger, Walter. *The Red Rover.* The notorious pirate known as the Red Rover, captain of the ship *Red Rover.*

Henley. "Heart." Father of the protagonist, Charlotte Henley.

Henley, Mrs. "Heart." Mother of the protagonist, Charlotte Henley.

Henley, Charlotte. "Heart." The beautiful and sensitive protagonist of the story, she remains single after her one love, George Morton, dies in youth.

Hennequin, Mlle. *Le Mouchoir.* Assumed name of Adrienne de la Rocheaimard.

Henri. *The Headsman.* A servant of the Bernardine convent.

Henry IV. *Mercedes of Castile.* King of Castile, in Spain, this historical figure dies early in the novel; also called Don Enriquez.

Herriefield, Lord. *Precaution.* Viscount and distant relative of Lady Chatterton, this elderly debauchee weds Catherine Chatterton.

Herriefield, Lady. *Precaution.* See Chatterton, Catherine.

Herring, Luke. *Wyandotté.* Suitor for the hand of Maud Meredith; mentioned.

Hester. *The Redskins.* The cook at Ravensnest.

Hewlett, Demosthenes. *The Redskins.* Speaker at the anti-renters' Sunday public meeting at Ravensnest.

Heyward, Alice Munro. *The Last of the Mohicans.* Younger daughter of Colonel Munro, born to him by his first love but second wife, Alice Graham. She marries Duncan Heyward.

Heyward, Duncan. *The Last of the Mohicans.* Major in the British army, he is second in command at Fort William Henry. He marries Alice Munro.

Hicks. *The Ways of the Hour.* Resident of Biberry.

Hight, Joe. *Satanstoe.* A major in the British army, he is an old friend of Hugh Littlepage.

Hightail. *The Monikins.* Contemptuous young monikin noble, a friend of Lord Chatterino.

Hillson. *The Crater.* Incompetent second mate of the *Rancocus.*

Hintermayer, Berchthold. *The Heidenmauer.* The only child of Lottchen Hintermayer, he is the male romantic lead in the novel.

Hintermayer, Lottchen. *The Heidenmauer.* Widowed and financially ruined member of the burgher class in Deurckheim, she is the mother of Berchthold Hintermayer.

Hiram. *The Wept of Wish-Ton-Wish.* Settler at Wish-Ton-Wish.

Hist-oh-Hist. *The Deerslayer.* See Wah-ta-Wah.

Hitchcock, Nathan. *Miles Wallingford.* Yankee crewman on the *Dawn.*

Hitchcox, Jane. *Afloat and Ashore.* Sister-in-law of Wallace Mortimer Brigham.

Hofmeister, Peter. *The Headsman.* The hereditary bailiff of Vévey; long-time associate of Melchior de Willading; also called Peterchen.

Hollis, Rev. Mr. *Jack Tier.* Chaplain on the U.S. cruiser *Poughkeepsie.*

Hollister. *The Spy.* A sergeant, he is the only noncommissioned officer of the Virginia Dragoons mentioned by name. *The Pioneers.* Proprietor of the Bold Dragoon tavern and commander of the local militia, he is now called Captain Hollister.

Holmes. *The Redskins.* Tenant farmer at Ravensnest.

Holt. *Precaution.* Elderly friend and neighbor of Sir Edgar Egerton.

Holt, Andrew. *The Pioneers.* English attorney for Colonel Edward Effingham, he does not appear personally but only through his letters.

Homespun, Desire. *The Red Rover.* Termagant wife of Hector Homespun.

Homespun, Hector. *The Red Rover.* Lame tailor with the stereotyped cowardice of his trade, he nevertheless tries to assume heroic stature.

Honest Joe. *The Red Rover.* Ironic nickname of Joe Joram.

Honeysuckle. *The Wept of Wish-Ton-Wish.* Indian epithet for the captive Ruth Heathcote.

Honeysuckle of the Hills. *The Deerslayer.* Epithet applied to Wah-ta-Wah by her Delaware admirers.

Hoof, Stephen. *The Ways of the Hour.* Coachman of Dr. McBrain.

Hook, Stephen. *The Ways of the Hour.* A country loafer; mentioned.

Hopkins, Pardon. *The Red Rover.* Countryman whose conversation with Hector Homespun provides exposition at the opening of the novel.

Hopper. *Lionel Lincoln.* Crippled man with whom Lionel talks upon his arrival in Boston from England.

Hopper. *The Water-Witch.* Midshipman on the cruiser *Coquette.*

Hornblower, Rev. Mr. *The Crater*. Episcopalian clergyman who joins Mark
    Woolston's colony.
Horton, Daniel. *The Ways of the Hour*. Tavern owner in Biberry; men-
    tioned.
Horton, Nancy. *The Ways of the Hour*. Wife of Daniel Horton, she provides
    a key witness following Mary Monson's first trial.
Hosack, Dr. *Afloat and Ashore*. Physician mentioned by the Brighams.
Hosea. *The Bravo*. Jewish jeweler and moneylender, he is banished from
    Venice for his complicity in a plot against the life of Don Camillo
    Monforte.
Hosmer. *The Chainbearer*. A Baptist tenant at Ravensnest.
Houston, Mrs. *Home as Found*. Prominent New York City socialite.
Hover, Paul. *The Prairie*. A "bee hunter" along the frontier, he becomes
    the friend of Natty Bumppo and the husband of Ellen Wade.
Hovey, Thomas. *The Deerslayer*. A former pirate who uses the alias
    Thomas Hutter, he is the stepfather of Judith and Hetty Hutter.
    He is the first white man to settle at Lake Glimmerglass.
Howard, Captain. *The Red Rover*. One of the many aliases used by Walter
    Heidegger, the Red Rover.
Howard, Miss. *Precaution*. Elderly bridesmaid of Laura Stapleton.
Howard, Cecilia. *The Pilot*. An orphan, she lives with her uncle and
    guardian, Colonel Howard. She married Edward Griffith.
Howard, George. *The Pilot*. A retired colonel and a Tory, he returns to
    England from South Carolina during the Revolution. He is the
    guardian of his niece, Cecilia Howard, and of Katherine Plowden.
    Held hostage aboard an American frigate, he is killed by a shell
    fired by a British warship.
Howe, [William]. *Lionel Lincoln, Wyandotté, Satanstoe*. An historical figure, he
    was the British general who directed the evacuation of Boston;
    prominent during the first three years of the Revolution.
Howel, Thomas. *Home as Found*. An extreme Anglophile, he is an old friend
    of the Effinghams in Templeton.
Howell, Bell. *Precaution*. See Ives, Isabel.
Howell, Peter. *Precaution*. Deceased admiral, he was the maternal grand-
    father of Francis Ives; mentioned.
Hubbard. *The Redskins*. Attorney at Mooseridge; confirmed anti-renter.
Hubbs. *The Ways of the Hour*. Gossipy resident of Biberry; usually called
    Sam Tongue.
Hubert. *The Redskins*. German personal servant of young Hugh Roger
    Littlepage; mentioned.
Hugo. *The Heidenmauer*. Youthful monk at the Abbey of Limburg, he is the
    nephew of Father Arnolph.

Huguenin, Kitty. *Miles Wallingford.* Granddaughter of Mrs. Wetmore and niece of Moses Marble, she marries Horace Bright.

Hull, [William]. *The Oak Openings.* An historical figure, he was the governor of the Michigan Territory. He was also the general who was forced to surrender Detroit to the British during the War of 1812.

Humphreys. *Precaution.* Aged pensioner aided by George Denbigh (Earl of Pendennyss).

Hurry Harry. *The Deerslayer.* Nickname of Henry March.

Hurry Skurry. *The Deerslayer.* Nickname of Henry March.

Huskisson. *The Monikins.* Political sponsor in England for matters of mercantile policy; mentioned.

Hutter, Hetty. *The Deerslayer.* Younger stepdaughter of Thomas Hovey (alias Hutter), she is innocent, sweet-tempered, pious, but feeble-minded. Christened Esther, she is never called by that name.

Hutter, Judith. *The Deerslayer.* Elder stepdaughter of Thomas Hovey (alias Hutter). She is beautiful, courageous, and vivacious, but her prospect for happiness is ruined after a youthful affair taints her reputation.

Hutter, Thomas. *The Deerslayer.* Alias for Thomas Hovey.

Ignatius, Father. *The Prairie.* Priest who marries Inez and Captain Middleton.

Ilse. *The Heidenmauer.* Aged and verbose nurse of Meta Frey.

Indian John. *The Pioneers.* Pejorative epithet for Chingachgook or John Mohegan.

Inesella. *The Prairie.* Nurse of Inez Augustin Middleton.

Isabella. *Mercedes of Castile.* Half sister of Henry IV, this devout historical personage, occupying the throne of Castile, marries Ferdinand of Aragon and sponsors Columbus's discovery of the Indies; also called Doña Ysabel and the Catholic Queen.

Ives, Rev. Dr. *Precaution.* Parish rector; long-term friend of the Denbigh family and of the Moseleys, he is the husband of Isabel Ives (née Howell) and the father of Francis.

Ives, Francis (Frank). *Precaution.* A minister, the son of Rev. Dr. and Mrs. Ives, he marries Clara Moseley.

Ives, Isabel (Bell). *Precaution.* Only daughter of the late Admiral Peter Howell, she is the wife of Rev. Dr. Ives and the mother of Francis.

Jaaf. *The Redskins.* See Satanstoe, Jacob.

Jaap. *Satanstoe.* See Satanstoe, Jacob.

Jackson. *Precaution*. Former butler of the Moseleys' household, he is master of the Moseley Arms inn.

Jacob. *The Redskins*. Free Negro serving Hugh Roger Littlepage the elder; great-grandson of Jacob Satanstoe (Jaap).

Jacques. *The Wing-and-Wing*. Coxswain on the *Feu-Follet*.

Jarvis. *Home as Found*. New York City merchant and husband of the socialite Jane Jarvis.

Jarvis, Lady. *Precaution*. See Jarvis, Mrs. Timothy.

Jarvis, Henry (Harry). *Precaution*. A captain in the army, he is the son of Timothy Jarvis. To his family's annoyance, he marries an unnamed girl from an untitled family.

Jarvis, Jane. *Home as Found*. New York City socialite.

Jarvis, Mary. *Precaution*. Imperious older daughter of Mr. and Mrs. Timothy Jarvis, she elopes with Colonel Egerton; also called Polly; she assumes the title of Lady Egerton after her marriage.

Jarvis, Polly. *Precaution*. See Jarvis, Mary.

Jarvis, Sally. *Precaution*. See Jarvis, Sarah.

Jarvis, Sarah. *Precaution*. Younger daughter of Mr. and Mrs. Timothy Jarvis; also called Sally.

Jarvis, Timothy. *Precaution*. Honest, wealthy retired merchant, the husband of Mrs. Jarvis and father of Harry, Mary, and Sarah, he is subsequently Sir Timothy Jarvis.

Jarvis, Mrs. Timothy. *Precaution*. Ill-bred wife of Timothy Jarvis and mother of Harry, Mary, and Sarah, she assumes the title Lady Jarvis after her husband's elevation to Sir Timothy.

Jaw, John. *The Monikins*. Deceased monikin political agitator; mentioned.

Jenkins. *The Sea Lions*. Crewman on the *Sea Lion* of Martha's Vineyard.

Jennie. *The Pathfinder*. Wife of one Sandy of the British 55th Regiment, she is killed and scalped shortly after the same fate befalls her husband.

Jenny. *Home as Found*. Servant of Mrs. Abbott.

Jette. *The Ways of the Hour*. Deceased German housemaid of the Goodwins; also called Yetty.

Jim. *The Sea Lions*. Waterfront loafer at Oyster Point.

Joanna of Portugal. *Mercedes of Castile*. The second wife of Henry IV, this historical figure is merely mentioned.

Joanna, La Beltraneja. *Mercedes of Castile*. This historical figure, daughter of Joanna of Portugal and stepdaughter of Henry IV of Castile, defeated pretender to the Castilian throne, becomes a nun; mentioned.

João, Dom. *Mercedes of Castile*. See John II.

Job, Sir Joseph. *The Monikins*. A colleague of Thomas Goldencalf and dealer in stocks on the London Exchange, he commits suicide following his business failure.

Joe. *Afloat and Ashore*. Black cook on the *Crisis;* also called Yo.

Joe. *The Sea Lions*. Negro sea cook on the *Sea Lion* of Martha's Vineyard.

Johan, Father. *The Heidenmauer*. Fanatic and vindictive Benedictine monk, he dies in the flames which consume the church at the Abbey of Limburg.

John. *Precaution*. Coachman of Caroline Harris.

John. *The Redskins*. English footman in service at Ravensnest.

John II. *Mercedes of Castile*. King of Aragon, in Spain, and father of Ferdinand, this historical figure dies early in the novel; mentioned; also called John of Trastamara and Don Juan of Aragon.

John II. *Mercedes of Castile*. This historical figure, the King of Portugal, refuses to support the proposal of Christoval Colon for discovery of the Indies by sailing westward; also called Dom João.

John of Trastamara. *Mercedes of Castile*. See John II (King of Aragon).

John, Prestor [sic]. *Mercedes of Castile*. Twelfth-century legendary figure assumed to have established a Christian empire in the Orient; mentioned.

Johnson. *The Crater*. Crewman of the shipwrecked *Rancocus,* he is held captive by Waally until he escapes to join the colony of Mark Woolston.

Johnson. *The Ways of the Hour*. One of Timms's agents in Biberry.

Johnson, Sir John. *Wyandotté*. An historical figure, he was the son of Sir William Johnson; mentioned.

Johnson, Peter. *Precaution*. Compassionate steward and personal friend of his master, Roderic Benfield.

Johnson, Sir William. *Wyandotté*. An historical figure, he was an Indian trader and the superintendent of Indian affairs in central and western New York. A powerful and wealthy person; mentioned several times.

Joker, Jack. *The Pilot*. An American sailor.

Jones. *Precaution*. Female servant of the Jarvises.

Jones. *Precaution*. A captain in the regiment of Captain Jarvis; mentioned.

Jones. *The Crater*. Refugee from a whaler, he is captured by Waally, from whom he escapes to join Mark Woolston's Pacific colony.

Jones, Mrs. *The Ways of the Hour*. Clergyman's wife who temporarily houses Mary Monson.

Jones, Jared. *Miles Wallingford*. Miller at Clawbonny.

[Jones, John Paul]. *The Pilot.* An historical figure. Of the three characters who know his name, none ever uses his surname, and only one, his betrothed, uses his given name. His actions and the context in which they occur identify him unmistakably. He is always called the Pilot or Mr. Gray by everyone but Alice Dunscombe, his estranged fiancée.

Jones, Richard. *The Pioneers.* Cousin of Judge Temple. He manages the minor business affairs of the Temple household and is ultimately rewarded with a sheriff's commission.

Joram, Joe. *The Red Rover.* Seemingly pious, he is the hypocritical owner of the Foul Anchor inn and an agent of the Red Rover.

Joram, 'Keziah. *The Red Rover.* Wife of "Honest Joe" Joram.

Josef. *The Wing-and-Wing.* Seaman on the *Feu-Follet.*

Josh. *Jack Tier.* Negro steward on the *Molly Swash.*

Joyce. *Wyandotté.* A British sergeant who served under Captain Willoughby, he becomes an employee of Willoughby at the Hutted Knoll. After the captain's death, he accepts an appointment in the new American army.

Juan. *Mercedes of Castile.* Son of Pepe, a mariner with Christoval Colon, and his wife Monica; mentioned.

Juan of Aragon, Don. *Mercedes of Castile.* See John II (King of Aragon).

Judy. *The Red Rover.* Negro servant girl at the Foul Anchor inn.

Juliana, Lady. *Precaution.* Idolized and often-mentioned only love of Roderic Benfield, she is eventually seen as the dissolute Dowager Viscountess Haverford.

Julietta. *Home as Found.* Member of the New York City literati.

Jumper. *Satanstoe.* See Quissquiss.

June. *The Pathfinder.* Shortened form of Dew-of-June's name.

Juno. *Satanstoe.* Mrs. Legge's slave; mentioned.

Juno. *The Crater.* Slave of Bridget Yardley, she marries the Kannaka Unus.

Kant. *Home as Found.* A member of the New York City literati, he is always referred to as Captain Kant.

Katrinke. *Satanstoe.* An elderly slave of Anneke Mordaunt.

Kettletas. *The Chainbearer.* Husband of Mordaunt Littlepage's sister Anneke; mentioned.

Kettletas, Anneke Littlepage. *The Chainbearer.* Older sister of Mordaunt Littlepage; married to Mr. Kettletas before the beginning of the novel.

Keys, Phoebe. *The Two Admirals.* Housekeeper at Wychecombe Hall employed by elderly Sir Wycherly Wychecombe; mentioned.

Kingsborough. *The Ways of the Hour.* Legal client of Thomas Dunscomb; mentioned.

Kingsland, Ira. *The Ways of the Hour.* Twelfth juror empaneled for Mary Monson's first trial.

Kirby, Billy. *The Pioneers.* Hearty, good-natured Yankee woodman.

Kite. *Afloat and Ashore.* Second mate on the *John.*

Knighthead, Francis. *The Red Rover.* Second mate on the *Royal Caroline.*

Kunigunde. *The Heidenmauer.* Daughter of Count Emich Leininger; mentioned.

Lamb, Meek. *The Wept of Wish-Ton-Wish.* A descendant of Meek Wolfe, he too serves as minister at Wish-Ton-Wish. Removed from his harsh ancestor by more than a century in time, he is equally distant from him in temperament.

Lap-Ear. *The Deerslayer.* Delaware sobriquet for the youthful Natty Bumppo.

Larder. *The Two Admirals.* Cook at Wychecombe Hall.

Larocheforte, Madame de. *The Ways of the Hour.* See Millington, Mildred.

Larocheforte, Gabriel Jules Vincent Jean Baptiste de. *The Ways of the Hour.* Estranged husband of Mildred Millington (alias Mary Monson).

Last of the Mohicans, The. *The Last of the Mohicans.* Uncas, son of Chingachgook, he is not literally the last of his tribe but the last male member of its ruling family, the family which long ruled also the entire Delaware nation.

Latouche, Abbé. *The Heidenmauer.* A quasi-religious person, he is a politician within the church organization. Count Emich Leininger invites him to Hartenburg Castle to lend an air of religious respectability to that nobleman's designs on the property of the Abbey of Limburg.

Lawton, John. *The Spy.* Captain and second in command of the Virginia Dragoons, he is killed late in the Revolutionary War.

Le Compte. *Afloat and Ashore.* Captain of the wrecked French vessel *Pauline* and briefly of the captive *Crisis.* He is killed when the Americans recapture the *Crisis.*

Le Gros. *Miles Wallingford.* The officer on the French privateer *Pollison* who becomes the "prize master" of the captive *Dawn.*

Le Quoi. *The Pioneers.* French political exile, a refugee from the Reign of Terror, he operates a small general store in Templeton.

Leach, Thomas. *Homeward Bound, Home as Found.* First mate on the *Montauk.*

Leamington, Mrs. *Le Mouchoir.* New York City socialite; mentioned.

Leaping Panther. *The Wept of Wish-Ton-Wish.* Epithet for Miantonimoh.

Leather-Stocking. *The Pioneers.* Epithet for Natty Bumppo.

Lechmere, John. *Lionel Lincoln.* Deceased husband of Priscilla Lechmere; mentioned.

Lechmere, Priscilla. *Lionel Lincoln.* Aged widow of John Lechmere, she is the grandmother of the female romantic lead, Cecil Dynevor. She is also the villainess of the novel.

Lee. *The Sea Lions.* Youthful ship carpenter on the *Sea Lion* of Martha's Vineyard.

Lee, Charles. *Satanstoe.* A British army captain, he serves in the colony of New York.

Legend, Mrs. *Home as Found.* Patroness of the New York City literati.

Legge. *Satanstoe.* Corny Littlepage's uncle, a lawyer taking the popular side in politics.

Legge, Jane. *Satanstoe.* Corny Littlepage's maternal aunt on Manhattan Island.

Leininger, Emich. *The Heidenmauer.* Count of Hartenburg, he represents both the strengths and the weaknesses of the feudal aristocracy of Germany.

Leo. *Lionel Lincoln.* Nickname of Lionel Lincoln.

Light, Mrs. *Satanstoe, The Chainbearer.* Garrulous landlady at Kingsbridge inn, near Lilacsbush.

Lilacsbush, Miss. *The Chainbearer.* See Satanstoe, Mrs. Jacob.

Lily. *The Pathfinder.* Indian sobriquet for Mabel Dunham.

Lily of Clawbonny. *Miles Wallingford.* Epithet applied to Grace Wallingford, Miles's sister.

Lincoln, Lionel. *Lionel Lincoln.* An American by birth, he is a major in the British army during the Revolution. He is the son of Sir Lionel and inherits his father's title. The male romantic lead, he marries Cecil Dynevor.

Lincoln, Sir Lionel. *Lionel Lincoln.* A wronged man, he suffers intermittent fits of insanity. He is the father of the titular hero.

Lincoln, Priscilla. *Lionel Lincoln.* Deceased wife of Sir Lionel Lincoln, she was the mother of the titular hero; mentioned.

Lippet, Chester. *The Pioneers.* Lawyer who defends Natty Bumppo during his trial.

Little, Mrs. John. *Afloat and Ashore.* Salem lady living in New York, she corresponds with Mrs. Brigham while the latter is in Europe.

Little Jarvy. *The Two Admirals.* Sentimental sobriquet for Vice Admiral Sir Gervaise Oakes used, when no officers are present, by the sailors of his fleet.

Little Nel. *The Wing-and-Wing.* Nickname for Admiral Horatio Nelson.

Little Smash. *Wyandotté.* Nickname for Desdemona.

Littlepage, Madam. *Satanstoe, The Chainbearer.* Mother of Cornelius Littlepage and wife of Major Evans Littlepage; subsequently, widow of General Evans Littlepage and paternal grandmother of Anneke, Mordaunt and Katrinke Littlepage.

Littlepage, Cornelius. *Satanstoe, The Chainbearer, The Redskins.* Narrator and hero of *Satanstoe;* son of Major (later General) Evans Littlepage; lifelong friend of Dirck Van Valkenburgh; eventually husband of Anna Cornelia (Anneke) Mordaunt; usually called Corny; subsequently serves in Revolutionary War, awarded rank of brigadier general; father of Anneke, Mordaunt, and Katrinke. In *The Redskins* he is only mentioned.

Littlepage, Evans. *Satanstoe, The Chainbearer, The Redskins.* A major and later a general in the colonial British army, he is a respected member of the minor gentry in New York State. He dies of smallpox during the Revolution. In *The Redskins* he is only mentioned.

Littlepage, Evans. *Satanstoe.* Firstborn son of Major Evans Littlepage; died in infancy; mentioned.

Littlepage, Hodge. *Satanstoe.* See Littlepage, Hugh Roger [first Littlepage with these given names].

Littlepage, Hodge. *The Redskins.* See Littlepage, Hugh Roger, the elder.

Littlepage, Hugh Roger. *Satanstoe.* The first Littlepage with these given names, he is the grandfather of Cornelius Littlepage. He is also called Hodge.

Littlepage, Hugh Roger [the elder]. *The Redskins.* Second son of Mordaunt and Ursula Malbone Littlepage; uncle of Hugh Roger Littlepage the younger; inherits Satanstoe and Lilacsbush; also called Ro, Roger, Hodge, and Greisenbach.

Littlepage, Hugh Roger [the younger]. *The Redskins.* Son of Malbone Littlepage (deceased), and narrator of the novel; nephew of Hugh Roger Littlepage the elder; inherits Ravensnest; marries Mary Warren.

Littlepage, Kate. *The Chainbearer.* See Littlepage, Katrinke.

Littlepage, Katrinke. *The Chainbearer.* Younger sister of Mordaunt Littlepage and close friend of Priscilla Bayard; marries Thomas Bayard; usually called Kate.

Littlepage, Malbone. *The Redskins.* First son of Mordaunt and Ursula Malbone Littlepage and father of Hugh Roger Littlepage the younger, narrator of the novel; deceased; mentioned.

Littlepage, Martha. *The Redskins.* Sister of Hugh Roger Littlepage the younger; also called Patt and Patty.

Littlepage, Mordaunt. *Satanstoe, The Chainbearer, The Redskins*. Son of Cornelius and Anneke Mordaunt Littlepage (merely mentioned in *Satanstoe*), narrator of the novel *The Chainbearer;* brother of Anneke and Katrinke, and eventually husband of Ursula Malbone; attained rank of major at end of Revolutionary War; usually called Mordy; grandfather of Hugh Roger Littlepage [the younger], narrator of *The Redskins;* mentioned in *The Redskins*.

Littlepage, Patt (or Patty). *The Redskins*. See Littlepage, Martha.

Littlepage, Ro. *The Redskins*. See Littlepage, Hugh Roger, the elder.

Littlepage, Roger. *The Redskins*. See Littlepage, Hugh Roger, the elder.

Liturgy, Rev. Dr. *Lionel Lincoln*. Anglican clergyman, he is the rector of King's Chapel, Boston.

Liturgy, Rev. Dr. *The Monikins*. A colleague of Rev. Dr. Etherington; mentioned.

Livingston, Cato. *The Sea Lions*. Black cook on the *Sea Lion* of Oyster Point.

Livingston, R. N. [R.] *Afloat and Ashore*. An historical figure, this American minister to France helped negotiate the Louisiana Purchase; mentioned.

Llera, Conde de. *Mercedes of Castile*. See Bobadilla, Don Luis de.

Locker. *The Two Admirals*. Personal servant of Sir Gervaise Oakes.

Long Rifle. *The Last of the Mohicans*. Epithet for Natty Bumppo.

Longbeard, Baron. *The Monikins*. Chief justice of the High Criminal Court of Leaphigh.

Longinus. *Home as Found*. Pseudonym of a member of the New York City literati.

La Longue Carabine. The Last of the Mohicans. See Long Rifle.

Loping Dominie. *Satanstoe*. See Worden, Rev. Mr. Thomas.

Lord, Daniel. *The Ways of the Hour*. Colleague of Thomas Dunscomb.

Lorenza, Donna. *Precaution*. Widow of a Spanish officer and companion to Julia Fitzgerald.

Lorraine, Duke of. *Mercedes of Castile*. Rebellious Catalan leader; mentioned.

Le Loup Cervier. The Deerslayer. See Lynx.

Ludlow, Cornelius Van Cuyler. *The Water-Witch*. Captain of the British cruiser *Coquette*, he is the principal representative of royal authority. He marries Alida de Barbérie.

Ludwig. *The Heidenmauer*. Latin secretary for the town of Deurckheim.

Luff. *The Water-Witch*. Lieutenant on the cruiser *Coquette*.

Luis. *Mercedes of Castile*. See Bobadilla, Luis de.

Lumley. *Precaution*. See Denbigh, George (Earl of Pendennyss).

Lumley, Lord. *Precaution*. See Denbigh, George (Earl of Pendennyss).

Lumley, Marian. *Precaution*. Countess of Pendennyss and sole surviving child of the last Duke of Annerdale, she marries George Denbigh (son of General Frederick Denbigh) and bears George Denbigh (the Earl of Pendennyss) and Marian Denbigh; deceased before the novel begins.

Luther, Martin. *The Heidenmauer*. An historical figure, he was the monk of Wittenberg who initiated the Reformation. He does not appear in person in the novel, but his religious activity is discussed by his contemporaries, and it influences the course of the story.

Lynx. *The Deerslayer*. A Huron brave, the first human being killed by Natty Bumppo. He gives Natty the name Hawkeye.

Lynx, Vigilance. *The Monikins*. The duenna of Lady Chatterissa; both are monkeys (monikins).

Lyon. *The Wing-and-Wing*. Commander of the British sloop-of-war *Ringdove*.

McBean, Archy. *The Wing-and-Wing*. Lieutenant on the British sloop-of-war *Ringdove*.

McBrain, Dr. Edward. *The Ways of the Hour*. Close friend of Thomas Dunscomb and a key witness at the inquest and at Mary Monson's murder trials, he marries Widow Anna Updyke early in the novel.

McCarthy, Señora. *Precaution*. Deceased maternal grandmother of Julia Fitzgerald; mentioned.

M'Carthy y Harrison, Louis. *Precaution*. A general, he is the maternal uncle of Julia Fitzgerald.

M'Dee, Lord. *The Monikins*. Young Scottish viscount whose matrimonial proposal is rejected by Anna Etherington; mentioned.

M'Fuse, Dennis. *Lionel Lincoln*. Captain of the Royal Irish Grenadiers, he is shot by Job Pray at the Battle of Bunker Hill.

McGosh. *The Sea Lions*. Condemned pirate who reveals to Thomas Daggett the location of his buried treasure; mentioned.

McNab. *The Pathfinder*. Corporal of the British 55th Regiment, he is killed at a French and Indian ambush on one of the Thousand Islands.

McSwale, Terence. *Miles Wallingford*. Irish fisherman.

M'Twill, Sawny. *The Spy*. Suitor for the hand of Elizabeth Flanagan during her youth; mentioned.

Macy. *The Sea Lions*. First mate on the *Sea Lion* of Martha's Vineyard.

McYarn, Sandy. *The Two Admirals*. Master's mate on the British warship *Plantagenet*.

Magnet. *The Pathfinder*. Charles Cap's term of endearment for his niece, Mabel Dunham.

Magrath. *The Two Admirals*. Surgeon on the British warship *Plantagenet*.

Magua. *The Last of the Mohicans*. Huron chief who returns from exile among the Mohawks to head his people in support of the French in 1757. He is the principal antagonist of the novel.

Mahhah. *The Prairie*. Teton Sioux warrior slain by Hard-Heart.

Mahtoree. *The Prairie*. Teton Sioux chief, he is the chief antagonist to both the Pawnees and the white characters in the novel.

Malbone, Bob. *The Chainbearer*. Opportunistic father (deceased) of Ursula Malbone; mentioned.

Malbone, Dus (Duss). *The Chainbearer*. See Malbone, Ursula.

Malbone, Francis. *The Chainbearer*. Half brother of Ursula Malbone and eventually husband of Priscilla Bayard; usually called Frank.

Malbone, Frank. *The Chainbearer*. See Malbone, Francis.

Malbone, Ursula. *The Chainbearer, The Redskins*. Orphaned niece and ward of Andries Coejemans (Chainbearer), former schoolmate of Priscilla Bayard, and eventually wife of Mordaunt Littlepage; usually called Dus or Duss; mother of bachelor Hugh Roger Littlepage and grandmother of Hugh Roger Littlepage the younger, narrator of *The Redskins*.

Il Maledetto ["The Accursed"]. *The Headsman*. See Contini, Bartolomeo.

Manual. *The Pilot*. Captain of a marine company on an American frigate and later an army officer. He is killed, ironically, by one of his own sentinels.

Manytongues. *The Redskins*. Interpreter for the Indians visiting Susquesus.

Marble, Moses. *Afloat and Ashore, Miles Wallingford*. See Wetmore, Oloff Van Duzer.

Marcelli, Enrico. *The Headsman*. The traveling companion of Gaetano Grimaldi.

March, Henry. *The Deerslayer*. Handsome giant whose reckless and immoral behavior reflects the negative characteristics of frontiersmen as Natty Bumppo's qualities reflect the positive.

Marchena, Father Juan Perez de. *Mercedes of Castile*. A friar esteemed by and loyal to Christoval Colon, this character apparently combines two historical figures: Frey Juan Pérez and Antonio de Marchena; provides assistance for Colon at the convent of La Rabida; confessor of Christoval Colon.

Marco. *The Bravo*. Menial in the palace of the doge.

Marguerite. *The Headsman*. The wife of Balthazar, the mother of Christine, and adoptive mother of Gaetano Grimaldi the younger (alias Sigismund Steinbach).

Mari. *Wyandotté*. Negro slave, sister of Pliny the Elder, she is the cook at the Hutted Knoll. She is manumitted after Captain Willoughby's death.

Mari. *Satanstoe*. Anneke Mordaunt's slave and age-mate.

Markham, Miss. *Satanstoe*. A single lady of forty regularly toasted by Herman Mordaunt.

Marron, Mariette. *The Headsman*. The impersonator of the Priestess of Flora in the revels at Vévey.

Marston, Anne. *The Redskins*. A ward of Hugh Roger Littlepage the elder; a minor heiress; marries a friend of Hugh Roger Littlepage the younger.

Marston, Edward. *Afloat and Ashore*. Young man toasted by Grace Wallingford; mentioned.

Martha. *The Ways of the Hour*. Servant in Dr. McBrain's household; mentioned.

Martin. *Precaution*. Steward in the service of the Earl of Pendennyss.

Martin, Catherine. *The Sea Lions*. Widowed cousin of Deacon Pratt.

Martin, Juan. *Mercedes of Castile*. One of the two spokesmen for the would-be mutineers aboard the *Santa Maria*.

Martinez, Martin. *Mercedes of Castile*. Resentful and rebellious seaman aboard the *Santa Maria*.

Martyr, Peter [d'Anghiera]. *Mercedes of Castile*. An historical figure, he cares for and instructs the young nobles of Isabella's court; also called Señor Pedro Matir and Señor Matir.

Marvin. *The Ways of the Hour*. Attorney in Duke's County.

Maso. *The Headsman*. See Contini, Bartolomeo.

'Maso. *The Wing-and-Wing*. Shortened first name of Tommaso Tonti.

Mason, Tom. *The Spy*. Lieutenant of the Virginia Dragoons during the Revolution.

Mason, Tom. *The Spy*. Son of Tom Mason and also a lieutenant, he serves in the War of 1812.

Massasoit. *The Wept of Wish-Ton-Wish*. An historical figure, he was the Wampanoag chief noted for his friendliness to the Pilgrims; father of Metacom; mentioned.

Matir. *Mercedes of Castile*. See Martyr, Peter.

Matir, Pedro. *Mercedes of Castile*. See Martyr, Peter.

Mattinao. *Mercedes of Castile*. Attendant to the ambassador sent from Guacanagari to welcome Christoval Colon, he is both a cacique and the brother of the beautiful Ozema.

Medford. *The Wing-and-Wing*. British naval officer whose ship is not identified.

Medina Celi, Duke of. *Mercedes of Castile.* An historical figure, he appears in the novel as a kinsman of Mercedes de Valverde.

Medina Sidonia, Duchess of. *Mercedes of Castile.* An historical figure, she is a noble lady of the Spanish court; mentioned.

Meekly. *Miles Wallingford.* New York City attorney of Thomas Daggett.

Mendoza, Pedro Gonzalez de. *Mercedes of Castile.* Archbishop of Toledo, this historical figure leads the Spanish troops into conquered Granada; opposes Columbus's venture westward to Cathay.

Menneval. *Miles Wallingford.* Captain of the French frigate *Désirée.*

Mentoni, Olivia. *The Bravo.* Neighbor and friend of Violetta Tiepolo.

Mercedes. *Mercedes of Castile.* See Valverde, Maria de las Mercedes de.

Meredith. *Wyandotté.* British general who is the great-uncle of Maud Meredith.

Meredith, Lewellen. *Wyandotté.* Deceased father of Maud Meredith, he was a major in the British army; mentioned.

Meredith, Maud. *Wyandotté.* Orphaned daughter of Lewellen and Maud Yeardley Meredith, she is adopted by Hugh and Wilhelmina Willoughby. Maud becomes the female romantic lead in the novel and marries Robert Willoughby.

Meredith, Maud Yeardley. *Wyandotté.* Deceased mother of Maud Meredith; mentioned.

Meriton. *Lionel Lincoln.* Lionel Lincoln's valet.

Merry, Andrew. *The Pilot.* Midshipman on an American frigate during the Revolution, he is later promoted to lieutenant. He is a cousin of both Katherine Plowden and Cecilia Howard. He is killed in a duel with a foreign officer.

Merton, Rev. Dr. *The Red Rover.* Elderly British naval chaplain who secretly married Paul de Lacey and Mrs. Wyllys.

Merton. *Afloat and Ashore, Miles Wallingford.* Retired, half-pay British army major, father of Emily Merton.

Merton, Mrs. *Afloat and Ashore.* Wife of Major Merton and mother of Emily, she dies at Manila while traveling.

Merton, Lady Dolly. *Satanstoe.* Woman to whom Bulstrode proposes a toast; mentioned.

Merton, Emily. *Afloat and Ashore, Miles Wallingford.* Daughter of the British Major Merton, she is married first to Rupert Hardinge and then to an elderly affluent Italian named Montiera.

Metacom. *The Wept of Wish-Ton-Wish.* An historical figure (better known as King Philip), he succeeds his father, Massasoit, as sachem of the Wampanoags. Although historically more important than Conanchet, he plays a lesser role in the novel.

Miantonimoh. *The Wept of Wish-Ton-Wish*. An historical figure, he was the father of the Narragansett sachem Conanchet; mentioned.

Michael, Father. *The Headsman*. The Prior of the Bernardine convent.

Middleton, Duncan Uncas. *The Prairie*. The grandson of Duncan Heyward of *The Last of the Mohicans*, he is an army captain in the newly acquired Louisiana Purchase. He marries a Spanish heiress and becomes a good friend of Natty Bumppo.

Middleton, Inez Augustin. *The Prairie*. Only child of Don Augustin de Certevallos, she is kidnapped by Abiram White an hour after her wedding to Captain Duncan Uncas Middleton.

Milano, Stefano. *The Bravo*. Calabrian born on an estate of Don Camillo Monforte, he commands a felucca that often serves the Venetian senate on secret missions.

Mill, Mary (Marie). *The Ways of the Hour*. See Moulin, Marie.

Miller. "Imagination." Father of Anna Miller, he is a merchant whose economic problems force him to leave New York City to live less expensively on the banks of the Genesee.

Miller, Anna. "Imagination." Schoolmate and close friend of Julia Warren.

Miller, Harry. *The Redskins*. Older son of Tom Miller, farm manager at Ravensnest.

Miller, Kitty. *The Redskins*. Daughter of Tom Miller, Ravensnest farm manager.

Miller, Ralph Willet. *The Wing-and-Wing*. British naval captain to whose ship Admiral Nelson transferred during the battle of Cape St. Vincent; mentioned.

Miller, Tom. *The Redskins*. Conservative, loyal farm manager at Ravensnest.

Miller, Mrs. Tom. *The Redskins*. Wife of Tom Miller, farm manager for the Littlepages at Ravensnest.

Millington, Frank. *The Ways of the Hour*. Deceased father of Mildred Millington (alias Mary Monson); mentioned.

Millington, Mrs. Frank (née Millington). *The Ways of the Hour*. Deceased mother of Mildred Millington (alias Mary Monson); mentioned.

Millington, Mary. *The Ways of the Hour*. Deceased maternal grandmother of Mildred Millington; mentioned.

Millington, Michael. *The Ways of the Hour*. Legal apprentice of Thomas Dunscomb, he weds Sarah Wilmeter.

Millington, Mildred. *The Ways of the Hour*. Defendant in two murder trials, throughout the novel she uses the alias Mary Monson; also known by her married name, Madame de Larocheforte.

Miquon. *The Pioneers, The Last of the Mohicans.* Delaware Indian name for William Penn; mentioned.

Mohtucket. *The Wept of Wish-Ton-Wish.* Wampanoag traitor who leads English and Pequot-Mohican forces to the secret camp of Metacom.

Monaldi, Gino. *The Bravo.* Gondolier in the service of Don Camillo Monforte.

Monday. *Homeward Bound, Home as Found.* Alcoholic passenger aboard the *Montauk,* he is fatally wounded in a battle with Arabs.

Monforte, Don Camillo. *The Bravo.* Duke of Sant' Agata, he is the heir of an ancient Venetian family. He elopes with Violetta Tiepolo, ward of the Venetian state.

Monica. *Mercedes of Castile.* Wife of the seaman Pepe, she is won to Christoval Colon's cause by his determination to carry Christianity to the heathen.

Monson. *Le Mouchoir.* Wealthy father of Julia Monson.

Monson, Mrs. *Le Mouchoir.* Mother of Julia Monson.

Monson, John. *Le Mouchoir.* Brother of Julia Monson.

Monson, Julia. *Le Mouchoir.* Wealthy debutante, she is one of the five people who, at different times, own the titular character.

Monson, Mary. *The Ways of the Hour.* See Millington, Mildred.

Monson, Moll. *Le Mouchoir.* Infant sister of Julia and John Monson; mentioned.

Monson, Tote. *Le Mouchoir.* Infant sister of Julia and John Monson; mentioned.

Montcalm, Louis Joseph. *The Last of the Mohicans, Satanstoe.* An historical figure, he was Marquis of St. Véran and French commanding general during the French and Indian War. Credited with the capture of Fort William Henry, he was also held responsible for the Indians' massacre of its defenders after their surrender.

Montecorvino, Giovanni di. *Mercedes of Castile.* A bishop, deceased, said to have converted Prestor [sic] John; mentioned.

Montefalderon y Castro, Don Juan. *Jack Tier.* Mexican agent who purchases smuggled gunpowder from Stephen Spike. He drowns when thrown overboard from the yawl of the *Molly Swash.*

Monthly, Miss. *Home as Found.* Pseudonym of a member of the New York City literati.

Montiera, Signora. *Miles Wallingford.* Name of Emily Merton after her second marriage.

Montresor, Lord. *The Two Admirals.* Duke of Glamorgan, at whose death his younger brother, Lord Geoffrey Cleveland, assumes the title; mentioned.

Montrose. *The Spy.* British general said to be interested in Jeanette Peyton, the spinster aunt of the Wharton children; mentioned.

Moore, Dr. Benjamin. *Afloat and Ashore.* Episcopal bishop of New York; mentioned.

Moose. *The Deerslayer.* Huron warrior.

Mordaunt. *Satanstoe.* Father of Herman Mordaunt; mentioned.

Mordaunt, Madam. *Satanstoe.* Deceased wife of Herman Mordaunt and mother of Anneke Mordaunt; mentioned.

Mordaunt, Anna Cornelia. *Satanstoe, The Chainbearer.* Daughter of Herman Mordaunt, she marries Corny Littlepage, by whom she bears three children, Mordaunt, Anneke, and Katrinke. Usually called Anneke, she is also called Anne and Annie.

Mordaunt, Anne (or Annie). *Satanstoe.* See Mordaunt, Anna Cornelia.

Mordaunt, Anneke. *Satanstoe.* See Mordaunt, Anna Cornelia.

Mordaunt, Herman. *Satanstoe, The Chainbearer.* Prosperous and respected owner of Lilacbush estate and Ravensnest patent, he is the father of Anneke Mordaunt.

Moreland. *Home as Found.* New York City socialite.

Morgan. *Afloat and Ashore.* Miller at the Clawbonny grist mill.

Morganic, Lord. *The Two Admirals.* Earl, playboy, and captain of the British warship *Achilles,* he holds his naval rank through political influence; subsequent to the main action of the novel, he loses his ship, through mismanagement, to the French but by means of favoritism at court becomes a vice admiral.

Morton, George. "Heart." Male romantic lead, he dies in youth after incurring severe damage to his health while performing a charitable act. He is the one love in the life of the protagonist, Charlotte Henley.

Moseley. *Home as Found.* New York City socialite.

Moseley, Lady Anne. *Precaution.* Wife of Sir Edward Moseley; mother of John, Clara, Jane, and Emily, and only niece of Roderic Benfield.

Moseley, Clara. *Precaution.* Eldest daughter of Sir Edward and Lady Anne Moseley, she weds Francis, son of Rev. Dr. and Mrs. Ives.

Moseley, Sir Edward. *Precaution.* Baronet, brother of Charlotte Wilson, and husband of Lady Anne, he is the father of John, Clara, Jane, and Emily.

Moseley, Emily. *Precaution.* Female romantic lead; thoughtful, high-principled youngest daughter of Sir Edward and Lady Anne Moseley; sister of John, Clara, and Jane; she weds George Denbigh (the Earl of Pendennyss).

Moseley, Jane. *Precaution.* Romantically inclined second daughter of Sir

Edward and Lady Anne Moseley; deceived by Colonel Egerton, she remains single; also called Jenny.

Moseley, Jenny. *Precaution.* See Moseley, Jane.

Moseley, John. *Precaution.* Strong-willed but jocular son of Sir Edward and Lady Anne Moseley; brother of Clara, Jane, and Emily; eventually he marries Grace Chatterton.

Mosely. *Satanstoe.* British colonel, he is the friend of Uncle Legge; mentioned.

Mott, Arcularius. *The Sea Lions.* Green hand on the *Sea Lion* of Oyster Point.

Moulin, Marie. *The Ways of the Hour.* Swiss maidservant to Mildred Millington (alias Mary Monson) during the latter's imprisonment; also called Mary Mill and Marie Mill.

Mount, Peter. *The Sea Lions.* Green hand on the crew of the *Sea Lion* of Oyster Point.

Mowatt, John. *The Redskins.* A tenant at Ravensnest.

Moya, Marquesa de. *Mercedes of Castile.* See Bobadilla, Beatriz de.

Mudge, Moses. *Satanstoe.* Tenant at Ravensnest killed and scalped by Hurons.

Muir, David. *The Pathfinder.* Lieutenant and quartermaster of the British 55th Regiment, he is a spy employed by the French. Thrice married and advanced in years, he is an unsuccessful suitor for the hand of Mabel Dunham. He is fatally stabbed by Arrowhead.

Mulford, Henry. *Jack Tier.* Youthful romantic lead, he is first mate on the *Molly Swash* until he discovers military contraband in the ship's cargo. He marries Rose Budd.

Mull, Adam. *Jack Tier.* Captain of the U.S. cruiser *Poughkeepsie.*

Müller, Herr. *The Headsman.* See Balthazar.

Mundo, Sancho. *Mercedes of Castile.* Mercenary fifty-year-old expert mariner, he serves Christoval Colon faithfully, reducing opposition to the voyage and to Colon among the crew; also called Sancho of the Ship-Yard Gate.

Muños, Pedro. *Mercedes of Castile.* See Bobadilla, Don Luis de.

Munro. *The Last of the Mohicans.* Scottish lieutenant colonel in the British army, he is the commanding officer of Fort William Henry before its fall to the French.

Munro. *Satanstoe.* British troop leader; mentioned.

Munro, Alice. *The Last of the Mohicans.* See Heyward, Alice Munro.

Munro, Cora. *The Last of the Mohicans.* Elder daughter of Colonel Munro, born to his first wife, a woman of mixed British and Caribbean ancestry.

Munson. *The Pilot.* Captain of the central ship in the novel, an American frigate.

Murray, John. *Afloat and Ashore.* New York City businessman; mentioned.

Muskrat. *The Deerslayer.* Huron epithet for Thomas Hovey (alias Hutter).

Musquerusque. *Satanstoe.* Huron chief taken prisoner by Jaap during battle; also called Muss.

Muss. *Satanstoe.* See Musquerusque.

Myers. *Le Mouchoir.* Brother-in-law of the millionaire speculator Henry Halfacre; mentioned.

Nab. *Lionel Lincoln.* Nickname for Abigail Pray.

Nab. *The Red Rover.* Servant girl in the tailor shop of Hector Homespun.

Nameless. *The Oak Openings.* Epithet applied to Onoah.

Nanny. *Homeward Bound, Home as Found.* Familiar name for Ann Sidley.

Narra-mattah. *The Wept of Wish-Ton-Wish.* See Heathcote, Ruth.

Ned. *The Two Admirals.* A quartermaster on the British warship *Plantagenet.*

Nell. *The Prairie.* Nickname for Ellen Wade Hover.

Nelson, Horatio. *The Wing-and-Wing.* Historical British admiral of great fame, he held, among other honors, the British title of Viscount and the Italian title of Duke of Bronte [a province in Sicily].

Nesbitt. *Lionel Lincoln.* Colonel in command of the British 47th Regiment; mentioned.

Newcome, Jason. *Satanstoe, The Chainbearer, The Redskins.* Yale graduate and Yankee schoolmaster in Westchester; subsequently crafty tenant and agent of the Littlepages for Mooseridge and Ravensnest patents; also called Squire Newcome; merely mentioned in *The Redskins.*

Newcome, Mrs. Jason. *The Chainbearer.* Wife of Ovid Newcome and mother of Opportunity and Seneca Newcome; mentioned.

Newcome, Opportunity. *The Redskins.* Wife of Ovid Newcome, and mother of Opportunity and Seneca Newcome; mentioned.

Newcome, Opportunity. *The Redskins.* Daughter of Ovid and Opportunity Newcome, and a belle of Ravensnest; informs Hugh Littlepage about plans of anti-renters.

Newcome, Orson. *The Redskins.* Brother and business partner of Seneca Newcome.

Newcome, Ovid. *The Redskins.* Son of Jason Newcome, husband of Opportunity Newcome, and father of Opportunity and Seneca Newcome; mentioned.

Newcome, Seneca. *The Redskins.* Son of Ovid and Opportunity Newcome, brother of young Opportunity Newcome, and anti-rent activist; also called Squire Newcome.

Newcome, Squire. *The Chainbearer.* See Newcome, Jason.

Newcome, Squire. *The Redskins.* See Newcome, Seneca.

Nichols, Nicholas. *The Red Rover.* Captain of the *Royal Caroline* who is succeeded by Henry de Lacey, alias Harry Wilder.

Nicholson, Sir Herbert. *Precaution.* Lieutenant colonel, friend, and comrade-at-arms of George Denbigh (Earl of Pendennyss).

Nick. *The Pilot.* An American sailor.

Nick. *Wyandotté.* See Wyandotté.

Nightingale, Jack. *The Red Rover.* Boatswain of the *Red Rover.*

Niño, Pedro Alonzo [Peralonso]. *Mercedes of Castile.* This historical figure serves as one of the pilots on the *Santa Maria* during Christoval Colon's first voyage to the Indies.

Nipset. *The Wept of Wish-Ton-Wish.* See Ring, Whittal.

Noon, Biddy. *Jack Tier.* Nickname of Bridget Noon.

Noon, Bridget. *Jack Tier.* Irish maidservant of Mrs. Budd, she drowns when thrown overboard from the yawl of the *Molly Swash.*

Norton. *Miles Wallingford.* New York City friend of Rupert Hardinge and Andrew Drewett.

Norton, Miss-Mrs. [sic]. *The Monikins.* Anna Etherington's governess.

Nuñez. *Mercedes of Castile.* See Cabrera, Don Andres de.

Oakes, Sir Gervaise. *The Two Admirals.* Baronet of Bowldero, vice admiral throughout the action of the novel, and ultimately a full admiral, he is one of the two titular heroes of the book.

Oakes, Josselin. *The Two Admirals.* Elder brother from whom Sir Gervaise Oakes inherited the baronetcy of Bowldero; mentioned.

O'Flagherty, Honor. *Le Mouchoir.* Servant in the household of Henry Halfacre.

Ogilvie, Mrs. *Afloat and Ashore.* Mutual friend of Mrs. Drewett and Lucy Hardinge; mentioned.

O'Hearn, Michael. *Wyandotté.* A stereotype of the Irish immigrant in early America, he is a comic and grotesque character.

Ojeda, Alonzo de. *Mercedes of Castile.* Young Castilian courtier reputed to be the most expert lance in Spain.

Old Nab. *Lionel Lincoln.* Job Pray's nickname for his mother.

Oldcastle, Jack. *The Two Admirals.* Sailor on the *Plantagenet;* mentioned.

O'Leary, *The Wing-and-Wing.* Second lieutenant aboard the British frigate *Terpsichore.*

Oneida. *Satanstoe*. See Quissquiss.

O'Neil. *The Two Admirals*. Captain of the British warship *Dublin* during the main action of the novel, he is subsequently killed in a duel with a French officer.

Onoah. *The Oak Openings*. Although he is respected by many tribes, his own tribal origin is unknown. After exhorting Indians for twenty years to exterminate white settlers, he becomes a Christian convert. He is known as Scalping Peter.

Onondago. *Satanstoe*. See Susquesus.

Ooroony [the elder]. *The Crater*. Kannaka chief opposed by the treacherous Waally, he is the benefactor of Bob Betts and friend of the settlers in Mark Woolston's colony.

Ooroony [the younger]. *The Crater*. Young chief of the Kannakas deposed, after his father's death, by the hostile Waally. He is restored to power by Mark Woolston.

Oothout, Nicholas. *Satanstoe*. A British major of Dutch extraction, he is a neighbor of Major Evans Littlepage.

Open Hand. *The Last of the Mohicans*. Indian epithet for Major Duncan Heyward.

Orbitello, Juan de. *Mercedes of Castile*. Jealous noble of Isabella's court at the time of Christoval Colon's return from his first voyage to the Indies; his challenge to Colon prompts the Admiral's famous "egg trick."

Osborne, Mrs. *The Oak Openings*. Only child of Benjamin Boden and Margery Waring Boden.

Osborne, Dolly. *The Oak Openings*. See Osborne, Dorothy.

Osborne, Dorothy. *The Oak Openings*. Granddaughter of Benjamin and Margery Waring Boden.

Osborne, Margery. *The Oak Openings*. Granddaughter of Benjamin and Margery Waring Boden.

Osgood. "Heart." Father of Maria Osgood; mentioned.

Osgood, Maria. "Heart." Confidante and closest friend of the protagonist, Charlotte Henley, she marries Seymour Delafield.

Osgood, Mrs. "Heart." Mother of Maria Osgood; mentioned.

Ozema. *Mercedes of Castile*. Beautiful sister of the Haitian cacique Mattinao. Enamored of Luis de Bobadilla, she accompanies him on his return to Spain, where she dies of grief.

Pachecho. *Mercedes of Castile*. See Giron, Don Pedro.

Panther. *The Deerslayer*. Huron chief killed by Natty Bumppo.

Parker. *The Two Admirals.* Captain of the British warship *Carnatic* during the main action of the novel, he is subsequently elevated to the rank of rear admiral and knighted.

Pat, Peleg. *The Monikins.* Deceased monikin political agitator; mentioned.

Pathfinder. *The Pathfinder.* Nickname of Natty Bumppo in his role as scout.

Patroon of Kinderhook. *The Water-Witch.* Title of Oloff Van Staats.

Pedro, Don. *Afloat and Ashore.* Ecuadorean smuggler through whom the *Crisis* carries on contraband trade.

Peggy. *The Crater.* Nickname of Petrina.

Peñalosa, Juan de. *Mercedes of Castile.* Messenger sent from the Castilian court in Christoval Colon's behalf; mentioned.

Pendennyss, Earl of. *Precaution.* See Denbigh, George (Earl of Pendennyss).

Pendennyss, Lord. *Precaution.* See Denbigh, George (Earl of Pendennyss).

Penguillan, Benjamin. *The Pioneers.* Assumed name of Benjamin Stubbs, Penguillan being the name of the gentleman on whose estate he was born.

Pennock, John. *The Crater.* First colonist recruited by Mark Woolston, he later replaces Mark as governor.

People's Friend, Judas. *The Monikins.* Representative from the republic of Leaplow to the court at Leaphigh and John Goldencalf's informant on the respective societies.

Pepe. *Mercedes of Castile.* Young sailor from Palos de Moguer, he proves an excellent mariner and entirely loyal to Christoval Colon on the first westward voyage to Cathay.

Pepita. *Mercedes of Castile.* Nurse and chaperone of Mercedes de Valverde.

Pepperage. *The Wept of Wish-Ton-Wish.* English sobriquet for Miantonimoh.

Peraza, Inez [sic]. *Mercedes of Castile.* This historical figure [Beatriz de Peraza y Bobadilla], mother of the young Count of Gomera, entertains Colon and his chief officers at Gomera [in the Canary Islands] before their departure for the first westward voyage to Cathay.

Percy, Lord. *Lionel Lincoln.* Earl of Northumberland, he directs part of the British retreat from Lexington; mentioned.

Pero. *Mercedes of Castile.* Talkative shipmate aboard the *Santa Maria.*

Perot, Peggy. *Afloat and Ashore.* Day nurse in area around Clawbonny; mentioned.

Pete. *Satanstoe.* See Petrus.

Peter. *Home as Found.* Apprentice boy at Templeton.

Peter. *The Redskins.* Hired man on Ravensnest farm.

Peter. *The Ways of the Hour.* Negro servant in Dunscomb's household.

Peter. "The Lake Gun." Aged owner and operator of a sailboat on Seneca Lake.

Peterchen. *The Headsman.* See Hofmeister, Peter.

Peters. *The Pilot.* British soldier.

Peters. *The Crater.* Refugee from a whaler, he is captured by Waally, from whom he escapes to join Mark Woolston's Pacific colony.

Petrina. *The Crater.* Kannaka bride of Peters.

Petrus. *Satanstoe.* Guert Ten Eyck's slave, killed and scalped by Hurons; also called Pete.

Pettibone, Remarkable. *The Pioneers.* Yankee housekeeper at the mansion of Judge Temple.

Peyton, Jeanette. *The Spy.* A Virginian by birth, she is a cousin of Major Peyton Dunwoodie and the spinster aunt (as well as governess) of Sarah and Frances Wharton.

Philip, King. *The Wept of Wish-Ton-Wish.* An English sobriquet for the Wampanoag sachem Metacom.

Phoebe. *The Crater.* The woman brought by Mark Woolston from Philadelphia as a wife for Bill Brown.

Phyllis. *The Water-Witch.* Black slave of Myndert Van Beverout, she is the wife of Bonnie.

Pierre. *Home as Found.* Butler in the household of Edward Effingham.

Pietro. *The Bravo.* Venetian gondolier.

Pietro. *The Wing-and Wing.* Servant of Andrea Barrofaldi.

Pigeon. *The Deerslayer.* Delaware sobriquet for the youthful Natty Bumppo.

Pigeonswing. *The Oak Openings.* A Chippewa runner for the American army during the War of 1812, he befriends the central group of whites on the Michigan frontier.

Pilot. *The Pilot.* A pilot who, though unidentified by most of his colleagues, is obviously a man of much higher status than his masquerade would suggest. The only name he uses is Mr. Gray, but he is in reality John Paul Jones. Throughout the novel the word *pilot* is always capitalized when it refers to him.

Pindar. *Home as Found.* Pseudonym for a member of the New York City literati.

Pintard, Jules. *The Wing-and-Wing.* First lieutenant on the *Feu-Follet.*

Pinzon, Francisco Martin. *Mercedes of Castile.* An historical figure, he is one of the pilots on the first westward-to-Cathay voyage of Christoval Colon.

Pinzon, Martin Alonzo. *Mercedes of Castile.* An historical figure, this wealthy mariner and resident of Palos de Moguer commands the *Pinta* of Christoval Colon's first voyage to the Indies; dies of grief toward the end of the novel following his attempted treachery.

Pinzon, Vincente Yañez. *Mercedes of Castile.* An historical figure, this loyal commander of the *Niña* westward bound toward Cathay on the first voyage with Christoval Colon is a brother of the treacherous Martin Alonzo Pinzon.

Pippo. *The Headsman.* Neapolitan trickster and street juggler; rabble-rouser; one of the murderers of Jacques Colis.

Pitcairn. *Lionel Lincoln.* Major in command of a British marine company.

Pith. *Home as Found.* Pseudonym of a member of the New York City literati.

Pius [II], Pope [authorial confusion with Pope Paul II?]. *Mercedes of Castile.* Presumably furnishes the papal bull permitting the consanguineous marriage of Ferdinand and Isabella; mentioned.

Pledge, Lord. *The Monikins.* Political aspirant supported by John Goldencalf.

Pliny the Elder. *Wyandotté.* Negro slave in the household of Captain Hugh Willoughby; he is manumitted after the captain's death.

Pliny the Younger. *Wyandotté.* Negro slave in the household of Captain Willoughby, he is the son of Pliny the Elder. He is manumitted after the death of the captain.

Plowden, Katherine. *The Pilot.* Beautiful, high-spirited, and intelligent, she is an orphan, a ward of Colonel Howard. She marries Richard Barnstable.

Podestà. *The Headsman.* See Bourrit, Herr.

Poke, Noah. *The Monikins.* Penniless, shipwrecked sea captain and excellent mariner, he is John Goldencalf's comrade and nurse.

Poke, Mrs. Noah. *The Monikins.* Wife of Captain Noah Poke; mentioned.

Polwarth, Peter. *Lionel Lincoln.* The captain of a British light infantry company, he is a close friend of the titular hero. Fat and gregarious, he is a gourmet who judges people by their attitudes toward food.

Pompey. *The Pilot.* A Negro slave in the household of Colonel Howard.

Pompey. *Satanstoe.* Negro slave of Mrs. Jane Legge.

Pope, Abigail. *The Ways of the Hour.* Gossip who serves as a witness at the inquest.

Pope, Jane. *The Ways of the Hour.* Witness at the first Mary Monson trial [conceivably an authorial confusion for Abigail Pope].

Positive. *Miles Wallingford.* Colonel and editor of the New York *Federal Truth Teller,* a pro-British newspaper.

Post, Dr. *Afloat and Ashore, Miles Wallingford.* New York City physician who comes to Clawbonny to attend Grace Wallingford.

Powis, Paul. *Homeward Bound, Home as Found.* One of several names used by Paul Effingham before his real identity is established.

Powlett. *Miles Wallingford.* First lieutenant on the British frigate *Speedy.*

Prairiefire. *The Redskins.* An Indian visiting Susquesus.

Pratt, Ichabod. *The Sea Lions.* Ship owner and investor, he is an avaricious hypocrite referred to consistently as Deacon Pratt.

Pratt, Israel. *The Sea Lions.* Deceased father of Mary Pratt Gardiner and brother of Deacon Pratt; mentioned.

Pratt, Job. *The Sea Lions.* Brother of Deacon Pratt.

Pratt, Mary. *The Sea Lions.* Niece of Deacon Ichabod Pratt, she marries Roswell Gardiner.

Pray, Abigail. *Lionel Lincoln.* Impoverished and pathetic mother of the illegitimate simpleton Job, she is one of those responsible for the madness of Sir Lionel Lincoln, her former lover.

Pray, Job. *Lionel Lincoln.* Illegitimate son of Sir Lionel Lincoln and Abigail Pray, he is a wise fool far superior to the idiot he is sometimes thought to be. He is a half brother of the titular hero.

Prescott, [William]. *Lionel Lincoln.* An historical figure, he was a prominent American officer at the Battle of Bunker Hill.

Pump, Ben. *The Pioneers.* Nickname for Benjamin Stubbs, alias Benjamin Penguillan.

Putnam, [Israel]. *Lionel Lincoln.* An historical figure, he was a prominent American officer at the siege of Boston during the Revolution; mentioned.

Quill, Ready. *The Monikins.* Deceased monikin political agitator; mentioned.

Quintanilla, Alonzo de. *Mercedes of Castile.* An historical figure, this accountant-general of Castile is a firm supporter of Christoval Colon and his cause.

Quintero, Christoval. *Mercedes of Castile.* An historical figure, this co-owner of the caravel *Pinta* resents the commandeering of his vessel for Colon's voyage.

Quissquiss. *Satanstoe.* Indian hired by Corny Littlepage and Dirck Follock as hunter and messenger in exploring Mooseridge; killed by Hurons; also called Jumper and the Oneida.

Ralph. *Lionel Lincoln.* Alias used by Sir Lionel Lincoln.

Randolph, Rebecca. *The Two Admirals*. Mother of Wycherly Wychecombe, Virginia-born seventh baronet of Wychecombe; mentioned.

Ransom, Jared. *The Pioneers*. Owner of a maple-sugar business near Templeton.

Rascon, Gomez. *Mercedes of Castile*. Owner, with Christoval Quintero, of the caravel *Pinta*, a ship commandeered by the Spanish court for the use of Christoval Colon on the first westward voyage to Cathay.

Raven. *The Deerslayer*. Huron youth.

Reasono, Dr. Socrates. *The Monikins*. Highly cultivated senior male among the monkeys (monikins) met by John Goldencalf in Paris, he explains the philosophy and culture of Leaphigh.

Record. *The Two Admirals*. Professional colleague of Baron Thomas Wychecombe.

Red Crow. *The Deerslayer*. Young Huron warrior.

Red Rover. *The Red Rover*. See Heidegger, Walter.

Reed-That-Bends. *The Last of the Mohicans*. Cowardly Huron executed by his own people.

Reef. *The Water-Witch*. Officer on the cruiser *Coquette*.

Regulus. "Imagination." Code name for Henry Frederick St. Albans.

Le Renard Subtil. *The Last of the Mohicans*. See Cunning Fox.

Ricardo of Gloucester, Don. *Mercedes of Castile*. Fifth suitor for Isabella's hand; mentioned.

Richard. *The Two Admirals*. Groom employed by Sir Wycherly Wychecombe, the sixth baronet of Wychecombe.

Riddel, Jotham. *The Pioneers*. Restless and superstitious Yankee who dies of burns from a forest fire.

Ring, Miss. *Home as Found*. Meant to be a stereotype of an early American belle, she is a ridiculous flirt at a ball in New York City.

Ring, Abundance. *The Wept of Wish-Ton-Wish*. The wife of Reuben Ring, she lives up to her given name by bearing him seven sons, the last three being triplets.

Ring, Faith. *The Wept of Wish-Ton-Wish*. Shrewish sister of Reuben Ring and Whittal Ring, she marries Eben Dudley.

Ring, Reuben. *The Wept of Wish-Ton-Wish*. Brother of Faith and Whittal Ring, he is a sergeant in the defense forces at Wish-Ton-Wish.

Ring, Whittal. *The Wept of Wish-Ton-Wish*. A half-wit, he becomes completely Indianized during his years of captivity among the Narragansetts. His Indian name is Nipset.

Rittenstein, Odo von. *The Heidenmauer*. Baron who spends his mature years as a hermit in penance for a sacrilege, committed in his youth, at the Abbey of Limburg.

Rivenoak. *The Deerslayer*. A senior chief among the Hurons.

Robbins. *Afloat and Ashore*. Captain of the Indiaman *John*.

Robinson, Robert. *The Ways of the Hour*. Rejected as the twelfth juror for Mary Monson's first trial.

Roderick. *The Red Rover*. Cabin "boy" of the *Red Rover* who is actually a girl, the captain's mistress.

Roderigo. *The Bravo*. Alias used by Jacopo Frontoni.

Roderique. *Mercedes of Castile*. Soldier and member of the guard at Saragossa, capital of Aragon.

Rogers. *Satanstoe*. A provincial British major, he safeguards Corny Littlepage and his military party.

Rogerson. *The Water-Witch*. Seaman on the *Water-Witch*.

Roldan, Bartolomeo. *Mercedes of Castile*. An historical figure, he serves as a pilot on the *Niña* during Christoval Colon's first voyage to the Indies.

Roller. *The Wing-and-Wing*. Midshipman on the British frigate *Proserpine*.

Rotherham, Rev. Mr. *The Two Admirals*. Vicar of the church near the Wychecombe estate in Devonshire.

Rowley. *Miles Wallingford*. Captain of the British frigate *Briton*.

Rudiger. *The Heidenmauer*. Abbot of Our Lady of Hermits, the Benedictine convent at Einsieden, Switzerland.

Ruiz, Sancho [de Gama]. *Mercedes of Castile*. An historical figure, he serves as a pilot on the *Niña* on the first westward-to-Cathay voyage of Colon.

S. R. P. *Home as Found*. Pseudonym of a member of the New York City literati.

Sagamore. *The Last of the Mohicans*. Title for Indian wise man, applied most often in this novel to Chingachgook.

Sage, Dr. *The Sea Lions*. Country physician at Sag Harbor, New York.

Sage, Seth. *Lionel Lincoln*. Laconic Yankee landlord of quarters in Boston occupied by British officers, he is active in the patriot irregular army.

St. Albans, Henry Frederick. "Imagination." Imaginary admirer of Anna Miller.

St. Angel, Luis de. *Mercedes of Castile*. An historical figure, this receiver of the ecclesiastical revenues of the crown of Aragon is a strong supporter of Christoval Colon.

Saint James. *The Two Admirals*. Sobriquet used by Sir Wycherly Wychecombe, sixth baronet, for his second oldest brother, James, a fox-hunting clergyman.

Salt-Water. *The Pathfinder*. Sobriquet used to distinguish Charles Cap as a mariner of the seven seas rather than of the Great Lakes.

Sam. *The Pilot*. An American sailor.

Sam. *Satanstoe*. Hunter accompanying Corny Littlepage and Dirck Follock in surveying Mooseridge; killed and scalped by Hurons.

Sam. *Jack Tier*. Crewman on the U.S. cruiser *Poughkeepsie*.

Sam. *The Sea Lions*. Formerly a slave, he is a servant in the household of Deacon Pratt.

San Tommaso. *The Headsman*. See Contini, Bartolomeo.

Sanchez, Roderigo. *Mercedes of Castile*. An historical figure coming from Segovia, he is comptroller of Christoval Colon's fleet on the voyage to Cathay, sailing aboard the *Santa Maria*.

Sancho. *Mercedes of Castile*. Lay brother at the convent of La Rabida, near Palos de Moguer.

Sancho of the Ship-yard Gate. *Mercedes of Castile*. See Mundo, Sancho.

Sanford, Anthony. "Imagination." Coachman in the employ of a livery stable in New York City.

Sandon, Henry. *Homeward Bound*. Dissolute young man who pretends aboard the *Montauk* to be Sir George Templemore. He has absconded with £40,000 of government funds but is arrested and taken back to England for trial.

Sandy. *The Pathfinder*. Member of the British 55th Regiment killed at a French and Indian ambush on one of the Thousand Islands.

Sanford. *The Ways of the Hour*. County coroner conducting the inquest.

Sanglier. *The Pathfinder*. French captain who directs Indian attacks on British forces along the shores of Lake Ontario and the St. Lawrence River.

Santi, Tommaso. *The Headsman*. See Contini, Bartolomeo.

Satanstoe, Jacob. *Satanstoe, The Chainbearer, The Redskins*. Cornelius Littlepage's black personal slave and companion; later aide to Mordaunt Littlepage in subdividing Mooseridge and Ravensnest patents; husband of Miss Lilacsbush; eventually retires and lives with the Indian Susquesus at Ravensnest; also called Jaap, Jaaf, Yaap, Thick-Lips, Yop, and Yop Littlepage.

Satanstoe, Mrs. Jacob. *The Chainbearer*. Wife of Jacob Satanstoe; calls herself Miss Lilacsbush.

Saucy Nick. *Wyandotté*. See Wyandotté.

Saunders. *Precaution*. Butler in the Moseleys' household.

Saunders. *Homeward Bound*. Steward on the *Montauk*.

Saunders. *The Crater*. Seaman who joins Mark Woolston's colony after being stranded in Canton. He becomes captain of one of the colony's ships.

Saunders, Charles. *The Two Admirals*. Schoolboy friend of the titular heroes of the novel; mentioned.

Sausaman. *The Wept of Wish-Ton-Wish*. A traitor who reveals to the colonists Metacom's military plans. His execution by Metacom leads indirectly to the conflict known as King Philip's War; mentioned.

Say and Do, Lord. *The Monikins*. English noble in the government ministry; mentioned.

Scalping Peter. *The Oak Openings*. See Onoah.

Schuyler, Madam. *Satanstoe*. Aunt of Philip Schuyler.

Schuyler, Philip. *Wyandotté, Satanstoe, The Chainbearer*. An historical figure, he was the general in command of the Continental forces in the northeastern colonies at the beginning of the Revolutionary War.

Scipio. *The Ways of the Hour*. Negro servant at the Duke's County jail; also called Sip.

Scupperton, Lord. *The Two Admirals*. Neighbor of Sir Gervaise Oakes at the latter's Bowldero estate; mentioned.

Seadrift. *The Water-Witch*. Name assumed by Eudora Van Beverout while, disguised as a man, she serves as agent for the *Water-Witch*.

Seal. *Homeward Bound*. English attorney who boards the *Montauk* at Portsmouth in search of a debtor.

See-wise. "The Lake Gun." An evil demagogue among the Seneca Indians who is cursed by the Great Spirit, transformed into a log, and condemned to float on Seneca Lake for a thousand years.

[Seneca Indian]. "The Lake Gun." Otherwise unidentified, he is one of the two characters whose dialogue carries the burden of the satire of the tale.

Sennit. *Miles Wallingford*. Ill-mannered supernumerary lieutenant on the British frigate *Speedy*.

Serrani, Cristofero. *The Headsman*. A confederate of Pantaleone Serrani and confirmer of the fact that Maso [Bartolomeo Contini] was fathered by Gaetano Grimaldi.

Serrani, Pantaleone. *The Headsman*. Abductor of the infant Gaetano Grimaldi, he is executed as a murderer by Balthazar after surrendering the child for adoption by the headsman; mentioned.

Sharp. *Homeward Bound*. Alias used by Sir George Templemore aboard the *Montauk*.

Shearflint. *Lionel Lincoln*. Captain Peter Polwarth's valet.

Shebear. *The Deerslayer*. Aged Huron squaw who guards the captive Wah-ta-Wah.

Shipwith. *The Spy*. Cornet (minor officer) of the Virginia Dragoons.

Shoreham, Betts. *Le Mouchoir*. The male romantic lead, he is a prosperous New Yorker who marries Adrienne de la Rocheaimard.

Short, Dr. *The Ways of the Hour*. Country doctor who testifies at the inquest.

Short, Joshua. *The Sea Lions*. Seaman on the *Sea Lion* of Oyster Point.

Shout, Plausible. *The Monikins*. Deceased monikin political agitator; mentioned.

Sidley, Ann. *Homeward Bound, Home as Found*. Nurse for Eve Effingham.

Siegfried, Father. *The Heidenmauer*. Benedictine monk at the Abbey of Limburg.

Sigismund. *The Headsman*. Deceased firstborn son of Balthazar and Marguerite; replaced by Balthazar (without Marguerite's knowledge) by young Gaetano Grimaldi, renamed Sigismund Steinbach.

Silky. *Le Mouchoir*. A self-styled "colonel," he is a silent partner in the firm of Bobbinet and Gull.

Silverpenny, Oliver. *The Monikins*. Neighbor of Thomas Goldencalf in Cheapside; mentioned.

Silvy. *Satanstoe*. Female slave of Herman Mordaunt.

Simon. *Jack Tier*. Negro cook on the *Molly Swash*.

Singleton. *The Spy*. Colonel, American staff officer, he is the father of Isabella and Captain George Singleton.

Singleton, George. *The Spy*. Captain in the Virginia Dragoons, he is wounded seriously early in the novel.

Singleton, Isabella. *The Spy*. Daughter of Colonel Singleton and sister of Captain George Singleton, she is killed by a bullet aimed at Captain Lawton.

Sip. *The Ways of the Hour*. See Scipio.

Sitgreaves, Anna. *The Spy*. Deceased sister of Dr. Archibald Sitgreaves; mentioned.

Sitgreaves, Dr. Archibald. *The Spy*. Grotesquely comic military surgeon attached to the Virginia Dragoons.

Sixtus IV, Pope. *Mercedes of Castile*. This historical figure grants ex post facto the proper dispensation for the marriage of Ferdinand and Isabella; mentioned.

Skimmer of the Seas, The. *The Water-Witch*. Epithet for Thomas Tiller.

Skip, Harry. *Lionel Lincoln*. Drill officer of a light infantry company in the British 47th Regiment; mentioned.

Skipping Fawn. *The Prairie*. See Tachechana.

Slit-Nose. *Afloat and Ashore*. Indian with whom the crew of the *Crisis* trades on the Canadian Pacific coast.

Smees. *The Wing-and-Wing*. Italian pronunciation for the pseudonym *Smith* used by Raoul Yvard.

Smith. *The Sea Lions.* Carpenter at Oyster Point.

Smith, Betty. *The Redskins.* Widow of the old coachman at Ravensnest; provides for the aged Jacob Satanstoe and Susquesus.

Smith, Jack. *The Wing-and-Wing.* Pseudonym used by Raoul Yvard. He himself pronounces Smith as *Smeet;* the Italians pronounce it *Smees.*

Smith, John. *The Redskins.* Speaker at the anti-renters' Sunday public meeting at Ravensnest.

Smith, Robert. *The Sea Lions.* Green hand on the crew of the *Sea Lion* of Oyster Point.

Smith, Tom. *Homeward Bound.* Seaman of the *Montauk* killed by Arabs.

Smudge. *Afloat and Ashore.* Canadian Indian leader hanged for his treachery by Moses Marble.

Smut, Bob. *The Monikins.* Cabin boy aboard the *Walrus,* he subsequently is titled Prince Royal of Great Britain in Leaphigh and serves as political spokesman in Leaplow.

Socrates. *The Crater.* A slave owned by Bridget Yardley, he is a competent seaman and harpooneer.

Somers. *The Pilot.* Lieutenant in the U.S. Navy.

Soranzo, Giulietta. *The Bravo.* Beautiful wife of Senator Paolo Soranzo.

Soranzo, Paolo. *The Bravo.* Youthful, idealistic senator who replaces Alessandro Gradenigo on the Council of Three. His corruption by the senate seems inevitable.

Soundings. *The Two Admirals.* Sailing master on the British warship *Plantagenet.*

Spike, Mary Swash. *Jack Tier.* Deserted wife of Stephen Spike, she is called Jack Tier throughout the novel.

Spike, Stephen. *Jack Tier.* Dissolute captain of the *Molly Swash.*

Sponge, Tom. *The Two Admirals.* Aged gunner on the *Plantagenet.*

Spriggs. *The Wing-and-Wing.* First lieutenant on the British frigate *Terpsichore.*

Stanley, Edward. "Imagination." Imaginary admirer of Julia Warren.

Stapleton, Lord Henry. *Precaution.* A young sailor attracted to Emily Moseley, he is the brother of Lady Laura Stapleton and a friend of the Earl of Pendennyss.

Stapleton, Lady Laura. *Precaution.* Eldest sister of the Marquis of Eltringham and of Lord Henry Stapleton and a friend of Emily Moseley, she becomes the wife of Colonel George Denbigh.

Stapleton, Lady Sarah. *Precaution.* Sister of the Marquis of Eltringham and Lord Henry Stapleton and Lord William Stapleton.

Stapleton, Lord William. *Precaution.* Young man formerly a messenger of Colonel Egerton, he is a brother of the Marquis of Eltringham, Lady Laura Stapleton, and Lord Henry Stapleton.

Steele, Patty. *Precaution.* Young lady wooed but not won by Peter Johnson; mentioned.

Steen, Moses. *The Ways of the Hour.* Resident of Biberry; mentioned.

Steinbach, Sigismund. *The Headsman.* See Grimaldi, Gaetano [the younger].

Sterling. *The Two Admirals.* Captain of the British warship *Blenheim* during the main action of the novel, he is subsequently killed in action.

Stevens, Dr. *Precaution.* Rector at Bolton preceding Francis Ives but now deceased; mentioned.

Stevenson. *Precaution.* Household servant of the Earl of Pendennyss.

Stimson, Stephen. *The Sea Lions.* Sturdy and devout old mariner aboard the *Sea Lion* of Oyster Point.

Stingy Tom. *Lionel Lincoln.* Derisive patriot epithet for the royal governor Thomas Gage.

Stone, Mrs. *The Sea Lions.* Neighbor of Deacon Pratt and Betsy White, she is a widow.

Stothard. *The Wing-and-Wing.* Second lieutenant on the British frigate *Terpsichore.*

Stowel. *The Two Admirals.* Captain of Rear Admiral Richard Bluewater's flagship, *Caesar,* during the main action of the novel; subsequently he goes down with his ship in a storm on the Baltic.

Straight-Tongue. *The Deerslayer.* Earliest of the Delaware epithets for Natty Bumppo.

Strand. *The Wing-and-Wing.* Boatswain on the British frigate *Proserpine.*

Strand, Jack. *Jack Tier.* Crewman on the *Molly Swash.*

Stratton, Mrs. *The Chainbearer.* Female friend of Ursula Malbone's mother, she rears and educates the orphaned Ursula until her own death; mentioned.

Streak o' Lightning. *The Redskins.* Pseudonym for an unidentified anti-renter; he is a leader of the "Injins."

Strides, Joel. *Wyandotté.* Yankee overseer of the farm on the Willoughby patent, he is a selfish, treacherous villain.

Strides, Lyddy. *Wyandotté.* Apparently the daughter of Joel Strides.

Strides, Phoebe. *Wyandotté.* Wife of Joel Strides.

Stubbs, Benjamin. *The Pioneers.* A retired British sailor, he is a comic figure who works in the household of Judge Temple. He is usually called Ben Pump.

Submission. *The Wept of Wish-Ton-Wish.* One of the regicides responsible for the execution of Charles I, he has fled to America where he spends his life in hiding. Supplied with necessities by the Heathcote family, he comes to the aid of Wish-Ton-Wish during periods of crisis. His real name is never revealed.

Le Subtil. The Last of the Mohicans. Shortened form of *Le Renard Subtil.* See
　　Cunning Fox.
Succetush. *Satanstoe.* See Susquesus.
Sumach. *The Deerslayer.* Sister of Huron chief Panther and widow of Lynx.
Summerfield. *Home as Found.* New York City socialite.
Sus. *The Redskins.* See Susquesus.
Susquesus. *Satanstoe, The Chainbearer, The Redskins.* Indian guide and hunter
　　hired by Cornelius Littlepage and Dirck Van Valkenburgh. He is a
　　long-term friend of the Littlepages and of Andries Coejemans.
　　Respected by both Indians and whites, he eventually lives in
　　retirement with Jacob Satanstoe (Yop Littlepage) at Ravensnest.
　　He is also called Trackless, Onondago [sic], and Withered Hemlock
　　That Still Stands.
Sutton, Manners. *The Monikins.* Speaker of the British House of Com-
　　mons; mentioned.
Swash, Molly. *Jack Tier.* Maiden name (nickname) of Mary Swash Spike.
Sweeney. *Afloat and Ashore.* British customs officer.
Sweeny, Michael. *Miles Wallingford.* Irish fisherman.
Sweet-Water. *The Pathfinder.* Sobriquet used to distinguish Jasper West-
　　ern as a freshwater rather than a saltwater mariner.
Swimming Seneca. "The Lake Gun." Epithet for See-wise.
Swooping Eagle. *The Prairie.* Teton Sioux warrior.

Tachechana. *The Prairie.* Youngest widow of Mahtoree but rejected by
　　him before his death. She later marries Hard-Heart.
Talavera, Fernando de. *Mercedes of Castile.* An historical figure, he is the
　　Archbishop of Granada, directed to determine the feasibility of
　　Christoval Colon's plan for the discovery of the Indies. He is the
　　friend and tool of Ferdinand of Aragon.
Talcott, Roger. *Afloat and Ashore.* Third mate on the *Crisis.*
Tamamamaah, King. *The Monikins.* Dealer in sandalwood; mentioned.
Tamenund. *The Last of the Mohicans.* An historical person, he was the
　　Delaware chief who welcomed William Penn. He is a venerable
　　figure in the novel.
Tarry Bob. *The Red Rover.* Sobriquet for Bob Bunt.
Tecumseh. *The Oak Openings.* An historical person, he was a Shawnee
　　chief who tried to unite all Indians in the old Northwest Territory
　　to halt further settlement in that area; mentioned.
Temple, Elizabeth. *The Pioneers.* Daughter of Judge Marmaduke Temple,
　　she marries young Oliver Effingham. She is the leading female
　　character in the novel.

Temple, Marmaduke. *The Pioneers.* Founder and most prominent citizen of the frontier village of Templeton, he holds the position of judge. He is the father of Elizabeth Temple.

Templemore, Sir George. *Homeward Bound, Home as Found.* English baronet who travels under the name of Sharp, he marries Grace Van Cortlandt.

Ten Eyck, Guert. *Satanstoe.* Mischievous but brave young Dutchman of Albany, he is Cornelius Littlepage's closest friend. He is a suitor of Mary Wallace, in whose arms he dies after being struck by a stray bullet during the defense of Ravensnest.

Terence. *Lionel Lincoln.* An Irish grenadier, he is wounded alongside Lionel Lincoln during the Battle of Bunker Hill.

Tetao. *The Prairie.* Teton Sioux warrior slain by Hard-Heart.

Thick-Lips. *The Redskins.* See Satanstoe, Jacob.

Thomas. *The Crater.* Captain of one of the colony's ships.

Thomas, Jane. *The Sea Lions.* Sister of Deacon Pratt.

Thompson, Caesar. *The Spy.* Negro slave in the Wharton household.

Thompson, Dinah. *The Spy.* Wife of Caesar Thompson.

Thompson, Jack. *The Sea Lions.* Seaman, next-to-last survivor of the crew that discovered the rich sealing island where most of the novel's action is set; mentioned.

Thompson, Nathan. *The Sea Lions.* Seaman on the *Sea Lion* of Oyster Point.

Thornton, Arthur. *The Deerslayer.* Young British officer.

Thoughtful, Mrs. *Le Mouchoir.* Chairwoman of the Widow's and Orphan's Society; mentioned.

Thousandacres, Aaron. *The Chainbearer.* See Timberman, Aaron.

Thousandacres, Daniel. *The Chainbearer.* See Timberman, Daniel.

Thousandacres, Jedediah. *The Chainbearer.* See Timberman, Jedediah.

Thousandacres, Jeruthy. *The Chainbearer.* See Timberman, Jeruthy.

Thousandacres, Lavinia. *The Chainbearer.* See Timberman, Lavinia.

Thousandacres, Moses. *The Chainbearer.* See Timberman, Moses.

Thousandacres, Nab. *The Chainbearer.* See Timberman, Nab.

Thousandacres, Nathaniel. *The Chainbearer.* See Timberman, Nathaniel.

Thousandacres, Prudence. *The Chainbearer.* See Timberman, Prudence.

Thousandacres, Sampson. *The Chainbearer.* See Timberman, Sampson.

Thousandacres, Tobit. *The Chainbearer.* See Timberman, Tobit.

Thousandacres, Mrs. Tobit. *The Chainbearer.* See Timberman, Mrs. Tobit.

Thousandacres, Zephaniah. *The Chainbearer.* See Timberman, Zephaniah.

Thunder Cloud. *The Oak Openings.* A Pottawattamie chief.

Thurston, Tom. *Le Mouchoir.* Fortune seeker who courts Julia Monson.

Tiepolo, Violetta. *The Bravo.* Orphaned heiress of a renowned patrician family, she is a captive of the state, which plans to marry her to its own political and economic advantage. She elopes with Don Camillo Monforte.

Tier, Jack. *Jack Tier.* Alias of Mary Swash Spike.

Tiller, Thomas. *The Water-Witch.* A free-trader who owns and commands the *Water-Witch,* he is known as the Skimmer of the Seas.

Tim. *The Wing-and-Wing.* Cabin boy on the British frigate *Proserpine.*

Timberman, Aaron. *The Chainbearer.* Old Vermont squatter illegally lumbering at Mooseridge, he is killed mysteriously. He is usually called Aaron Thousandacres.

Timberman, Daniel. *The Chainbearer.* One of the sons of Aaron and Prudence Timberman, he is usually called Daniel Thousandacres.

Timberman, Jedediah. *The Chainbearer.* One of the sons of Aaron and Prudence Timberman, he is usually called Jedediah Thousandacres.

Timberman, Jeruthy. *The Chainbearer.* Youngest daughter of Aaron and Prudence Timberman, she is usually called Jeruthy Thousandacres; mentioned.

Timberman, Lavinia. *The Chainbearer.* A daughter of Aaron and Prudence Timberman, she is usually called Lowiny Thousandacres. She is helpful to Mordaunt Littlepage, and she leaves her family to serve Ursula Malbone Littlepage.

Timberman, Moses. *The Chainbearer.* A son of Aaron and Prudence Timberman, he is usually called Moses Thousandacres.

Timberman, Nab. *The Chainbearer.* Eldest daughter of Aaron and Prudence Timberman, she is usually called Nab Thousandacres; mentioned.

Timberman, Nathaniel. *The Chainbearer.* A son of Aaron and Prudence Timberman, he is usually called Nathaniel Thousandacres.

Timberman, Prudence. *The Chainbearer.* Wife of Aaron Timberman, she is usually called Prudence Thousandacres.

Timberman, Sampson. *The Chainbearer.* A son of Aaron and Prudence Timberman, he is usually called Sampson Thousandacres.

Timberman, Tobit. *The Chainbearer.* Eldest and most formidable son of Aaron and Prudence Timberman, he is usually called Tobit Thousandacres.

Timberman, Mrs. Tobit. *The Chainbearer.* Daughter-in-law of Aaron and Prudence Timberman, she is usually called Mrs. Tobit Thousandacres.

Timberman, Zephaniah. *The Chainbearer.* A son of Aaron and Prudence Timberman, he is usually called Zephaniah Timberman. He is a rejected suitor of Ursula Malbone.

Timms. *The Ways of the Hour.* Coarse country lawyer who assists Thomas
Dunscomb in Mary Monson's defense. He courts Mary Monson
without success. He is also called Squire Timms.

Timms, Squire. *The Ways of the Hour.* See Timms.

Tinkum, Mrs. *The Chainbearer.* Gossipy, penny-pinching squatter landlady
of a log tavern near the Ravensnest patent.

Tin-Pot. *Afloat and Ashore.* Indian with whom the crew of the *Crisis* trades
on the Canadian Pacific coast.

Titus, Peter. *The Ways of the Hour.* One of Timms's agents in Biberry.

Toast. *Homeward Bound.* Assistant steward on the *Montauk.*

Todd, Dr. Elnathan. *The Pioneers.* Yankee doctor of dubious medical
training.

Todd, Marcus. *The Sea Lions.* Seaman on the *Sea Lion* of Oyster Point.

Todd, Pulaski. *The Redskins.* Secretary of the anti-renters' public meeting
which approves a set of resolutions submitted to young Hugh
Roger Littlepage.

Tom. *Precaution.* Servant at Moseley Arms inn.

Tom. *Lionel Lincoln.* Orderly in Captain Polwarth's company of light
infantry.

Tom. *Home as Found.* Servant at the Wigwam.

Tom. *The Two Admirals.* A junior lieutenant on the British warship
Plantagenet.

Tom. *Satanstoe.* Second hunter and axe-man of Corny Littlepage and
Dirck Follock's surveying crew, he is shot and scalped by Hurons.

Tom. *Jack Tier.* Old seaman on the *Molly Swash.*

Tongue, Sam. *The Ways of the Hour.* See Hubbs.

Tonti, Tommaso. *The Wing-and-Wing.* Retired seaman and supposedly
wise old man at Portoferraio, Elba.

Torti, Annina. *The Bravo.* Daughter of the wine seller Tommaso Torti, she
is an agent of the Venetian secret police.

Torti, Giuseppe. *The Bravo.* Son of Tommaso Torti and brother of Annina.

Torti, Tommaso. *The Bravo.* A wine seller in Venice, he is the father of
Annina and Giuseppe Torti.

Tourniquet. *The Pilot.* A naval surgeon.

Town. *The Ways of the Hour.* Client in a lawsuit; mentioned.

Trackless. *Satanstoe.* See Susquesus.

Traverse. *Satanstoe.* Surveyor of the Mooseridge patent, he is killed and
scalped by Hurons.

Treviño, Count of. *Mercedes of Castile.* Host to Ferdinand's entourage en
route to Valladolid.

Tribeless. *The Oak Openings.* Epithet applied to Onoah.

Trimmer, Tim. *The Chainbearer*. A boy at 'Nest Village.

Trott, Hezekiah. *The Redskins*. A tenant at Ravensnest, he is one of the three men chosen to present a list of grievances to the landlord, young Hugh Roger Littlepage, of Ravensnest.

Trotter, Mrs. *Le Mouchoir*. New York City socialite; mentioned.

Truck, John. *Homeward Bound, Home as Found*. Able and resolute Yankee captain of the packet ship *Montauk*.

Truman, Ira. *The Ways of the Hour*. Second juror empaneled for the first Mary Monson trial.

Trysail, Ben. *The Water-Witch*. Sailing master of the cruiser *Coquette*.

Tubbs, Shabbakuk. *The Redskins*. Tenant farmer at Ravensnest. His first name is also spelled *Shabbakuck*.

Ulrich, Father. *The Heidenmauer*. Benedictine monk at the Abbey of Limburg.

Uncas. *The Last of the Mohicans*. The last male member of the Mohican family that long ruled all of the tribes of the Delaware or Lenni-Lenape nation. He is killed by the evil Magua.

Uncas. *The Wept of Wish-Ton-Wish*. Mohican chief, ally of the English settlers; his warriors capture Conanchet, deliver him to the colonists for trial, and later execute him. Not a personal name, the word *Uncas* refers to a whole dynasty of Mohican chiefs.

Ungque. *The Oak Openings*. Indian orator and demagogue.

Unus. *The Crater*. A Kannaka, brother of Petrina, he joins the white colony and marries the slave girl Juno.

Updyke, Widow Anna. *The Ways of the Hour*. Mother of young Anna Updyke, she marries Dr. McBrain early in the novel.

Updyke, Anna. *The Ways of the Hour*. Confidante of Sarah Wilmeter and of Mary Monson, she weds John Wilmeter.

Updyke, Frank. *The Ways of the Hour*. Son of Widow Anna Updyke; mentioned.

Upright Onondago [sic]. *The Redskins*. Epithet applied to Susquesus by the visiting Indians.

Uttawa. *The Last of the Mohicans*. Delaware warrior who delivers elegy over the grave of Uncas.

Valverde, Maria de las Mercedes de. *Mercedes of Castile*. Pious young female romantic lead, she is the relative and adopted daughter of Beatriz de Bobadilla; she eventually marries Luis de Bobadilla. She is usually called Mercedes or Mercedes de Valverde.

Valverde, Mercedes de. *Mercedes of Castile.* See Valverde, Maria de las Mercedes de.

Van Beverout, Eudora. *The Water-Witch.* Long-lost daughter of Myndert Van Beverout, she dresses as a man to serve as agent for the *Water-Witch,* whose owner-captain she marries.

Van Beverout, Myndert. *The Water-Witch.* Prosperous Dutch fur merchant and alderman of New York City.

Van Cortlandt, Grace. *Home as Found.* Niece and ward of Edward Effingham, she marries Sir George Templemore.

Van der Heyden, Mrs. *Satanstoe, The Chainbearer.* Anneke Mordaunt's widowed cousin in Kinderhook; in *The Chainbearer* she is merely mentioned.

Van der School, Dirck. *The Pioneers.* Lawyer and district attorney at Templeton.

Van Rensselaer, Jeremiah. *Satanstoe.* Patroon of Albany.

Van Staats, Oloff. *The Water-Witch.* A sturdy and stolid Dutch youth, he is the Patroon of Kinderhook.

Van Tassel. *Miles Wallingford.* Rapacious moneylender.

Van Valkenburgh, Abraham. *Satanstoe, The Chainbearer.* A major in the British colonial army, he is the father of Dirck Van Valkenburgh. He is also called Brom Follock, Colonel Follock, and Volleck.

Van Valkenburgh, Dirck. *Satanstoe, The Chainbearer.* Lifelong friend of Corny Littlepage, he is an undeclared suitor of Anneke Mordaunt.

Van Valtenberg, Abraham. *Afloat and Ashore.* Pilot of the Hudson River sloop *Gull.* He is familiarly known as Brom Follock.

Van Vechten, Abraham. *Miles Wallingford.* Prominent Albany attorney; mentioned.

Varse, Rev. Mr. *The Oak Openings.* Clergyman who edits the autobiographical notes of Benjamin Boden; mentioned.

Vecchio, Antonio. *The Bravo.* Foster brother of Senator Alessandro Gradenigo, he is a poor fisherman. For his efforts to win liberation of his grandson from galley duty he is assassinated by the state.

Verplanck. *Wyandotté.* Suitor for the hand of Maud Meredith; mentioned.

Vervillin, Comte de. *The Two Admirals.* French admiral.

Viefville, Mademoiselle. *Homeward Bound, Home as Found.* French governess of Eve Effingham.

Villa, Pedro de. *Mercedes of Castile.* A seaman, he is an historical figure.

Viner, John. *Afloat and Ashore.* New York City socialite mentioned by the Brighams.

Viti, Vito. *The Wing-and-Wing*. Magistrate at Portoferraio, Island of Elba.

Vivero, John de. *Mercedes of Castile*. Proud Castilian noble, lord of Valladolid, in whose palace young Isabella seeks seclusion.

Volleck. *Satanstoe*. See Van Valkenburgh, Abraham.

Voorhees. *Miles Wallingford*. Crewman on the *Dawn*, he is impressed into service on a British frigate, the *Speedy*.

Waally. *The Crater*. Treacherous Kannaka chief, he is the rival of Ooroony and his son.

Wad, Sam. *The Two Admirals*. A quartermaster on the British warship *Plantagenet*.

Wade, Ellen. *The Prairie*. Niece of Esther Bush, she marries Paul Hover.

Wagner, Nicklaus. *The Headsman*. Prosperous, avaricious Bernese peasant drowned during a storm on Lake Leman (Geneva).

Wah-ta-Wah. *The Deerslayer*. Delaware girl betrothed and later married to Chingachgook.

Walker. *Precaution*. Young attorney for Sir William Harris and others; mentioned.

Walker. *The Crater*. A Nantucket seaman, he becomes captain of the colony's first whaler.

Wallace. *Jack Tier*. Second lieutenant on the U.S. cruiser *Poughkeepsie*.

Wallace, Mary. *Satanstoe, The Chainbearer*. Anneke Mordaunt's intimate friend and Herman Mordaunt's ward, she is courted by Guert Ten Eyck but remains unmarried. She lives in the household of Anneke Mordaunt Littlepage, where she is often called Aunt Mary.

Wallingford, Mrs. *Afloat and Ashore*. Mother of Miles and Grace, she dies early in the novel.

Wallingford, Grace. *Afloat and Ashore, Miles Wallingford*. Sister of the protagonist, Miles, she dies during the second of the two novels.

Wallingford, Grace. *Miles Wallingford*. Elder daughter of Miles and Lucy Hardinge Wallingford.

Wallingford, John (Jack). *Afloat and Ashore, Miles Wallingford*. Bachelor cousin who bequeaths Miles Wallingford an estate valued at more than $200,000.

Wallingford, Lucy. *Miles Wallingford*. Younger daughter of Miles and Lucy Hardinge Wallingford.

Wallingford, Miles. *Afloat and Ashore, Miles Wallingford*. Narrator and hero of both novels.

Wallingford, Miles. *Afloat and Ashore*. Father of the protagonist, he is killed in a mill accident.

Wallingford, Miles. *Miles Wallingford.* Son of Miles and Lucy Hardinge Wallingford.

Wallingford, Thomas. *Wyandotté.* British general who in his younger years was a military colleague of Captain Willoughby; mentioned.

Walther, Conrad. *The Heidenmauer.* Potential suitor for the hand of Meta Frey; mentioned once.

Walton, Mrs. "Imagination." Married sister of Anna Miller; mentioned.

Walton. *The Two Admirals.* Lieutenant who led the unsuccessful attempt to capture the French lugger *Voltigeuse;* mentioned.

Walton. *Afloat and Ashore.* Second mate on the *Dawn.*

Walworth. *Home as Found.* New York City socialite.

Wandering Jew. "The Lake Gun." Sobriquet of the white settlers for Seewise after his transformation to a log.

Warbler. *Miles Wallingford.* Colonel and editor of the New York *Republican Freeman,* a pro-French newspaper.

Ward, [Artemas]. *Lionel Lincoln.* An historical general, he was second in command to Washington during the siege of Boston; mentioned.

Ward, Sir Hotham. *Miles Wallingford.* Commanding officer of the British frigate *Black Prince.*

Waring, Dolly. *The Oak Openings.* See Waring, Dorothy.

Waring, Dorothy. *The Oak Openings.* Wife of Gershom Waring, she is usually called Dolly.

Waring, Gershom. *The Oak Openings.* An alcoholic of Yankee extraction, he is a hapless trader along the frontier.

Waring, Margery. *The Oak Openings.* Sister of Gershom Waring and the female romantic lead, she marries Benjamin Boden.

Warley, Thomas. *The Deerslayer.* British officer who takes Judith Hutter as mistress.

Warner. *The Crater.* Settler who initiates the first lawsuit in the colony.

Warren, Rev. Mr. *The Redskins.* Rector of the church at Ravensnest, this widower is the father of Mary Warren.

Warren, [Joseph]. *Lionel Lincoln.* An historical figure, he was a prominent American officer killed during the Battle of Bunker Hill; mentioned.

Warren, Julia. "Imagination." Adolescent protagonist of the story, she eventually marries Charles Weston.

Warren, Mary. *Le Mouchoir.* Friend of Julia Monson.

Warren, Mary. *The Redskins.* Daughter of the widower Rev. Mr. Warren, she is courted and won by young Hugh Roger Littlepage.

Warren, Peter. *The Two Admirals.* Schoolboy friend of the titular heroes of the novel; mentioned.

Warrington. *The Crater.* First judge to be appointed in Mark Woolston's colony.

Wart, Joe. *Home as Found.* Apprentice boy at Templeton.

Washington, George. *The Spy, Lionel Lincoln, Wyandotté.* An historical figure, he was the commander-in-chief of the Continental army during the Revolution. He is known throughout *The Spy* by the alias Mr. Harper. Although mentioned frequently in the two later novels, he does not appear in person among the other characters.

Watch, Rev. Mr. *The Ways of the Hour.* Minister in Biberry; mentioned.

Waters, Joan. *The Crater.* Sister of Martha Waters, she marries the seaman Jones.

Waters, Martha. *The Crater.* Quaker woman who marries Bob Betts.

Watson. *The Sea Lions.* Second mate of the *Sea Lion* of Martha's Vineyard.

Watson, Tom. *Satanstoe.* Colonial colonel from Massachusetts; mentioned.

Watson, Tom. *Satanstoe.* Son of old Colonel Tom Watson; mentioned.

Wattles, James. *The Crater.* Crewman of the shipwrecked *Rancocus,* he is held captive by Waally until he escapes to join the colony of Mark Woolston.

Wattles, Jonas. *The Ways of the Hour.* First juror empaneled for Mary Monson's first trial.

Wa-wa-nosh. *The Oak Openings.* Name given to Onoah by the Ojibways.

Weasel. *The Oak Openings.* Sobriquet for Ungque.

Webb. *The Last of the Mohicans.* An historical figure, he was the British general in command of Fort Edward during the French and Indian War.

Weeks, David. *The Sea Lions.* Ship carpenter on the *Sea Lion* of Oyster Point.

Wellmere. *The Spy.* A supercilious British colonel, he would have become a bigamist if his marriage to Sarah Wharton had not been canceled at the altar.

Wenham. *Home as Found.* A provincial resident of Templeton, he makes himself ridiculous by insisting on American superiority in taste, refinement, morals, and intelligence.

Western, Jasper. *The Pathfinder.* A freshwater seaman, he is master of the *Scud,* a British cutter on Lake Ontario. He is a close friend of Pathfinder.

Weston, Charles. "Imagination." Male romantic lead of the story, he marries the protagonist, Julia Warren.

Weston, Jane. *The Wing-and-Wing.* Fiancée and later wife of Jack Clinch.

Wetmore, George. *Miles Wallingford.* Deceased father of Oloff Van Duzer Wetmore (alias Moses Marble); mentioned.

Wetmore, Katharine. *Miles Wallingford.* Widow of George Wetmore, she is the mother of Oloff Van Duzer Wetmore (alias Moses Marble).

Wetmore, Oloff Van Duzer. *Afloat and Ashore, Miles Wallingford.* This is the real name of Moses Marble. He is one of the protagonist's closest friends, a stereotyped rough old seaman with a heart of gold. His identity and parentage are not known until the time of the second novel.

Weucha. *The Prairie.* A Teton warrior, he is dastardly even in the Indian context.

Wharton. *The Spy.* Father of Sarah, Frances, and Captain Henry Wharton, he is the owner of The Locusts.

Wharton, Frances. *The Spy.* Younger daughter of Mr. Wharton, she is patriot in sympathy while the rest of the family remains Loyalist. She marries Major Peyton Dunwoodie.

Wharton, Henry. *The Spy.* A captain in the British army, he is captured behind American lines and convicted of espionage. He ultimately attains the rank of general.

Wharton, Sarah. *The Spy.* Older daughter of Mr. Wharton, she becomes deranged when, at the altar, her betrothed, Colonel Wellmere, is revealed to be already married.

Whipple, Kate. *The Red Rover.* Former wife of Richard Fid.

Whiskey Centre. *The Oak Openings.* Nickname for Gershom Waring.

White. *Precaution.* Neighbor of Roderic Benfield; mentioned.

White, Abiram. *The Prairie.* Kidnapper and murderer, he is the villainous brother of Esther Bush.

White, Abraham. *The Crater.* Quaker owner of the *Rancocus.*

White, Betsy. *The Sea Lions.* Widow at Oyster Point who houses the dying Thomas Daggett.

White, Jonas. *The Ways of the Hour.* A country loafer; mentioned.

Whittle, Rev. Mr. *The Sea Lions.* Parson of the small church at Oyster Point.

Wigram, Miss. *Precaution.* Card-playing companion of Lady Juliana.

Wild Rose. *The Deerslayer.* Sobriquet given to Judith Hutter by both the Delawares and the Hurons.

Wilder, Harry. *The Red Rover.* Alias used by Henry de Lacey.

Wilhelm of Venloo. *The Heidenmauer.* Abbot of Limburg, a Benedictine convent, he is known in the religious community as Bonifacius.

William. *Precaution.* Servant of the Jarvises.

William. *Precaution.* Servant in the Moseley household.

Williams. *Afloat and Ashore.* Captain of the armed merchantman *Crisis.*

Williams, Bayard. *Afloat and Ashore.* New York City businessman; mentioned.

Williams, Dick. *The Ways of the Hour.* See Williams, Frank.

Williams, Frank. *The Ways of the Hour.* Clever Duke's County lawyer, he is retained by Jesse Davis in the Mary Monson trial. He is also called Dick Williams and Saucy Williams.

Williams, Saucy. *The Ways of the Hour.* See Williams, Frank.

Williamson. *The Two Admirals.* First lieutenant on the British warship *Carnatic.*

Willis. *Precaution.* Servant of Lady Chatterton.

Willis. *The Chainbearer.* Tenant farmer at Ravensnest.

Willoughby, Beulah. *Wyandotté.* Daughter of Hugh and Wilhelmina Willoughby, she marries Colonel Evert Beekman. She is killed by a stray bullet during an Indian attack on the Hutted Knoll.

Willoughby, Sir Harry. *Wyandotté.* A cousin from whom Captain Hugh Willoughby inherits a baronetcy; mentioned.

Willoughby, Hugh. *Wyandotté.* Retired captain of the British army, he is the owner of the patent in Central New York where most of the action of the novel occurs. He is murdered by the titular hero of the book.

Willoughby, Robert. *Wyandotté.* The male romantic lead in the novel, he marries Maud Meredith. A British major when the Revolution begins, he eventually becomes a lieutenant general; he also inherits a baronetcy.

Willoughby, Wilhemina. *Wyandotté.* Wife of Hugh Willoughby, and mother of Beulah and Robert Willoughby.

Wilmeter, Lady. *The Two Admirals.* Noblewoman who befriended the youthful Martha Dutton (née Ray) and accepted her as a companion to her own daughters; mentioned.

Wilmeter, John. *The Ways of the Hour.* Nephew and legal apprentice of Thomas Dunscomb, he marries Anna Updyke. He is also called Jack and Jack Wilmington [sic].

Wilmeter, Sarah. *The Ways of the Hour.* Orphaned niece of Thomas Dunscomb, she marries Michael Millington. She is also called Sally and Sally Wilmington [sic].

Wilmington, Jack. *The Ways of the Hour.* See Wilmeter, John.

Wilmington, Sally. *The Ways of the Hour.* See Wilmeter, Sarah.

Wilmot. *The Crater.* A merchant who joins Mark Woolston's colony.

Wilmot, Mrs. *Precaution.* Neighbor of young Lord and Lady Chatterton (Astley Cooper and his bride) in London; mentioned.

Wilson, Dr. *Afloat and Ashore.* Clergyman toasted at a party given by Mrs. Bradfort; mentioned.

Wilson, Charlotte. *Precaution.* Prudent childless sister of Sir Edward

Moseley and widow of General Wilson, she is the social and spiritual mentor of Emily Moseley.

Wilton. *The Ways of the Hour.* A general cited as an example of one who, reputed to be wealthy, dies a debtor; mentioned.

Winchester. *The Wing-and-Wing.* First lieutenant on the British frigate *Proserpine.*

Withered Hemlock That Still Stands. *The Redskins.* Epithet applied to Susquesus by visiting Indians.

Wolfe, Meek. *The Wept of Wish-Ton-Wish.* A vindictive clergyman, he is responsible for the punitive expedition that captures and executes Conanchet while that Indian chief is on a peacemaking mission.

Wolfeye. *The Oak Openings.* A Pottawattamie brave.

Wolfgang. *The Heidenmauer.* Aged burgher of Deurckheim.

Wompawisset. *The Wept of Wish-Ton-Wish.* A savage from whom Conanchet saves the infant Ruth Heathcote.

Wood, George. *The Ways of the Hour.* Colleague of Thomas Dunscomb.

Woods, Rev. Mr. Jedediah. *Wyandotté.* Anglican clergyman and former military chaplain, he is a resident member of the Willoughby household at the Hutted Knoll.

Woolston, Dr. *The Crater.* Physician at Bristol, Pennsylvania, he is the father of Mark Woolston and his siblings.

Woolston, Abraham. *The Crater.* A brother of Mark Woolston, he becomes the first Secretary of the Woolston colony.

Woolston, Anne. *The Crater.* Sister of Mark Woolston and confidante of Bridget Yardley, she marries Dr. John Heaton.

Woolston, Charles. *The Crater.* A brother of Mark Woolston, he becomes the first Attorney General of the Woolston colony.

Woolston, Mark. *The Crater.* Youthful first mate of the *Rancocus,* he is shipwrecked on a volcanic reef in the Pacific and later founds a thriving colony there. He marries Bridget Yardley.

Worden, Rev. Mr. Thomas. *Satanstoe.* Rector of St. Jude's, he is also Cornelius Littlepage's preparatory-school teacher. In Albany he is often called the Loping Dominie.

Wren of the Woods. *The Deerslayer.* Chingachgook's term of endearment for Wah-ta-Wah.

Wriggle, Gilded. *The Monikins.* Social pretender in Bivouac, Leaplow.

Wright. *The Deerslayer.* British sergeant.

Wright. *The Ways of the Hour.* Assistant to the District Attorney in the Mary Monson trial.

Writ. *Home as Found.* Lawyer who delivers the Fourth of July oration at Templeton.

Wurtz, Dr. *Miles Wallingford*. One of the physicians attending the dying Grace Wallingford.

Wyandotté. *Wyandotté*. Titular hero of the novel, he is a Tuscarora chief cast out by his own tribe. He is also called Nick and Saucy Nick.

Wychecombe, Agnes. *The Two Admirals*. Daughter of the Virginian Sir Wycherly Wychecombe, seventh baronet of Wychecombe, and Mildred Bluewater Wychecombe.

Wychecombe, Charles. *The Two Admirals*. Third oldest brother of Sir Wycherly Wychecombe (sixth baronet), he was an army officer killed in action before the time of the novel; mentioned.

Wychecombe, Gregory. *The Two Admirals*. The youngest of the four brothers of Sir Wycherly Wychecombe (sixth baronet), he was the grandfather of the male romantic lead, Lieutenant Wycherly Wychecombe (later seventh baronet); mentioned.

Wychecombe, Rev. Mr. James. *The Two Admirals*. Second oldest brother of Sir Wycherly Wychecombe (sixth baronet), he was a clergyman killed in a fox hunt before the action of the novel; mentioned.

Wychecombe, Sir Michael. *The Two Admirals*. He was the first member of the family to hold the baronetcy of Wychecombe, an honor conferred upon him in 1611 by James I; mentioned.

Wychecombe, Mildred. *The Two Admirals*. Daughter of the Virginian Sir Wycherly Wychecombe (seventh baronet) and Mildred Bluewater Wychecombe.

Wychecombe, Sir Reginald. *The Two Admirals*. Present head of the branch of the family descended from Sir Michael Wychecombe's younger son. His estate is in Hertfordshire.

Wychecombe, Lord Thomas. *The Two Admirals*. Lawyer, judge, and baron, he is a bachelor who fathers three illegitimate children. He dies before his elder brother, Sir Wycherly Wychecombe (sixth baronet).

Wychecombe, Thomas. *The Two Admirals*. Eldest of Lord Thomas Wychecombe's three illegitimate sons.

Wychecombe, Sir Wycherly. *The Two Admirals*. The sixth baronet of Wychecombe, he dies during the novel at the age of eighty-four.

Wychecombe, Wycherly. *The Two Admirals*. Virginia-born, he is the son of Gregory Wychecombe and the father of Sir Wycherly Wychecombe, seventh baronet.

Wychecombe, Wycherly. *The Two Admirals*. A Virginian by birth, he is the male romantic lead in the novel, marrying Mildred Bluewater. A lieutenant in the British navy, he later inherits the family title to become Sir Wycherly Wychecombe, the seventh baronet.

Wychecombe, Wycherly. *The Two Admirals*. Son of the Virginian Sir

Wycherly Wychecombe, seventh baronet, and Mildred Bluewater Wychecombe.

Wyllys, Mrs. *The Red Rover*. Mother of Henry de Lacey, wife of Paul de Lacey, and sister of the Red Rover. Only at the end of the novel are her relationships with Henry de Lacey and the Red Rover recognized.

Xavier, Father. *The Headsman*. Genial Augustine monk and clavier of the Bernardine convent, he performs the marriage rites uniting Adelheid de Willading and Gaetano Grimaldi the younger (alias Sigismund Steinbach).

Yaap. *Satanstoe*. See Satanstoe, Jacob.

Yardley, Dr. *The Crater*. Rival of Dr. Woolston, he disapproves of the marriage of his daughter, Bridget, to Mark Woolston.

Yardley, Bridget. *The Crater*. Sixteen-year-old daughter of Dr. Yardley, she weds Mark Woolston secretly and without their parents' consent.

Yarn, Robert. *The Water-Witch*. Sailor on the *Coquette*.

Yelverton. *The Wing-and-Wing*. Third lieutenant on the British frigate *Proserpine*.

Yetty. *The Ways of the Hour*. See Jette.

Yo. *Afloat and Ashore*. Variant for the name of Joe, the black cook on the *Crisis*.

Yocommo. *The Deerslayer*. Delaware deserter who kidnaps Wah-ta-Wah and then joins the Hurons. He is most often referred to as Briarthorn, the English translation of his name.

Yoke, Sam. *The Two Admirals*. Coxswain on the British warship *Caesar*.

Yop. *The Redskins*. See Satanstoe, Jacob.

Young Eagle. *The Pioneers*. Delaware nickname for Edward Oliver Effingham.

Ysabel, Doña. *Mercedes of Castile*. See Isabella.

Yvard, Raoul. *The Wing-and-Wing*. Commander of the French privateer *Feu-Follet*, he is cited throughout the novel as "our hero." He is killed in a battle with British sailors near Sorrento.

Zantzinger, Friedrich. *The Heidenmauer*. Potential suitor for the hand of Meta Frey; mentioned once.

Zephyr. *The Water-Witch*. Ten-year-old cabin boy of the *Water-Witch*.